2007-2008

# Standard COMPANION DEVOTIONS

*The flowers appear on the earth; the time of the singing of birds is come, and the voice of the turtle is heard in our land.*
*–Song of Solomon 2:12, (KJV)*

Volume 5

Cincinnati, Ohio

Gary Allen, *editor*
Margaret Williams, *editor*
Jonathan Underwood, *senior editor*

The "Spotlight" and "Search the Word" features were written by the following: Kenneth Beck, Cheryl Frey, and Ronald G. Davis, Cover by DesignTeam.

Published by Standard Publishing, Cincinnati, Ohio
www.standardpub.com

# September

# GOD CREATES A PERSON

*O* Lord, *our Lord, how majestic is your name in all the earth!*
—Psalm 8:1

*Photo © istock*

# Powerful Reminder

*God blessed them and said, "Be fruitful and increase in number and fill the water in the seas, and let the birds increase on the earth"* (Genesis 1:22).

Scripture: Genesis 1:20-23

Song: *"His Eye Is on the Sparrow"*

***From this meditation today, I will pray . . .***

Adoration ______________________________

______________________________

______________________________

Confession ______________________________

______________________________

______________________________

Thanksgiving ______________________________

______________________________

______________________________

Supplication ______________________________

______________________________

______________________________

***From this meditation today, I will . . .***

Think ______________________________

______________________________

______________________________

Say ______________________________

______________________________

______________________________

Do ______________________________

______________________________

______________________________

September 1–2. ***Cos Barnes,*** *a freelance writer living in Southern Pines, North Carolina, has three children, seven grandchildren, and is an avid handbell ringer.*

"Mom, guess what?" my daughter said when I answered the telephone. Not waiting for a reply, she rushed on, "Today I saw a baby being born."

Sharing my daughter's excitement, I felt goose bumps rising on my arms and legs. My daughter, a third-year nursing student, was learning rapidly.

"It was a perfect baby girl," she continued. "And the parents were so thrilled."

"You have seen God's greatest miracle," I said. "Many people never do. And you assisted in that miracle."

I read more in my daughter's words than the reassurance that she would make a fine nurse; I witnessed the enduring power of God's command to be fruitful on the earth. For at no time are we more aware of the call upon our lives to acknowledge our creaturehood—and to lift thankful hearts to our creator—than at the birth of a child.

Creator of All, *thank You for filling the earth with all good things for my enjoyment. Keep me mindful this day of my origin in You and my constant need to depend on Your grace and care. In Jesus' name, amen.*

**SPOTLIGHT**

***Next Week's Lesson***

At creation God set the laws of birth in place. They still work.

# What a Heritage!

*God made the wild animals according to their kinds, the livestock according to their kinds, and all the creatures that move along the ground according to their kinds. And God saw that it was good* (Genesis 1:25).

The first chapter of Genesis has been called a doxology—a hymn of praise to God as creator. In these two verses the repeated phrase "their kinds," is especially meaningful to me these days, as I have been diligently pursuing my genealogy. I recently met a long-lost cousin, and he shared with me some papers written by a kindred ancestor who was a book publisher in seventeenth-century London.

Holding those precious documents, I was overcome with emotion. As I studied the archaic English, the logo of his print business, and the pictures of his shop in St. Paul's Square, I gasped, "I feel a connection to this forebearer! All my life I have loved pretty stationery, ink, newsprint—anything to do with the printed word. Now I know why—it's in my blood!"

Similarly, the accounts of Genesis portray an entire family's character by detailing its origins. When we see God in those pages, we see our holy heritage, all that we are meant to be in Him and in His Son.

My Father, *You created me to bring You glory in all I do and say. Work in me today a little more of Your matchless character! Through Christ, amen.*

**SEARCH THE WORD**

*God made the kinds; then He empowered the kinds to reproduce themselves.*

Scripture: Genesis 1:24, 25

Song: *"Praise God, from Whom All Blessings Flow"*

***From this meditation today, I will pray . . .***

Adoration ______________________________

______________________________

______________________________

Confession ______________________________

______________________________

______________________________

Thanksgiving ______________________________

______________________________

______________________________

Supplication ______________________________

______________________________

______________________________

***From this meditation today, I will . . .***

Think ______________________________

______________________________

______________________________

Say ______________________________

______________________________

______________________________

Do ______________________________

______________________________

______________________________

______________________________

______________________________

September 3

# Gazing in Love

*Lift your eyes and look to the heavens: Who created all these? He who brings out the starry host one by one, and calls them each by name* (Isaiah 40:26).

Scripture: Isaiah 40:25-31

Song: *"The Wonder of It All"*

***From this meditation today, I will pray . . .***

Adoration ______________________________

______________________________

______________________________

Confession ______________________________

______________________________

______________________________

Thanksgiving ______________________________

______________________________

______________________________

Supplication ______________________________

______________________________

______________________________

***From this meditation today, I will . . .***

Think ______________________________

______________________________

______________________________

Say ______________________________

______________________________

______________________________

Do ______________________________

______________________________

______________________________

September 3–9. ***Pat S. Johnson,*** *a speaker and freelance writer, served for 20 years as a missionary in the Middle East. She now lives in Temple City, California.*

As a child I loved stargazing. I lived in a small Oregon town with few streetlights to blur my view of the heavens. My whole family would stretch out on the grass and admire the night's brilliant display.

Dad pointed out the constellations and tried to teach me their names. I only mastered locating the Big Dipper and the Little Dipper. I quickly recognized the North Star being at the end of the Little Dipper's handle, and I later learned that some 88 constellations could be recognized. (Never by me, however.)

Today's Scripture not only tells us that God created the sun, moon, and stars, He also named each one of them. Each is in its place, fulfilling the purpose for which it was designed—bringing light to the world. None are missing.

The God who named the stars also knows us by name. Therefore let us never forget: we are constantly in His loving gaze, through the day and also through the night.

Lord, *help me trust Your love and concern for me in a deeper way. Every time I enjoy Your star-spangled sky, let me lift up the eyes of my heart to Your kind gaze. Thank You, in Jesus' name. Amen.*

**SPOTLIGHT**

***Next Week's Lesson***

To see the stars
is to see God's early work.
Amazing, isn't it?

# Looking Like God

*God created man in his own image . . .*
*male and female he created them*
(Genesis 1:27).

While growing up I was perplexed by the idea of being made in God's image. I just didn't look like the illustrations of God's Son in my Sunday school papers! That full-bearded man with the piercing blue eyes and authoritative posture was not me.

Later, of course, I realized that being made in God's image had little to do with my physical attributes. I came to understand my *personhood* as a reflection of God's own nature; I too was a being with intellect, emotions, and will. And my actions were to reflect God's character too. But I would never look like Him.

My initial interpretation of God-like living included never disappointing God in any action or attitude. Therefore, I often felt my self-serving responses to life's irritations and disappointments demonstrated spiritual weakness. As I yearned to develop the attributes of God in my own character, I grew into a transformed understanding of what it means to live as one made in His image. It's about allowing God free reign in my life, to guide and direct me in His ways. Only then can I truly reflect His image to those I meet each day.

Dear Heavenly Father, *help me respond to Your Spirit's leading in my life so I can truly mirror You in my world. In Jesus' name, amen.*

**SEARCH THE WORD**

*Looking like God is not physical, for He is not. Looking like God is spiritual, for He is Spirit.*

Scripture: Genesis 1:26, 27
**Song:** *"O to Be Like Thee!"*

*From this meditation today, I will pray. . .*

Adoration ______________________

______________________

______________________

Confession ______________________

______________________

______________________

Thanksgiving ______________________

______________________

______________________

Supplication ______________________

______________________

______________________

*From this meditation today, I will . . .*

Think ______________________

______________________

______________________

Say ______________________

______________________

______________________

Do ______________________

______________________

______________________

______________________

______________________

# Every Good Landscape

*God saw all that he had made, and it was very good* (Genesis 1:31).

Scripture: Genesis 1:28-31
Song: *"For the Beauty of the Earth"*

In my 34 years as a missionary, I was blessed to live in different parts of the world. My first assignment was Lebanon—often called the "Switzerland of the Middle East." Its snow-capped mountains, bubbling springs, tide-licked coastline, and fertile gardens reflected creation's beauty in every season.

Our move to Jordan brought a dramatic change to the landscape. Because of the meager yearly rainfall, rolling, rock-strewn hills with little vegetation covered most of the country. The sun's rays reflecting off dust-filled air produced sunsets which were winners on a regular basis. My time in Papua, New Guinea, introduced me to the world of the jungle. There tropical fruits abounded: pineapples, mangoes, bananas, passion fruit, and guavas. It was easy to revel in the land's lush abundance.

In every land where I've lived, I learned to appreciate the beauty of God's earth. When He made this world, He proclaimed it good. We too—if we keep our eyes open to the miracle of life in all its variety—will see the good hand of God in every landscape to which He leads us.

Lord, *I have seen Your world, and it is good. Help me to be a responsible steward and caretaker as I partake of its bounty and enjoy its beauty. In the name of Jesus, my Savior, I pray. Amen.*

***From this meditation today, I will pray . . .***

Adoration ______________________________

______________________________

______________________________

Confession ______________________________

______________________________

______________________________

Thanksgiving ______________________________

______________________________

______________________________

Supplication ______________________________

______________________________

______________________________

***From this meditation today, I will . . .***

Think ______________________________

______________________________

______________________________

Say ______________________________

______________________________

______________________________

Do ______________________________

______________________________

______________________________

______________________________

______________________________

**SPOTLIGHT**
***Next Week's Lesson***

Being in God's image is good; violating His image is not.

# Rules or Rest?

*God blessed the seventh day and made it holy*
(Genesis 2:3).

I grew up in a rather strict and conservative religious family. Our Christian lifestyle was controlled by a long list of "don't!" rules. Some of these rules centered on keeping Sunday holy. In my home, for example, we were forbidden to read the Sunday newspaper. It never made sense to me that we could listen to the Sunday news on the radio or watch a news program on television; we just dare not touch that newspaper!

After my husband and I married we developed our own Sunday schedule. It included a Bible study class as well as worship services. We'd sing in the choir, help in the nursery, and bring food for potlucks. (And I must confess, we'd read the Sunday comics in the afternoon.)

When our children were old enough, we began teaching them to give thanks at mealtime and to join in family devotions before bedtime. We also taught them the importance of setting aside Sunday to focus on God. Our family's routine included Sunday school class and morning and evening church services. My point is simple: focusing on worship—going beyond rules—made Sunday holy to us, and still does today.

God, *I am thankful that You rested on the seventh day of creation and called us to emulate Your example. May my Sunday activities reflect just that desire—to rest, not just from work but in You. Through Christ, amen.*

**SEARCH THE WORD**

*Worship, not works, sanctifies the Lord's Day.*

Scripture: Genesis 2:1-3

Song: *"Brethren, We Have Met to Worship"*

*From this meditation today, I will pray . . .*

Adoration ______________________________

Confession ______________________________

Thanksgiving ______________________________

Supplication ______________________________

*From this meditation today, I will . . .*

Think ______________________________

Say ______________________________

Do ______________________________

# Let's Go Outside

*The heavens declare the glory of God . . .*
*Their voice goes out into all the earth*
(Psalm 19:1, 4).

Scripture: Psalm 19:1-6
Song: *"This Is My Father's World"*

***From this meditation today, I will pray . . .***

Adoration ______________________________

Confession ______________________________

Thanksgiving ______________________________

Supplication ______________________________

***From this meditation today, I will . . .***

Think ______________________________

Say ______________________________

Do ______________________________

I am the oldest of six children. You'd think it would take a mighty big voice to call us all into supper when we were kids. But Mom's soft, husky tone was designed for polite conversation, not yelling. Nevertheless, she knew exactly how to get our attention—she whistled! It didn't matter whether we were in our own backyard, at the neighbor's house, or at the park, we immediately responded to her one-of-a-kind trill.

Our heavenly Father uses more than words to get our attention. For example, the beauty of the heavens speak for Him, as the psalmist so eloquently proclaims. It's as if a voice from the Lord calls to us, amazing us with a cycle of light and dark, thrilling us in a celestial revelation of His power and glory. God's majesty is declared in the blazing sun by day, the soft light of a changing moon by night, and the myriad stars lighting up the universe from beyond time.

I've decided to go outside this very night and admire God's handiwork. I want to revel in His marvelous creation, feel His presence and power. Won't you join me?

Father in Heaven, *thank You for Your beautiful creation. Best of all, thank You for letting me hear Your voice through it. In the name of Jesus, Lord and Savior of all, I pray. Amen.*

**SPOTLIGHT**
***Next Week's Lesson***

God loves beauty. To be in His image, one must also love and appreciate beauty.

# Reflect His Compassion

*The LORD is compassionate and gracious, slow to anger, abounding in love*
(Psalm 103:8).

The psalmist tells us that God abounds in love. And because we are to reflect God's image in our world, we also have the great privilege of abounding in love. But how do we do it?

It's easy to love the lovable—those gracious people who say "Please" and "Thank you" and live up to our expectations. It's the *others,* though—the folks who fall into the category of unappreciative or selfish or malicious—that give us our love-challenge. However, choosing whom *to* love and whom *not* to love isn't an option. The very idea of "abounding" precludes that kind of choice.

We are to love whoever comes our way, constantly enlarging our circle of care and concern. That way, our love reaches out to an ever-growing number of people with the kind of compassion and grace we ourselves have received.

Not easy! It requires asking God for a fresh supply of love for each day. Only then do we find the fruit of love ripening and cheering the people in our lives. And what a joyful way to live!

Gracious God, *how great is Your goodness to me over the years! Help me reach out to those in need around me as one who, like them, was rescued by Your compassion through no merit of my own. Through Christ, amen.*

**SEARCH THE WORD**

*Love can never be used up as long as it is given away.*

Scripture: Psalm 103:1-14

Song: *"The Love of God"*

***From this meditation today, I will pray . . .***

Adoration ______________________________

______________________________

______________________________

Confession ______________________________

______________________________

______________________________

Thanksgiving ______________________________

______________________________

______________________________

Supplication ______________________________

______________________________

______________________________

***From this meditation today, I will . . .***

Think ______________________________

______________________________

______________________________

Say ______________________________

______________________________

______________________________

Do ______________________________

______________________________

______________________________

______________________________

______________________________

# Crowning of a King

*The LORD has established his throne in heaven, and his kingdom rules over all* (Psalm 103:19).

Scripture: Psalm 103:15-22

Song: *"The Lord Jehovah Reigns"*

***From this meditation today, I will pray . . .***

Adoration ______________________________

Confession ______________________________

Thanksgiving ______________________________

Supplication ______________________________

***From this meditation today, I will . . .***

Think ______________________________

Say ______________________________

Do ______________________________

It's a big day for a country when it crowns a new king. Pomp and circumstance rule. Parade routes are marked and security measures checked. Streets are swept, tree branches trimmed, and curbs refreshed with new coats of color. It's a public holiday in celebration of the occasion, and leaders from neighboring countries make it a point to attend. At least that's what happened at the 1999 coronation of his majesty, King Abdullah II of the Hashemite Kingdom of Jordan.

I was there, watching the school children excitedly pressing against each other on the curbs, chanting "Long live King Abdullah!" The enthusiastic crowds lining the parade route held bobbing balloons and billowing banners. A formation of fighter planes streaked through the sky above, their roar mingled with the shouts of the crowd. It was a day for the history books.

However, the reign of all earthly kings will end one day. All pomp and glory will pale in the splendor of His Majesty, king of the universe!

*Your reign,* my Heavenly King, *is eternal and all-encompassing. Therefore, let me acknowledge Your undisputed rule within my heart in this quiet moment. In the name of the Father, the Son, and the Holy Spirit, I pray. Amen.*

**SPOTLIGHT**

***Next Week's Lesson***

Being in the image of God immediately bestows royalty; we are princes and princesses.

# He's There!

*Listen to me, all who hope for deliverance, who seek the Lord! Consider the quarry from which you were mined, the rock from which you were cut!* (Isaiah 51:1, *The Living Bible*).

Northwest of Thermopolis, Wyoming, on State Highway 120, a series of rock formations thrusts out alongside the road. A few miles down that road, these same formations, buried several thousand feet below the surface, produce hydrocarbons—one of earth's most important natural resources because of the energy produced when burned.

We sometimes forget that our Lord is like these rock formations. He can be buried far below the surface of our consciousness, but He also rises to the surface of our lives in our actions and words. He provides the foundation for our production of fruit in His kingdom.

In Isaiah, the Lord reminded the Israelites that they were cut from His quarry and He alone could deliver them. May we too always remember that God is our rock—the rock of all ages—dwelling within us by His Spirit. In every fearful circumstance we can call upon Him for help and deliverance.

Lord, *when I'm blinded by the day-to-day problems of my world, open my eyes to Your abiding presence through Your loving Word. I pray through my deliverer, the Lord Jesus Christ. Amen.*

**SEARCH THE WORD**

*Being cut from His quarry gives us His attributes. We can't be sandstone if we come from a diamond mine.*

Scripture: Isaiah 51:1-5

Song: *"The Rock That Is Higher Than I"*

*From this meditation today, I will pray . . .*

Adoration ______________________________

______________________________

______________________________

Confession ______________________________

______________________________

______________________________

Thanksgiving ______________________________

______________________________

______________________________

Supplication ______________________________

______________________________

______________________________

*From this meditation today, I will . . .*

Think ______________________________

______________________________

______________________________

Say ______________________________

______________________________

______________________________

Do ______________________________

______________________________

______________________________

September 10-16. ***Kristi Stingley,*** *a retired engineer and lawyer, now dedicates her time to writing Christian novels and inspirational nonfiction books.*

September 11

# Lord of the Stars

*He took him outside and said, "Now look toward the heavens, and count the stars, if you are able to count them." And He said to him, "So shall your descendants be"* (Genesis 15:5, *New American Standard Bible*).

Scripture: Genesis 15:1-6
Song: *"Blessed Assurance"*

*From this meditation today, I will pray . . .*

Adoration ______________________________

______________________________

______________________________

Confession ______________________________

______________________________

______________________________

Thanksgiving ______________________________

______________________________

______________________________

Supplication ______________________________

______________________________

______________________________

*From this meditation today, I will . . .*

Think ______________________________

______________________________

______________________________

Say ______________________________

______________________________

______________________________

Do ______________________________

______________________________

______________________________

______________________________

______________________________

When did you last look into the heavens and marvel at the number of stars? I would do this often as a child, but *counting* the stars never entered my mind. Who could count that high?

I imagine God taking Abraham outside on one of those clear, moonless nights that always invite a meditative upward gaze. He pointed to the stars and told His servant to count them. I might have said under my breath, "Are you kidding?"

But the Lord delivered on His promise to Abraham, as the apostle Paul confirmed centuries later: "Be sure that it is those who are of faith that are sons of Abraham," (Galatians 3:7, *NASB*). What a vast family God has given this one who believed such an awesome promise as he stood under a cloudless night sky! All through the ages, from his day to ours, Abraham's sons and daughters have been lifting their praise to the Lord of the stars.

Dear Father in Heaven, *just as I can't count the stars in the sky, I can't count all the ways You touch and bless my life. Make me ever grateful for Your many blessings and show me Your will in all I will say and do this day. In the name of Jesus, my Lord and Savior, I pray. Amen.*

**SPOTLIGHT**
***Next Week's Lesson***

Abraham and Sarah could count their "stars" on no fingers. At that time Isaac was just a "twinkle."

# Now We Live in Gratitude

*God said to Abraham, "As for Sarai your wife, you shall not call her name Sarai, but Sarah shall be her name"* (Genesis 17:15, *New American Standard Bible*).

Have you ever wished you could be someone different? Would you like to change your name and start over again? Many European immigrants desiring a new life in America change their names, hoping to assimilate into society with more ease.

The Lord provided Abram and his wife with new names but for a different reason. Abram became *Abraham,* and Sarai become *Sarah,* in order to signify their new roles in God's world-saving plan. They would become the father and mother of many nations, and the great, great . . . great grandparents of the one in whom the Lord God would establish His new covenant—Jesus Christ.

We are a part of it all! The Lord gives us new names when we enter the waters of baptism. We're no longer just John or Jane Doe in some no-name family. We are God's adopted sons and daughters, chosen ones, the recipients of eternal life (see Ephesians 1:5). From now on the life of gratitude is the only life for us.

Dear Lord, *thank You for making me new in Your name, for giving me a new identity—one that glorifies Your precious name. Keep working in me, transforming me into the likeness of Your Son, Jesus, until I see Him face-to-face. I pray these things in His precious name. Amen.*

**SEARCH THE WORD**

*A name change becomes significant only when a life change accompanies it.*

Scripture: Genesis 17:15-22

Song: *"A Child of the King"*

*From this meditation today, I will pray . . .*

Adoration ______

Confession ______

Thanksgiving ______

Supplication ______

*From this meditation today, I will . . .*

Think ______

Say ______

Do ______

September 13

# Bow to Him

*[Abraham] said, "My lord, if now I have found favor in your sight, please do not pass your servant by"* (Genesis 18:3, *New American Standard Bible*).

Scripture: Genesis 18:1-8
Song: *"All Creatures of Our God and King"*

***From this meditation today, I will pray . . .***

Adoration ________________________________

________________________________

________________________________

Confession ________________________________

________________________________

________________________________

Thanksgiving ________________________________

________________________________

________________________________

Supplication ________________________________

________________________________

________________________________

***From this meditation today, I will . . .***

Think ________________________________

________________________________

________________________________

Say ________________________________

________________________________

________________________________

Do ________________________________

________________________________

________________________________

________________________________

________________________________

The stewardship ministry team in our congregation recently produced a play titled *Come to the Castle.* In it, crowds gather to hear the announcement of the king's return. On his journey to the castle, a sty warden ("pig boy" to most) encounters many who shy away from him due to his distinct odor, while others treat him with respect and kindness. In the end it is revealed that the sty warden is the king himself!

In our Scripture today, three men visit Abraham. Unlike those in our stewardship play, Abraham instantly recognizes his king. He bows down at the visitors' feet and asks them not to pass him by but to let him provide for their refreshment.

It makes me consider: What do I do when the Lord calls me? Do I let Him pass by because I just don't recognize Him? Or do I immediately know His voice and bow down in service?

Lord of my life, *all glory and praise to Your holy name! Give me an open heart that is ready to hear and receive Your guidance. And when You call, may I, like Abraham, recognize Your presence and answer Your call with all that You have given me—with my time, my abilities, and my money. In the name of Your Son, my Savior, I pray. Amen.*

**SPOTLIGHT**

***Next Week's Lesson***

Genealogy begins with two parents and a child. Abraham, Sarah, and baby Isaac—the beginning of the genealogy of the godly.

# Surpassing Greatness

*"Is anything too difficult for the Lord?"*
(Genesis 18:14, *New American Standard Bible*).

I have friends whose daughter was in a car accident. At the hospital, after being told their daughter was brain dead, they were asked to donate her organs. What a request! Could you do it?

What is the most difficult thing you have been asked to do? In our Scripture, God tells Abraham and Sarah that at their advanced age they would become parents. They couldn't believe it. Sarah laughed, thinking it sounded ridiculous. But God responded, "Is anything too difficult for the Lord?"

Sometimes we ask ourselves: can God really help with this mess I'm in? As the Lord reminds Abraham and Sarah—and reminds us too—nothing falls beyond the bounds of His abilities. He remains eternally omnipotent and omniscient—all-powerful and all-knowing.

Whatever your struggle today, whether big or small, simple or complex, let the one who can handle anything handle it for you. In so doing, you honor Him, glorify His name, and witness to His surpassing greatness.

Lord, *You can do anything; nothing is too large or too small, too simple or complex for Your loving attention. Help me to remember that whatever my struggle, You can help me overcome and be victorious. For Your name's sake, I pray. Amen.*

**SEARCH THE WORD**

*He is the God who specializes in doing the improbable and the impossible. He is. He can.*

Scripture: Genesis 18:9-15
Song: *"He Will Make a Way"*

***From this meditation today, I will pray . . .***

Adoration ______________________

______________________

______________________

Confession ______________________

______________________

______________________

Thanksgiving ______________________

______________________

______________________

Supplication ______________________

______________________

______________________

***From this meditation today, I will . . .***

Think ______________________

______________________

______________________

Say ______________________

______________________

______________________

Do ______________________

______________________

______________________

______________________

______________________

September 15

# Joy with Me!

*Sarah said, "God has made laughter for me; everyone who hears will laugh with me"* (Genesis 21:6, *New American Standard Bible*).

Scripture: Genesis 21:1-8

Song: *"Down in My Heart"*

***From this meditation today, I will pray . . .***

Adoration ______________________________

Confession ______________________________

Thanksgiving ______________________________

Supplication ______________________________

***From this meditation today, I will . . .***

Think ______________________________

Say ______________________________

Do ______________________________

I have two sisters. As children, sometimes while playing or joking around, we would break out in uncontrollable laughter. Our dad said, "Who gave you the giggle gas?" This, of course, made us laugh even harder.

Sarah laughed at God when He told her she would bear a child, but it was a somewhat sarcastic laugh. After bearing the promised child, Sarah's laughter turned to a bubbling joyfulness—an infectious kind of laughter like the kind my sisters and I shared.

In fact laughter can be catching. Often people walking in on the end of a joke will start to chuckle, even though they don't know exactly why. Isn't it interesting that God made laughter with such a contagious quality?

He's not our giggle-gas, though. For even when we can't laugh, when joking is clearly inappropriate, when we're immersed in serious pain or heartache, He is the source of a deep-down joy that remains through it all. That joy, of course, goes beyond humor to form a solid basis for all our fellowship and worship.

Lord, *help me always remember that You are my source of joy. When I rely on circumstances for happiness, keep me ever mindful that You alone bring true happiness to my life by Your abiding presence. In Jesus' name. Amen.*

**SPOTLIGHT**

***Next Week's Lesson***

Because nothing is too hard for God, joy and laughter are always at hand for the godly.

# Step Out in Faith

*Abraham trusted God, and when God told him to leave home and go far away to another land which he promised to give him, Abraham obeyed. Away he went, not even knowing where he was going* (Hebrews 11:8, *The Living Bible*).

Have you noticed that faith can lead us to do many things we might not otherwise do?

I ventured over 700 miles away from my hometown in Nebraska to attend college in New Mexico. I believed I would get the education I needed to propel me into a successful and prosperous career as an engineer. My faith was rewarded.

Abraham believed God when He said He would give him a new home, even though Abraham had never seen the place. Abraham also believed God when He said Abraham would be the father of many nations. Through Abraham's obedience, we have an example of how we can demonstrate our faith in the Lord.

Never fear or be ashamed to show your Christian faith because it isn't the popular thing to do. By expressing faith openly, we glorify the Lord (and might just make "faithing it" a little more popular).

**Almighty Lord,** *make my faith as strong and reliable as Abraham's. Help me never fear or be ashamed to show those around me that I am a Christian and that You are my Savior. And when I hear Your call to go, let my feet be swift to answer! In the precious name of Jesus, I pray. Amen.*

**SEARCH THE WORD**

*Faith may be blind,*
*but it is never sightless.*

Scripture: Hebrews 11:8-12

Song: *"Faith of Our Fathers"*

*From this meditation today, I will pray . . .*

Adoration ______________________

______________________

______________________

Confession ______________________

______________________

______________________

Thanksgiving ______________________

______________________

______________________

Supplication ______________________

______________________

______________________

*From this meditation today, I will . . .*

Think ______________________

______________________

______________________

Say ______________________

______________________

______________________

Do ______________________

______________________

______________________

______________________

______________________

# Everybody Else's Fault

*Then Sarai said to Abram, "You are responsible for the wrong I am suffering. I put my servant in your arms, and now that she knows she is pregnant, she despises me"* (Genesis 16:5).

**Scripture: Genesis 16:1-6**

**Song: *"My Tribute"***

***From this meditation today, I will pray . . .***

Adoration ____________________

Confession ____________________

Thanksgiving ____________________

Supplication ____________________

***From this meditation today, I will . . .***

Think ____________________

Say ____________________

Do ____________________

September 17–23. ***Terry Magee*** *is a writer living in Pennsylvania, where he serves his church while attending school. He is married and has two grown children.*

Confronted by my manager about a late project, I was ready with excuses. "It was the customers! They didn't know what they wanted and didn't support me. And those people working with me! They didn't do their share, so I had to do both my job and theirs. And, besides, you're always giving me too much to do!" I could go on, but I think you get the general idea.

Notice that everybody else was to blame except me. Even if those other people shared in the blame, I refused to take my share. I was "victimized" by them instead of owning up to my own failings. I was living the old adage, "To err is human; to blame it on others is even more human."

Even though Sarai allowed Hagar to be with Abram, she still blamed him for the problems that followed. There was enough blame for everybody, but she refused to take her share. But then, I thoroughly understand how that could happen.

**Dear God,** *help me to take responsibility for what I have done instead of blaming others. Through Christ I pray. Amen.*

**SPOTLIGHT**

***Next Week's Lesson***

Who's to blame for Ishmael? God? Sarah? Abraham? Hagar? Blame anyone but God!

# We Are Not Alone

*The angel of the Lord also said to her: "You are now with child and you will have a son. You shall name him Ishmael, for the Lord has heard of your misery"*
(Genesis 16:11).

The television show *Hee Haw* featured a recurring song that recounted the cast members' dreadful state of life, filled with gloom, despair, and agony. They were poking fun at misery, but it can be easy for any of us to wallow in a woe-is-me attitude during tough times This is especially true when we feel that nobody notices or cares—or even that God has turned His back on us.

Yet a common experience of those who seek God with fervent hearts is that they will, at some point, enter what's known as the dark night of the soul. God may indeed feel absent at those times, but our feelings don't give us the true picture. For Christ has promised to be with us always, even when we don't feel Him. And the indwelling Holy Spirit intercedes for us, even when prayerful words won't come to our lips.

All of this to say: Just as the Lord heard Hagar, he constantly beholds us and hears our own hearts. He hears and cares whether we're experiencing joy or misery, gloom or gladness. That we grow to be more like His Son is what matters most to Him.

Dear God, *thank You for never abandoning me! Help me enjoy your presence even now. Thank You, in Jesus' name. Amen.*

**SEARCH THE WORD**

*The Lord never abandons the miserable, but the miserable often ignore His presence.*

Scripture: Genesis 16:7-16

Song: *"Praise to the Lord, the Almighty"*

*From this meditation today, I will pray . . .*

Adoration ______________________________

______________________________

______________________________

Confession ______________________________

______________________________

______________________________

Thanksgiving ______________________________

______________________________

______________________________

Supplication ______________________________

______________________________

______________________________

*From this meditation today, I will . . .*

Think ______________________________

______________________________

______________________________

Say ______________________________

______________________________

______________________________

Do ______________________________

______________________________

______________________________

______________________________

______________________________

# Lasting Inheritance

*"Get rid of that slave woman and her son, for that slavewoman's son will never share in the inheritance with my son Isaac"* (Genesis 21:10).

Scripture: Genesis 21:9-13

Song: *"One Pure and Holy Passion"*

***From this meditation today, I will pray . . .***

Adoration ____________________

Confession ____________________

Thanksgiving ____________________

Supplication ____________________

***From this meditation today, I will . . .***

Think ____________________

Say ____________________

Do ____________________

Dying childless, the old woman left a sizeable estate. Her surviving family members eagerly awaited the reading of the will, expecting everything to be divided among them.

Not so! Shock preceded anger as they all discovered she'd left everything to one relative. Angry accusations flew, followed by silence, as family members refused to speak to one another. Years later, the rift remains.

Sarai refused Ishmael a share in the inheritance she felt belonged solely to Isaac. She saw that anything given to Ishmael would diminish Isaac's portion.

Many families are permanently broken by money or inheritance struggles. However, we have an inheritance that is limitless in Christ. What we have received from Him can flow out in boundless grace among countless peoples. And since there is more than enough for all, how important that we share it every day of our lives!

Dear God, *help me remember today that everything in my earthly life is limited and temporary. Anything I acquire here I will soon leave behind. Therefore, let me live with a view to what is most important: pleasing You in word and deed, living by Your Spirit each moment. Help me do it! I pray this prayer in the name of Jesus, my merciful Savior and Lord. Amen.*

**SPOTLIGHT**

***Next Week's Lesson***

Ishmael would not share Isaac's inheritance, but God would give him one of his own; God is good even when people "go bad."

# Doing Compassion

*She went off and sat down nearby, about a bowshot away, for she thought, "I cannot watch the boy die"*
(Genesis 21:16).

According to news reports, the family was enjoying a bike ride along a tour road in the Florida Everglades when disaster struck. Their 6-year-old son fell off his bike and landed in an alligator's nest. The mother alligator, reacting to an apparent attack on her offspring, clamped onto the boy. The boy's mother, seeing her son in the alligator's jaws, rushed to his defense, beating the alligator with her bare hands to save her child. Thankfully, everyone survived this rare alligator attack.

Compassion for our young is built into us by God. We show it by risking our lives when they are attacked or by simply being in misery as Hagar was. She felt helpless to stop her son's suffering, yet she did stay nearby to watch over him.

Every parent knows this protective instinct. However, all of us, whether we have children or not, are surrounded by the young, defenseless, or suffering. Hagar knew of no response but to feel compassion. May we ourselves go even further—and *do* compassion.

**Dear Father,** *Your Son always had time to put His compassion into action. Give me the discernment to see those suffering around me. But also help me put my feelings of compassion into action. Help me reach out in the most practical forms of help. In Jesus' name I pray. Amen.*

**SEARCH THE WORD**

*Hagar knew something about how God felt when His Son hung dying on the cross. God knew her anguish too.*

**Scripture: Genesis 21:14-16**
**Song:** *"Comfort, Comfort Ye My People"*

***From this meditation today, I will pray . . .***

Adoration ______________________

______________________

______________________

Confession ______________________

______________________

______________________

Thanksgiving ______________________

______________________

______________________

Supplication ______________________

______________________

______________________

***From this meditation today, I will . . .***

Think ______________________

______________________

______________________

Say ______________________

______________________

______________________

Do ______________________

______________________

______________________

______________________

______________________

# Seeing or Just Looking?

*Then God opened her eyes and she saw a well of water*
(Genesis 21:19).

Scripture: Genesis 21:17-19
Song: *"See, Jesus, Thy Disciples See"*

***From this meditation today, I will pray . . .***

Adoration ______________________________

______________________________

______________________________

Confession ______________________________

______________________________

______________________________

Thanksgiving ______________________________

______________________________

______________________________

Supplication ______________________________

______________________________

______________________________

***From this meditation today, I will . . .***

Think ______________________________

______________________________

______________________________

Say ______________________________

______________________________

______________________________

Do ______________________________

______________________________

______________________________

______________________________

______________________________

"Where are the car keys?" I asked my wife as I was rushing to leave for an appointment.

"On the dresser," she replied from the next room.

I searched again, including the drawers. "I still can't find them!" I called impatiently. "Are you sure they're here?" She came into the room and, pointing to the dresser, said, "Open your eyes; they're right in front of you!" Just like magic, those keys had appeared on the dresser!

Except that it wasn't magic, was it? I was *looking* without *seeing.*

Of course, it's all too easy to go through life missing the obvious—that God is constantly with us, that people around us long for kind words, that our neighbor might need a little help.

The well didn't magically appear for Hagar; it had been there all along. She just needed God to open her eyes, to show her the source of her survival. What kinds of opportunities and blessings would you like Him to show you this week?

Dear God, *thank You for seeing and knowing everything. It is too easy for me to miss what should be obvious. Open my eyes and help me to see everything around me with Your eyes, both opportunities to serve and special blessings from You. In the name of Your Son, I pray. Amen.*

**SPOTLIGHT**
***Next Week's Lesson***

Even when Hagar despaired—
as we all do—
God offered hope.

# Everyday Presence

*God was with the boy as he grew up. He lived in the desert*
(Genesis 21:20).

The golfer had been given a remarkable gift. When his ball was on the green, an imaginary line appeared only to him, a line he could follow to hit his ball in the hole. He was able to use this wonderful gift to join the professional golf tour and fulfill his life's ambition.

I sometimes dream of having some remarkable gift—especially if I could know that it came directly from God's hand.

The Bible speaks of God being with Ishmael as Ishmael grew up, yet it doesn't relate any miraculous examples of God's grace during this time. No doubt God's goodness was unfolding, though, in the mundane, normal activities of his life.

We look for God in miraculous events. But isn't He more commonly present in the ordinary ones? God is just as powerful when working in subtle, almost hidden ways as when He works in dramatic and miraculous ways. In the most ordinary of our daily activities, we can find the Lord of our lives.

Lord of my every moment, *thank You for being with me amid all the routines of my life. Help me enjoy this fellowship with You throughout the day as I learn to pray always. In the name of the Father, the Son, and the Holy Spirit, I pray. Amen.*

**SEARCH THE WORD**

*What more could a parent want for a child than God's abiding presence?*

Scripture: Genesis 21:20, 21
**Song:** *"Lead Us On"*

***From this meditation today, I will pray . . .***

Adoration ______________________

______________________

______________________

Confession ______________________

______________________

______________________

Thanksgiving ______________________

______________________

______________________

Supplication ______________________

______________________

______________________

***From this meditation today, I will . . .***

Think ______________________

______________________

______________________

Say ______________________

______________________

______________________

Do ______________________

______________________

______________________

______________________

______________________

# Proud Legacy—or Not?

*His descendants settled in the area from Havilah to Shur, near the border of Egypt, as you go toward Asshur. And they lived in hostility toward all their brothers* (Genesis 25:18).

Scripture: Genesis 25:12-18

Song: *"Let Everything That Has Breath"*

*From this meditation today, I will pray . . .*

Adoration ______________________________

______________________________

______________________________

Confession ______________________________

______________________________

______________________________

Thanksgiving ______________________________

______________________________

______________________________

Supplication ______________________________

______________________________

______________________________

*From this meditation today, I will . . .*

Think ______________________________

______________________________

______________________________

Say ______________________________

______________________________

______________________________

Do ______________________________

______________________________

______________________________

______________________________

______________________________

I constantly struggled with the heavy traffic and aggressive driving behavior while living in New Jersey. And I often responded by blasting my horn and yelling unkind things at other drivers. I was both surprised and humbled one day when my 2-year-old son, upon hearing a car horn in the distance, yelled "You turkey!"

Children watch us all the time and pick up our behaviors—good and bad. I couldn't pick and choose when my son watched me. I couldn't stop and say, "Don't do what I'm doing, because it's wrong." No, children are like sponges, soaking in everything around them.

Ishamel was born and raised in strife. And he passed that strife on to his children, who lived in hostility with those around them.

We're building a legacy each and every day of our lives. The question is, would it make us proud?

Dear Lord, *help me to be aware that I am not alone, that my actions affect and influence those around me. Let me continue to reflect Your love and grace with everyone I know, so that I might build a legacy that brings honor to my family and glory to Your name. Especially keep me mindful of the little ones looking on, learning from me how to live. I pray this prayer in the name of Jesus, the one who died for my sins. Amen.*

**SPOTLIGHT**

***Next Week's Lesson***

Children learn what they live. Strife begets strife as surely as grace begets grace.

# Can You Loosen Up?

*"The Lord . . . will send his angel before you so that you can get a wife for my son from there"*
(Genesis 24:7).

When I was a girl, one of my greatest joys was skating. Gliding across the rink made me feel so light and graceful.

But initially learning how to skate had been another matter. My legs were rigid, and my knees were constantly locked tight for fear of falling. I thought that if I could just control my legs and knees, I'd get the hang of it. But then my sister told me to "just let go" and loosen up. When I did, I relaxed—and finally knew the joy of moving across the ice with a free spirit.

Life is like that. We have family or work problems, and our first inclination is to try to seize control of the situation and fix things. We lock our jaws and rigidly "clamp down." Like Abraham's servant, we want to cover all our bases, so we develop a contingency plan.

God's way, though, is to invite us to relax and let Him work out the details. We are simply called to trust and obey Him. When we do that, our walk of faith becomes as graceful as a skater floating across the rink.

Father, *I know You are fully capable of guiding me without my constant suggestions. Help me trust You more fully! Through Christ, amen.*

**SEARCH THE WORD**

*God always goes in front.*
*He doesn't push faith;*
*He only calls for it.*

Scripture: Genesis 24:1-9

Song: *"I Will Serve Thee"*

***From this meditation today, I will pray . . .***

Adoration ______________________________

______________________________

______________________________

Confession ______________________________

______________________________

______________________________

Thanksgiving ______________________________

______________________________

______________________________

Supplication ______________________________

______________________________

______________________________

***From this meditation today, I will . . .***

Think ______________________________

______________________________

______________________________

Say ______________________________

______________________________

______________________________

Do ______________________________

______________________________

______________________________

September 24–30. ***Lisa Konzen*** *is an administrative assistant for United Way in Janesville, Wisconsin. She also writes health articles for her local newspaper.*

# All About Attitude

*After she had given him a drink, she said, "I'll draw water for your camels too, until they have finished drinking"* (Genesis 24:19).

Scripture: Genesis 24:10-21

Song: *"The Servant"*

***From this meditation today, I will pray . . .***

Adoration __________________________

Confession __________________________

Thanksgiving __________________________

Supplication __________________________

***From this meditation today, I will . . .***

Think __________________________

Say __________________________

Do __________________________

Like most people, I'm not a fan of household chores. But they've become a little easier for me since I learned that I could do them in two different ways. The first way was to view every task as a drudgery; just get them done and move on.

The other way? I found I could offer every mundane chore as an act of service in thanksgiving to God. For instance, as I took up that attitude, washing dishes became more than a cleaning duty. It was now a loving act of caring for the family God had given me.

It's all in the attitude, isn't it? It seems to me that Rebekah invested her chores with meaning too. When Abraham's servant asked her for a sip of water from her jar, she didn't just give it to him. She went beyond what was asked of her and watered the camels too. Her willingness to be kind and generous won the approval of the servant. And her gracious spirit also prepared her for her role as Isaac's wife.

Small things done with love can make wondrous changes in our lives. Just ask Rebekah.

Loving Father, *remind me that You care more about the quality of my heart than the length of my good works list. Through Christ I pray. Amen.*

**SPOTLIGHT**

***Next Week's Lesson***

Jesus later prescribed the behavior one sees in Rebekah: the "second mile" of kindness.

# Driving Directions

*"As for me, the LORD has led me on the journey to the house of my master's relatives"* (Genesis 24:27).

When my sister moved into her new home on the other side of town, I had to call her for detailed directions to her house. She told me all the turns to make and even gave me landmarks to observe so I'd be sure of traveling in the right direction.

When we set out on a journey to an unfamiliar destination, it helps to consult a road map. Or do as I did, and call ahead for directions. Without instructions, the journey can be frustrating or even frightening, and we're likely to get lost.

Abraham's servant knew how to find the wife God intended for Isaac. Why? Because he knew he wasn't traveling blindly. God directed him each step of the way, and he was able to find Rebekah without any trouble.

We too have a road map to follow on the Christian journey. God's Word shows us the way, pointing out the turns we must take and the landmarks that will indicate whether we're headed in the right direction. We don't have to go it alone.

**Dear Father in Heaven,** *You have given me the great privilege of knowing You through Your revealed Word. Help me to be faithful in my Bible reading and devotional times, so I'll be able to follow wherever You lead. In the name of Your Son, my Savior, I pray. Amen.*

**SEARCH THE WORD**

*Every successful saint can say, "The Lord has led me on the journey."*

Scripture: Genesis 24:22-27

Song: *"Follow On"*

*From this meditation today, I will pray . . .*

Adoration ____________________

Confession ____________________

Thanksgiving ____________________

Supplication ____________________

*From this meditation today, I will . . .*

Think ____________________

Say ____________________

Do ____________________

# All That Glitters

*As soon as he had seen the nose ring, and the bracelets on his sister's arms . . . he went out to the man and found him standing by the camels near the spring. "Come, you who are blessed by the LORD," he said* (Genesis 24:30, 31).

Scripture: Genesis 24:28-32

Song: *"Little Is Much When God Is in It"*

***From this meditation today, I will pray . . .***

Adoration ______________________

Confession ______________________

Thanksgiving ______________________

Supplication ______________________

***From this meditation today, I will . . .***

Think ______________________

Say ______________________

Do ______________________

Movie stars are rich, so they must be doing something right. Correct? Maybe if we could look more like them or buy the products they endorse, we could get in on the blessings they have. Right?

Rebekah's brother Laban also judged by appearances. When he saw the expensive jewelry, he was impressed. If Abraham is rich, he thought, maybe I can get in on that blessing too.

But all that glitters is not always gold. A person's net worth has nothing to do with his or her relationship with God. Although it's true that Abraham was wealthy and that he was a righteous person, his righteousness certainly didn't make God bless him. God blessed him with wealth and righteousness because He chose to do so.

Abraham couldn't earn God's blessings, and neither can we. Affluence isn't necessarily a sign of God's influence in a person's life. In fact, faithful service done in gratitude shines brighter than all the gold in the world.

Giver of all good gifts, *I thank You for the greatest gift of all—Your Son Jesus Christ. May I adorn myself with His grace today, the one who loved me enough to die for me. In His name I pray. Amen.*

**SPOTLIGHT**

***Next Week's Lesson***

Impressed by "bling" or impressed by godliness and God's plan? That's the choice Laban had; that's the choice I have too.

# Friend for the Journey

*"The Lord, before whom I have walked, will send his angel with you and make your journey a success, so that you can get a wife for my son from my own clan and from my father's family"* (Genesis 24:40).

My sister is a nervous highway driver, so when she had to travel the 30-mile journey from her home to an appointment with a lawyer, she asked me to accompany her. Somehow, just having me nearby made her calmer, and she actually enjoyed the trip.

What are some of the frightening things you face in life? Isn't it always better to have a friend with you?

A companion may not actually protect us, but having him or her with us calms our fears and helps us face our challenges with greater courage and perhaps even humor.

We can be faithful friends to those around us who face challenges in their walks of faith. Just being there, encouraging and loving them, can help make their journey successful. The same Lord who sent His angel as a companion to Abraham's servant also sends us as messengers to those around us, calling us to convey His peace, hope, and love.

Father, *thank You for the people in my life who have held my hand along the way. Help me, in return, offer my own hand in friendship to fellow travelers on their way home to You. In Christ's holy name I pray. Amen.*

**SEARCH THE WORD**

*When God is in an endeavor, there is no doubt of its success.*

Scripture: Genesis 24:33-41

Song: *"Traveling Home"*

***From this meditation today, I will pray . . .***

Adoration ______________________

______________________

______________________

Confession ______________________

______________________

______________________

Thanksgiving ______________________

______________________

______________________

Supplication ______________________

______________________

______________________

***From this meditation today, I will . . .***

Think ______________________

______________________

______________________

Say ______________________

______________________

______________________

Do ______________________

______________________

______________________

______________________

______________________

September 29

# Wonderful Counselor

*Laban and Bethuel answered, "This is from the LORD; we can say nothing to you one way or the other"* (Genesis 24:50).

Scripture: Genesis 24:42-51

**Song:** *"Open My Eyes That I May See"*

***From this meditation today, I will pray . . .***

Adoration ______________________

______________________

______________________

Confession ______________________

______________________

______________________

Thanksgiving ______________________

______________________

______________________

Supplication ______________________

______________________

______________________

***From this meditation today, I will . . .***

Think ______________________

______________________

______________________

Say ______________________

______________________

______________________

Do ______________________

______________________

______________________

______________________

______________________

Have you ever struggled to discern God's will for you? It would be nice if God would send down a giant neon sign flashing, "Here I am, and here's what I want you to do." But God doesn't usually work that way. So what are we to do?

I find an important clue in today's Scripture passage. Laban and Bethuel listened carefully to what Abraham's servant told them. They had a tough decision to make about Rebekah's future, but they were able to make it easily because they knew God had arranged it all. They knew Abraham's servant was obeying the Lord, and that was enough for them.

When we face our own important decisions, we can be certain that God has given us many faithful counselors to help point the way. Our families, ministers, and other church members will often provide helpful wisdom. But the most important and authoritative guide of all is the Holy Spirit, who speaks to us in Scripture and in our hearts. When we study the Word and listen to His leading, we will know the next step to take.

Lord, *I face so many choices every day. Help me find direction in Your Word and be very attentive to Your still voice within. In the name of the Father, the Son, and the Holy Spirit, I pray. Amen.*

**SPOTLIGHT**

***Next Week's Lesson***

Rebekah's family had a hard decision, but once they saw God's will, the decision became easy.

# Love Through the Generations

*The LORD is good and his love endures forever;*
*his faithfulness continues through all generations*
(Psalm 100:5).

My father is 84 years old and quite frail. During his most recent hospitalization, he had some trouble with memory, so the doctors frequently asked him questions like "Where are you now?" and "Who are these people in the room with you?" Often it would be my sisters and I, and then my dad would tell the doctors about his seven children and how proud he was of them. He couldn't remember much else, but he knew his legacy of love lived on in us.

God's love is alive and well in us too. God has always loved, and He always will love. That constancy has not wavered throughout history. From Adam to Abraham, from Moses to David, from the birth of Christ to His future glorious appearing, God's love is eternal.

And just as my dad's love lives on in his children, so too God's love is lived out in the daily lives of His children. Whenever we help our neighbor, we allow God's love to be shared in our generation and in the generations to come.

God of eternity, *Your great love causes me to sing Your praises and to offer my whole life as a witness to You. Help me this day to be faithful in serving You as You have always been faithful in loving me. I pray this prayer in the name of Jesus, my Savior and Lord. Amen.*

**SEARCH THE WORD**

*Reading Genesis, one quickly discovers this truth: God is faithful to His word.*

Scripture: Psalm 100

Song: *"Great Is Thy Faithfulness"*

*From this meditation today, I will pray . . .*

Adoration ______________________________

______________________________

______________________________

Confession ______________________________

______________________________

______________________________

Thanksgiving ______________________________

______________________________

______________________________

Supplication ______________________________

______________________________

______________________________

*From this meditation today, I will . . .*

Think ______________________________

______________________________

______________________________

Say ______________________________

______________________________

______________________________

Do ______________________________

______________________________

______________________________

______________________________

______________________________

*Enter his gates
with thanksgiving
and his courts with praise;
give thanks to him and
praise his* name.
—Psalm 100:4

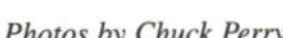

*Photos by Chuck Perry*

## October

# GOD'S PEOPLE INCREASE

*Let the hearts of those who seek the LORD rejoice.*
—Psalm 105:3

*Photo © Jupiterimages*

October 1

# Give Him the Glory

*According as it is written, He that glorieth, let him glory in the Lord* (1 Corinthians 1:31, *King James Version*).

Scripture: 1 Corinthians 1:26-31
Song: *"To God Be the Glory"*

***From this meditation today, I will pray . . .***

Adoration ____________________________

Confession ____________________________

Thanksgiving ____________________________

Supplication ____________________________

***From this meditation today, I will . . .***

Think ____________________________

Say ____________________________

Do ____________________________

October 1–7. ***Richard Robinson*** *is a minister in Denver, Colorado, and Bible teacher on The Holy Ground Radio Broadcast, aired daily throughout the state.*

On April 29, 1962, President John F. Kennedy made the following comment at a dinner honoring the Nobel Prize winners of the Western Hemisphere: "I think this is the most extraordinary collection of talent, of human knowledge, that has ever been gathered together at the White House—with the possible exception of when Thomas Jefferson dined alone." That witty remark gave perspective to those specially chosen honorees. They were among the world's best and brightest, but the brilliant impact of one man—Jefferson—gave them all a nation that could appreciate and appropriate what they had done.

Paul told the Corinthian believers they'd been specially chosen by the Lord. However, for most of them, at least in the world's eyes, their main distinction was their seeming *lack* of any distinction! But God used the ordinary to do the extraordinary. And, as usual, the Lord deserves all the credit for developing lesser abilities in humble circumstances. When we gather for worship, it is not to congratulate ourselves but to give Christ the glory.

Dear Savior, *thank You for Your special calling and using me beyond what was even thought possible. In Jesus' name, amen.*

**SPOTLIGHT**
***Next Week's Lesson***
Twins usually have a special bond; for Esau and Jacob that bond would turn to rivalry. Bonded or broken? That's the choice.

# Guided, Gracious, Grand Life

*Laban and Bethuel answered and said, The thing proceedeth from the LORD: we cannot speak unto thee bad or good* (Genesis 24:50, *King James Version*).

The beautiful story of Abraham's servant finding a wife for Isaac presents three striking features. First, we see how this faithful servant was guided by God. As Rebekah's family heard how God precisely answered the servant's prayer, they knew that the events had been issued from the Lord. Like the servant, we should say to all would-be helpers in the drama of God's will, "Hinder me not, seeing the LORD hath prospered my way" (v. 56, *KJV*).

Second, we see how gracious all the parties were in their interactions with each other. Obviously, the right attitude always helps.

Third, notice the grand undertones of this whole story. We sense it from the servant's spontaneous worship, from Rebekah's sweet surrender, even from Laban and Bethuel's reluctant blessing, saying, "Thou art our sister; be thou the mother of thousands of millions" (v. 60, *KJV*). Like them, we all need expanded views of God's will and work. Are we indeed caught up in something bigger than ourselves?

Dear Lord, *help me to walk by faith and experience Your guidance, graciously doing Your will in Your grand plan for my life. I pray this prayer in the name of Jesus, my wonderful Savior and Lord. Amen.*

**SEARCH THE WORD**

*O for the wisdom to say, "This proceeds from the Lord; we cannot speak ill of it!"*

Scripture: Genesis 24:50-61

Song: *"The Guiding Hand"*

*From this meditation today, I will pray . . .*

Adoration ______________________

Confession ______________________

Thanksgiving ______________________

Supplication ______________________

*From this meditation today, I will . . .*

Think ______________________

Say ______________________

Do ______________________

# A Sigh of Relief

*Isaac . . . took Rebekah, and she became his wife; and he loved her: and Isaac was comforted after his mother's death*
(Genesis 24:67, *King James Version*).

Scripture: Genesis 24:62-67
Song: *"O Perfect Love"*

***From this meditation today, I will pray . . .***

Adoration ____________________

Confession ____________________

Thanksgiving ____________________

Supplication ____________________

***From this meditation today, I will . . .***

Think ____________________

Say ____________________

Do ____________________

Picture Isaac seeing the camel caravan off in the distance. In anticipation, he went to meet the traveling party. Rebekah saw him walking toward them, inquired of the servant, and was told that it was his master—and her new husband! Upon meeting them, Isaac heard the whole amazing story of God's guidance. With appropriate tenderness, Isaac took his new bride into his mother's tent to consummate their marriage.

The void in the patriarch's heart after his mother's death was finally filled by the love and comfort that Rebekah extended to Isaac. Only the right woman matched to the right man could produce this right result—and at just the right time!

God brought Isaac and Rebekah together across a vast space, closing the distance at the appointed time. As Proverbs 18:22 says, "Whoso findeth a wife findeth a good thing, and obtaineth favor of the LORD" *(KJV)*. That kind of favor always ends, as it did for Isaac, with a sweet sigh of relief.

God, *thank You for the way You bring others into my life, especially when that special someone is sent to bring comfort. Through Christ, I pray. Amen.*

**SPOTLIGHT**
***Next Week's Lesson***

The love and comfort of a good marriage is sometimes broken by children gone wrong—as with Isaac and Rebekah's sons.

# A Shining Moment

*Isaac entreated the Lord for his wife . . . and the Lord was entreated of him, and Rebekah his wife conceived*
(Genesis 25:21, *King James Version*).

Theodore Roosevelt delivered a speech on April 10, 1899, titled "The Strenuous Life" and made this observation: "If we are to be a really great people, we must strive in good faith to play a great part in the world. We cannot avoid meeting great issues. All that we can determine for ourselves is whether we shall meet them well or ill."

These words describe Isaac's situation in today's Scripture. Isaac had now reached a comfortable stage in his life, a peaceful and predictable time. But his wife's barrenness was a growing concern to both of them. This led the easygoing, calm-natured patriarch to entreat the Lord for his wife (v. 21, *KJV*). The word *entreat* conveys the idea of pleading, and this prayer was so intense and persuasive that God granted his request. Soon after, the happy couple was expecting.

As Roosevelt pointed out, there is no avoiding "great issues," even in the most secure, well-to-do homes. But we can meet them as Isaac did—by rising to the occasion with our finest prayers. It was Isaac's shining moment.

Father God, *in my prayers give me the perseverance and urgency of an Isaac. Let me learn for myself what it means to entreat the Lord with an open and sincere heart. Thank You, in Jesus' name. Amen.*

**SEARCH THE WORD**
*God understands the urgency of our prayers. Sometimes He does not respond until He sees our sense of urgency.*

Scripture: Genesis 25:19-23
**Song:** *"I Must Tell Jesus"*

**From this meditation today, I will pray . . .**

Adoration ______________________________

______________________________

______________________________

Confession ______________________________

______________________________

______________________________

Thanksgiving ______________________________

______________________________

______________________________

Supplication ______________________________

______________________________

______________________________

***From this meditation today, I will . . .***

Think ______________________________

______________________________

______________________________

Say ______________________________

______________________________

______________________________

Do ______________________________

______________________________

______________________________

______________________________

______________________________

October 5

# Destiny of Two Boys

*The boys grew: and Esau was a cunning hunter, a man of the field; and Jacob was a plain man, dwelling in tents*
(Genesis 25:27, *King James Version*).

Scripture: Genesis 25:24-28
Song: *"Children of the Heavenly Father"*

***From this meditation today, I will pray . . .***

Adoration ______________________________

______________________________

______________________________

Confession ______________________________

______________________________

______________________________

Thanksgiving ______________________________

______________________________

______________________________

Supplication ______________________________

______________________________

______________________________

***From this meditation today, I will . . .***

Think ______________________________

______________________________

______________________________

Say ______________________________

______________________________

______________________________

Do ______________________________

______________________________

______________________________

______________________________

______________________________

After Rebekah gave birth to twin boys, the prophecy given earlier began to be fulfilled (see v. 23, *KJV*). Two nations developed, as opposite as the boys themselves. Esau became an avid outdoorsman with a taste for adventure, tending toward the worldly and secular.

Jacob preferred the domestic circle over the great outdoors. He was less active but just as ambitious, using his mind more than his muscle. Jacob also possessed the raw materials of spiritual leadership and became God's chosen patriarch-in-the-making.

These two boys remind all parents that a child's destiny begins in childhood. Several people have been credited with saying, "Give me a child for the first seven years, and you may do what you like with him afterwards." It's true! Young children respond to training—of any kind, from any person, whether good or bad. Thankfully, good parenting still shapes the child who shapes the future. Yet, as Isaac and Rebekah demonstrate, only when parents work together will the future of children be bright.

Dear Lord, *may all those with children depend on Your wisdom and grace, remembering that the future of many lives is at stake. In the holy name of Jesus, my Lord and Savior, I pray. Amen.*

**SPOTLIGHT**
***Next Week's Lesson***
Early differences may portend later difficulties whether in marriage, with siblings, or even in friendships.

# Birthright at a Bargain

*Jacob said, Swear to me this day; and he sware unto him: and he sold his birthright unto Jacob*
(Genesis 25:33, *King James Version*).

Compared to the secretive, scheming Jacob, Esau seemed like an open book, freely sharing what was on his mind. When he came in from the field tired and hungry, Jacob was ready for him. With the delicious aroma of a fresh pot of stew hitting his nostrils, Esau immediately wanted some. Jacob simply said to his brother, "Sell me this day thy birthright" (v. 31, *KJV*).

Esau reacted impulsively with no thought of the consequences and swiftly agreed to the deal. He sold his birthright, ate the stew, and went his way. The Bible puts the whole transaction in its true light: Esau *despised* his birthright, something of inestimable value.

Like Esau, we all have a birthright, those special privileges granted only to children of God. Praying, teaching, counseling, leading, serving, giving—these all tap into our spiritual inheritance. But if we give in to our fleshly appetites, we are prodigal children squandering our birthright. Jacob drove a hard bargain that day, which Esau later regretted. May we never sell our birthright at any price!

Heavenly Father, *keep me from foolish, impulsive, and short-sighted compromises that defraud me of spiritual blessings. I pray in Jesus name, amen.*

**SEARCH THE WORD**

*Understanding the value of one's gifts—there's the foundation for spiritual success.*

Scripture: Genesis 25:29-34

Song: *"Falter Not"*

*From this meditation today, I will pray . . .*

Adoration ______________________

______________________

______________________

Confession ______________________

______________________

______________________

Thanksgiving ______________________

______________________

______________________

Supplication ______________________

______________________

______________________

*From this meditation today, I will . . .*

Think ______________________

______________________

______________________

Say ______________________

______________________

______________________

Do ______________________

______________________

______________________

______________________

______________________

October 7

# He Got What He Wanted

*When Esau heard the words of his father, he cried with a great and exceeding bitter cry, and said unto his father, Bless me, even me also, O my father. And he said, Thy brother came with subtilty, and hath taken away thy blessing* (Genesis 27:34, 35, *King James Version*).

Scripture: Genesis 27:30-40

Song: *"Take the World, but Give Me Jesus"*

*From this meditation today, I will pray . . .*

Adoration ____________________

Confession ____________________

Thanksgiving ____________________

Supplication ____________________

*From this meditation today, I will . . .*

Think ____________________

Say ____________________

Do ____________________

Intense human emotion drips from this story. Esau finally arrived to receive his father's highest blessing, reserved for the firstborn—only to discover that Jacob had gotten there first! Yes, the schemer had already tricked his father into giving him the best blessing. Esau begged his father to bless him anyway, which he did, but not with the great patriarchal blessing.

As it turned out, Esau ended up getting exactly what he wanted. He valued worldly success and material things, so his father blessed him with "the fatness of the earth, and of the dew of heaven from above" (v. 39, *KJV*). God gave him his heart's real desire, but at the awful price of constant striving and a forfeited birthright (v. 40, *KJV*).

It makes me realize that I ought to be very careful what I ask for. I just might get it!

**Blessed Father,** *it is so tempting to choose immediate gratification over the promise of future rewards. But remind me, Lord, that Your promise is sure and unfailing. So cleanse my heart from inordinate affections here on earth, the love of the world and the lusts of the flesh. Instead, let me desire only Your will and glory for as long as I live. In Jesus' name, amen.*

**SPOTLIGHT**

***Next Week's Lesson***

Deceit always ends in a rush of bitter anguish. Either the deceived or the deceiver or both will wilt in tears.

# Say, Can You Sing?

*Sing to him, sing praise to him; tell of all his wonderful acts* (Psalm 105:2).

Recently, our school district hosted a motivational seminar for a few hundred teachers. At one point our energetic speaker instructed us, "Raise your hand if you can sing." Perhaps 20 hands braved an answer. Amazing! Only that many people regard themselves as singers?

I considered my classroom of 6-year-olds. All sing. All paint. All write. In fact, they regard themselves as experts at everything.

How could a singing child mature into an adult incapable of carrying a tune in a bucket? Perhaps mind-set is the answer. Some of us adopt the notion we're inept because we're not the best in the field. However, the Lord never asks us to sing to Him only if we're trained vocalists or if our albums top the charts.

We bless God when we offer melodies from a grateful heart. Today's passage details several of God's attributes worthy of including in a song of worship. We may not be experts in all things, but we've been given so much. A song of gratitude waits to praise Him. Who will sing it?

Lord, *thank You for the goodness You've brought to my life. I want to praise You with heartfelt words, whether spoken or sung. In Jesus' name, amen.*

**SEARCH THE WORD**

*Melody and poetry—how befitting the God who speaks in both languages!*

Scripture: Psalm 105:1-6

**Song:** *"O Worship the King"*

***From this meditation today, I will pray . . .***

Adoration ____________________

Confession ____________________

Thanksgiving ____________________

Supplication ____________________

***From this meditation today, I will . . .***

Think ____________________

Say ____________________

Do ____________________

October 8–14. ***Vicki Hodges*** *teaches first grade and writes from her home in the Colorado Rockies.*

# Imagination Express

*"To you I will give the land of Canaan as the portion you will inherit"* (Psalm 105:11).

Scripture: Psalm 105:7-11

Song: *"Holy, Holy, Holy"*

A few weeks ago a friend asked, "What is the best thing you can imagine?" A lifetime supply of chocolate, of course! Maybe I should have answered visits with loved ones, traveling to all the places on *my list,* or always being in sound health. Pause a few moments to explore your own response.

Someone has rightly noted that our most important thoughts are those of God and Heaven. Today's Bible passage overflows with significant descriptions of God. He is the Lord our God, just, faithful, a promise keeper, and our benefactor. Just as God promised Abraham's descendants the land of Canaan as their inheritance, all followers of Jesus are promised Heaven as an inheritance by their faithful, promise-keeping Lord.

In his letter to the Ephesians, Paul proclaims that God "is able to do immeasurably more than all we ask or imagine" (3:20). That includes taking us to Heaven, of course. Thoughts of Heaven always stretch my mind, but God isn't interested in just confirming my finite thoughts. He continually exceeds my imagination, for Heaven is far better than the best we can envision.

Lord, *You are not limited even by my highest thoughts. I am so eager to experience the best You can create. Praise to You in Christ's name! Amen.*

***From this meditation today, I will pray . . .***

Adoration ______________________________

______________________________

______________________________

Confession ______________________________

______________________________

______________________________

Thanksgiving ______________________________

______________________________

______________________________

Supplication ______________________________

______________________________

______________________________

***From this meditation today, I will . . .***

Think ______________________________

______________________________

______________________________

Say ______________________________

______________________________

______________________________

Do ______________________________

______________________________

______________________________

______________________________

______________________________

**SPOTLIGHT**

***Next Week's Lesson***

If Jacob had been offered a choice, what might he have asked for? God knows and plans something better.

# Glowing in Grace

*Esau held a grudge against Jacob because of the blessing his father had given him. He said to himself, "The days of mourning for my father are near; then I will kill my brother Jacob"* (Genesis 27:41).

Fire needs four ingredients: oxygen, fuel, a heat source, and a chemical reaction. When one of those is missing, flames can't exist. This year at my workplace, some drastic policy changes have produced relational wildfires. Staff tempers grew short, attitudes flared, and production plummeted. And I'm sorry to say, my own bad attitude has contributed to the blaze.

Esau kindled a personal wildfire. Disappointment, anger, and hatred—all natural emotions—fueled his desire to kill his brother. This unchecked seething caused him to become disordered, virtually psychopathic. Twisted thoughts of Jacob's demise consoled Esau, though he could have chosen to enjoy God's goodness instead.

Esau's experience teaches me much. Just as God would have delighted to show grace to Esau, He would also be pleased to shower my life with grace. The climate at work would likely be improved if I would set aside my seemingly justified reactions and choose to let Christ transform my attitudes.

Lord, *help me surrender my frustration and anger to You today. By Your example and indwelling Spirit, put out these fires! In Jesus' name, amen.*

**SEARCH THE WORD**

*Esau's emotional steam would burn him more than it would others. That's almost always the case.*

Scripture: Genesis 27:41-45

Song: *"And Can It Be That I Should Gain?"*

***From this meditation today, I will pray . . .***

Adoration ______________________________

Confession ______________________________

Thanksgiving ______________________________

Supplication ______________________________

***From this meditation today, I will . . .***

Think ______________________________

Say ______________________________

Do ______________________________

# Never Give a Good Gift

*Rebekah said to Isaac, "I'm disgusted with living because of these Hittite women. If Jacob takes a wife from among the women of this land, from Hittite women like these, my life will not be worth living"* (Genesis 27:46).

Scripture: Genesis 27:46–28:5

Song: *"The Gifts of Love"*

*From this meditation today, I will pray . . .*

Adoration ________________________________

________________________________

________________________________

Confession ________________________________

________________________________

________________________________

Thanksgiving ________________________________

________________________________

________________________________

Supplication ________________________________

________________________________

________________________________

*From this meditation today, I will . . .*

Think ________________________________

________________________________

________________________________

Say ________________________________

________________________________

________________________________

Do ________________________________

________________________________

________________________________

________________________________

________________________________

The skillet sizzled with melted butter and fresh fish. I considered the size of this gift. Our friend drove several miles and spent a couple of hours to catch his legal limit of salmon. When he arrived at our house, the fish were cleaned, skinned, filleted, and packaged. He could have handed over a dripping stringer of slimy fish for us to prepare, but he chose to give a *better* gift.

Rebekah was a giver of good gifts. When she learned of Esau's plot to kill Jacob, she insisted her husband send Jacob away. Of course, she diluted the truth by saying she didn't want Jacob marrying a Canaanite. Even though this plan spared Jacob from certain death, Rebekah's means were deceitful. She endowed Jacob with a good gift: the gift of life. However, she could have afforded a better gift: the gift of honesty.

When deciding between a good and better gift, which will we choose? Do we donate the worn-out or the new? Do we prefer the best for ourselves or give it away?

Father, *thank You for giving Your best gift, Your Son, Jesus, at great sacrifice. My tendency is to give when it's convenient and doesn't cost too much. By Your power, help me to follow Your example. Through Christ, amen.*

**SPOTLIGHT**

***Next Week's Lesson***

Jacob wasn't actually sent by his parents; he was called by God.

# Motives and Actions

*Esau then realized how displeasing the Canaanite women were to his father Isaac* (Genesis 28:8).

Josh was a boy in one of my elementary classes years ago. He tripped over his untied shoes, had a runny nose and mussed hair. Kids frequently tattled on his abrasive behavior, and he rarely completed class assignments. When his single mom, mired in a custody battle, asked me to write a letter indicating her positive influence on his grades, cleanliness, and behavior, I told her the evidence wouldn't allow me to accommodate the request.

The next day a clean Josh brought me a bouquet of shriveled aspen leaves. The following day he slipped me a purple-crayoned drawing of two stick people holding hands. Now when turning in his homework, he says, "I love you. You're my favorite teacher." (If he'd fork over some chocolate, I might cut a deal!)

What motivated Josh to change? Perhaps it was the same thing that urged Esau to shift gears. He realized what it would take to please his parent.

While we likely don't approve of either rationale, both guys made decisions for positive change. Sometimes it takes time for a noble motivation to catch up with our actions. And vice versa.

Lord, *do Your work in my heart, for You know my own actions are often driven by selfishness more than virtue. In Your holy name, I pray. Amen.*

**SEARCH THE WORD**

*A lightbulb moment—"O, now I realize"—regarding our sins is the first step toward repentance.*

Scripture: Genesis 28:6-9

**Song:** *"Fairest Lord Jesus"*

*From this meditation today, I will pray . . .*

Adoration ____________________

Confession ____________________

Thanksgiving ____________________

Supplication ____________________

*From this meditation today, I will . . .*

Think ____________________

Say ____________________

Do ____________________

# The Best Calling Plan

*He was afraid and said, "How awesome is this place! This is none other than the house of God; this is the gate of heaven"* (Genesis 28:17).

Scripture: Genesis 28:10-17

Song: *"Be Thou My Vision"*

***From this meditation today, I will pray . . .***

Adoration ______________________________

Confession ______________________________

Thanksgiving ______________________________

Supplication ______________________________

***From this meditation today, I will . . .***

Think ______________________________

Say ______________________________

Do ______________________________

Both our daughters worked abroad during the summer, but geography hardly separated us. While we missed them greatly, phone calls and e-mails helped us stay in touch. We shared news and expressions of love. Though we were physically apart, we remained connected.

When Jacob left home he spent a night in what seemed an arbitrary location. He settled in for the night, sleeping on a rock pillow, dreaming of angels ascending and descending from a stairway bridging earth and Heaven. From above the top step, God spoke to Jacob, establishing His identity and reassuring Jacob that He would be *his* God, as well as being the God of Abraham and Isaac. Imagine Jacob's surprise at finding God in such a random place!

Where do we expect to find God? He is a thought away. Prayer, instant communication between earth and Heaven, is our great privilege. And Jesus, our resident intercessor, bridges both realms as He constantly talks with the Father on our behalf (see Romans 8:34).

Lord, *thank You for Your constant presence. You always listen to me and speak wisdom. Teach me to explore Your mind until I come into agreement with Your heart. Through Christ, my Lord, I pray. Amen.*

**SPOTLIGHT**

***Next Week's Lesson***

Jacob's dream is a testimony to God's omnipresence; do you see Him in the hard places?

# Memory Rocks!

*Early the next morning Jacob took the stone he had placed under his head and set it up as a pillar and poured oil on top of it* (Genesis 28:18).

When our family vacations, we generally collect a rock to remind us of the trip, and a section of our front yard is designated for those special souvenirs. We have jade, quartz, petrified wood, copper-streaked stones, a desert rose, agate, rose quartz, lava, sandstone, flint, and a kidney-shaped stone. Each rock holds a special memory, except for the kidney. None of us remembers where we got it.

I think Jacob would have liked our rock garden. After his amazing dream of angels and God's conversation with him, Jacob called that area "God's house" (v. 22). He promptly erected a small memorial from the stone pillow he had used the night before and anointed the top of it with oil. This memory-rock served to commemorate God's promise to bless and multiply Jacob's descendants. It was also a reminder of the vow Jacob made to God.

Any significant encounter with the Lord is cause for celebration, isn't it? Whether we anoint our own memory-rock by journaling, or just by telling family and friends, the remembrance is an important faith-builder.

Heavenly Father, *You are my rock and my salvation. May You always be my best memory, as well! In the precious name of Jesus, I pray. Amen.*

**SEARCH THE WORD**

*Every Christian needs a "rock garden" to commemorate meetings with God.*

Scripture: Genesis 28:18-22

**Song: *"Come, Thou Fount"***

*From this meditation today, I will pray . . .*

Adoration ______________________________

______________________________

______________________________

Confession ______________________________

______________________________

______________________________

Thanksgiving ______________________________

______________________________

______________________________

Supplication ______________________________

______________________________

______________________________

*From this meditation today, I will . . .*

Think ______________________________

______________________________

______________________________

Say ______________________________

______________________________

______________________________

Do ______________________________

______________________________

______________________________

______________________________

______________________________

# Finally, Breathing!

*He will cover you with His pinions, and under His wings you may seek refuge; His faithfulness is a shield and bulwark* (Psalm 91:4, *New American Standard Bible*).

Scripture: Psalm 91

Song: *"Under His Wings"*

***From this meditation today, I will pray . . .***

Adoration ______________________________

Confession ______________________________

Thanksgiving ______________________________

Supplication ______________________________

***From this meditation today, I will . . .***

Think ______________________________

Say ______________________________

Do ______________________________

October 15–21. ***Phillis Harris Brooks*** *is an experienced devotional writer who enjoys the aspens of Colorado with her husband and son.*

Growing up as a member of a large family that normally rode Greyhound buses for extended trips, I surprised no one when I fell wildly in love with flying at a young age. I equated safety with those huge wings and always looked forward to any flight. However, by the time September 2001 arrived, I'd taken too many business trips to retain my childhood wonder at flying.

About a week after September 11, while flying from the Southwest back eastward, I realized I'd unconsciously held my breath ever since the fall of the Twin Towers. Sheepishly, I admitted to a friend my reluctance to board a plane ever again. She advised, "Read Psalm 91. It's one of my favorites."

Reading that psalm flooded me with the image of our powerful God enfolding me within huge, divine, omnipotent wings. I read those blessed, lyric lines, wept . . . and finally exhaled.

O God, *forgive me for sometimes losing sight of how grand You are. You are always there with Your loving arms and omnipotent care. All glory to You, in the name of the Father, the Son, and the Holy Spirit. Amen.*

**SPOTLIGHT**

***Next Week's Lesson***

Psalm 91 pictures God's love—the model for all human love, even Jacob's for Rachel.

# If Nothing Else

*It came about, when Jacob saw Rachel the daughter of Laban his mother's brother, and the sheep of Laban his mother's brother, that Jacob went up, and rolled the stone from the mouth of the well, and watered the flock of Laban his mother's brother* (Genesis 29:10, *New American Standard Bible*).

Imagine a kiss causing death. A news story told of a teenage girl with extreme allergies. One of those allergies involved a reaction to peanut oil. She died after kissing her boyfriend, who had eaten a peanut butter sandwich.

Love requires mindfulness, if nothing else. What does mindfulness look like? In the case of Jacob, it could involve rolling a stone away from a well for his cousin Rachel. Yet, in his case, mindfulness may have taken a back-seat to pride. Jacob probably longed to favorably impress his attractive cousin. Perhaps current day mindfulness, for us, might entail investing the necessary time to better appreciate a close friend.

I know that such mindfulness can draw me into closer fellowship with God, as well. If I embrace Him as the lover of my soul, then my soul needs to strive to mirror that which would please my love. And how do I begin to know what would please God? By not being afraid to spend time alone with Him and His Word.

Lord, *help me set my mind on You today. Even if I can only spare five minutes, let those moments be genuine and precious. In Jesus' name, amen.*

**SEARCH THE WORD**

*Good deeds can be done to impress. Good deeds can be done to bless. Which will it be?*

Scripture: Genesis 29:1-12

Song: *"Take Time to Be Holy"*

***From this meditation today, I will pray . . .***

Adoration ____________________

Confession ____________________

Thanksgiving ____________________

Supplication ____________________

***From this meditation today, I will . . .***

Think ____________________

Say ____________________

Do ____________________

October 17

# No-Boundary Loving?

*Jacob served seven years for Rachel and they seemed to him but a few days because of his love for her* (Genesis 29:20, *New American Standard Bible*).

Scripture: Genesis 29:13-20

Song: *"Love Lifted Me"*

***From this meditation today, I will pray . . .***

Adoration ______________________________

______________________________

______________________________

Confession ______________________________

______________________________

______________________________

Thanksgiving ______________________________

______________________________

______________________________

Supplication ______________________________

______________________________

______________________________

***From this meditation today, I will . . .***

Think ______________________________

______________________________

______________________________

Say ______________________________

______________________________

______________________________

Do ______________________________

______________________________

______________________________

______________________________

______________________________

Our family learned a lot about the heaviness of time this previous year. As though under siege, we catapulted from one challenge to another. A favorite aunt died. After 19 years, a brother questioned his marriage. Spring found me recovering from quadruple bypass surgery, only to have another blockage surface in my leg. And diagnosed with breast cancer early in the year, a younger sister then confronted brain cancer 11 months later.

The disappointments and heartaches of the year reduced time's speed to the slowness of a dance in quicksand. Against such a backdrop, it isn't at all difficult to understand how Jacob's seven year labor of love, heightened by anticipation, would assume the sensation of warp speed for him. Joy and anticipation can color an attitude so that no sacrifice looms too great.

I wonder if it's possible to live for God in the same manner. In this day and age, with its encouragement to set boundaries, that might constitute a pretty scary thought —loving God without any boundaries!

*No matter what the cost,* Lord, *whether health, time, or family, I give my days and years to You. They were never mine anyway; I have always belonged to You. In Christ's holy name, I pray. Amen.*

**SPOTLIGHT**

***Next Week's Lesson***

"Tempus fugit," (time flies) the Romans declared. But for Jacob, the days couldn't go by fast enough for his love.

# Entitlements

*It came about in the morning that, behold, it was Leah! And he said to Laban, "What is this you have done to me? Was it not for Rachel that I served with you? Why then have you deceived me?"*
(Genesis 29:25, *New American Standard Bible*).

How often we've heard the outraged accusation "That's not *fair!*" No matter our age, we all have a keen sense of what constitutes fair play. Don't kick a person when she's down. Share, and share alike.

Many of us appreciate the concept of Camelot, with its Knights of the Round Table, to enforce the concept that might doesn't make right. Our expectation is that, having agreed to certain terms, the other parties will do the right thing to fulfill their obligations as well.

We really should be grateful, though, that God isn't quite the stickler for rules we sometimes tend to be. God sees each of us believers as His beloved adopted children. He overlooks our tantrums in the midst of adversity, cradles each sobbing child until he's comforted enough to run, play, and . . . throw tantrums again.

Sounds quite a bit like parenting, doesn't it? Yes, we all know how much fairness a good daddy expects to receive.

Father in Heaven, *regardless of the experiences I may have had as a child, inspire me to approach You as the loving parent I've desired. I ask this in the name of Your Son, Jesus the Christ. Amen.*

**SEARCH THE WORD**

*We expect everyone to be fair except for God. Him we expect to be gracious and forgiving.*

Scripture: Genesis 29:21-25a

Song: *"Have Thine Own Way, Lord"*

***From this meditation today, I will pray . . .***

Adoration ______________________________

Confession ______________________________

Thanksgiving ______________________________

Supplication ______________________________

***From this meditation today, I will . . .***

Think ______________________________

Say ______________________________

Do ______________________________

# Wrong Direction?

*But Laban said, "It is not the practice in our place, to marry off the younger before the first-born"* (Genesis 29:26, *New American Standard Bible*).

Scripture: Genesis 29:25b-30
Song: *"Pure Within"*

***From this meditation today, I will pray . . .***

Adoration ____________________

Confession ____________________

Thanksgiving ____________________

Supplication ____________________

***From this meditation today, I will . . .***

Think ____________________

Say ____________________

Do ____________________

One of my coworkers lives for competition. If I'm not careful, I'll occasionally fall into the trap of trying to outshine her. Of course, once I enter into that game, then we fuel each other's egos. The result: the project doesn't turn out quite as well, requires more time, and leaves me with a general sense of dissatisfaction.

I'm pretty sure my disquiet has more to do with my behavior than with the results of my performance. Why? Because I know that I know better. My allowing others to goad me into purely selfish behavior says much more about me than about them.

God deliberately equipped us with consciences to act as moral compasses. Perhaps Laban misplaced his compass! Otherwise, he'd have fulfilled his promise to Jacob, rather than continuing this sad competition for his daughters. In fact, as soon as any of us begin to suspect that we've tarted in the wrong direction, we can immediately stop and ask God's assistance to regain our ethical bearings.

Lord, *You know how quickly I falter, so remind me that when I stumble, You remain at my side to catch me. In the holy name of Jesus, my Lord and Savior, I pray. Amen.*

**SPOTLIGHT**
***Next Week's Lesson***

Truth sometimes comes later than it should. When it does, it stands very close to being a lie.

# Just Thank Him

*She conceived again and bore a son and said, "This time I will praise the Lord." Therefore she named him Judah. Then she stopped bearing* (Genesis 29:35, *New American Standard Bible*).

The Christmas when I was 10 years old, after I'd prayed for a great toy, someone gave me a pair of what had to be the ugliest shoes in the world. They were candy-apple red, complete with bone-crushing pointed toes. They looked as though they'd escaped the set of *The Wizard of Oz.* Because of their glitter, passersby found it difficult, if not impossible, to rip their gazes from them.

How I hated those shoes! Yet my mother eventually demanded to know when I intended to write the thank-you note for them. I looked at her in astonishment. Why in the world would I thank someone for giving me something so impractical and embarrassing?

Naturally, my mother's outlook differed significantly. "You needed shoes," she said. "And we don't tell God how to answer our prayers. We just thank Him." It took some time before I could take up her outlook as my own. But as Leah must have discovered so long ago, I too have begun to realize that "No" also represents a divine response. Ingratitude only serves to chill my relationship with the one who always answers my prayers.

Giver of every good thing, *help me never discard Your greater gifts for the easier way. In the name of Christ, I pray. Amen.*

**SEARCH THE WORD**

*God answers prayers, not always as we hoped and anticipated but always as we need.*

Scripture: Genesis 29:31-35

Song: *"Now Thank We All Our God"*

*From this meditation today, I will pray . . .*

Adoration ______________________________

______________________________

______________________________

Confession ______________________________

______________________________

______________________________

Thanksgiving ______________________________

______________________________

______________________________

Supplication ______________________________

______________________________

______________________________

*From this meditation today, I will . . .*

Think ______________________________

______________________________

______________________________

Say ______________________________

______________________________

______________________________

Do ______________________________

______________________________

______________________________

______________________________

______________________________

# Missing the Alarm?

*Then God remembered Rachel,*
*and God gave heed to her and opened her womb*
(Genesis 30:22, *New American Standard Bible*).

**Scripture: Genesis 30:22-24; 35:16-21**

Song: *"Brighten the Corner Where You Are"*

***From this meditation today, I will pray . . .***

Adoration ______________________________

______________________________

______________________________

Confession ______________________________

______________________________

______________________________

Thanksgiving ______________________________

______________________________

______________________________

Supplication ______________________________

______________________________

______________________________

***From this meditation today, I will . . .***

Think ______________________________

______________________________

______________________________

Say ______________________________

______________________________

______________________________

Do ______________________________

______________________________

______________________________

______________________________

______________________________

None of us read the signals my sister's body had sent. Her brow would pucker and she'd admit to one of us, "I don't remember how to get there." We chalked it up to her busy lifestyle or her habit of overextending herself. Thoroughly organized, she made it a point to have her doctor's office conveniently located up the street from where she worked.

One day while at work, she confessed to one of her coworkers, "I don't feel well. I should go to the doctor, but I can't remember where his office is." The alarms had finally transformed into loud warning gongs for our family; she had brain cancer.

There's a sense in which God sends us alarms regularly—those inner longings or feelings of uneasiness—may be God tugging at our sleeves. God's persistence in getting our attention is His way of reminding us that He has not moved but we may have wandered from Him. It is the wandering that leads to our forgetfulness about His constant, abiding presence, no matter our situations.

**Light of the world,** *when I wander from You, my world becomes a darker place. Remind me that Your brightness is ever near, and I need only turn homeward to feel the warmth of Your presence. In Jesus' name, amen.*

**SPOTLIGHT**

***Next Week's Lesson***

Years of invested love are always blessed by God.

# Why Worry?

*"Save me, I pray, from the hand of my brother Esau, for I am afraid he will come and attack me, and also the mothers with their children"* (Genesis 32:11).

In October of 1942, Eddie Rickenbacker was forced to crash land his B-17 bomber into the Pacific Ocean. He and his crew were out of radio range, so prospects for rescue were dim. After eight days of floating in a small raft, the crew members had run out of rations and were growing hungry. That morning, after their daily devotional time, Rickenbacker leaned his head back and pulled his hat over his eyes. A seagull landed on his head. Rickenbacker caught it, and the crew ate it while using the bird's intestines for bait to catch fish with hooks provided in their survival kits.

A seagull 900 miles from land? Rickenbacker had a simple explanation for their deliverance: "We prayed."

Fearful circumstances often drive us to our knees, don't they? Jacob feared his brother was seeking vengeance, and so we read "Then Jacob prayed" (vv. 9-12).

Any trouble worth worrying about is worth praying about. And once we've prayed about it, why worry?

Dear Lord, *strengthen my faith that I might always recognize Your presence in my most fearful times. In Christ's holy name, I pray. Amen.*

**SEARCH THE WORD**

*Specific prayers get specific answers.*

Scripture: Genesis 32:3-12

Song: *"A Prayer for God's Blessing"*

***From this meditation today, I will pray . . .***

Adoration ______________________________

______________________________

______________________________

Confession ______________________________

______________________________

______________________________

Thanksgiving ______________________________

______________________________

______________________________

Supplication ______________________________

______________________________

______________________________

***From this meditation today, I will . . .***

Think ______________________________

______________________________

______________________________

Say ______________________________

______________________________

______________________________

Do ______________________________

______________________________

______________________________

October 22–28. ***Dan Nicksich*** *is a minister who writes articles and devotionals from his home in Somerset, Pennsylvania.*

# Time to Reconcile

*"You are to say, 'They belong to your servant Jacob. They are a gift sent to my lord Esau, and he is coming behind us'"* (Genesis 32:18).

Scripture: Genesis 32:13-21

Song: *"Brothers, Joining Hand to Hand"*

***From this meditation today, I will pray . . .***

Adoration ______________________________

Confession ______________________________

Thanksgiving ______________________________

Supplication ______________________________

***From this meditation today, I will . . .***

Think ______________________________

Say ______________________________

Do ______________________________

I need to get even with my brother. First, he drove a rental truck 500 miles to help pack and move our household goods. Now he hosts family gatherings and opens his swimming pool to us on hot summer days. I really do need to get even with him.

Of course, it wasn't always this way. As a younger brother, I constantly felt I was being abused and harassed by him during our childhood years. Getting even (in a different way) seemed to be a constant, consuming passion. How a little maturity changes such perspectives!

One of the saddest funerals I ever conducted was that of a young man whose brothers and sisters experienced a kind of reunion because of his tragic death. "He'll never know how he got us all together for the first time in years," one sister told me through her tears. How sad it is when we carry such harsh feelings toward others without making an effort to reconcile before death.

Jacob had once outrageously cheated his brother. He'd been a wily deceiver. Now he sought reconciliation. Good for him!

Dear Lord, *if there is someone with whom I have had a falling out, grant me the wisdom and courage to seek reconciliation. In Jesus' name, amen.*

**SPOTLIGHT**
***Next Week's Lesson***

Jacob's plan, as elaborate as it was, could not anticipate Esau's welcome—open arms and tears.

# Expecting the Worst?

*Esau ran to meet Jacob and embraced him; he threw his arms around his neck and kissed him. And they wept* (Genesis 33:4).

When I entered the hospital room, the elderly couple sat side by side on the bed, holding hands and crying. They had just received good news, no sign of his suspected cancer. They were both in their 80s.

Jacob was expecting the worst. He put his wives and their children in the back of his procession to give them a better chance of escape. His beloved Rachel and favorite son, Joseph, were bringing up the rear—the safest place, should violence erupt.

What joy Jacob must have felt as his brother ran to meet him and overwhelmed him with an affectionate embrace and kiss! Jesus would paint a similar picture in a parable involving reunion between a father and his wayward son (see Luke 15:11-32).

The Bible says that God can bring good from evil (see Genesis 50:20). He has a way of extending His blessings, even when we expect the worst: a clean bill of health despite the gloomy prognosis, peace and love where once bitterness ruled.

Dear Heavenly Father, *sometimes I expect the worst and then experience Your wonderful blessings instead. Help me to trust You always, even when the days seem darkest. I pray in the name of Jesus my Savior. Amen.*

**SEARCH THE WORD**

*Expecting the worst is false expectation, when God is involved.*

Scripture: Genesis 33:1-4

Song: *"Count Your Blessings"*

***From this meditation today, I will pray . . .***

Adoration ______________________________

______________________________

______________________________

Confession ______________________________

______________________________

______________________________

Thanksgiving ______________________________

______________________________

______________________________

Supplication ______________________________

______________________________

______________________________

***From this meditation today, I will . . .***

Think ______________________________

______________________________

______________________________

Say ______________________________

______________________________

______________________________

Do ______________________________

______________________________

______________________________

______________________________

______________________________

October 25

# The Other Side of Giving

*"Please accept the present that was brought to you, for God has been gracious to me and I have all I need." And because Jacob insisted, Esau accepted it* (Genesis 33:11).

Scripture: Genesis 33:5-11

**Song:** *"Give of Your Best to the Master"*

***From this meditation today, I will pray . . .***

Adoration ____________________________________

Confession ____________________________________

Thanksgiving ____________________________________

Supplication ____________________________________

***From this meditation today, I will . . .***

Think ____________________________________

Say ____________________________________

Do ____________________________________

The church wanted to provide Thanksgiving dinners to some of their senior members, and everything was now in place—volunteers to cook meals, others to deliver them. But then they hit a snag. Many of the intended recipients refused the offer; a few even appeared offended.

While the church often teaches on giving, it may be that we also need to instruct our people in the art of receiving. One cannot give what another refuses to receive. A gracious acceptance completes the exercise of gift-giving.

Jacob insisted, Esau accepted. Most people I know are accustomed to being the giver: the caregiver, the gift giver, the willing helper in a time of need. Once the roles are reversed, they struggle to receive. But God says there will be times when those with plenty must supply the needs of others so that, in turn, the roles may be reversed in due season.

Perhaps this is a time of plenty for you, and you are helping provide for others. But are you also willing to be the needful one at times? How else would it be possible ever to experience love, grace, and caring?

*Humble me,* Lord, *that my pride might not hinder the gifts of those who seek only to give of their best to You. Thank You, in Jesus' name. Amen.*

**SPOTLIGHT**

***Next Week's Lesson***

Esau received the best gift—his brother. Everything else was icing.

# Seeking Favor

*"Just let me find favor in the eyes of my lord"*
(Genesis 33:15).

Ben Franklin once felt that a certain individual seemed to harbor ill feelings toward him, though he could think of no offense or disagreement that had arisen between them. He thought it might have been some perceived, but unintended, slight, or simply a personality clash.

Franklin sent word to the other man, asking whether he could borrow a certain book from his personal library. The book was promptly sent, and thereafter relations between the two were cordial. Franklin's wise approach was to create a situation wherein he was indebted to his potential adversary. He treated the other man as a person of value and worth, and so attained his favor.

Jesus said that even when we are the offended party, we need to take the initiative and seek reconciliation. Of course, this runs contrary to human nature. Shouldn't the offending party bear the burden? But those who simply seek the favor of another will find a way to forgive and move forward.

Esau and Jacob were once again going their separate ways. Once they had departed in anger. Now they departed in peace.

Lord, *may it be that my departure from others would always be in peace. May the regret I feel always be that of the pain of separation and never the pain of unresolved differences. In Jesus' name I pray. Amen.*

**SEARCH THE WORD**

*Nothing more is desirable in a relationship than the favor of the other party.*

Scripture: Genesis 33:12-15

Song: *"Blest Be the Tie That Binds"*

*From this meditation today, I will pray . . .*

Adoration ______________________________

______________________________

______________________________

Confession ______________________________

______________________________

______________________________

Thanksgiving ______________________________

______________________________

______________________________

Supplication ______________________________

______________________________

______________________________

*From this meditation today, I will . . .*

Think ______________________________

______________________________

______________________________

Say ______________________________

______________________________

______________________________

Do ______________________________

______________________________

______________________________

______________________________

______________________________

October 27

# Not Really Foolish

*There he set up an altar and called it El Elohe Israel* (Genesis 33:20).

Scripture: Genesis 33:16-20

Song: *"Freely, Freely"*

*From this meditation today, I will pray . . .*

Adoration ____________________

Confession ____________________

Thanksgiving ____________________

Supplication ____________________

*From this meditation today, I will . . .*

Think ____________________

Say ____________________

Do ____________________

I once read a delightful story called "The Foolish Offering." Whenever confronted with an unexpected expense or potential time of financial hardship, this couple would make what they dubbed their foolish offering. They made a special offering, beyond their weekly gift to their church, some mission, or other worthy cause. They gave in faith, anticipating that God would provide for them in their time of need.

I heard of a church once that operated on the same principle. Whenever things were tightest financially, one of their elders was sure to say, "Time to give more to missions."

It's appropriate that Jacob's journey, including his time of reconciliation with his brother, ends in worship. God's actions on our behalf should bring corresponding acts of praise, thanksgiving, and worship. Some are so confident that they respond to God *in anticipation of blessings yet to come*. How fitting that we not forget God once we've actually reaped His favor!

Lord, *I know that You give all good things at just the right time. Help me give praise and thanks to You whenever You have blessed me. But help me also to give in faith beforehand, anticipating Your sure blessings in Christ. In His precious name I pray. Amen.*

**SPOTLIGHT**

***Next Week's Lesson***

Worship and reconciliation are partners. We can't have one without the other.

# Precious Oil!

*How good and pleasant it is when brothers live together in unity!* (Psalm 133:1).

We purchase perfume by fractions of an ounce. Yet a woman once poured a whole pint of expensive perfume on Jesus, an amount worth more than a year's wages. Some proclaimed this a waste, but Jesus praised her generous act of devotion (see Mark 14:3-9).

It's difficult to relate to the picture of precious oil running down over Aaron's head to the extent that his beard and even the collar of his robes are drenched. Yet the point that comes through is awesome: there are times for a bit of extravagance in our worship of God.

What inspires the outpouring of God's blessings like so much precious oil? Simply this—brothers living together in unity (v. 1). Yet the Bible abounds with brothers who experienced disunity—Cain and Abel, Esau and Jacob, Joseph and his brothers, and the sons of David. You could probably pencil in a few names yourself. You may even know a few examples of brothers or sisters in your own extended family who never seem to reconcile. Thus the precious oil of God's blessing is withheld.

Dear Lord, *thank You for the blessings that appear in my world. But wherever there has been injury or disunity, make me an instrument of peace that others would come to know the abundant outpouring of Your blessings. In the name of the Father, the Son, and the Holy Spirit, I pray. Amen.*

**SEARCH THE WORD**

*"Lets be extravagant in the worship of God!"*

Scripture: Psalm 133

Song: *"Together, Lord, We Come to Thee"*

***From this meditation today, I will pray . . .***

Adoration ______________________

______________________

______________________

Confession ______________________

______________________

______________________

Thanksgiving ______________________

______________________

______________________

Supplication ______________________

______________________

______________________

***From this meditation today, I will . . .***

Think ______________________

______________________

______________________

Say ______________________

______________________

______________________

Do ______________________

______________________

______________________

______________________

______________________

October 29

# Child in His Old Age

*Israel loved Joseph more than any of his other sons, because he had been born to him in his old age; . . . When his brothers saw that their father loved him more than any of them, they hated him* (Genesis 37:3, 4).

Scripture: Genesis 37:1-4
Song: *"God Moves in a Mysterious Way"*

***From this meditation today, I will pray . . .***

Adoration ______________________________
______________________________
______________________________

Confession ______________________________
______________________________
______________________________

Thanksgiving ______________________________
______________________________
______________________________

Supplication ______________________________
______________________________
______________________________

***From this meditation today, I will . . .***

Think ______________________________
______________________________
______________________________

Say ______________________________
______________________________
______________________________

Do ______________________________
______________________________
______________________________

October 29–31. ***Dell Smith-Klein*** *shares Bible truths in the form of stories that touch the hearts of hearers. She lives in the Weaver Mountains of Arizona.*

After his wife died, Hank remarried to a woman almost 25 years younger than he. When their son, Sam, was born, the 50-year-old father doted on the boy. He bought him lots of toys, played with him in the park after work, and took him fishing on the weekends.

But what about Hank's older children? They became jealous of little Sam. Their dad hadn't bought them lots of fancy toys. Nor had he spent as much time with them.

Joseph's brothers were jealous of him too. Their hatred must have hurt. But both boys, Joseph and Sam, were loved deeply by their fathers. Little Sam, like Joseph, could not know what the future held for him, but he knew he could always depend on the love of his father. In the same way, we are loved by our heavenly Father. We can't know what the future holds, but His unchanging love keeps us secure.

Dear Heavenly Father, *I know You hold the future in Your hands. I ask that You help me expect and accept, as Your plan, those difficult circumstances that come into my life. In Jesus' name, amen.*

**SPOTLIGHT**
***Next Week's Lesson***

Love is always good.
Jealousy never is.

# Scorned by His Brothers

*His brothers were jealous of him,*
*but his father kept the matter in mind*
(Genesis 37:11).

Joseph had another dream and felt compelled to share it with his family. His brothers could have begun praising God for revealing something very important to the boy; instead, they succumbed to envy and hatred. And as time went by, they began to scheme against young Joseph.

As I pondered this Bible story, I came up with this scenario: What if someone at church volunteered to be in charge of the children's choir, even though I have always been the choir director? Would I respond with joy that God is working through this person?

In Joseph's case, God was preparing him for leadership long before the need appeared. Joseph didn't know that, nor did his brothers. All they had was Joseph's strange dream about the sun, moon, and stars bowing before him.

It would be hard to figure out the truth if that was all we had to go on—a little brother's dream. After thinking about that children's choir volunteer, I had to ask, "Am I a dreamer like Joseph or a schemer like his brothers?"

Dear God, *thank You for guiding me, even when I don't understand the meaning of the difficult events in my life. With all my heart I lean on You and believe that You have my best interest in mind each step of the way. I pray this prayer in the name of Jesus, my Savior and Lord. Amen.*

**SEARCH THE WORD**

*Some men dream;*
*some men scheme.*
*Both are "could-be" plans.*
*Which do you want?*

Scripture: Genesis 37:5-11
Song: *"Love Is the Theme"*

***From this meditation today, I will pray . . .***

Adoration __________

Confession __________

Thanksgiving __________

Supplication __________

***From this meditation today, I will . . .***

Think __________

Say __________

Do __________

# Helped to Glory

*A man found him wandering around in the fields and asked him, "What are you looking for?" He replied, "I'm looking for my brothers. Can you tell me where they are grazing their flocks?"*

(Genesis 37:15, 16).

Scripture: Genesis 37:12-17

**Song:** *"All the Way My Savior Leads Me"*

***From this meditation today, I will pray . . .***

Adoration ______________________

______________________

______________________

Confession ______________________

______________________

______________________

Thanksgiving ______________________

______________________

______________________

Supplication ______________________

______________________

______________________

***From this meditation today, I will . . .***

Think ______________________

______________________

______________________

Say ______________________

______________________

______________________

Do ______________________

______________________

______________________

______________________

______________________

Stories abound of people who've been helped by an unknown stranger. Some have claimed that the benevolent visitor was an angel, but most of the time the helper is just a good-hearted soul willing to lend a hand in difficult times.

One summer, my husband was driving about 50 miles from home when he saw an older couple parked at the side of the road. He stopped to help and found two very weary 80-year-olds. My husband tried a simple fix on their car, but the couple only drove a few miles before it broke down again. This time, my husband drove all the way home, got the part they needed, and drove back to replace it for them. He wasn't an angel; just a stranger who felt led by God to help.

Joseph knew where his brothers were to be camped, but when he got there, they were gone. A kind stranger directed him to their new location—and to Joseph's rather painful immediate future. But the unfolding of his entire life was in God's hands. And what eventual glory!

Father, *I don't know the motives of others, but I know that I can trust You to bring about what is best in my life. I thank You in Jesus' name. Amen.*

**SPOTLIGHT**

***Next Week's Lesson***

Finding his brothers was Joseph's quest; finding his brothers was Joseph's disaster.

# November

# GOD'S PEOPLE RE-CREATED

*May all who seek you rejoice and be glad in you; . . . "Let God be exalted!"*
—Psalm 70:4

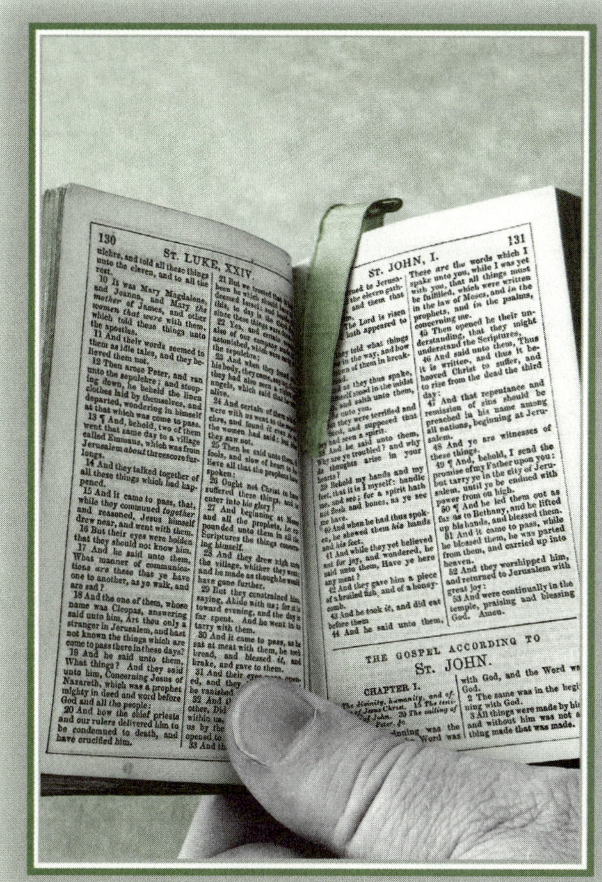


*Photo © istock*

November 1

# Where Will You Serve?

*When Reuben heard this, he tried to rescue him from their hands. "Let's not take his life," he said*
(Genesis 37:21).

Scripture: Genesis 37:18-24

Song: *"Servant of God, Well Done!"*

***From this meditation today, I will pray . . .***

Adoration ____________________

Confession ____________________

Thanksgiving ____________________

Supplication ____________________

***From this meditation today, I will . . .***

Think ____________________

Say ____________________

Do ____________________

November 1–4. ***Dell Smith-Klein*** *shares Bible truths in the form of stories that touch the hearts of hearers. She lives in the Weaver Mountains of Arizona.*

I once had a friend, raised in a minister's home, who sensed from an early age that his gifts for leadership and teaching ought to be used in the church. Instead he went into sales.

For years nothing seemed to work out for him in the business world. When he was in his 50s, he realized that he had tried to thwart an essential calling on his life. After a long session on his knees, he signed up for Bible college. Within a few years he became the minister of a church in a small town where he was truly needed.

Joseph's brothers were so consumed with hatred that they didn't take time to think about what they were planning. They saw Joseph coming and let their anger get the best of them.

They couldn't, of course, thwart God's work in Joseph's life. Nor can His plans for us be thwarted as we seek His guidance day by day. Our part is to assess the spiritual gifts we've been given and then put them to use in His kingdom. The Spirit will lead us to just the right place.

Lord, *help me to know myself well enough to know where and how I can serve You best. Then lead me there! In Jesus' name, amen.*

**SPOTLIGHT**

***Next Week's Lesson***

Occasionally, good—such as Reuben's intention—is overwhelmed by evil plans. But God will not let it be permanent.

# Painfully, Gloriously Awesome

*When the Midianite merchants came by, his brothers pulled Joseph up out of the cistern and sold him for twenty shekels of silver* (Genesis 37:28).

When I was about 8 years old, my cousins shut me in the tack house at my family's ranch. They thought it was pretty funny. There I stood, locked in with dusty saddles, bridles, saddle soap, and curry combs. But surely, my cousins would come back for me soon!

It wasn't funny for me. My heart pounded and my legs shook as I hollered for them to let me out.

Joseph must have felt like that. I imagine he sat on the musty-smelling floor of that dry well waiting in fear, maybe calling out from time to time. Surely his crazy brothers would come back and lift him out.

I was only locked in the tack house a short time before my teasing cousins pulled the door open, but Joseph's story ended differently. When his brothers finally hauled him out of the pit, he realized their scheme included a business transaction. He watched Midianite merchants count 20 shekels of silver into his brothers' eager palms. What an awesome thing to witness! And even more awesome: though he didn't know at the time, it was all in God's plan.

Lord, *sometimes I feel as if I've landed in a pit of despair. It's not very comfortable there. Help me to a deeper trust today, in Jesus' name. Amen.*

**SEARCH THE WORD**

*In the pit, the pendulum of time swings very slowly.*

Scripture: Genesis 37:25-28

**Song:** *"Where He Leads Me"*

***From this meditation today, I will pray . . .***

Adoration ______________________________

______________________________

______________________________

Confession ______________________________

______________________________

______________________________

Thanksgiving ______________________________

______________________________

______________________________

Supplication ______________________________

______________________________

______________________________

***From this meditation today, I will . . .***

Think ______________________________

______________________________

______________________________

Say ______________________________

______________________________

______________________________

Do ______________________________

______________________________

______________________________

______________________________

______________________________

# A Father's Grief

*All his sons and daughters came to comfort him, but he refused to be comforted. "No," he said, "in mourning will I go down to the grave to my son." So his father wept for him* (Genesis 37:35).

Scripture: Genesis 37:29-36

Song: *"The Grave Itself a Garden Is"*

***From this meditation today, I will pray . . .***

Adoration ____________________

Confession ____________________

Thanksgiving ____________________

Supplication ____________________

***From this meditation today, I will . . .***

Think ____________________

Say ____________________

Do ____________________

In October 2005, the body of a World War II airman was found in a glacier at Kings Canyon National Park. He was apparently part of a crew that crashed in those mountains 63 years earlier. The airman's family knew his plane had gone down, but searchers had never recovered his body. Thus, a family spokesperson said the family's grief had had no ending—until now.

After Joseph's brothers sold him to a traveling band of traders heading toward Egypt, they lied to their father, saying a wild animal had killed his favorite son. Their father's grief was so deep he couldn't be comforted—even when surrounded by all his other children. Never again to look upon, or hold, his child was beyond this father's capacity to bear.

Yet, God's purpose was unfolding. There would come a day in the lives of Joseph's brothers when they would be grateful Joseph hadn't died in that pit. In the meantime, they watched their father mourn the death of a son who was just as alive as you or me.

God, *sometimes my grief is so deep! But thanks for walking with me through it. In You I find comfort and peace. In Jesus' name, amen.*

**SPOTLIGHT**

***Next Week's Lesson***

Part of Joseph's abuse by his brothers was knowing that his father would be cut to the soul. How cruel sin is.

# Look and See!

*You are my help and my deliverer; O* L*ORD*, *do not delay* (Psalm 70:5).

Even though his angry brothers tried to destroy Joseph and God's plan, they couldn't do it. And when Reuben tried to rescue Joseph, he couldn't do that either. God had it in control. Every step of the way, from the time of his youth, God's hand was upon Joseph, directing and delivering.

Once when my children were small, we camped in the forest together. At dusk we took a little walk, and I became so interested in showing the children the moss on the rocks and the minnows in the stream that I failed to keep an eye on the setting sun. At dark we were still some distance from our campsite.

It was a moonless night, and we couldn't see the path. My heart pounded as I walked along carrying the 3-year-old and leading the 5-year-old. Then another camper, flashlight in hand, stepped up beside us. He shined his light on our path and walked with us all the way to our campsite. I was so grateful!

Even when we can't recognize God's direction, it's there. He shines His light on our dark pathway and delivers us. When we look, will we truly see?

Lord God, *I praise You as I think how You have, time and time again, led me through dangerous situations. Glory to You, through Christ! Amen.*

**SEARCH THE WORD**

*Death waits for God's timing. Kill Joseph? God would decide when Joseph's life was complete.*

Scripture: Psalm 70

Song: *"Deliverance Will Come"*

***From this meditation today, I will pray . . .***

Adoration ______________________

Confession ______________________

Thanksgiving ______________________

Supplication ______________________

***From this meditation today, I will . . .***

Think ______________________

Say ______________________

Do ______________________

November 5

# One Path to Success

*The* Lord *was with Joseph, so he became a successful man* (Genesis 39:2, *New American Standard Bible*).

Scripture: Genesis 39:1-6a
Song: *"Spend One Hour with Jesus"*

***From this meditation today, I will pray . . .***

Adoration ______________________________

______________________________

______________________________

Confession ______________________________

______________________________

______________________________

Thanksgiving ______________________________

______________________________

______________________________

Supplication ______________________________

______________________________

______________________________

***From this meditation today, I will . . .***

Think ______________________________

______________________________

______________________________

Say ______________________________

______________________________

______________________________

Do ______________________________

______________________________

______________________________

November 5-11. ***Marjorie Vawter,*** *of Westminster, Colorado, loves to write and has authored several published devotionals and book reviews.*

Remember the story of King Midas, who requested that everything he touched would become gold? He soon discovered the gift was actually a curse—when his beloved daughter turned to solid gold at his touch! We could say that Joseph had a kind of Midas touch. His benefactor was God, and the gift wasn't a curse at all.

The prophet Jeremiah penned the words revealing God's wonderful touch upon His people: He knows His plans for us, plans to prosper us, to give us hope and a future (see Jeremiah 29:11).

God certainly knew what He had planned for Joseph from the beginning. And while it may not have seemed a blessing to be sold by his brothers into slavery—going from the pampered son of a wealthy rancher to a slave doing menial tasks—God had a purpose in it all.

We know the story of Joseph's success and his eventual rulership in Egypt. The thing we must never forget, though, is this: Joseph had nothing to do with his success other than being a willing, obedient servant of God.

Lord, *help me see that even in the most difficult circumstances, You have my good in mind. I pray through my deliverer, Jesus. Amen.*

**SPOTLIGHT**

***Next Week's Lesson***

Fill in your own name: "The Lord was with ____________, so he/she became a successful man/woman."

# Plan Ahead!

*"How then could I do such a wicked thing and sin against God?"* (Genesis 39:9).

As a teacher in a Christian high school, I enjoyed the frequent opportunity to sit under wonderful, godly preaching in our twice-weekly chapel services. Many of the preachers taught our young people the importance of being morally pure. The best piece of advice I heard came from our youth minister: "In order to stand firm in temptation, make the decision to please God *long before* the temptation comes."

Joseph recognized that the temptation he faced would, in reality, lead to a sin against God. God had blessed Joseph with such great stewardship responsibility that Potiphar had no idea what he owned; it was all trusted to Joseph's wise management. The only thing or person Potiphar withheld from Joseph was . . . Mrs. Potiphar! Sadly, Mrs. Potiphar was obsessed with Joseph's good looks.

But isn't all sin ultimately an affront to God? Spurning His wonderful blessings, we choose immediate gratification over long-term peace. But knowing how this grieves God's heart, we can determine far ahead of time our plan of escape.

Father God, *help me determine ahead of time to stand firm on the principles of Your Word when I face temptation. In Jesus' name, amen.*

**SEARCH THE WORD**

*Every wicked thing is a sin. Every sin is an insult to God.*

Scripture: Genesis 39:6b-10

Song: *"Thy Word Have I Hid in My Heart"*

***From this meditation today, I will pray . . .***

Adoration ______________________________

______________________________

______________________________

Confession ______________________________

______________________________

______________________________

Thanksgiving ______________________________

______________________________

______________________________

Supplication ______________________________

______________________________

______________________________

***From this meditation today, I will . . .***

Think ______________________________

______________________________

______________________________

Say ______________________________

______________________________

______________________________

Do ______________________________

______________________________

______________________________

______________________________

______________________________

# Try a Footrace!

*He left his garment in her hand and fled*
(Genesis 39:12, *New American Standard Bible*).

Scripture: Genesis 39:11-20
**Song:** *"Yield Not to Temptation"*

*From this meditation today, I will pray . . .*

Adoration ____________________

____________________

____________________

Confession ____________________

____________________

____________________

Thanksgiving ____________________

____________________

____________________

Supplication ____________________

____________________

____________________

*From this meditation today, I will . . .*

Think ____________________

____________________

____________________

Say ____________________

____________________

____________________

Do ____________________

____________________

____________________

____________________

____________________

In general the Bible tells us to stand firm and resist our temptations. However in certain sudden, sticky situations, its best just to . . . *run!*

Literally. Like Joseph did.

In the New Testament, Paul encouraged Timothy to flee the lusts of youth and chase after godly virtues, such as righteousness, faith, love, and peace (see 2 Timothy 2:22).

Joseph did just that, leaving his garment in Mrs. Potiphar's hand. He may not have anticipated her anger when she didn't get what she wanted. And he may not have expected to end up in prison. But Joseph did the right thing.

Writer Jerry Bridges, in *The Pursuit of Holiness,* tells us that John's view of holiness (not sinning) was different from his own goal (not sinning *very much*). It would be like a soldier going into battle with the aim of not getting hit *very much.* If this is our aim in life, we can be sure the darts of temptation will hit us over and over again. A good old-fashioned footrace has a much better chance of success.

Lord, *no matter how hot the battle, keep me close to You in pursuing holiness. When it's time to run, help me do it. Through Christ I pray. Amen.*

**SPOTLIGHT**
***Next Week's Lesson***

Unrobed and running, Joseph looks humiliated. But God would exalt him at the right time.

# Waiting for Refining

*Two years later, Pharaoh dreamed that he was standing on the bank of the Nile River*
(Genesis 41:1, *New Living Translation*).

Have you noticed how difficult it is to wait on God? Yet God uses those times of waiting to mold and refine us, preparing us to accomplish His plans in our lives. When Habakkuk wondered how long it would be before God fulfilled His promises of deliverance to Israel, God answered: "These things I plan won't happen right away. Slowly, steadily, surely, the time approaches. . . . If it seems slow, wait patiently, for it will surely take place. It will not be delayed" (Habakkuk 2:3, *NLT*).

We don't know much about Joseph's wait in prison other than that he interpreted the dreams for Pharaoh's chief cupbearer and baker. We don't even know how long his imprisonment lasted. But it was another two years before God was ready to release him and exalt him to the No. 2 position in the land of Egypt.

God used the time well, however: He prepared Joseph for the tasks ahead, even though the waiting must have been hard for the young man. Perhaps Job said it best amid all his patient sufferings: "He knows where I am going. And when he has tested me like gold in a fire, he will pronounce me innocent" (Job 23:10, *NLT*).

**Lord,** *help me each day to wait patiently for you to mold me into a vessel fit for the work You've placed at hand. In Jesus' name, amen.*

**SEARCH THE WORD**

*"How long?" the weary one of God asks. God says, "The wait is part of the plan!"*

Scripture: Genesis 41:1-8
Song: *"How Firm a Foundation"*

***From this meditation today, I will pray . . .***

Adoration ____________________

____________________

____________________

Confession ____________________

____________________

____________________

Thanksgiving ____________________

____________________

____________________

Supplication ____________________

____________________

____________________

***From this meditation today, I will . . .***

Think ____________________

____________________

____________________

Say ____________________

____________________

____________________

Do ____________________

____________________

____________________

____________________

____________________

# Can You Focus Like This?

*"Now as for the repeating of the dream to Pharaoh twice, it means that the matter is determined by God, and God will quickly bring it about"* (Genesis 41:32, *New American Standard Bible*).

Scripture: Genesis 41:25-36

Song: *"If You Will Only Let God Guide You"*

***From this meditation today, I will pray . . .***

Adoration ______________________________

______________________________

______________________________

Confession ______________________________

______________________________

______________________________

Thanksgiving ______________________________

______________________________

______________________________

Supplication ______________________________

______________________________

______________________________

***From this meditation today, I will . . .***

Think ______________________________

______________________________

______________________________

Say ______________________________

______________________________

______________________________

Do ______________________________

______________________________

______________________________

______________________________

______________________________

What is our usual first reaction when we've been wronged? For me, as soon as I get a chance, I go into defense mode. "This isn't fair! Justice should be done. My rights have been violated."

I'm impressed that Joseph didn't say any of these things when he came before Pharaoh. He didn't talk about being imprisoned on trumped-up charges. He didn't confront the cupbearer for forgetting him those two long years. Instead he focused on Pharaoh's request and kept his eyes on God. Three times in this passage Joseph tells Pharaoh that God sent the dream because God was ready to work in Egypt and the surrounding lands.

Joseph also refused to take credit for his ability to interpret dreams, again pointing his hearers to the sovereign God. Then he followed the dream's interpretation with words of counsel, not realizing God was going to use him to fulfill the plan of action he suggested. If I could keep everything focused on God like that, I know my life would bring greater glory to Him. How is it with you?

Father, *Your Son, Jesus, suffered every injustice as my perfect high priest. Let me focus on honoring Him today as I pray in His name. Amen.*

**SPOTLIGHT**

***Next Week's Lesson***

Fresh out of prison, Joseph didn't feel exalted yet. But coronation is near. It is for the Christian too.

# Finally, Justice!

*Pharaoh said, "Since God has revealed the meaning of the dreams to you, you are the wisest man in the land! I hereby appoint you to direct this project"* (Genesis 41:39, 40, *New Living Translation*).

Have you ever wondered how Joseph felt when Pharaoh spoke these words? In a single day, Joseph went from being a prisoner to holding the second highest position in the land of Egypt—from the chains of imprisonment to the soft raiment and jewels of royalty.

While Joseph's thoughts and words about it aren't recorded, we can know that he recognized God's hand in all of this. Years earlier he'd dreamed about holding this rulership above his family. And Jacob had rebuked him for his pride.

Yet now God fulfilled the dream. After all the years of testing, learning, and waiting, Joseph was ready for the job God had for him. I'm quite sure that God's ultimate justice helped him forget all the cruel injustices done to him. And we can do the same—but with some difficulty. For, as William Penn once said: "Justice is the insurance which we have on our lives and property. Obedience is the premium which we pay for it."

God, *You indeed are good! You bring us out of the fire and exalt us above our enemies—in this life or in the next. You work all things together for good to those who love You. For this I praise You, in Christ's name. Amen.*

**SEARCH THE WORD**

*God's justice is sure, for He is holy. God's grace is available, for He is love.*

Scripture: Genesis 41:37-45

Song: *"God Is So Good"*

*From this meditation today, I will pray . . .*

Adoration ______________________________

______________________________

______________________________

Confession ______________________________

______________________________

______________________________

Thanksgiving ______________________________

______________________________

______________________________

Supplication ______________________________

______________________________

______________________________

*From this meditation today, I will . . .*

Think ______________________________

______________________________

______________________________

Say ______________________________

______________________________

______________________________

Do ______________________________

______________________________

______________________________

______________________________

______________________________

# Tested Character

*Until the time came to fulfill his word, the LORD tested Joseph's character* (Psalm 105:19, *New Living Translation*).

Scripture: Psalm 105:16-22

Song: *"Rejoice in the Lord Always"*

***From this meditation today, I will pray . . .***

Adoration ______________________________

______________________________

______________________________

Confession ______________________________

______________________________

______________________________

Thanksgiving ______________________________

______________________________

______________________________

Supplication ______________________________

______________________________

______________________________

***From this meditation today, I will . . .***

Think ______________________________

______________________________

______________________________

Say ______________________________

______________________________

______________________________

Do ______________________________

______________________________

______________________________

______________________________

______________________________

The writer of Hebrews tells us that Jesus learned obedience. How? Through suffering (see 5:8). Think of it—the perfect Son of God had to *learn* obedience.

Joseph was a teenager when his brothers sold him into slavery. But even that initial trial resulted in his being an honored servant to Potiphar, captain of Pharaoh's guard. But to truly test his character, God allowed Joseph to be imprisoned on a charge of rape. We're told that he was in fetters that bruised his feet and bound him around his neck. His entire being—body, soul, and spirit—was tested by those chains and the years he was in prison.

Even after the chains were removed, Joseph must have borne the marks of those fetters. Through all of this, Joseph's character was refined. I believe God allowed him the dream of ruling over his parents and brothers to sustain him in his darkest hours. Even Joseph's own testimony to his brothers spoke of understanding that God's way, though hard, is always best: "As far as I am concerned, God turned into good what you meant for evil" (Genesis 50:20, *NLT*).

Lord, *help me remember that what seems bad to me, whatever is unfair in my life, whatever chains bind me—these things are opportunities to recall Your presence and draw on Your strength. Through Christ, amen.*

**SPOTLIGHT**

***Next Week's Lesson***

Earthly suffering is nothing.
Heavenly exaltation is everything.

# Listening, Then Loving

*I will listen to what God the LORD will say; he promises peace to his people* (Psalm 85:8).

I turned off the TV news with a sigh. It was bad news again. Besides another devastating earthquake, I'd watched reports of disturbing crimes committed against innocent children. I couldn't stand to know anymore. I picked up my Bible and began to read. A hundred years ago it took a lot longer for such news to reach us. But in our instant media society, it is hard to avoid contact with the pain of others. How do we deal with all this suffering in the world?

The psalmist helps me here. If I focus on listening to the Lord, I will find personal peace. It is an act of the will to stop and listen to Him.

As we open to His inner peace, we will be strengthened to reach out to others with the first small steps of compassion. We can't save the whole world at once, but we can offer a cup of cold water to the one suffering next door. That is my prayer this day—that I will listen to the Lord and then reach out with the power of His peace.

Lord, *I thank You that You desire to speak to me—even more than I want to listen. Help me to hear Your voice in the many ways You communicate with me every day. Then move me into loving service in Jesus' name. Amen.*

**SEARCH THE WORD**

*"I've Got Peace Like a River," the songwriter wrote. God is the source of the stream.*

Scripture: Psalm 85

Song: *"Lord, Speak to Me"*

*From this meditation today, I will pray . . .*

Adoration ______________________________

______________________________

______________________________

Confession ______________________________

______________________________

______________________________

Thanksgiving ______________________________

______________________________

______________________________

Supplication ______________________________

______________________________

______________________________

*From this meditation today, I will . . .*

Think ______________________________

______________________________

______________________________

Say ______________________________

______________________________

______________________________

Do ______________________________

______________________________

______________________________

November 12–18. ***Janet Bair*** *is a freelance writer and a children's librarian. She lives in Ansonia, Connecticut, with her husband and two daughters.*

November 13

# Remember Me?

*Although Joseph recognized his brothers, they did not recognize him*
(Genesis 42:8).

Scripture: Genesis 42:1-20

Song: *"Face to Face with Christ, My Savior"*

***From this meditation today, I will pray . . .***

Adoration ____________________

Confession ____________________

Thanksgiving ____________________

Supplication ____________________

***From this meditation today, I will . . .***

Think ____________________

Say ____________________

Do ____________________

Has anyone ever come up to you and exclaimed, "Hi, remember me? I almost didn't recognize you." And as he or she talks on and on . . . you are still wondering who, exactly, *is* this person?

Sometimes we recognize that sudden stranger, and sometimes, like Joseph's brothers, we don't. The person's looks may have changed significantly over the years. Simply growing up changes a person's face.

Joseph was 17 years old when his brothers sold him into slavery, and about 25 years had passed before they met again. Pharaoh had given him robes of fine linen and put a gold chain about his neck. At age 42, Joseph not only looked different but he was in a totally unexpected place when his brothers saw him again.

While we may have the same problem of recognizing people we knew long ago, there is one person we should always be able to recognize—Jesus. Someday when we see Him face-to-face in Heaven, we will know Him by His love for us. We will recognize His character. We will see the marks on His hands and feet. We will remember all He has done for us, and we will be eternally thankful.

Lord, *as I learn more about You every day, help me to learn more of You in this wonderful relationship. In Your precious name I pray. Amen.*

**SPOTLIGHT**

***Next Week's Lesson***

Joseph knew there was a best time to reveal the truth. Oh, for the wisdom to choose the best time.

# Don't Delay!

*As it is, if we had not delayed,*
*we could have gone and returned twice*
(Genesis 43:10).

Carol frowned as she looked at her long To Do list. She couldn't put off doing those chores any longer—the phone calls to make, a costume to alter, grocery shopping to do, and a huge yard of leaves to rake before it rained.

Procrastination! We're all guilty at times.

Joseph's brothers delayed going back to Egypt after their first visit during the famine. Even though Simeon was waiting in prison, they ate all of the grain before they went back. Judah finally reminded his father that they could have already gone—and come back twice—in the time it was taking Jacob to make a decision!

Sometimes I too hesitate to get moving. When the Lord prompts me to do something, it's usually pretty clear. God's still, small voice may nudge me to go and talk to a lonely neighbor or give some money to a struggling college student I know. It may be a small or a big thing. It may not make sense at the time. But the Lord has His own purposes and plans. And I long to be a part of the solution rather than a cause of delay.

Lord God in Heaven, *help me with my procrastinating tendencies. I know that if I follow Your leading, the plans You have for Your kingdom will be accomplished in my small part of the world. Thank You for using me today. In the name of the Father, the Son, and the Holy Spirit, amen.*

**SEARCH THE WORD**

*The procrastinator surely delays anguish, but he also delays joy.*

Scripture: Genesis 43:1-15

Song: *"The Savior Is Waiting"*

*From this meditation today, I will pray . . .*

Adoration ______________________

______________________

______________________

Confession ______________________

______________________

______________________

Thanksgiving ______________________

______________________

______________________

Supplication ______________________

______________________

______________________

*From this meditation today, I will . . .*

Think ______________________

______________________

______________________

Say ______________________

______________________

______________________

Do ______________________

______________________

______________________

______________________

______________________

November 15

# Don't Finish This

*Deeply moved at the sight of his brother, Joseph hurried out and looked for a place to weep. He went into his private room and wept there* (Genesis 43:30).

Scripture: Genesis 43:16-34

Song: *"Father, Make Us Loving"*

*From this meditation today, I will pray . . .*

Adoration ______________________________

________________________________________

________________________________________

Confession ______________________________

________________________________________

________________________________________

Thanksgiving ____________________________

________________________________________

________________________________________

Supplication _____________________________

________________________________________

________________________________________

*From this meditation today, I will . . .*

Think __________________________________

________________________________________

________________________________________

Say ____________________________________

________________________________________

________________________________________

Do _____________________________________

________________________________________

________________________________________

________________________________________

________________________________________

Have you ever been to a large family reunion with relatives you haven't seen in a long time? At such times, we wonder why we waited so long to get together.

Sometimes you want to cry for joy at seeing everyone again. The great Joseph wept when he saw his beloved brother Benjamin. In spite of the fact that his brothers had sold him into slavery, he was overcome with emotion upon seeing his family reunited again. Now Joseph was a tough man, ruling over thousands in Egypt, but he had a tender heart for his family.

God calls all of His people to have caring, reconciling hearts. As Hebrews 12:14 tells us: "Make every effort to live in peace with all men." Family reunions offer us the opportunity to resolve conflicts as we reconnect. God gives us these special times of great food and conversation to catch up on news but also to show how we can pray for one another and build one another up. As humorist Don Marquis once quipped: "I would rather start a family than finish one."

Lord, *thank You for the families and friends that You have placed with me. Help me to be a good listener and to see their true needs, praying for them with discernment. In Your name I pray. Amen.*

**SPOTLIGHT**

***Next Week's Lesson***

Joseph was a man of full and deep emotion. He could cry. He could laugh. O for men like Joseph today.

# Another Test

*Put my cup, the silver one, in the mouth of the youngest one's sack, along with the silver for his grain*
(Genesis 44:2).

In a sermon one Sunday, Chrissy heard the story of how Joseph forgave his brothers. The closing prayer included an invitation to forgive any family member who had caused hurt. Later that day, Chrissy's forgiveness capability was tested. Another family member yelled and berated her at a party. Surprisingly, Chrissy was able to keep quiet and walk away. Later she realized the power of God had been at work in her life. For it is incredibly difficult to forgive while the sting of hurt or embarrassment still simmers in our hearts.

There are many tests in the Christian life, though most aren't as elaborate or as planned as Joseph's. When he had his own silver cup put in Benjamin's sack, he wanted to see whether his brothers really had changed. Would they abandon Benjamin as they had heartlessly left Joseph himself so long ago?

God will test our faithfulness too. But not for the purpose of failing us. Rather He will confirm and strengthen our faith through each trial. As Job proclaimed: "When he has tested me, I will come forth as gold" (Job 23:10).

Lord, *let forgiveness always be on my heart and lips. And thank You for growing me toward maturity, even through the tough times. In the holy name of Jesus, my Lord and Savior, I pray. Amen.*

**SEARCH THE WORD**

*God always tests for change not to confirm it to Himself—He knows—but to confirm it for the one changed.*

Scripture: Genesis 44:1-13

Song: *"Wonderful Grace of Jesus"*

*From this meditation today, I will pray . . .*

Adoration ______________________________

______________________________

______________________________

Confession ______________________________

______________________________

______________________________

Thanksgiving ______________________________

______________________________

______________________________

Supplication ______________________________

______________________________

______________________________

*From this meditation today, I will . . .*

Think ______________________________

______________________________

______________________________

Say ______________________________

______________________________

______________________________

Do ______________________________

______________________________

______________________________

______________________________

______________________________

November 17

# Launched Back to Joy

*"What can we say? How can we prove our innocence? God has uncovered your servants' guilt"*
(Genesis 44:16).

Scripture: Genesis 44:14-34

Song: *"My Sins Are Blotted Out, I Know!"*

***From this meditation today, I will pray . . .***

Adoration ______________________________

Confession ______________________________

Thanksgiving ______________________________

Supplication ______________________________

***From this meditation today, I will . . .***

Think ______________________________

Say ______________________________

Do ______________________________

"Did you finish your dinner?" Mom would ask as she was busy cleaning up. *Well* . . . I used to sneak those hated lima beans to our cat under the table. And my little brother would hide his unwanted food in a napkin and then throw it out. Funny how, so many years later, I can remember doing a little thing like that. I am sure I told my mother "Oh yes, I ate it all."

Secret sins stick with us, big or small.

Joseph's brothers had a secret sin that loomed large before them. When they met Joseph again 25 years later and things weren't going well for them, their consciences quickly prodded them. They felt uncovered, soul-naked in their guilt.

Unconfessed sin can plague us like that. And it's a good thing it does! Then we can take it as a gracious call to open our hearts to God, to let Him know the hurts, the desires, the alienation that drove us to some sad form of self-destructiveness. There, at His feet, we obtain sweet mercy—and the courage to launch into life again with joy.

Heavenly Father, *how I wish to serve You in all purity and perfection! But when I fail, help me run to You with unguarded heart to receive Your forgiveness. I pray through my deliverer, Jesus. Amen.*

**SPOTLIGHT**
***Next Week's Lesson***

Conscience, if it reflects God's indwelling Spirit, is good.

# A Reconciliation Model

*It was not you who sent me here, but God. He made me father to Pharaoh, lord of his entire household and ruler of all Egypt* (Genesis 45:8).

Cindy sat down with her preschool class and began to color with the children. As soon as she started coloring her picture, two of the kids began watching her intently. They used the same colors she used and copied her picture—even down to the blue and green stripes she added on the boy's shirt.

Cindy was stunned to see how quickly they wanted to emulate her every move. She thought, "What else do the children copy?" She was humbled to find herself such a powerful public role model!

Children model adults as if it were second nature; they do need patterns to follow as they grow up. Joseph's forgiveness of his brothers—and their final reconciliation—is a good family model for any of us to copy. No matter how serious the offense, family members can work towards reconciliation. And it will benefit all concerned. As someone once put it: "When chickens quit quarrelling over their food, they often find there is enough for all of them."

Lord, *thank You for Joseph's model of reconciliation. In my family where there are hurts, help us to take them to the cross where all is forgiven. In the name of the Father, the Son, and the Holy Spirit, I pray. Amen.*

**SEARCH THE WORD**

*When good things happen, who gets the credit? God, of course!*

Scripture: Genesis 45:1-15

Song: *"Others, Lord"*

***From this meditation today, I will pray . . .***

Adoration ______________________________

______________________________

______________________________

Confession ______________________________

______________________________

______________________________

Thanksgiving ______________________________

______________________________

______________________________

Supplication ______________________________

______________________________

______________________________

***From this meditation today, I will . . .***

Think ______________________________

______________________________

______________________________

Say ______________________________

______________________________

______________________________

Do ______________________________

______________________________

______________________________

______________________________

______________________________

# Big Promises

*"Never mind about your belongings, because the best of all Egypt will be yours"* (Genesis 45:20).

Scripture: Genesis 45:16-20

Song: *"Standing on the Promises"*

***From this meditation today, I will pray . . .***

Adoration ______________________________

______________________________

______________________________

Confession ______________________________

______________________________

______________________________

Thanksgiving ______________________________

______________________________

______________________________

Supplication ______________________________

______________________________

______________________________

***From this meditation today, I will . . .***

Think ______________________________

______________________________

______________________________

Say ______________________________

______________________________

______________________________

Do ______________________________

______________________________

______________________________

November 19–25. ***Phillip H. Barnhart,*** *writer of 14 books, retired in 2002 after 45 years in ministry. He lives on Perdido Bay, Florida, with his wife, Sharon.*

God makes great big promises. Read the New Testament and see: We are promised fire that burns hot. We are promised wind that blows strong and light like that of a city set on a hill. God adds to those promises the startling radiance of a marriage banquet.

Pharaoh promised Joseph's family land in Egypt. It was a promise that eased an old past and pointed to a new future; a promise they could trust, invest their lives in, and look forward to. It was a promise they knew would come true. But Pharaoh promised even more: the most excellent land in Egypt.

God's promises are true and they are tremendous. Read the New Testament. It is the fatted calf and the best robe. It is abundant grace and unspeakable joy. It is a pearl of great price and a great big box full of treasure. God's promises are true. They are also excessive, extravagant, and exceedingly abundant.

Dear God, *thank You for wrapping Your strong arms around me, pouring out Your great love into my life, and lifting me up to the highest mountain of gift and blessing. Thank You for wide doors through which to pass and large rooms in which to stand. In the name of Christ, I pray. Amen.*

**SPOTLIGHT**

***Next Week's Lesson***

Pharaoh's promises to Israel were great; God's promises to Israel were greater.

# Our God Speaks

*God spoke to Israel in a vision at night and said, "Jacob! Jacob!"*
(Genesis 46:2).

It is no problem for God to speak to us. We are made in God's image, so God communicating with us is not unlike us communicating with one another. As God spoke to Jacob on his way to Egypt for a family reunion, He also speaks to us in all sorts of circumstances.

Besides the obvious—Bible meditation and prayer—we hear from God in the when and where and what of how things go in life. A road taken here, a page turned there, and we look back to see God's voiceprint all over our decisions and choices.

God is keen on self-revelation, isn't He? He likes to make himself known to us. It gives Him joy to plop down in our lives in ways we are foolish to deny. I've noticed that He occasionally likes to send a friend my way with a word for me that could have only come from Him. He likes to stir up a favorite emotion and speak to me from the wind that blows in the heart of my feelings. The point is, no venue is out of bounds for the voice of God.

My Father in Heaven, *You are knowable to me. Every day, any place, I can hear from You. I am glad You aren't secretive about yourself! Of all the things You reveal, the most important are the incomparable aspects of Your character. And since You never quit speaking, may I never stop listening. In the name of Your Son, my Savior, I pray. Amen.*

**SEARCH THE WORD**

*The voice of God is never silent; the ears of men are often dull.*

Scripture: Genesis 46:1-4

**Song:** *"Speak to My Soul"*

***From this meditation today, I will pray . . .***

Adoration ____________________

Confession ____________________

Thanksgiving ____________________

Supplication ____________________

***From this meditation today, I will . . .***

Think ____________________

Say ____________________

Do ____________________

# What a Hug!

*Joseph got in his chariot and went to meet his father. When they met, Joseph hugged his father around the neck and cried for a long time* (Genesis 46:29, *Contemporary English Version*).

Scripture: Genesis 46:28-34

Song: *"God Be with You Till We Meet Again"*

***From this meditation today, I will pray . . .***

Adoration ______________________________

Confession ______________________________

Thanksgiving ______________________________

Supplication ______________________________

***From this meditation today, I will . . .***

Think ______________________________

Say ______________________________

Do ______________________________

Joey was 13 months old when his estranged father kidnapped him and took him to a faraway state to live. Years later as Joey visited an Internet chat room, a couple became curious about him. Joey's story sounded like another they'd heard. The couple contacted the police and, not long afterward, the FBI showed up on Joey's doorstep to tell him his mother had been searching for him for the past 14 years. Just before Christmas of that year, Joey and his mother were joyfully reunited.

In our Bible passage, Jacob is on his way to Egypt to be reunited with his son Joseph. It is a glorious journey as every step he puts down on the road leaves a footprint of joyful anticipation. He can't wait to see his boy again. Upon approaching Joseph, he throws his arms wide open, runs with abandon toward his son, and puts a hug on Joseph that will not let go. There is shouting, crying, dancing. There is the immeasurable joy of reunion.

I like to imagine how it will be when we, His long lost brothers and sisters, finally see Jesus face-to-face. What will that hug be like?

Dear God, *no matter how far I roam, I will come home to You. Thank You for Your ready arms of welcome. In Jesus' name, amen.*

**SPOTLIGHT**

***Next Week's Lesson***

Reuniting with one's father—that's the grand hope of Heaven.

# Family Time

*Joseph also provided his father and his brothers and all his father's household with food, according to the number of their children* (Genesis 47:12).

Little Mikey asked his mother, "Where was I born?" The answer came, "In Michigan." Another question had queued up behind the first one. "Where was sister born?" So Mom replied, "She was born in Wisconsin."

Little Mikey was not through. "How about you and Daddy?" Mikey's mother accommodated her son. "I was born in Georgia, and your dad was born in Oregon." Mikey thought about all of that information for a minute and then said, "Isn't it great we could all get together?"

After years of separation, Joseph gets together with his father and brothers. They are reunited and Joseph takes advantage of the reunion to give his family everything they need. His generosity celebrates his love for each and all of them. It is family time in Egypt, and like the best of family time everywhere, love communicates and joy dominates. No matter what the future holds, it's OK because the caring family is together. Each member rests in a haven of safety and security. Everyone knows this is where they belong, and these are the people they can count on. There's no time like family time.

*Thank You,* Dear Father, *for giving me a place in Your family. In this family, I am Yours and You are mine. Through Christ the Lord, amen.*

**SEARCH THE WORD**

*God's family has everything they need, for He is a loving Father.*

Scripture: Genesis 47:7-12

Song: *"The Family of God"*

*From this meditation today, I will pray . . .*

Adoration ______________________________

______________________________

______________________________

Confession ______________________________

______________________________

______________________________

Thanksgiving ______________________________

______________________________

______________________________

Supplication ______________________________

______________________________

______________________________

*From this meditation today, I will . . .*

Think ______________________________

______________________________

______________________________

Say ______________________________

______________________________

______________________________

Do ______________________________

______________________________

______________________________

______________________________

______________________________

# Going Home

*"When I rest with my fathers, carry me out of Egypt and bury me where they are buried"* (Genesis 47:30).

Scripture: Genesis 47:27-31

Song: *"On Jordan's Stormy Banks I Stand"*

***From this meditation today, I will pray . . .***

Adoration ______________________

______________________

______________________

Confession ______________________

______________________

______________________

Thanksgiving ______________________

______________________

______________________

Supplication ______________________

______________________

______________________

***From this meditation today, I will . . .***

Think ______________________

______________________

______________________

Say ______________________

______________________

______________________

Do ______________________

______________________

______________________

______________________

______________________

I have decided what I want engraved on my tombstone. Put my name, year of birth and death, and then put, "To Be Continued."

When I die I will pass across the threshold of death into the storehouse of life forever. My sequence begun in the heart of God continues in the presence of God. I pray for the kingdom to come and for me to come to the kingdom.

When Jacob dies he wants to go home, to end up in his homeland, not in a foreign land. Joseph promises his father he will go home, just as God promises us that we will go home.

Yes, we will go home where the light never fails because the sun never sets. We will go home where the little chords we hear on earth become full-scale symphonies of beauty and majesty. We will go home where our speculations and intimations become absolute certainties. Heaven is the destination, the completion of a journey, the fulfillment of a promise. Heaven is home.

O Lord, *You are God of earth and Heaven. You are God of beginnings, endings, and continuings. You are God of yesterday, today, and tomorrow. You are the God who comes and never leaves. You are God who always finishes Your sentences with the exclamation point of forever! In the holy name of Jesus, my Lord and Savior, I pray. Amen.*

**SPOTLIGHT**

***Next Week's Lesson***

Joseph's journey, with all its blessings and curses, would end where it began: home. Isn't that what every person of God wants?

# Bountiful Blessings

*Jacob told him that in the future the people of Israel would ask God's blessings on one another by saying, "I pray for God to bless you as much as he blessed Ephraim and Manasseh"* (Genesis 48:20, *Contemporary English Version*).

Every time someone tells me I'm lucky about something, I say, "Not lucky—*blessed.*" I consider any so-called good fortune to originate in the heart of God's love for me. All the goodness of my life has its source in God's grace, and that grace shows up in full benevolent apparel at the beginning of each day. Each day that I wake up is a beautiful day, and I am blessed in it.

Jacob blessed Ephraim and Manasseh in such a way that people talked about it for generations. Similarly, God blesses me with the gift of life that opens my mouth in celebration and praise. That gift of good life takes many shapes, has many embodiments, and soaks itself into me everywhere.

There have been many times in my life when I have been pretty much blessed off my rocker! Times when I drink out of my saucer because my cup has overflowed. Times when I sit at God's table and am filled with God's blessings—but still He says to me, "Here, have another one."

Dear God, *each and every blessing You pour out to me in grace and love, I give back to You in thanksgiving and praise. In Jesus' name, amen.*

**SEARCH THE WORD**

*Every person is blessed by God. So few realize it.*

Scripture: Genesis 48:8-21

Song: *"There Shall Be Showers of Blessing"*

***From this meditation today, I will pray . . .***

Adoration ______________________________

______________________________

______________________________

Confession ______________________________

______________________________

______________________________

Thanksgiving ______________________________

______________________________

______________________________

Supplication ______________________________

______________________________

______________________________

***From this meditation today, I will . . .***

Think ______________________________

______________________________

______________________________

Say ______________________________

______________________________

______________________________

Do ______________________________

______________________________

______________________________

______________________________

______________________________

# Tell It All

*I will exalt you, my God the King;*
*I will praise your name for ever and ever*
(Psalm 145:1).

Scripture: Psalm 145:1-13a
Song: *"Praise Him! Praise Him!"*

***From this meditation today, I will pray . . .***

Adoration ______________________________

Confession ______________________________

Thanksgiving ______________________________

Supplication ______________________________

***From this meditation today, I will . . .***

Think ______________________________

Say ______________________________

Do ______________________________

I cannot offer enough praises to God. I get paper and pencil to itemize the blessings for which I praise Him, but I run out of paper and my pencil wears down to a tiny nub. The most prevalent position for my arms and hands on any given day is a vertical one. They are lifted up, as my heart is elevated in appreciation for what God does and who God is. I am forever a psalmist, raising my praise to God.

Yes, the hard times come too. But let us be faithful in our adoration—not spasmodic and intermittent, but steady and consistent—showing up every day to praise God who gives us what we have and makes us who we are. Why not be exuberant in our adoration!

I've begun to see there is no better use of my vocal chords than utilizing them to express my thankfulness to God. Therefore, I want to be prolific in my adoration, go on a rampage of praise every now and then, and mention everything great and small that comes to mind. Yes, in the next few moments, I'm going to tell it all to God.

Dear God, *I am far more concerned about what You do for me than I am about what I can do for You. I realize how You bless me. I see how You guide me. I know how You make me more able than I am. How I thank You, in the name of Jesus, my Savior and Lord. Amen.*

**SPOTLIGHT**
***Next Week's Lesson***
Jacob blessed his family
because God had blessed him.
He knew the right thing to do:
blessings for blessings.

# Compliment Him

*Say to God, "How awesome are your deeds!*
*So great is your power that your enemies cringe before you"*
(Psalm 66:3).

"See, I told you. Things never work out for me." Linda used those words often, to the extent that they gradually became an overused phrase, a cliché that her friends tuned out. Soon people quit listening altogether. Sadly, they no longer heard Linda's cries for help.

Linda had experienced many disappointments. Because of this, she focused on her problems, undesirable circumstances, and past failures—most of them not her fault. Yet her perceptions often made bad situations even worse.

Then one day Linda met a Christian woman named Sandy. Sandy listened past the clichés and heard the cry of Linda's heart. Sandy suggested that Linda change the way she prayed. Instead of complaining to God, compliment Him. Her outlook on life changed dramatically. It didn't take long for her friends to notice the improvement.

God is a patient listener. He hears us when we talk about our problems, bemoan our circumstances, or complain about all the evil in the world. Even so, God surely enjoys our praises too!

Dear Lord, *I am so thankful that You listen to my hurts and concerns. Help me to lift up my praises this day as well. Through Christ, amen.*

**SEARCH THE WORD**

*Praise is simple and profound, happy and necessary. The psalmist knew it; so do all God's children.*

Scripture: Psalm 66:1-4

Song: *"Praise the Lord, for He Is Good"*

***From this meditation today, I will pray . . .***

Adoration ______________________________

______________________________

______________________________

Confession ______________________________

______________________________

______________________________

Thanksgiving ______________________________

______________________________

______________________________

Supplication ______________________________

______________________________

______________________________

***From this meditation today, I will . . .***

Think ______________________________

______________________________

______________________________

Say ______________________________

______________________________

______________________________

Do ______________________________

______________________________

______________________________

November 26–30. ***Charles E. Harrel*** *has been a minister for more than 30 years. He currently directs His Place Outreach in Portland, Oregon.*

November 27

# All That He Commanded

*Both of them were upright in the sight of God, observing all the Lord's commandments and regulations blamelessly* (Luke 1:6).

Scripture: Luke 1:5-7

Song: *"Go Forth at Christ's Command"*

*From this meditation today, I will pray . . .*

Adoration ______________________________

______________________________

______________________________

Confession ______________________________

______________________________

______________________________

Thanksgiving ______________________________

______________________________

______________________________

Supplication ______________________________

______________________________

______________________________

*From this meditation today, I will . . .*

Think ______________________________

______________________________

______________________________

Say ______________________________

______________________________

______________________________

Do ______________________________

______________________________

______________________________

______________________________

______________________________

As a 10-year-old, I visited my Uncle Mel and Aunt Millie one summer. Since Mel was a preacher, I knew that meant going to church. Not exactly my idea of a vacation, rating only slightly higher than going to the dentist. On Sunday morning, I put on my coat and tie. "Why are you wearing that stuff?" my uncle asked. "You better change into some blue jeans and grab a cowboy hat—you might need them later." Now he had my attention.

My aunt and uncle were a dedicated couple who obeyed God in all things. They sponsored a youth out-reach with riding horses on Sunday afternoons. They also hosted a carnival on the church grounds every summer. Some members thought they were foolish; others left the church. The complaining stopped, however, when revival spread to the surrounding churches and nearby cities.

Following God and living uprightly has benefits. Elizabeth and Zechariah conceived a child of promise. For Mel and Millie, God granted what they wanted most: salvation for their young nephew and revival for their city.

Precious Lord, *teach me to live my life in obedience to Your will. Even when Your ways seem unconventional to some, may I always follow the path You have marked out for me. In Jesus' name I pray. Amen.*

**SPOTLIGHT**

***Next Week's Lesson***

Old age is a blessing from God. Elizabeth and Zechariah discovered God's special blessing of being needed for His plan.

# Your Prayers Are Heard

*The angel said to him: "Do not be afraid, Zechariah; your prayer has been heard. Your wife Elizabeth will bear you a son, and you are to give him the name John"* (Luke 1:13).

Laura wanted another child. She and her husband were happy with their two girls; still, she dreamed of having one more. God heard the cry of her heart. Although she was nearing the age when most women stop having children, she felt she had God's assurance to proceed. It even seemed that God gave her a name—a boy's name.

When she told her husband, Charles, he was less than sympathetic. "Are you sure? How do you know God wants us to have another child? What about hospital costs?" Charles had many concerns. However, when Laura mentioned that God had given her a name, he settled down and listened. She explained that God wanted this baby to have a special heritage and a name that pointed back to the Redeemer. With fears alleviated, they put their faith and love to work. Nine months later, little Christopher came into the world.

Sometimes it seems as if God forgets us, even ignores our prayers. But that is never the case. He listens to our every word. Even our thoughts are known to Him. Zechariah's prayers reached Heaven, and so do ours.

Dear God, *teach me to trust You in all things. Whenever doubts arise, remind me that You always hear my prayers. In Jesus' name, amen.*

**SEARCH THE WORD**

*Prayers are heard. Zechariah would have solid evidence. Everyone who prays will have.*

Scripture: Luke 1:8-13

Song: *"The God of Salvation Hears"*

***From this meditation today, I will pray . . .***

Adoration ______________________________

______________________________

______________________________

Confession ______________________________

______________________________

______________________________

Thanksgiving ______________________________

______________________________

______________________________

Supplication ______________________________

______________________________

______________________________

***From this meditation today, I will . . .***

Think ______________________________

______________________________

______________________________

Say ______________________________

______________________________

______________________________

Do ______________________________

______________________________

______________________________

______________________________

______________________________

# Forerunners Still Needed

*He will go on before the Lord, in the spirit and power of Elijah, to turn the hearts of the fathers to their children and the disobedient to the wisdom of the righteous—to make ready a people prepared for the Lord* (Luke 1:17).

Scripture: Luke 1:14-17

Song: *"I'll Go Where You Want Me to Go"*

***From this meditation today, I will pray . . .***

Adoration ________________________

Confession ________________________

Thanksgiving ________________________

Supplication ________________________

***From this meditation today, I will . . .***

Think ________________________

Say ________________________

Do ________________________

Johann Gutenberg designed a printing press with replaceable wooden or metal letters. His press furthered the gospel message by printing Gutenberg Bibles, the first books published in volume. In 1803, Lewis and Clark led an expedition across a newly acquired land, most of it unexplored; their efforts paved the way for a great westward expansion in America. The Wright brothers and their Wright Flyer became the first heavier-than-air machine to achieve controlled flight with a pilot aboard; their design opened wide the doors to modern aviation.

All these people, and countless others like them, were forerunners. They blazed new trails or repaired old ones, setting the stage for those who followed them. And thus was John the Baptist. His messages turned the hearts of many people back to God and prepared them for the arrival of Jesus the very Son of God.

God still uses forerunners today. They preach a common message: Get ready; Jesus is coming back.

God and Father of my Lord Jesus Christ, *I may not have the fame as others do, but I can still reach out to my neighbors and befriend them. Help me do it with all graciousness for Your glory. In Jesus' name, amen.*

**SPOTLIGHT**

***Next Week's Lesson***

"Onward, Christian soldiers . . . with the cross of Jesus going on before."

# Age Doesn't Matter

*Zechariah asked the angel, "How can I be sure of this? I am an old man and my wife is well along in years" (Luke 1:18).*

I never knew her first name. Everyone at church simply called her Lady J. Her husband had passed away years before, and her grown children lived out of town, wrapped up in their own lives. Although Lady J stayed busy, loneliness filled her days. What she missed most was being a mother.

One Sunday after church, the minister asked asked her to teach a class for young married couples. With his offer came the opportunity to be a "mother" again! God used Lady J in the senior years of her life. She wasn't given just one child to raise like Zechariah and Elizabeth; she was given many. Her nurturing and parental guidance inspired the class to serve Christ. In fact, most of her students became ministers, including me.

Zechariah thought he was too old for a blessing, but age doesn't determine our eligibility. The call of God doesn't depend on age either. The Lord can fill the barren places in our lives with a wave of His hand. If He wants to bless you, just believe and never ask why.

Lord God, *Your promises are sure words that never fail. They do not weaken withage, nor do they expire with time. Throughout the ages, Your promises have blessed so many—eternal testimony to Your awesome loving kindness. Thank You, in the precious name of Jesus. Amen.*

**SEARCH THE WORD**

*Even old people of faith still have doubts; God understands.*

Scripture: Luke 1:18-23

Song: *"After the Mist and Shadow"*

*From this meditation today, I will pray . . .*

Adoration ______________________________

______________________________

______________________________

Confession ______________________________

______________________________

______________________________

Thanksgiving ______________________________

______________________________

______________________________

Supplication ______________________________

______________________________

______________________________

*From this meditation today, I will . . .*

Think ______________________________

______________________________

______________________________

Say ______________________________

______________________________

______________________________

Do ______________________________

______________________________

______________________________

______________________________

______________________________

*One generation will commend your works to another; they will tell of your mighty acts. . . . and joyfully sing of your righteousness.*
*—Psalm 145:4, 7b*

# December

# GOD'S CALL IN CHRIST

*Praise be to God,*
*who has not rejected my prayer.*
—Psalm 66:20

*Photo © istock*

# Pondering God's Purpose

*After this his wife Elizabeth became pregnant and for five months remained in seclusion* (Luke 1:24).

Scripture: Luke 1:24, 25
Song: *"Alone with God"*

I needed a break—or at least a short sabbatical. Maybe our church building project had affected me more than I realized. Although I enjoyed being a minister, my heart was somewhere else these days. My interests were changing. After decades of ministry, did God have other plans for me? Why would God ask me to start writing now?

I needed time to mull things over. I remembered that the apostle Paul sought solitude after his conversion experience on the Damascus Road. He allowed time for God's message to saturate his heart (see Galatians 1:16-18). Moses spent time on Mount Sinai. Elijah rested by a brook. Jesus himself sought out the quietness of the wilderness. In seclusion, they all communed with the Father. Similarly, Elizabeth remained by herself to reflect on the favor of God.

We today also need time alone with God. Thankfully, He draws us to "isolated places" in our lives that we might simply wait on Him. In the quiet, we can ponder His goodness and learn more of His purposes.

*Draw me away,* O Lord, *to that secret place of prayer. Help me listen closely for Your still, small voice. In Christ Jesus, I pray. Amen.*

***From this meditation today, I will pray . . .***

Adoration ______________________________

______________________________

______________________________

Confession ______________________________

______________________________

______________________________

Thanksgiving ______________________________

______________________________

______________________________

Supplication ______________________________

______________________________

______________________________

***From this meditation today, I will . . .***

Think ______________________________

______________________________

______________________________

Say ______________________________

______________________________

______________________________

Do ______________________________

______________________________

______________________________

December 1, 2. ***Charles E. Harrel*** *has been a minister for more than 30 years. He currently directs His Place Outreach in Portland, Oregon.*

**SPOTLIGHT**
***Next Week's Lesson***

Seclusion and stillness before God will help us find our way.

# Just Tell It

*Come and listen, all you who fear God;*
*let me tell you what he has done for me* (Psalm 66:16).

The gold-plated fishhook on the man's shirt collar grabbed my attention. It reminded me of my dad; he often pinned his favorite fishing fly or lure on his hat. After I'd snuck several glances, the man walked over and introduced himself. Our conversation soon turned to fishing.

I discovered this gold hook was John's favorite one; he had caught more fish with it than any other. He told me that he once hooked a 200-pounder with it!

John always kept his favorite hook handy in case he saw a fish. In fact, he said, he had one on the line now (and he started to tug on his collar as if a fish were nibbling). That's when I realized John had been fishing for me. With his hook set, John told me the story of his own experience of being caught—by the greatest fisherman of all.

Our witness matters. People may dismiss our doctrine or disagree with our beliefs, but they cannot deny what God has done in our lives. If we'll just tell them how God has graciously reached into our hearts, we can let Him take care of the rest.

Father, *I know we all have different stories. Some have experienced Your healing, others a wonderful answer to prayer. But all of us have known Your unconditional favor through Christ's work of atonement. Help me to tell of Your great goodness in my life. In Jesus' name, amen.*

**SEARCH THE WORD**

*Find someone to tell your personal story of God's grace.*

Scripture: Psalm 66:16-20
Song: *"I Love to Tell the Story"*

*From this meditation today, I will pray . . .*

Adoration ______________________

______________________

______________________

Confession ______________________

______________________

______________________

Thanksgiving ______________________

______________________

______________________

Supplication ______________________

______________________

______________________

*From this meditation today, I will . . .*

Think ______________________

______________________

______________________

Say ______________________

______________________

______________________

Do ______________________

______________________

______________________

______________________

______________________

December 3

# Trusting for Each Step

*Blessed is the man who makes the Lord his trust, who does not look to the proud, to those who turn aside to false gods* (Psalm 40:4).

**Scripture: Psalm 40:1-5**

**Song:** *"I Could Not Do Without Thee"*

*From this meditation today, I will pray . . .*

Adoration ______________________

______________________

______________________

Confession ______________________

______________________

______________________

Thanksgiving ______________________

______________________

______________________

Supplication ______________________

______________________

______________________

*From this meditation today, I will . . .*

Think ______________________

______________________

______________________

Say ______________________

______________________

______________________

Do ______________________

______________________

______________________

December 3–9. ***Gerry Kershner*** *writes from his home in Lancaster County, Pennsylvania. In addition to devotionals, he writes poetry and magazine articles.*

As I read Psalm 40 for my morning devotions, the fourth verse really seemed to stand out. I realized how often I am tempted to trust in people or things more than the Lord. Why? For one thing, we're constantly bombarded by media messages calling us to find our security elsewhere—with all kinds of appealing false gods.

And those gods come in many forms, don't they? Yet science and technology can't solve all of our problems. And mere possessions won't deliver a solid and settled joy. Even modern medicine—a great boon to civilization—can subtly pull us away from ultimate trust in God for our well-being. As educator Harold W. Dodds once said: "The way to be safe is never to be secure. . . . Each one of us requires the spur of insecurity to force us to do our best." Perhaps that is why God calls us to walk by faith and not by sight, one step at a time.

Dear Lord, *I live in a world filled with so much that is questionable—or downright evil. Help me resist the allure of finite pleasures and trust You, instead, for every good thing. In the holy name of Jesus, my Lord and Savior, I pray. Amen.*

**SPOTLIGHT**

***Next Week's Lesson***

Mary put her trust in God's amazing promise to her.

# Troubled by Good News?

*Mary was greatly troubled at his words and wondered what kind of greeting this might be* (Luke 1:29).

Mary later exhibited tremendous joy and faith concerning this miraculous event. But why was she initially so troubled at Gabriel's words, wondering "what kind of greeting this might be"? This sudden introduction was a great surprise, of course—even a bit shocking. And no doubt Mary needed time to adjust to her new role.

We too may initially react to good news with a troubled spirit. In a wonderful 1983 film about redemption, *Tender Mercies,* the main character (played by Robert Duvall) is baptized and changed forever. But he later says to the lady who brought him into the church: "I prayed last night to know: *Why?* . . . I don't know why I wandered to this part of Texas, and you took me in, pitied me, and helped me to straighten out. . . . Why did that happen? You see, I don't trust happiness. I never did and never will."

We may not be able to explain (or fully trust) the sudden goodness of God in our lives, for sometimes that grace enters in almost shocking ways. We are right to be troubled—at least for awhile—until our consternation turns to unspeakable joy.

Dear Father, *during this season when we celebrate the birth of Your Son, I am overwhelmed with Your sudden entrance into this world. Help me to accept Your many good gifts with joy. In Jesus' name, amen.*

**SEARCH THE WORD**

*Believe in God's grace even though it seems too good to be true.*

Scripture: Luke 1:26-29

Song: *"Joy to the World"*

*From this meditation today, I will pray . . .*

Adoration ____________________

Confession ____________________

Thanksgiving ____________________

Supplication ____________________

*From this meditation today, I will . . .*

Think ____________________

Say ____________________

Do ____________________

December 5

# Let the Kingdom Show Through!

*He will reign over the house of Jacob forever; his kingdom will never end* (Luke 1:33).

Scripture: Luke 1:30-33

Song: *"There's a Song in the Air"*

***From this meditation today, I will pray . . .***

Adoration ____________________________

Confession ____________________________

Thanksgiving ____________________________

Supplication ____________________________

***From this meditation today, I will . . .***

Think ____________________________

Say ____________________________

Do ____________________________

Like many other Christians, I'm distressed by the crass commercialism and secular activities associated with Christmas in our culture. Every year we seem to experience less of the true meaning of Christ's incarnation.

As I read Luke 1:33, I wonder what the angel Gabriel means when he says that Jesus' kingdom will never end. Then I'm reminded that (at least for now) Jesus' realm is not a political, earthly kingdom. He refused political rule during His time on earth. No, Jesus reigns forever in the hearts of His followers, a kingdom that will never end.

As followers of Jesus we can share His love, His joy, and His peace with others during the Christmas season and throughout the year. We can do this no matter how others celebrate. In this way we can be a part of maintaining Jesus' kingdom and even helping spread it in our neighborhoods and throughout the world. As Jesus himself said, "The kingdom of God is within you" (Luke 17:21). But will we let His reign in our hearts be visible in the most practical and loving forms of outreach?

Lord, *help me to keep my eyes, mind, and heart on You, continually reminding me that Your kingdom is within me. And do move me to share Your love, Your joy, and Your peace with others during this Christmas season. In the name of Jesus, who came as Lord and Savior of all, I pray. Amen.*

**SPOTLIGHT**

***Next Week's Lesson***

Earthly kings die and their rule ends;
King Jesus will reign for all eternity.

# Back to Basics

*The holy one to be born will be called the Son of God*
(Luke 1:35).

For many of us, the Christmas season is harried and hurried. We have gifts to make or buy, boxes to wrap, cards to address and send, parties to plan, food to buy and prepare, and church activities to fit into our busy schedules. Most of these activities are good, but I'm thinking of "going back to the basics."

I'm starting with the basic question, "What is Christmas all about?" In today's verse the angel tells Mary that the child to be born will be called the Son of God. In that brief announcement we can see that Christmas is really the most important event in the history of the world. God came to the world as a flesh-and-blood human being!

In light of this amazing truth, all of our Christmas activities take on new meaning. The gifts, cards, food, parties, and church activities now all become our part of celebrating the radical entrance of the Son of God. What a birthday this is—calling us to slow down, to contemplate its miraculous unfolding, to make room for many silent nights of praise.

Dear Father in Heaven, *I come to You during this harried and hurried season, asking You to help me get back to the basics. Keep me focused on the great miracle of Your Son coming in person to love Your world. And help me love Him with all my heart in return. In His name, I pray. Amen.*

**SEARCH THE WORD**

*Remember this simple yet sublime truth: God came to earth as a baby.*

Scripture: Luke 1:34, 35
**Song:** *"Silent Night"*

*From this meditation today, I will pray . . .*

Adoration ____________________

Confession ____________________

Thanksgiving ____________________

Supplication ____________________

*From this meditation today, I will . . .*

Think ____________________

Say ____________________

Do ____________________

December 7

# Mary, the Lord's Servant

*"I am the Lord's servant," Mary answered. "May it be to me as you have said"* (Luke 1:38).

Scripture: Luke 1:36-38

Song: *"Mary, Did You Know?"*

***From this meditation today, I will pray . . .***

Adoration ______________________________

______________________________

______________________________

Confession ______________________________

______________________________

______________________________

Thanksgiving ______________________________

______________________________

______________________________

Supplication ______________________________

______________________________

______________________________

***From this meditation today, I will . . .***

Think ______________________________

______________________________

______________________________

Say ______________________________

______________________________

______________________________

Do ______________________________

______________________________

______________________________

______________________________

______________________________

Rereading the wonderful story of Christmas in the first chapter of Luke's gospel, I am struck by Mary's humble acceptance of the angel's dramatic announcement that she is to be pregnant. And her child was to be called the Son of the Most High!

After all this fanfare, she simply answers, "I am the Lord's servant. May it be to me as you have said" (1:38). Yes, she may have been a bit confused, or troubled, but she apparently did not need to know all of the minor details and long-term implications, as I usually do. God said it, and that was enough. Such childlike faith is a lesson I often need to relearn.

I think any of us can learn much from Mary. We don't normally receive angelic visitations, but we do often experience God moving in ways we do not understand. And this is where we can remember Mary's example. Rather than trying to understand the big picture all at once, we can simply take the next step with God.

Dear Lord and Master, *thank You so much for Mary and the many other biblical role models You've given me, that I may lead a life pleasing to You. I too am Your servant. So help me live with simple, childlike faith in Your good will and guidance in my life. In the name of the Father, the Son, and the Holy Spirit, I pray. Amen.*

**SPOTLIGHT**

***Next Week's Lesson***

When next faced with a daunting task from God, can you say, "I am your servant"?

# Elizabeth's Joy and Faith

*As soon as the sound of your greeting reached my ears, the baby in my womb leaped for joy*
(Luke 1:44).

We can hardly imagine the joy that Elizabeth felt when Mary visited her. She who had been childless during her normal childbearing years was now pregnant. She must have been overjoyed when she immediately recognized that her relative, Mary, was also pregnant in a miraculous way. Elizabeth's joy in the autumn of her life must have been especially sweet.

Yet through all those childless years, Elizabeth kept her strong faith in God. She was upright in the sight of God. She observed all of the commandments and regulations blamelessly. Later, she believed that the one who made the promise would keep the promise. Simply put, she kept the faith.

Many of us have dreams that remain unfulfilled, causing us, at times, to doubt God's goodwill toward us. Yet, like Elizabeth, we need to keep the faith, because our faith is more important than our dreams. As writer Henry Thoreau once said: "The smallest seed of faith is better than the largest fruit of happiness."

Dear Lord, *strengthen my faith. Help me to remain true and faithful even when I have no visible evidence, like Elizabeth during her childless years. Help me to keep the faith so I may also experience joy as Elizabeth did. In Jesus' name I pray. Amen.*

**SEARCH THE WORD**

*Great rewards come to those who patiently wait for God to keep His promises.*

Scripture: Luke 1:39-45

Song: *"My Faith Looks Up to Thee"*

*From this meditation today, I will pray . . .*

Adoration ______________________

______________________

______________________

Confession ______________________

______________________

______________________

Thanksgiving ______________________

______________________

______________________

Supplication ______________________

______________________

______________________

*From this meditation today, I will . . .*

Think ______________________

______________________

______________________

Say ______________________

______________________

______________________

Do ______________________

______________________

______________________

______________________

______________________

# Mary's Song of Praise

*My soul glorifies the Lord and my spirit rejoices in God my Savior* (Luke 1:46, 47).

Scripture: Luke 1:46-56
Song: *"How Majestic Is Your Name"*

*From this meditation today, I will pray . . .*

Adoration ____________________

Confession ____________________

Thanksgiving ____________________

Supplication ____________________

*From this meditation today, I will . . .*

Think ____________________

Say ____________________

Do ____________________

I am humbled by Mary's song of praise in these ten verses, traditionally called the *Magnificat.* After a spontaneous outburst of praise for her personal blessing, she continues to praise God for His mercy, power, and goodness in the past as well as the present.

I must confess that far too often I do not praise God and give Him the glory for the small, and sometimes even the larger, blessings in my life. Oh yes, I pray on a daily basis like many other Christians. But my prayer requests often far outnumber my praise items. Obviously, Mary had many personal prayer needs at this time, but none of them are included in this short song of praise.

Study of this song has convinced me to make a deliberate, personal effort to include more and more praise in my prayer life. In fact, I hope it will become a spontaneous and constant part of my relationship with God. After all, prayer is primarily an opening of hearts up to God, just as Mary did. Sometimes it is simply a wordless adoration or a period of silent listening for Him. But couldn't many of us use a little boost to our prayer lives by adding small songs of praise to our daily devotional times?

Dear Lord, *You are so good! Help me to praise you spontaneously and sincerely this day. In Your holy name I pray. Amen.*

**SPOTLIGHT**
***Next Week's Lesson***

"I will extol the Lord at all times; his praise will always be on my lips" (Psalm 34:1).

# Messengers

*See, I will send my messenger, who will prepare the way before me* (Malachi 3:1).

When I feel unimportant, I recall the words I once heard a minister preach: "You may be the only Bible some people will ever read." John the Baptist must have understood this thoroughly. He was the messenger God chose to prepare the way for Jesus' arrival.

On the face of it, John was unimpressive. He lived in the wilderness, ate bugs, and wore strange clothes. Yet people flocked to hear the message of repentance he preached. They came, not because John was attractive, but because he was a faithful messenger, telling the people what God wanted them to know.

We may never know the impact we have on the people we encounter, day in and day out. A kindness done to a stranger, a hug given a stressed-out coworker, or time spent with a little child may seem like simple, unnoticeable acts. But to God, they are a witness to the world of Christ's love. When we allow God to use us as messengers of the gospel, we may even amaze ourselves.

Lord, *I feel so unworthy of the calling to be a messenger of Your good news. Help me be faithful in word and deed—and be on the lookout for those in any kind of need. In the name of Christ I pray. Amen.*

**SEARCH THE WORD**

*The lives we lead can help prepare others to receive God's message.*

Scripture: Malachi 3:1-4

Song: *"If Jesus Goes with Me"*

***From this meditation today, I will pray . . .***

Adoration ____________________

Confession ____________________

Thanksgiving ____________________

Supplication ____________________

***From this meditation today, I will . . .***

Think ____________________

Say ____________________

Do ____________________

December 10–16. ***Lisa Konzen*** *works for United Way in Janesville, Wisconsin. She also writes health articles for seniors in her local newspaper,* The Janesville Gazette.

December 11

# Standing Up

*But his mother spoke up and said, "No! He is to be called John"* (Luke 1:60).

Scripture: Luke 1:57-61

Song: *"Stand Up, Stand Up for Jesus"*

***From this meditation today, I will pray . . .***

Adoration ______________________________

______________________________

______________________________

Confession ______________________________

______________________________

______________________________

Thanksgiving ______________________________

______________________________

______________________________

Supplication ______________________________

______________________________

______________________________

***From this meditation today, I will . . .***

Think ______________________________

______________________________

______________________________

Say ______________________________

______________________________

______________________________

Do ______________________________

______________________________

______________________________

______________________________

______________________________

I used to be quite a pushover. If my food was served cold at a restaurant, I'd meekly eat it instead of sending it back. If I wasn't satisfied with something I bought, I'd stash it away in my closet instead of returning it to the store for a refund.

But not anymore. What made the difference? The day I realized that some things are worth standing up for. My father was in the hospital, and because he had many health problems, full and complete information about his status wasn't always communicated very well. I had to approach doctors and nurses rather assertively for the answers I needed.

It taught me a valuable lesson: Sometimes, you just have to be tough. Not unkind, and certainly not violent. But tough. It all depends on what you're standing up for. I imagine Elizabeth trembled a little when her relatives challenged her decision to name her son John. But she knew that was what God wanted her to do. So, despite being a woman in a society that did not highly value a woman's opinion, Elizabeth stood up for God.

Holy God, *too often I've been timid when I should have been bold. Yet You are the source of all my courage. Fill me with Your presence to the extent that I have no room left for fear. In the name of Jesus, amen.*

**SPOTLIGHT**

***Next Week's Lesson***

When we have no doubt, we'll be able to speak out.

# Tongue Un-Tied

*Immediately his mouth was opened and his tongue was loosed, and he began to speak, praising God* (Luke 1:64).

Have you ever been tongue-tied when trying to talk about your faith? You know you should say something, but it's so difficult. Maybe you're going through a rough time, and bearing witness for God seems to require more faith than you feel you have.

Zechariah knew about being tongue-tied. When the angel Gabriel told him his elderly, barren wife Elizabeth would bear a son, he asked for proof. His lack of trust was met with a stern promise from Gabriel that Zechariah would not be able to speak until the child was born. And sure enough, Zechariah was mute until the day he said, "His name is John" (1:63).

I think we can learn a lesson from Zechariah. His lack of trust in God led him to mute ineffectiveness. Similarly, when our faith falters, we may find it difficult to speak about the good news of the gospel. But the same Holy Spirit who loosened Zechariah's tongue and restored his faith can do the same for us. Our simple willingness to be used by Him is the first movement toward a full-bodied trust that won't falter.

Word of God, *speak through me. My tongue is dry, and my heart is empty without You. But when You dwell in me, rivers of blessings pour forth from my lips as I sing Your praises! In the name of Jesus, amen.*

**SEARCH THE WORD**

*Lord, loosen my tongue and help me declare Your truth.*

Scripture: Luke 1:62-66

**Song:** *"Praise the Savior"*

*From this meditation today, I will pray . . .*

Adoration ____________________

Confession ____________________

Thanksgiving ____________________

Supplication ____________________

*From this meditation today, I will . . .*

Think ____________________

Say ____________________

Do ____________________

December 13

# Without Fear

*He has raised up a horn of salvation . . . to rescue us from the hand of our enemies, and to enable us to serve him without fear* (Luke 1:69, 74).

Scripture: Luke 1:67-75
Song: *"All Your Anxiety"*

*From this meditation today, I will pray . . .*

Adoration ______________________________

______________________________

______________________________

Confession ______________________________

______________________________

______________________________

Thanksgiving ______________________________

______________________________

______________________________

Supplication ______________________________

______________________________

______________________________

*From this meditation today, I will . . .*

Think ______________________________

______________________________

______________________________

Say ______________________________

______________________________

______________________________

Do ______________________________

______________________________

______________________________

______________________________

______________________________

You've probably heard of the fight-or-flight response. It's the wonderful system God designed in our bodies that helps us react to dangerous situations. When we're in crisis, the hormone adrenaline is released. For example, a grizzly bear challenges us in the woods. We can either try to tackle him to the ground or . . . run away. Fast!

We rarely face grizzlies in modern living today. Yet our bodies react the same way when we feel under pressure day after day or experience even a minor conflict with a coworker or spouse. Adrenaline still shoots into our hearts; we react with fear—and fight or flee.

Problem is, when the crisis passes, many of us can't seem to turn off the response! Chronic fear can contribute to the development of generalized anxiety, depression, and a host of physical maladies, including heart disease. Our hectic lives have turned what was once a blessing from God into a curse.

But it doesn't have to be that way. In Christ, we are set free. We'll still face stress, but as we cast our cares upon our Savior, we can let go and let God rescue us.

Dear God, *it's so easy to become afraid these days. But You asked me to cast my cares upon You, so that's what I'm going to do. Through Christ, amen.*

**SPOTLIGHT**
***Next Week's Lesson***

In what wonderful ways could we serve the Lord if we were truly free from fear?

# Knowing the Word

*To give his people the knowledge of salvation through the forgiveness of their sins*
(Luke 1:77).

The minister of my church is a strong believer in Bible study, and with good reason. Because he is so faithful in teaching the truth of God's Word, we know the history and mystery of our faith. History, because he painstakingly presents the narrative of the Scripture, exploring the time lines and themes.

But he goes way beyond that, teaching us the mystery of the grace of our Savior, Jesus Christ, and the way His life, death, and resurrection free us to serve Him joyfully.

And serve Him we do. From hunger walks to "Christmas in July" fund raisers for the local food pantry, our church practices what our minister preaches. New ministries inside and outside of the church are continually springing up. But if all this sounds like bragging, that's because it is. Not about our members, or even about our minister. We're just responding to the gift of salvation freely given that we learn about as we study Scripture. All the praise, glory, and honor go to Jesus, the Word of Life who writes His gospel across the lives of His people. For without Him, we can do nothing.

O Lord, *help me to rededicate myself to studying the Scripture each day. I want to be knowledgeable so I can share the treasures of Your truth with every openhearted person I meet. In Jesus' name, amen.*

**SEARCH THE WORD**

*Study Scripture or serve others? Let's do both!*

Scripture: Luke 1:76-80
Song: *"More About Jesus"*

*From this meditation today, I will pray . . .*

Adoration ______________________

______________________

______________________

Confession ______________________

______________________

______________________

Thanksgiving ______________________

______________________

______________________

Supplication ______________________

______________________

______________________

*From this meditation today, I will . . .*

Think ______________________

______________________

______________________

Say ______________________

______________________

______________________

Do ______________________

______________________

______________________

______________________

______________________

# Pedigree or Mutt?

*Do not begin to say to yourselves, "We have Abraham as our father." For I tell you that out of these stones God can raise up children for Abraham* (Luke 3:8).

Scripture: Luke 3:7-14

Song: *"A Child of the King"*

***From this meditation today, I will pray . . .***

Adoration ______________________________

Confession ______________________________

Thanksgiving ______________________________

Supplication ______________________________

***From this meditation today, I will . . .***

Think ______________________________

Say ______________________________

Do ______________________________

All my life we've had dogs. I remember Bagel, so named because we were told she was a beagle, only to learn later that she was a Pit Bull mix. Peggy was a black Labrador retriever, who was so smart and loving. And Princess Su Linn, a Lhasa Apso, was the only purebred dog our family ever had.

Pedigreed or mutt, it really doesn't matter. What matters with dogs is not who their parents were, but the love given by their owners. A dog won't snub us because his sire was a best in show. Dogs stand on their own four paws, protecting and loving us because they're part of our family.

We can learn a lot from our pooch pals. It doesn't matter what our name is, where we're from, or how much money sits in our bank account. What matters in the church is that we're all part of God's family. It has nothing to do with any effort on our part. God adopted us and calls us to love each other as brothers and sisters in Christ.

Heavenly Father, *thank You for adopting me into Your family as a precious child. Help me to remember the pure grace that made it possible—and therefore to love unconditionally all my siblings in the faith. I pray this prayer in the name of Jesus, my merciful Savior and Lord. Amen.*

**SPOTLIGHT**

***Next Week's Lesson***

What a privilege to be adopted into God's family.

# Proud to Be Humble

*John answered them all, "I baptize you with water. But one more powerful than I will come, the thongs of whose sandals I am not worthy to untie"* (Luke 3:16).

Have you ever heard someone complain about having to play second fiddle? Perhaps it was an employee whose coworker was just promoted. "I hate playing second fiddle to him," the disgruntled worker might grumble. Playing second fiddle means you are not the one in charge, not the one getting all the attention.

But have you ever wondered what the phrase literally means? An orchestra has sections and subsections. Within the strings are violins, in subsets of first and second violins (violins being the dressed-up name for fiddles). The role of the second violins is to support the work of the first violins, enhancing them with glorious harmony.

John the Baptist wasn't ashamed to play second fiddle to Jesus. He knew he had a job to do, and he wasn't in it for the limelight. For him, playing second fiddle was right because he knew Jesus was the Savior whose sacrifice would save him and the world. Perhaps next time we're asked to serve in the shadows, we'll remember the prophet in the wilderness who was proud to be humble.

Dear God and Father, *may my thoughts, words, and actions take the spotlight off me and glorify You. Let me bring harmony to Your kingdom. Through Your precious Son, Jesus Christ, I pray. Amen.*

**SEARCH THE WORD**

*A little humility never hurts.*

Scripture: Luke 3:15-20

Song: *"The Unveiled Christ"*

*From this meditation today, I will pray . . .*

Adoration ______________________________

______________________________

______________________________

Confession ______________________________

______________________________

______________________________

Thanksgiving ______________________________

______________________________

______________________________

Supplication ______________________________

______________________________

______________________________

*From this meditation today, I will . . .*

Think ______________________________

______________________________

______________________________

Say ______________________________

______________________________

______________________________

Do ______________________________

______________________________

______________________________

______________________________

______________________________

# Making a List

*Sing to the* L*ORD* *a new song. . . . Splendor and majesty are before him; strength and glory are in his sanctuary* (Psalm 96:1, 6).

Scripture: Psalm 96:1-6
Song: *"Glorious Is Thy Name"*

***From this meditation today, I will pray . . .***

Adoration ______________________________

______________________________

______________________________

Confession ______________________________

______________________________

______________________________

Thanksgiving ______________________________

______________________________

______________________________

Supplication ______________________________

______________________________

______________________________

***From this meditation today, I will . . .***

Think ______________________________

______________________________

______________________________

Say ______________________________

______________________________

______________________________

Do ______________________________

______________________________

______________________________

December 17–23. ***Susan Miholer,*** *a grandmother and special education assistant, owns Picky, Picky Ink, her editorial service in Salem, Oregon.*

I'm a year-round list-maker. Lists keep me focused—especially at Christmas time. Let's see, what do I need to do in order to be ready? Cards, decorations, gifts, parties, programs . . . and on it goes.

I do something similar when I study God's Word. If I come to a passage that includes a list of God's attributes or commands, I love to list them in my journal. Then I might use a Bible dictionary to jot some definitions next to each item. Even the subtle differences I find between quite similar words give me much food for thought. The next step is to consider how to apply what I've learned.

A particular favorite this time of year is the list of names in Isaiah 9:6: Wonderful Counselor, Mighty God, Everlasting Father, Prince of Peace. Even today's passage lends itself to such a word study with phrases like: praise His name, proclaim His salvation, declare His glory, splendor and majesty, strength and glory. What do each of these mean to you?

Lord, *Your Word is so rich. May I pause at even familiar words and find in them a new song to sing Your praise. Through Christ my Lord, amen.*

**SPOTLIGHT**
***Next Week's Lesson***

At this time of year it's especially easy to find reasons to praise God.

# The Trinity of the Slide

*Give him the name Jesus, because he will save his people from their sins* (Matthew 1:21).

"Grandma, come get me!" Four-year-old Nicholas was at the top of the slide at a fast-food restaurant, too scared to come down. I assumed some uncomfortable positions as I crawled through the not-quite-adult-sized tunnels to get to him, and then I rode down the slide with him. Not my most dignified grandmotherly moment! He, on the other hand, thought it was great fun. I kept envisioning the newspaper headline: "Grandmother Stuck—Fire Department Summoned."

I didn't feel very god-like that day; in fact, I was glad there were few witnesses to my actions and attitude. But later I saw the whole episode as a picture of what God did for us. As the Father, He saw our need of a Savior. As the Son, He assumed the uncomfortable positions of the Incarnation to rescue me. And as the Holy Spirit, He rides with me through the twists and turns of this slide-ride we call life.

Jesus. There's just something about that name—something that tells us so much about God that we can never comprehend it all.

Heavenly Father, *when I consider how You reached down through Your Son, I'm humbled that You included me in Your great plan of salvation. Thank You for the sacrifice of the incarnation! In Jesus' name, amen.*

**SEARCH THE WORD**

*Jesus—*
*name above all names.*

Scripture: Matthew 1:18b-21

Song: *"The Name of Jesus"*

*From this meditation today, I will pray . . .*

Adoration ______________________________

______________________________

______________________________

Confession ______________________________

______________________________

______________________________

Thanksgiving ______________________________

______________________________

______________________________

Supplication ______________________________

______________________________

______________________________

*From this meditation today, I will . . .*

Think ______________________________

______________________________

______________________________

Say ______________________________

______________________________

______________________________

Do ______________________________

______________________________

______________________________

______________________________

______________________________

# A New Chapter

*So Joseph also went . . . to Bethlehem. . . . He went there to register with Mary* (Luke 2:4, 5).

Scripture: Luke 2:1-5

Song: *"O Little Town of Bethlehem"*

During the last few weeks of my pregnancies, waddling anywhere was a challenge. Travel for any reason other than essential errands and appointments was pretty much out of the question.

Mary probably wasn't eager to travel from Nazareth to Bethlehem in her condition. But regardless of the discomforts involved, she was no doubt relieved to be getting away from the whispers and judgmental stares in her old neighborhood. She was probably both exhilarated and frightened about her new role as mother too—a new chapter in her life. Bethlehem might well provide a clean slate for her and Joseph.

When God ushers in a new chapter in our lives, we often experience the same emotional mix—the exhilaration, yet the questions about what is happening and why things are unfolding the way they are. And, like Mary, we can face the challenge with a similar response: "May it be to me as you have said" (Luke 1:38).

Facing a life-change in this season of your life? Look to God as He leads you into a new chapter.

*Thank You, God, that You have gone before me into the unknown of my life. Allow me to trust You for the grace, strength, and wisdom to face today's challenges. In the name of Jesus, my Savior, I pray. Amen.*

***From this meditation today, I will pray . . .***

Adoration ____________________

Confession ____________________

Thanksgiving ____________________

Supplication ____________________

***From this meditation today, I will . . .***

Think ____________________

Say ____________________

Do ____________________

**SPOTLIGHT**

***Next Week's Lesson***

Together Mary and Joseph faced the challenges God gave them.

# No Room in the Family?

*There was no room for them in the inn*
(Luke 2:7).

At the birth of my first grandchild, we grandparents practically elbowed each other out of the way to be first in the room to see our new baby boy. But Scripture is strangely silent about Mary and Joseph's families. I would think that several members of Joseph's family would have been in Bethlehem. Didn't they have to go there to register as well? If this was Joseph's ancestral home, I'd expect there may have been relatives in Bethlehem with whom they could have stayed. But they seemed so alone in that place.

I know Scripture doesn't give us all the details, but I'm wondering if Mary's circumstances had ostracized Joseph and Mary so much that even close family members wouldn't extend hospitality to them—or at least some loving concern. That would take the phrase "no room for them in the inn" (2:7) to another level, wouldn't it? Not only was there no room in the inn, there may have been no room in the family circle.

Yet Jesus' earthly parents model for me the response I should have when I feel cut off from others. Follow God anyway.

Father, *I sometimes feel there's no room for me in certain situations because I've chosen to follow You along the narrow way. At those times, may I rest assured that You are always with me. Through Christ, amen.*

**SEARCH THE WORD**

*When everyone else leaves, God is there.*

Scripture: Luke 2:6, 7
Song: *"No Room in the Inn"*

***From this meditation today, I will pray . . .***

Adoration __________

Confession __________

Thanksgiving __________

Supplication __________

***From this meditation today, I will . . .***

Think __________

Say __________

Do __________

December 21

# Creative Announcement

*Today in the town of David a Savior has been born to you; he is Christ the Lord* (Luke 2:11).

Scripture: Luke 2:8-14

**Song:** *"Angels We Have Heard on High"*

***From this meditation today, I will pray . . .***

Adoration ______________________

______________________

______________________

Confession ______________________

______________________

______________________

Thanksgiving ______________________

______________________

______________________

Supplication ______________________

______________________

______________________

***From this meditation today, I will . . .***

Think ______________________

______________________

______________________

Say ______________________

______________________

______________________

Do ______________________

______________________

______________________

______________________

______________________

People have gotten creative with birth announcements lately, as the computer provides all kinds of new ways to announce a baby's entrance into the world. Families design entire Web sites to share the news. I've even seen custom-printed wrappers that slip over a regular chocolate bar. The front of the label (and its color) let people know the baby's vital statistics. And the parents' names replace the standard ingredients label.

But the most creative of all birth announcements occurred on a hillside over 2,000 years ago as a bunch of ordinary (and probably scruffy) shepherds settled their sheep and themselves for the night. As they adjusted their cloaks to ward off the evening chill and breathed that last relaxed sigh of impending sleep, an angel amid the glory of the Lord delivered awesome good news. And then the sky seemed to explode as the heavenly host underscored the grand message.

No other birth in history has been announced in such magnificent style. Nor has any other birth in history had the same eternal consequences. No wonder the angels praised God!

Eternal God, *may I, like the angels, praise You and say, Glory to God in the highest! In the name of the incarnate Christ I pray. Amen.*

**SPOTLIGHT**

***Next Week's Lesson***

Let us join the angels in giving glory to God for His magnificent gift.

# Different Reactions

*Mary treasured up all these things and pondered them in her heart* (Luke 2:19).

Different people react differently to good news. Some clap, some cry, some dance, and some just stand there looking surprised. I've done all four—and sometimes two or three at the same time.

Recovering from the spectacle of God's glory and the good news of Christ's birth, the shepherds couldn't get to Bethlehem fast enough. Having seen the baby, their exuberance bubbled over as they told everyone of the angel's announcement and what they had seen. People were astonished. Even without e-mail, the news traveled quickly. But Mary, precious Mary, the one who had known for months whose child this was, quietly pondered what was happening, filing away memories of her Son.

Emotions run high at Christmas time. Like the shepherds, we may push and shove to get there first. We may be so excited about the good news of Christmas that we sing the familiar carols with new enthusiasm, astonished by the discovery of new facets in the familiar story. But like Mary, I also want to carve out times of quiet reflection upon who Jesus really is—my Lord and my God.

Dear Father, *the birth of Your Son changed the course of history. May I understand a piece of the Christmas story in a new way this year. Keep my focus on who Christ is and why He came. In His name I pray. Amen.*

**SEARCH THE WORD**

*Use this quiet moment to reflect on what happened that first Christmas night.*

Scripture: Luke 2:15-20

Song: *"O Come, Let Us Adore Him"*

***From this meditation today, I will pray . . .***

Adoration ______________________

______________________

______________________

Confession ______________________

______________________

______________________

Thanksgiving ______________________

______________________

______________________

Supplication ______________________

______________________

______________________

***From this meditation today, I will . . .***

Think ______________________

______________________

______________________

Say ______________________

______________________

______________________

Do ______________________

______________________

______________________

______________________

______________________

December 23

# Who's the Author?

*Ascribe to the Lord the glory due his name; bring an offering and come into his courts* (Psalm 96:8).

Scripture: Psalm 96:7-13

Song: *"Creation's Lord, We Give Thee Thanks"*

*From this meditation today, I will pray . . .*

Adoration ______________________

______________________

______________________

Confession ______________________

______________________

______________________

Thanksgiving ______________________

______________________

______________________

Supplication ______________________

______________________

______________________

*From this meditation today, I will . . .*

Think ______________________

______________________

______________________

Say ______________________

______________________

______________________

Do ______________________

______________________

______________________

______________________

______________________

We don't use the word *ascribe* very often anymore. The dictionary says it suggests an "inferring or conjecturing of cause, quality, or authorship." If you're a Shakespearean scholar or an expert on Picasso, you know what to look for in a specific play or work of art to indicate its creator. Sometimes, though, even the experts don't agree as to whom a particular work ought to be ascribed.

But there is no disagreement in today's passage about who is responsible for, who is the author of, all the beauty in nature. Every aspect of the natural world—the seas, the hills, the forests, even the living beings—point us toward their creator. And that same author is the author of our salvation, the baby whose birth we celebrate at this time of year.

Born in obscurity, He is the author of this world and everything in it. And if anything good and admirable blossoms within our hearts . . . He is the author of all of those virtues too. For our heart is the place He has chosen to make His dwelling place. Ascribe glory to Him!

My Father in Heaven, *Your Son came to the earth to be the author of my salvation. Thank You, from the bottom of my heart. I want to worship You in the same spontaneous way Your creation does, pointing others to You. In the name of the Father, the Son, and the Holy Spirit, I pray. Amen.*

**SPOTLIGHT**

***Next Week's Lesson***

Simeon and Anna both worshiped God as they beheld the promised Messiah.

# The First Christmas Gift-giver

*That you may bring my salvation to the ends of the earth* (Isaiah 49:6).

Our familiar white-bearded Santa harks back to a third-century bishop born in Turkey. Renowned for his humility and generosity, Nicholas became the patron saint of many nations, causes, and groups, including sailors and children. A body of legend grew around his person, including the idea that he dressed in red and gave gifts at Christmas time.

Poet Clement Moore leaned on such legends as he wrote the whimsical, "A Visit from St. Nicholas" in 1832 to amuse his children. But the reindeer-powered Christmas Eve trip around the world was Moore's unique idea. His poem gained immediate fame and imposed a curious persona on humble Nicholas that would have amazed him.

We need not fuss about the folklore from many lands that colors our Christmas celebrations. But tree lights, holly, and mistletoe must not overshadow the manger, where the true Gift-giver was born. He offers His gift to the ends of the earth, not once a year, but every day—and throughout all generations to every tribe and tongue.

*Thank You,* Lord, *for offering Your gift of eternal life to all, whether they have been naughty or nice. All praise to You, in Christ's name. Amen.*

**SEARCH THE WORD**

*"Every good and perfect gift is from above, coming down from the Father"* (James 1:17).

Scripture: Isaiah 49:5, 6

Song: *"It Came Upon the Midnight Clear"*

***From this meditation today, I will pray . . .***

Adoration ______________________________

______________________________

______________________________

Confession ______________________________

______________________________

______________________________

Thanksgiving ______________________________

______________________________

______________________________

Supplication ______________________________

______________________________

______________________________

***From this meditation today, I will . . .***

Think ______________________________

______________________________

______________________________

Say ______________________________

______________________________

______________________________

Do ______________________________

______________________________

______________________________

December 24–30. ***Lloyd Mattson*** *is a retired minister and author of Christian camping books. He and his wife, Elsie, live in Duluth, Minnesota.*

# Poor Joseph and Mary!

*Joseph and Mary took him to Jerusalem to present him to the Lord . . . and to offer a sacrifice in keeping with what is said in the Law of the Lord* (Luke 2:22, 24).

Scripture: Luke 2:21-24

Song: *"Thou Didst Leave Thy Throne"*

***From this meditation today, I will pray . . .***

Adoration ______________________________

Confession ______________________________

Thanksgiving ______________________________

Supplication ______________________________

***From this meditation today, I will . . .***

Think ______________________________

Say ______________________________

Do ______________________________

Joseph and Mary came to the temple with birds, the sacrifice of the poor. Similarly, throughout His ministry, Jesus depended on others for food and shelter. Yet we seldom think of Jesus or His family as poor. After all, poverty is relative; our poorest seem rich beyond imagining to earth's millions who are starving.

While Jesus placed no premium on poverty, He spoke often about greed. That's why Christmas appeals move us to give to the needy, and we rightly feel good about doing so. The Magi, too, presented gifts, but we can't know the worth of those gifts until we know what they had left.

What do we have left? Our benevolent giving marks us as among earth's most generous people, yet America has little cause for pride. Consider what we keep! The American dream wears a dollar sign, and a good Christmas usually means retailers sold more than they did the year before.

The point is, giving isn't really giving until it costs us something. And at Christmas time we can remember: We celebrate the birth of a man who owned nothing.

Heavenly Father, *that I might embrace Your presence in me to the fullest, please help me loosen my grip on everything else. In Jesus' name, amen.*

**SPOTLIGHT**

***Next Week's Lesson***

How rich beyond measure were those "poor" parents to whom God entrusted His Son.

# A Devout Nobody

*Now there was a man in Jerusalem, called Simeon, who was righteous and devout. He was waiting for the consolation of Israel, and the Holy Spirit was upon him* (Luke 2:25).

A remarkable man, Simeon. He held no office or honors, yet the Holy Spirit was upon him. How could that be? Pentecost was at least three years away. Was not that the day the Holy Spirit came?

We tend to arrange God's affairs according to our limited understandings, keeping Him safely within the boundaries of our doctrinal preferences. We ought not do that, for the sovereign God works where, when, and among whom He chooses, and that truth abides today.

Simeon came to the temple at just the right time. As far as he knew, it was an ordinary day. Many people, priests, Levites, scribes, and teachers of the law bustled about. Did any of them long for Messiah's coming? But Simeon had a God-ward heart, and the Holy Spirit had given him a remarkable promise.

That day Simeon's longing was fulfilled. And the least of Jesus' followers can draw comfort from Simeon, a devout nobody who longed to see the Christ.

Dear Father above, *grant me holy desires this day. And thank You for Your gift of the Holy Spirit, who fulfills the desires of my heart. I pray this prayer in the name of Jesus, my merciful Savior and Lord. Amen.*

**SEARCH THE WORD**

*Waiting, watching, praying, praising—Simeon's faithfulness finally paid off.*

Scripture: Luke 2:25, 26

Song: *"Spirit of Faith, Come Down"*

*From this meditation today, I will pray . . .*

Adoration ______________________

______________________

______________________

Confession ______________________

______________________

______________________

Thanksgiving ______________________

______________________

______________________

Supplication ______________________

______________________

______________________

*From this meditation today, I will . . .*

Think ______________________

______________________

______________________

Say ______________________

______________________

______________________

Do ______________________

______________________

______________________

______________________

______________________

December 27

# Take Him to Your Heart

*When the parents brought in the child Jesus to do for him what the custom of the Law required, Simeon took him in his arms and praised God* (Luke 2:27, 28).

Scripture: Luke 2:27, 28
Song: *"Into My Heart"*

***From this meditation today, I will pray . . .***

Adoration ______________________

______________________

______________________

Confession ______________________

______________________

______________________

Thanksgiving ______________________

______________________

______________________

Supplication ______________________

______________________

______________________

***From this meditation today, I will . . .***

Think ______________________

______________________

______________________

Say ______________________

______________________

______________________

Do ______________________

______________________

______________________

______________________

______________________

I once read a little anecdote about a shabby lad who rushed into a department store on Christmas Eve, just before the store's closing. Out of breath, he pled, "Could we borrow your Jesus? Ours got busted." That line was irresistible, and I later wrote a story about a clumsy young man who knocked over a Christmas tree and shattered the porcelain pieces of a nativity scene. The story's theme: We all need our own special relationship with Jesus

Simeon experienced this when Mary came to the temple bearing a precious, six-weeks-old bundle. The baby's humanity and deity wasn't the issue, nor was His transcendent holiness. Moving beyond theology, Simeon simply took the mystery of incarnation into his arms. For those moments, he had his very own Jesus.

We can take Jesus to our heads and acknowledge His historic reality. That is well and good—and quite necessary. We can assign Him the highest place of transcendence in our doctrines and worship. But day by day, do we keep Him at the center of our lives? Simeon, a simple, devout man, took Jesus to heart—and praised God.

Father in Heaven, *grant me each day a continuing sense of Your presence in my life, through the indwelling Christ. In His name I pray. Amen.*

**SPOTLIGHT**
***Next Week's Lesson***

Hold Jesus close to your heart today.

# Marvelous Pronouncement

*The child's father and mother marveled at what was said about him* (Luke 2:33).

A quiet, elderly woman came to our small church. Though she had had no formal Bible training, she eventually became our favorite Sunday school teacher. One day my wife asked where she had gained such heartwarming, intriguing insights. The woman replied, "Elsie, it takes a lifetime to know the Scriptures." She might have added, "It takes a lifetime—and beyond—to know Jesus."

Joseph and Mary marveled at Simeon's song, and little wonder. They were ordinary folks; how could those things be?

Joseph had taken Mary to be his wife at great risk. Who would believe her story? She had endured birth pangs and held the newborn to her breast in a stable. She had not yet digested the angel Gabriel's mysterious words or the song of her cousin Elizabeth. Now would the new parents not marvel at Simeon's prophetic pronouncement?

We, too, will marvel as we grow in the grace and knowledge of our Lord. There is much, much more to Jesus than our quaint renditions of the Christmas story. It will take a lifetime and more to learn it all.

*Thank You, Lord, for the privilege of knowing You. As I open my heart to You daily in prayer, lead me into an ever deeper knowledge of Your presence and purpose in my life. In the name of my precious Savior, I pray. Amen.*

**SEARCH THE WORD**

*Let us dedicate our lives to learning all we can about Jesus.*

Scripture: Luke 2:29-33

Song: *"My Savior First of All"*

*From this meditation today, I will pray . . .*

Adoration ______________________________

______________________________

______________________________

Confession ______________________________

______________________________

______________________________

Thanksgiving ______________________________

______________________________

______________________________

Supplication ______________________________

______________________________

______________________________

*From this meditation today, I will . . .*

Think ______________________________

______________________________

______________________________

Say ______________________________

______________________________

______________________________

Do ______________________________

______________________________

______________________________

______________________________

______________________________

December 29

# Couldn't Lie to Her

*(And a sword will pierce through your own soul also), that thoughts out of many hearts may be revealed*
(Luke 2:35, *Revised Standard Version*).

Scripture: Luke 2:34, 35

Song: *"Grace and Truth Shall Mark the Way"*

***From this meditation today, I will pray . . .***

Adoration ______________________________

______________________________

______________________________

Confession ______________________________

______________________________

______________________________

Thanksgiving ______________________________

______________________________

______________________________

Supplication ______________________________

______________________________

______________________________

***From this meditation today, I will . . .***

Think ______________________________

______________________________

______________________________

Say ______________________________

______________________________

______________________________

Do ______________________________

______________________________

______________________________

______________________________

______________________________

I could not bring myself to lie to Mother. I lied easily to my sister, and I could stretch a point with my father, but I could not lie to Mother. A quiet, small woman, Mother seemed able to read my thoughts. I believed that because I knew her character. I could depend on her, and I couldn't imagine her telling a lie. I fully believed lying to her was useless; she would know the truth.

We were not an overtly religious household, and few Christian artifacts hung on our walls. We attended church faithfully, though, and rarely missed a mealtime prayer. The Bible was prominent, faith in Christ was genuine, and Mother was warm and affirming. She embodied what I imagined Jesus to be.

An early memory finds me snuggling close to Mother's breast in an heirloom rocking chair. As we rocked, "Jesus Loves Me" resonated from her. Mother loved me, she loved Jesus, and so did I, even at age three. Yes, even then I understood that nothing was hidden from Mother, nor from God.

Lord, *we are all the products of what we've been taught by people we trust. Thank You for my own teachers. May I be trustworthy, so that those who follow me will be following You. Through Christ I pray. Amen.*

**SPOTLIGHT**

***Next Week's Lesson***

Even at this early stage in His life, the painful truth about Jesus' future was predicted.

# A Touch from the Old

*She was very old . . . . She never left the temple but worshiped night and day* (Luke 2:36, 37).

August was old and dying. I was his young, green minister. He told me one day he had seen Jesus. It seems the Lord was standing in the meadow just beyond a small stream on his old country farm, beckoning. "I will go home soon," August said.

I smiled at the old man's odd vision and prepared to read a psalm. A thin, pale hand slipped over the page. "Read from your heart, my brother." That I couldn't do, and so he led me, verse by verse, through the beloved passage, his words tinged with the gentle accent of his homeland. Within a few days, August died.

Cherish your godly elders! They are wiser and closer to Heaven than younger people can be. Come to think of it, those who have eternal life can never grow old. They will change dwelling places, but they can never age. I think often of August. I'm glad Jesus came to him when he was very old, so he could touch the heart of a young, green minister.

*Thank You,* Lord, *for elderly friends. Throughout the new year, nudge me to spend more time with them, so they can minister to me in their special way. And help me to never look down on those who are close to seeing You, face to face. I pray this prayer in the name of Jesus my Savior. Amen.*

**SEARCH THE WORD**

*Only those who abide in God's presence become older and wiser.*

Scripture: Luke 2:36-38

Song: *"Beyond the Sunset"*

***From this meditation today, I will pray . . .***

Adoration ______________________

______________________

______________________

Confession ______________________

______________________

______________________

Thanksgiving ______________________

______________________

______________________

Supplication ______________________

______________________

______________________

***From this meditation today, I will . . .***

Think ______________________

______________________

______________________

Say ______________________

______________________

______________________

Do ______________________

______________________

______________________

______________________

______________________

December 31

# Praise from Deep Within

*Praise the* Lord *from the earth, you great sea creatures and all ocean depths* (Psalm 148:7).

Scripture: Psalm 148:7-14

Song: *"All Creatures of Our God and King"*

***From this meditation today, I will pray . . .***

Adoration ______________________

______________________

______________________

Confession ______________________

______________________

______________________

Thanksgiving ______________________

______________________

______________________

Supplication ______________________

______________________

______________________

***From this meditation today, I will . . .***

Think ______________________

______________________

______________________

Say ______________________

______________________

______________________

Do ______________________

______________________

______________________

December 31. ***Brian J. Waldrop*** *is a freelance writer and professional copy editor. Originally from Champaign, Illinois, Brian now resides in Mt. Healthy, Ohio.*

Beneath the ocean's depths exists an amazing world of God's creation that most of us will never see. Yet even nature unseen functions as a testimony to God and offers its praise to the one who sees it, created it, and maintains it. The depths of the earth's oceans, and the creatures contained within, cause us to marvel. So many small creatures, such as jellyfish, sand dollars, starfish, and sea horses. So many grand creatures, such as manatees, dolphins, sharks, and whales. So many shapes and sizes and colors of marine life grace the seas. Even in a fallen world, God's creation is breathtaking.

Like the creatures of the sea, we too praise the one who intricately designed and assembled us, He who maintains us and sustains us. We worship Him who knows us and loves us despite our sin.

The unseen in us? He sees our deepest hurts and cares. And like the rest of creation, we too praise God, especially when we live according to our ultimate purpose on earth: to become more and more like His Son, Jesus.

Sovereign God of all Creation, *I worship You. And as I live each day on earth, may my life reflect Your greatness. In Jesus' name, amen.*

**SPOTLIGHT**

***Next Week's Lesson***

"All things were created by him and for him" (Colossians 1:16).

# January

# INSPIRED BY GOD'S CALL

*His name alone is exalted; his splendor is above the earth and the heavens.*
—Psalm 148:13

*Photo © Photodisc*

January 1

# Celebrate!

*Have the Israelites celebrate the Passover*
(Numbers 9:2).

Scripture: Numbers 9:1-5
Song: *"Celebrate Jesus"*

*From this meditation today, I will pray . . .*

Adoration ______________________________

Confession ______________________________

Thanksgiving ____________________________

Supplication ____________________________

*From this meditation today, I will . . .*

Think ______________________________

Say ______________________________

Do ______________________________

The Israelites were commanded to celebrate the Passover, their deliverance from Egypt. It's crazy, but sometimes—even most of the time—people need to be reminded to celebrate: to appreciate, to be thankful, to remember.

Celebrations are fun but often mean a lot of work. For example, the Passover feast required many preparations. Lambs had to be slaughtered, and other specific rituals precisely followed. Concerning the Passover, verse 3 says to "celebrate it at the appointed time, at twilight on the fourteenth day of this month, in accordance with all its rules and regulations." Most celebrations don't have to be so elaborate, but they still require a concerted effort to make them meaningful.

Surprisingly, celebration comes hard for many Christians. Rather than being party people, we're often seen as sober killjoys. Yet of all people, we have the best reasons to celebrate, for God has come into our world by His Son to bring us new life. And if we are going to celebrate that, then New Year's Day is a great time to start!

Lord, *throughout the coming year, help me remember who You are and what You have done—and respond in celebration. In Jesus' name, amen.*

**SPOTLIGHT**
***Next Week's Lesson***

Celebrating the Passover feast in Jerusalem each year was a big part of Jesus' family life.

January 1-6. ***Brian J. Waldrop*** *is a freelance writer and professional copy editor. Originally from Champaign, Illinois, Brian now resides in Mt. Healthy, Ohio.*

# Passed Over

*When I see the blood, I will pass over you*
(Exodus 12:13).

"Duck, duck, duck, duck, *goose!*" As a child playing Duck Duck Goose, I never liked being the goose. In that situation, I considered being "passed over" a good thing. The Jews celebrated a feast called Passover, commemorating their release from Egyptian bondage. Why that name? The Israelites' release occurred after the final plague, the death of Egypt's firstborn. The firstborn of the Israelites were spared because their families obeyed God and put lamb's blood on the door frames of their homes, a sign for the death angel to "pass over" them.

God's essential character of holiness and justice won't allow Him to merely pass over our sins as if nothing has happened. Christians are indeed forgiven, however, because of the blood of their Passover lamb, Jesus Christ. Thus, like the Israelites escaping the tyranny of Egyptian slavery, we are freed from the eternal consequences of our sins. By His blood, we escape the impossible tyranny of attempting to earn God's acceptance by good works. As the writer to the Hebrews put it: "He entered the Most Holy Place once for all by his own blood, having obtained eternal redemption" (Hebrews 9:12).

God, *I breathe a sigh of relief at being passed over, escaping the judgment for sin. Praise You for sending Jesus, my Passover lamb! May I always live gratefully and obediently, in light of His sacrifice. In His name, amen.*

**SEARCH THE WORD**
*Instead of Passover, Christians have the Lord's Supper to remind us of the saving power of the blood.*

Scripture: Exodus 12:11-14
Song: *"There Is Power in the Blood"*

***From this meditation today, I will pray . . .***

Adoration ______________________

______________________

______________________

Confession ______________________

______________________

______________________

Thanksgiving ______________________

______________________

______________________

Supplication ______________________

______________________

______________________

***From this meditation today, I will . . .***

Think ______________________

______________________

______________________

Say ______________________

______________________

______________________

Do ______________________

______________________

______________________

______________________

______________________

January 3

# Got Some Growing Up to Do?

*The child grew and became strong;*
*he was filled with wisdom, and the grace of God was upon him*
(Luke 2:40).

Scripture: Luke 2:39-45
Song: *"The Guiding Hand"*

***From this meditation today, I will pray . . .***

Adoration ______________________________

______________________________

______________________________

Confession ______________________________

______________________________

______________________________

Thanksgiving ______________________________

______________________________

______________________________

Supplication ______________________________

______________________________

______________________________

***From this meditation today, I will . . .***

Think ______________________________

______________________________

______________________________

Say ______________________________

______________________________

______________________________

Do ______________________________

______________________________

______________________________

______________________________

______________________________

It was a simple, loving act springing from the innocent heart of a little girl. Without saying a word, she walked over to my father and unlocked the seat belt he was having trouble unfastening from a fun-park ride. It was a gesture of the heart, not done for a sticker or a prize.

A child's tender, trusting heart is often more gracious than our own. For example, young children usually aren't as skeptical as we adults are. When words come from a trusted source, such as a parent or a teacher, children believe what they are told. They haven't yet been scarred by the deceptions of the unscrupulous.

We, as adults, need to regain a simple trust in God and His Word. Jesus himself, in His human nature, had to grow in wisdom and maturity—and respond positively to the grace that came from the Father. We may be adults, but I suspect we each have such growing up to do. The key, for us, is to keep our hearts open to all that God desires to do within us and through us. It's the only way to grow strong in the spiritual life.

Dear God, *help me recapture the wonder, purity, and innocence of a child-like trust in Your goodness and guidance. I long to be filled with Your wisdom and motivated by Your Kingdom plans. And by Your grace, let me act graciously toward others, as well. Thank You, in Jesus' name. Amen.*

**SPOTLIGHT**
***Next Week's Lesson***

Like the boy Jesus, let us have a strong desire to know more about our heavenly Father.

# An Amazing God

*Everyone who heard him was amazed*
(Luke 2:47).

Even as a mere boy, Jesus wowed people by what He said and did. These same reactions would follow Jesus throughout His adult life: "The people were amazed at his teaching" (Mark 1:22). "The disciples were amazed at his words" (Mark 10:24). "The men were amazed and asked, 'What kind of man is this?'" (Matthew 8:27).

In a time of cold religion and oppressive rules, Jesus' insights into God's law and character refreshed the weary. Christ's authentic walk with God contrasted with the stagnant lives of many religious leaders of the day. His compassion toward the unpopular and unattractive astonished people who were used to harsh judgment.

Jesus' miracles? Naturally, they produced surprise and elation. And both His crucifixion and resurrection, though unexpected and shocking, resulted in whispers of awe and shouts of freedom.

Today we still stand in awe of the Master. We're astonished at Jesus' ability to transform messed-up lives. We're humbled by His pity and love for us. We're simply amazed by His grace.

Heavenly Father, *I'm amazed not only by Your ability to save me from the penalty of my sins but by Your unconditional willingness to do so. By Your Son You have adopted me into Your family and given me Your indwelling Holy Spirit. I will stand amazed forever! Through Christ, amen.*

**SEARCH THE WORD**

*May our response to Jesus also be awe and amazement.*

Scripture: Luke 2:46-50

Song: *"I Stand Amazed in the Presence"*

*From this meditation today, I will pray . . .*

Adoration ____________________

____________________

____________________

Confession ____________________

____________________

____________________

Thanksgiving ____________________

____________________

____________________

Supplication ____________________

____________________

____________________

*From this meditation today, I will . . .*

Think ____________________

____________________

____________________

Say ____________________

____________________

____________________

Do ____________________

____________________

____________________

____________________

____________________

# Perfect Obedience

*Then he went down to Nazareth with them and was obedient to them*
(Luke 2:51).

Scripture: Luke 2:51, 52
Song: *"Lamb of God"*

***From this meditation today, I will pray . . .***

Adoration ______________________________
______________________________
______________________________

Confession ______________________________
______________________________
______________________________

Thanksgiving ______________________________
______________________________
______________________________

Supplication ______________________________
______________________________
______________________________

***From this meditation today, I will . . .***

Think ______________________________
______________________________
______________________________

Say ______________________________
______________________________
______________________________

Do ______________________________
______________________________
______________________________
______________________________
______________________________

What are those last words of reminder (or warning) so often uttered by parents before departing from their children? "Be good!"

Whether Mary and Joseph ever said these words to Jesus is unknown. One thing we do know: Our text records that Jesus was an obedient child.

Jesus' perfect childhood obedience, however, isn't just a nice little note in the Gospel text. That obedience was crucial to the plan of salvation. Without His having lived a perfect human life, Jesus would not have been qualified to serve as the unblemished lamb of God who would take away the sins of the world (see John 1:29).

Even at this early period in the life of Christ, the perfection that would be exchanged for the penalty of our sins was in full development. When Jesus died, He took our sins and gave us His righteous standing before God. When our heavenly Father sees us, He sees us as perfectly obedient sons and daughters. His obedience has become our obedience. It's the only way we could ever be good enough for Heaven.

Lord, *because You are good I am accounted good, though I know my daily life often shows otherwise. By Your grace may I strive to be in practice what I have already become in position. Through Christ, amen.*

**SPOTLIGHT**
***Next Week's Lesson***

What an exchange—
my sins for Jesus' perfection.
Thank You, Lord!

# Why Limit the Praise?

*Praise him, sun and moon,*
*praise him, all you shining stars*
(Psalm 148:3).

Mankind walking on the moon, rovers roaming the surface of Mars, and now an unmanned spacecraft on its way to Pluto—these are marvelous feats, but they only reach the outer fringes of one solar system in God's vast universe.

Ever wonder why God created galaxies that no one may ever see? Perhaps it's simply because He can. When we stop to consider the seemingly infinite size of the universe, we realize how awesome and mighty its creator must be. In Psalm 8:3, 4, King David says, "When I consider your heavens, the work of your fingers, the moon and the stars, which you have set in place, what is man that you are mindful of him?" A big universe proclaims a big God.

The enormous size of the universe also serves as a reminder of the limitlessness of God's attributes: His unlimited love, unlimited grace, and unlimited forgiveness for those who believe. Such infinite attributes remind us that God deserves . . . our unlimited praise.

Lord God of Creation, *when I see the stars I am reminded of how big You are and how small I am in comparison. I acknowledge that You alone are the King of the Universe, and I invite You to make my soul, more and more, a territory fully conquered by Your loving reign. In the name of the Father, the Son, and the Holy Spirit, I pray. Amen.*

**SEARCH THE WORD**

*Is there anything too hard for the God who created the universe?*

Scripture: Psalm 148:1-6

Song: *"Praise God from Whom All Blessings Flow"*

*From this meditation today, I will pray . . .*

Adoration ______________________

______________________

______________________

Confession ______________________

______________________

______________________

Thanksgiving ______________________

______________________

______________________

Supplication ______________________

______________________

______________________

*From this meditation today, I will . . .*

Think ______________________

______________________

______________________

Say ______________________

______________________

______________________

Do ______________________

______________________

______________________

______________________

______________________

# No Fair?

*Be still before the LORD and wait patiently for him; do not fret when men succeed in their ways, when they carry out their wicked schemes* (Psalm 37:7).

Scripture: Psalm 37:1-11

Song: *"Be Still and Know"*

***From this meditation today, I will pray . . .***

Adoration ______

Confession ______

Thanksgiving ______

Supplication ______

***From this meditation today, I will . . .***

Think ______

Say ______

Do ______

January 7-13. ***Charlotte Mize*** *has three published books and often speaks at retreats and seminars. She loves hiking in the mountains and doing needlework.*

A big-rig truck driver was lying in his hospital bed, worried not about his recovery from a rollover but about how he would pay the hospital bill. His company refused to pay for his treatment. He was being held at fault for the accident caused by a load shift—even though he hadn't loaded the flatbed. More fines to pay and more points on his license. "It's not fair!" he shouted, startling the nurse working at his side. Here was the end of a career.

We all face an unfair life, in which ruthless and unprincipled people may well prosper while honest folk will suffer. Yet God's counsel to us is patience. Just be still and wait.

How hard to do! We want to "get back at them, and make them pay." But God says, "Wait." This approach will pay off—eventually—as a glimpse at the final verse of today's reading clearly reveals: "The meek will inherit the land and enjoy great peace." Let us trust God to right the wrongs, in His way, in His time.

O God, *You are so gracious in the midst of an ungracious world. Thank You that judgment does not rest on our shoulders. In Jesus' name, amen.*

**SPOTLIGHT**

***Next Week's Lesson***

It will always pay off in the end to do things God's way.

# Stop That!

*Do not hate your brother in your heart.*
*Rebuke your neighbor frankly so you will not share in his guilt*
(Leviticus 19:17).

Her 18-year-old stepbrother was headed for her younger brother with hatred in his eyes. Ten-year-old Jana stepped between them. "Don't hit him; he's little." Jason took another step closer, with Jana the first in line for a punch.

Hearing the ruckus, Jason's father rushed into the room. "Stop that!"

Jason halted, then whirled around and left the room. Jana was shaking. "Jana, you should have called me. You can't stop Jason by yourself," her stepfather said as he hugged both of the younger children.

The scene moved me to reflect: While trying to right the wrongs of the world, don't we often neglect to call upon the one who can save both us and our brothers from abuse? We may be called to rebuke the raging hater, but we must allow only our Father to chasten him. What a fine line between protecting the weak and usurping God's role! Thankfully, we can learn to let go of grudges and allow Him to fulfill—in His way and time—His promise: "It is mine to avenge; I will repay" (Romans 12:19).

Dear Father, *how like a child I act, rushing into Your role! Help me distinguish between standing up for the right and overstepping Your authority. For You alone are the only perfect judge. In Christ's name, amen.*

**SEARCH THE WORD**

*Even when it goes against the grain, give your grudges to God.*

Scripture: Leviticus 19:17, 18
Song: *"Be Still, My Soul"*

*From this meditation today, I will pray . . .*

Adoration ____________________

Confession ____________________

Thanksgiving ____________________

Supplication ____________________

*From this meditation today, I will . . .*

Think ____________________

Say ____________________

Do ____________________

# Good for Evil?

*I tell you who hear me: Love your enemies, do good to those who hate you* (Luke 6:27).

Scripture: Luke 6:27, 28
Song: *"I Love You with the Love of the Lord"*

***From this meditation today, I will pray . . .***

Adoration ______________________

______________________

______________________

Confession ______________________

______________________

______________________

Thanksgiving ______________________

______________________

______________________

Supplication ______________________

______________________

______________________

***From this meditation today, I will . . .***

Think ______________________

______________________

______________________

Say ______________________

______________________

______________________

Do ______________________

______________________

______________________

______________________

______________________

Cindy questioned every decision I made. She clothed it as "constructive criticism," but it felt like insubordination. It was hard for me to lead a group of 12 support staff in our office, providing motivation, training, and encouragement to them. Cindy's constant carping undermined my confidence and leadership. I often heard secondhand complaints about her grumbling.

It was time for salary reviews. Our support staff was woefully underpaid, so I went to the CEO on their behalf. He asked whether I thought all of my staff people were working up to their potential. Here was my chance to let him know of Cindy's uncooperative spirit! Somehow, though, God stilled my voice, and I was able to recommend raises for all of them. Cindy never knew that her raise came because I went to bat for her.

It's hard to bless those who curse us. It's even more difficult to pray for them. I do pray for Cindy, since her work habits will no doubt land her in trouble some day. I also pray for myself, that I can love her in spite of my own hurt. After all, Jesus loves and blesses me, even when I fail Him.

Father, *it is because of Your Son's intercession for me that I am right with You. Help me learn to love as You love. Through Christ my Lord, amen.*

**SPOTLIGHT**
***Next Week's Lesson***

Love our enemies?
Only with God's help can we do what seems impossible.

# Above and Beyond

*If someone strikes you on one cheek, turn to him the other also. If someone takes your cloak, do not stop him from taking your tunic* (Luke 6:29).

Have you ever been honored for going "above and beyond"? One company I worked for gave unexpected monetary awards to employees who performed well beyond their job descriptions. Of course, those extra tasks were usually done voluntarily and willingly. Still, it was nice to be recognized. And it was exciting to have senior management troop into one's office, smiling—and bearing an envelope with cash inside.

Jesus deals with a different situation: the times when we're coerced and mistreated. Even under duress we are to go above and beyond what is required of us. Under these circumstances, we will not be rewarded or even recognized—at least not by our tormentors! In fact, we may be ridiculed for being easy prey.

However, we are to yield willingly, offering more than is required. The reward comes not from those around us but from Jesus himself. He understands the stress we endure, and He recognizes our sacrifice. He too was coerced but willingly acquiesced for our benefit.

Father, *life often requires more of me than I expect. Help me to look beyond my own "rights." May I willingly lay down my possessions to be generous, in Your name, even to those who exploit me. Through Jesus, amen.*

**SEARCH THE WORD**

*Demanding our "rights" will never make us right with God.*

Scripture: Luke 6:29, 30

Song: *"Is Your All on the Altar?"*

*From this meditation today, I will pray . . .*

Adoration ______________________

______________________

______________________

Confession ______________________

______________________

______________________

Thanksgiving ______________________

______________________

______________________

Supplication ______________________

______________________

______________________

*From this meditation today, I will . . .*

Think ______________________

______________________

______________________

Say ______________________

______________________

______________________

Do ______________________

______________________

______________________

______________________

______________________

# Treat Them Right

*Do to others as you would have them do to you*
(Luke 6:31).

Scripture: Luke 6:31
Song: *"Love One Another"*

***From this meditation today, I will pray . . .***

Adoration ______________________________

______________________________

______________________________

Confession ______________________________

______________________________

______________________________

Thanksgiving ______________________________

______________________________

______________________________

Supplication ______________________________

______________________________

______________________________

***From this meditation today, I will . . .***

Think ______________________________

______________________________

______________________________

Say ______________________________

______________________________

______________________________

Do ______________________________

______________________________

______________________________

______________________________

______________________________

Yesterday my husband came home irritated at the day's events. My child was angry with an apparently unfair world, and my mother complained about her arthritis acting up again.

*Why don't they just get over it?* I thought. Everybody has troubles, but I wish they wouldn't take it out on me.

Today I'm the one irritated, angry, and complaining. Without a word, my husband gives me a hug. My daughter offers to clean up the kitchen. My mother smiles and pats my cheek. All this kindness bothers me a bit. Why? Because they are treating me the way they wanted me to treat them the day before.

Often I would like to rewind the tape of life a couple of days. I would offer my husband a glass of iced tea and a quiet moment in his recliner. I would allow my child to vent her understandable frustrations in a safe environment. I would offer my mother a cup of hot cocoa and a gentle back rub.

But life doesn't rewind! I need to respond to opportunities as they arise—the privilege of simply treating others as I would like to be treated.

God, *forgive my impatience with family members. Help me feel their pain and respond in the same way I want them to respond to me. In this small way, let me be a servant in Your name. Through Christ I pray. Amen.*

**SPOTLIGHT**
***Next Week's Lesson***

The truth of Jesus' Golden Rule still gleams brightly today.

# Generosity

*Love your enemies, do good to them, and lend to them without expecting to get anything back. Then your reward will be great, and you will be sons of the Most High, because he is kind to the ungrateful and wicked* (Luke 6:35).

We tend to think of generosity in connection with our friends or family. As usual, Jesus turns our thinking upside down: He expects us to be generous to our enemies.

First, then, we must identify whom we consider to be an enemy. Is it a coworker, a neighbor, a government agent, a foreigner, a wealthy oppressor? Then we must ask, "How can I be generous to this person?"

One way is simply to be liberal with forgiveness. What greater or more costly gift can we offer someone than our complete forgiveness, whether or not they request it? Another way is to supply what is lacking. If my adversary needs anything I can offer, Jesus tells me to provide it without expecting repayment. And how about imparting an unexpected kindness—a helping hand, a meal, a smile, or an encouraging word?

The supreme gift, though, is love. Can I sincerely love my enemy as I love my family or myself? If I can do that, I am truly reflecting the character of God. As His child, I have "inherited" His traits of kindness and mercy.

Dear Giver of Everything, *I want to emulate Your unconditional love. Help me see every enemy as a potential friend. In Jesus' name, amen.*

**SEARCH THE WORD**

*Take your enemy by surprise—use a sneak attack of kindness.*

Scripture: Luke 6:34-36

Song: *"Let the Beauty of Jesus Be Seen in Me"*

*From this meditation today, I will pray . . .*

Adoration ______________________________

______________________________

______________________________

Confession ______________________________

______________________________

______________________________

Thanksgiving ______________________________

______________________________

______________________________

Supplication ______________________________

______________________________

______________________________

*From this meditation today, I will . . .*

Think ______________________________

______________________________

______________________________

Say ______________________________

______________________________

______________________________

Do ______________________________

______________________________

______________________________

______________________________

______________________________

# Ultimate Safety Net

*The salvation of the righteous comes from the LORD;*
*he is their stronghold in time of trouble*
(Psalm 37:39).

Scripture: Psalm 37:35-40
**Song:** *"You Are My Hiding Place"*

*From this meditation today, I will pray . . .*

Adoration ______________________________

______________________________

______________________________

Confession ______________________________

______________________________

______________________________

Thanksgiving ______________________________

______________________________

______________________________

Supplication ______________________________

______________________________

______________________________

*From this meditation today, I will . . .*

Think ______________________________

______________________________

______________________________

Say ______________________________

______________________________

______________________________

Do ______________________________

______________________________

______________________________

______________________________

______________________________

In 1989 a powerful earthquake shook San Francisco. Highways collapsed in tiers, sandwiching vehicles and drivers between layers of concrete. Buildings erupted in flames, sending firework-like embers skyward. Humanity poured out of downtown buildings, fleeing destruction.

It wasn't a good time for us to be visiting the city! Engulfed in a throng of commuters trying to get home, we didn't know the area well enough to navigate the interruptions in public transportation so we could return to our hotel many miles away. We were vulnerable to physical danger and to opportunists who might see a chance to exploit some naive out-of-towners.

After several hours of wandering the streets, we came upon a hotel employee who offered us a place to spend the night in the reinforced basement of his brand new hotel. We were safe once again.

Earthquake-like trials of life can assault us to the point that we become extremely vulnerable. The ruthless seem to flourish during these times, but we flounder. Yet God promises us a refuge during both physical and emotional upheavals. He alone is our place of ultimate safety.

Dear Father, *thank You for being my refuge in the time of trial. Help me let go of my self-sufficiency and turn only to You. In Jesus' name, amen.*

**SPOTLIGHT**
***Next Week's Lesson***

Afraid and in danger?
Prayer is the key that unlocks
the door into God's shelter.

# Shields Up!

*The Lord is my strength and my shield;*
*my heart trusts in him, and I am helped*
(Psalm 28:7).

A starship glides gracefully through the eternal night of outer space. It passes through fields of stars, smearing streaks of light against the velvety blackness. All is serene. Without warning, an unseen enemy dives to the attack, pummeling the spacecraft with powerful lasers that could rip the ship in half. The seasoned crew reacts instantly, raising an invisible force field as thunderous explosions rock the craft.

It might be a scene from any science fiction movie. In reality, Christians are much like that starship crew sailing through the black night. Our unseen enemy lurks, watching for a vulnerable moment, seeking to exploit our weaknesses. He targets our lives, minds, and emotions. Yet an invisible force field surrounds believers with an impenetrable protection that also fortifies from within. Nothing can pass through the shield except that which our Father allows. He is stronger than every enemy and will see us through our dark night.

O Lord, *You are El Shaddai, Almighty God, and there is no other like You. My heart sings for joy, knowing that no plan of Yours can be thwarted. Thank You for shielding me on every side. In Jesus' name, amen.*

**SEARCH THE WORD**

*"The Lord is the stronghold of my life—of whom shall I be afraid?"* (Psalm 27:1).

Scripture: Psalm 28:6-9

Song: *"How Firm a Foundation"*

*From this meditation today, I will pray . . .*

Adoration ______________________________

______________________________

______________________________

Confession ______________________________

______________________________

______________________________

Thanksgiving ______________________________

______________________________

______________________________

Supplication ______________________________

______________________________

______________________________

*From this meditation today, I will . . .*

Think ______________________________

______________________________

______________________________

Say ______________________________

______________________________

______________________________

Do ______________________________

______________________________

______________________________

January 14–20. ***Rhonda Brunea,*** *of Cherry Creek, New York, is a single mother of four. She loves reading and collecting amusing and fairly useless pets, like sheep.*

# Prodigal to Pray-er

*One day Jesus was praying in a certain place. When he finished, one of his disciples said to him, "Lord, teach us to pray, just as John taught his disciples"* (Luke 11:1).

Scripture: Luke 11:1-4
Song: *"He Knows"*

*From this meditation today, I will pray . . .*

Adoration ______________________________

______________________________

______________________________

Confession ______________________________

______________________________

______________________________

Thanksgiving ______________________________

______________________________

______________________________

Supplication ______________________________

______________________________

______________________________

*From this meditation today, I will . . .*

Think ______________________________

______________________________

______________________________

Say ______________________________

______________________________

______________________________

Do ______________________________

______________________________

______________________________

______________________________

______________________________

"Lying, stealing, gambling, novel-reading, licentiousness, extravagance, and almost every form of sin was indulged in by him," wrote biographer J. Gilchrist Lawson. "No one would have imagined that the sinful youth would ever become eminent for his faith in God and for his power in prayer."

Who was this miserable sinner? None other than the great nineteenth-century "prayer warrior" George Mueller—and that was before he went to jail for cheating an innkeeper out of a week's rent! In his own words, Mueller says of his youthful days: "I cared nothing for the Word of God."

Eventually, though, Mueller became known for never mentioning his needs to others; he laid everything before God with constant, patient intercession. And he kept precise records of his requests, to prove to the world that there is a God who hears His people.

Jesus had taught Mueller to pray. He will do the same for us, if we come to Him with an open heart, no matter the current state of our lives.

Lord, *teach me to pray with a humble and contrite spirit, that those around me will see Your faithfulness when You answer. In Jesus' name, amen.*

**SPOTLIGHT**
***Next Week's Lesson***

Who better to teach us how to talk to God than His own Son?

# Be Bold

*I tell you, though he will not get up and give him the bread because he is his friend, yet because of the man's boldness he will get up and give him as much as he needs* (Luke 11:8).

Two girls wanted to go to the local mall one Saturday. "Let's ask my father," said one.

"Oh, no! He'll be angry," the second girl replied. The first girl was puzzled. "Why would he be angry with us, just for asking?"

"Well . . . what if he says no?" The second girl's voice quavered a little. Her friend shrugged her shoulders. "Then he says no. He does sometimes. So what? He'll say yes if he can."

We sometimes fear to ask our heavenly Father for the desires of our hearts, as if we're suspicious of His reaction. Will He strike us down if we ask with wrong motives? Will He be angry if we request something we don't really need? Will He answer no? (We don't always ask wisely, and sometimes the answer ought to be no.) But God invites us to ask boldly. He knows our motives are less than pure. Still He loves us. And can't we trust this wonderful Father to sort our imperfect prayers and do whatever is best?

My Abba, *even the finest earthly father can't approach Your wisdom, patience, kindness, and love. Help me to keep my needs and desires before You, that our relationship might grow ever deeper. Through Christ, amen.*

**SEARCH THE WORD**
*Don't allow the failures of an earthly father to distort the reality of the Father's tender love.*

Scripture: Luke 11:5-8

Song: *"Abba Father"*

*From this meditation today, I will pray . . .*

Adoration ______________________

______________________

______________________

Confession ______________________

______________________

______________________

Thanksgiving ______________________

______________________

______________________

Supplication ______________________

______________________

______________________

*From this meditation today, I will . . .*

Think ______________________

______________________

______________________

Say ______________________

______________________

______________________

Do ______________________

______________________

______________________

______________________

______________________

# Too Easy?

*Everyone who asks receives; he who seeks finds; and to him who knocks, the door will be opened* (Luke 11:10).

Scripture: Luke 11:9-12

Song: *"Jesus Will Let You In"*

*From this meditation today, I will pray . . .*

Adoration __________

Confession __________

Thanksgiving __________

Supplication __________

*From this meditation today, I will . . .*

Think __________

Say __________

Do __________

A woman stood in the darkness before the large, well-lit house. Snow encrusted the toes of her costly leather boots. She had been making her unsteady way home when someone told her about a great party at this house.

She was told, though, that she had to change her clothes to join this gathering. "I paid a lot of money for my outfit," she mumbled, watching a straggly teenaged girl knock and then boldly step over the threshold into the bright interior. She folded her arms around herself, indignant, and kicked the snow from her boots.

Laughter and music flooded into the street each time the door swung wide to admit another. She watched a white-robed woman gently assist a grimy man still reeling with drink. "They'll let *anybody* in there!" It was dark, and growing colder. The hour was late. She should go home and forget about these freaks. Still, those leaving the house looked so peaceful. It seemed too easy—knock, walk in, join the party. The woman frowned, and the worry lines marring her brow deepened.

Gracious Lord, *may I never cease to wonder at Your wholehearted invitation to me—filthy rags and all. Thank You for clothing me in your righteousness through Your matchless grace. Please keep me alert to assist those still standing in the darkness. Through Christ I pray. Amen.*

**SPOTLIGHT**

***Next Week's Lesson***

What door do you need to be knocking on?

# Someone's Daughter

*I tell you the truth, anyone who will not receive the kingdom of God like a little child will never enter it* (Luke 18:17).

Her world is crashing around her, but Rachel hardly notices. She is three years old, and she's known only deep love and protection. Blissfully unaware of the trauma rocking her mother, Rachel spins and twirls in a joyful dance choreographed by her trusting heart. The weary mother watches her daughter. "Like a child," she thinks.

Rachel has no worries. All will be well because Mommy is here. Mommy guards her from monsters in the night, comforts her when she's sad, and gives her everything she needs. Mommy is always there, and somehow she always knows just what to do.

If only that were true! The young woman's shoulders sag with the weight of it all. Bewildering fears and dire possibilities clutch her mind and drag her down into a swamp of confusion. "I can't do this," she thinks. Rachel twirls up to her mother, plants a warm kiss on her cheek, and then leaps away again, laughing. For a moment, the ache eases, and the young woman remembers that she, too, is Someone's daughter.

Father, *help me remember that I am Your child. You love me with an everlasting love. You are always here, and always know what to do. I will dance with joy for such a Father. I will curl into Your strong arms and trust. I love You, my good Papa. In the name of Your Son, my Savior, I pray. Amen.*

**SEARCH THE WORD**

*We can give all our cares to Him because we know He cares for us.*

Scripture: Luke 18:1-17

Song: *"Be Still, My Soul"*

*From this meditation today, I will pray . . .*

Adoration ______________________

______________________

______________________

Confession ______________________

______________________

______________________

Thanksgiving ______________________

______________________

______________________

Supplication ______________________

______________________

______________________

*From this meditation today, I will . . .*

Think ______________________

______________________

______________________

Say ______________________

______________________

______________________

Do ______________________

______________________

______________________

______________________

______________________

# What a Great Day!

*When the day of Pentecost came, they were all together in one place* (Acts 2:1).

Scripture: Luke 11:13; Acts 2:1-4
**Song:** *"I've Got a River of Life"*

*From this meditation today, I will pray . . .*

Adoration ______________________________

______________________________

______________________________

Confession ______________________________

______________________________

______________________________

Thanksgiving ______________________________

______________________________

______________________________

Supplication ______________________________

______________________________

______________________________

*From this meditation today, I will . . .*

Think ______________________________

______________________________

______________________________

Say ______________________________

______________________________

______________________________

Do ______________________________

______________________________

______________________________

______________________________

______________________________

Behind a wall of shimmering heat, the lioness patiently stalks her prey—a large herd of antelope. There is strength in the unity of the herd, so she cannot attack them all at once. She might be trampled to death if she tried. She lurks until a single antelope strays from the safety of the herd. Only then does the lioness purr in anticipation of her feast. She crouches, gathering her strength for the chase, and launches her brutal attack.

The enemy of our souls also knows the power of unity. He seeks to divide in order to destroy us, one by one. Though each of us walks through life seemingly alone, no believer is ever truly alone. Our spirits gather at the Lord's table, and as we kneel before His glorious throne. Believers across the entire earth sing His praise as if from one throat.

Every follower of Jesus is part of a mighty fellowship that will never be broken. As our hearts gather in worship, His Spirit flows through us, and each of us is strengthened. All because of Pentecost, a great day indeed!

Dear Lord, *thank You for sending Your Spirit to strengthen and encourage us until we all go home. Help the family of believers always be all together in one place spiritually, so that You may work Your perfect plan through us. In the holy name of Jesus, my Lord and Savior, I pray. Amen.*

**SPOTLIGHT**
***Next Week's Lesson***

Comforter, Counselor, Companion—the Father's best gift to us is His indwelling Holy Spirit.

# Authentic Life

*Blessed are they who maintain justice, who constantly do what is right* (Psalm 106:3).

Once there lived an influential man. At first glance, no one would think him a person of importance. He possessed only modest means, dressing neatly but with no great style. He lived quietly in a humble home with a sweet-tempered wife, and he never did anything extraordinary. Yet when the man passed away, people came by the hundreds to pay their respects to his widow.

"Your husband was a good man," someone said. "I was in trouble once, and he was the only one to help me."

"I respected your husband more than anyone I've ever met," said another. "I don't remember ever hearing him speak an unkind word about anyone."

Another commented with a puzzled look, "He always seemed so peaceful, even when I knew he had troubles of his own." And one woman approached the widow with tears pooling in her eyes. "I always wanted to ask . . . what made your husband so different?"

To all these the widow smiled and replied, "My husband had a wise and faithful Friend. Come to our home this Sunday. I'll introduce you." And she did.

**Dear Lord,** *I ask that Your sweet fragrance saturate my life and draw seekers closer to You. Help me love You above all and live authentically for the sake of those who are watching. Thank You, in Jesus' name. Amen.*

**SEARCH THE WORD**

*The best inheritance to leave our children is the example of a life well lived.*

Scripture: Psalm 106:1-3

Song: *"Let Your Love Flow Through Me"*

*From this meditation today, I will pray . . .*

Adoration ______________________

______________________

______________________

Confession ______________________

______________________

______________________

Thanksgiving ______________________

______________________

______________________

Supplication ______________________

______________________

______________________

*From this meditation today, I will . . .*

Think ______________________

______________________

______________________

Say ______________________

______________________

______________________

Do ______________________

______________________

______________________

______________________

______________________

January 21

# Supposed Friends

*Free me from the trap that is set for me, for you are my refuge. Into your hands I commit my spirit; redeem me, O LORD, the God of truth* (Psalm 31:4, 5).

Scripture: Psalm 31:1-5

Song: *"A Shield About Me"*

***From this meditation today, I will pray . . .***

Adoration ________________________________________

Confession ________________________________________

Thanksgiving ________________________________________

Supplication ________________________________________

***From this meditation today, I will . . .***

Think ________________________________________

Say ________________________________________

Do ________________________________________

January 21–27. ***Daniel F. Varnell*** *is a part-time scientist and a church worker. He loves spending time with his wife and daughters, playing golf, and cooking chili.*

It seems strange now, but many years ago I found myself under surveillance as a scientist in a large company. The secret observation wasn't for something I had done but because of someone who worked in the laboratory with me. The young man had a family, a job, and was going to school at night to do even better. I often wondered how he had enough energy to do everything. One day the police came and took him away.

A comment he made a few days earlier struck me: "I shouldn't have trusted my supposed friends; they just used me." I later discovered that his friends were making and selling illegal drugs.

Psalm 31 is a study in contrasts. There is evil around us in the world and in people's hearts; we can get trapped. In contrast, there is the Lord, God of truth and love. Jesus entered this world of lies and deceit, but in dying He preached the message of a father He could trust—"Father, into your hands I commit my spirit" (Luke 23:46).

**Lord,** *I am so thankful that in You there is no deception. I commit my whole life into Your hands. All praise to You, in Christ's name. Amen.*

**SPOTLIGHT**

***Next Week's Lesson***

God never sets traps for His children; instead, He helps set us free.

# Of Great Worth

*Consider the ravens: They do not sow or reap, they have no storeroom or barn; yet God feeds them. And how much more valuable you are than birds!* (Luke 12:24).

My children love our young cat. They feed, hug, and spoil him constantly. So when he was about to die this past year, we had a very sad household. My wife and I spent a fairly large amount of money to save him. He was worth it—because he was loved.

Jesus told His disciples not to worry. Yet I still find that at times my mind is weighed down. Worries sneak in on me from all kinds of insecurities—like when I'm approaching my yearly performance appraisal at work.

Jesus started His teaching on worry with the key to breaking free. The key is our worth, our value, in God's eyes. Each and every one of us is a great and precious joy to God. If I provided an operation for a family cat, how much more will my heavenly Father take care of me?

And, of course, worry is mostly just a pure waste of emotional energy. As one anonymous quipster once put it: "Don't tell me that worry doesn't do any good. I know better; the things I worry about *never* happen."

Heavenly Father, *I accept the truth of Your Word that You love and care for me deeply. Let my burdens fall from my shoulders this day. Let my anxious thoughts be replaced by thoughts of Your care. Thank You, Lord, for Your great and awesome love. I pray through my deliverer, Jesus. Amen.*

**SEARCH THE WORD**

*Why does God love me so much? Not because of who I am, but who He is.*

Scripture: Luke 12:22-24

Song: *"O the Deep, Deep Love of Jesus"*

***From this meditation today, I will pray . . .***

Adoration ______________________

______________________

______________________

Confession ______________________

______________________

______________________

Thanksgiving ______________________

______________________

______________________

Supplication ______________________

______________________

______________________

***From this meditation today, I will . . .***

Think ______________________

______________________

______________________

Say ______________________

______________________

______________________

Do ______________________

______________________

______________________

______________________

______________________

# Always a Majority

*Who of you by worrying can add a single hour to his life? Since you cannot do this very little thing, why do you worry about the rest?* (Luke 12:25, 26).

Scripture: Luke 12:25, 26

**Song:** *"Breathe"*

***From this meditation today, I will pray . . .***

Adoration ______________________________

______________________________

______________________________

Confession ______________________________

______________________________

______________________________

Thanksgiving ______________________________

______________________________

______________________________

Supplication ______________________________

______________________________

______________________________

***From this meditation today, I will . . .***

Think ______________________________

______________________________

______________________________

Say ______________________________

______________________________

______________________________

Do ______________________________

______________________________

______________________________

______________________________

______________________________

I read the other day that the word *worry* comes from an old Anglo-Saxon word meaning "to strangle or choke." In my teens I woke one night unable to breathe because my sinuses and lungs were congested. After several minutes of gasping for air, I came through those scary moments, with the help of my parents. However, a deep worry filled my mind for years.

And, recently, after pushing myself and taking on too many commitments, I started having panic attacks. My throat would tighten up, and I worried about breathing. Apparently the old fear was still there.

Jesus taught that worry can't add anything to our lives, not even an hour. Yet, for God to add an hour is a simple thing. And for God to help us move through any tough circumstance—could that ever be too hard for Him?

As I have meditated upon the truths in these Scriptures about worry, I have felt my worries disappear. As the old saying goes: "Me plus God always equals a majority."

Dear Heavenly Father, *I praise You for Your awesome power. Since nothing is too hard for You, let me not be anxious but at peace, knowing that my life is in Your infinitely capable hands. I pray this prayer in the name of Jesus, my merciful Savior and Lord. Amen.*

**SPOTLIGHT**
***Next Week's Lesson***

Why worry
when you can pray?

# Growing Beautiful

*Consider the lilies, how they grow: they neither toil nor spin; and yet I say to you, even Solomon in all his glory was not arrayed like one of these* (Luke 12:27, *New King James Version*).

Every year I plant flower seeds, and they turn into beautiful, blossoming plants. It amazes me—all of that beauty lies within every tiny seed. The seeds had no say about how they'd be planted, nor the soil they would inhabit, nor how well (or not!) I might care for them. Nor did the seeds produce their own beauty from scratch. God had already placed that potential within them.

What of us? Jesus said we must fall to the ground and die spiritually (John 12:24), be born again of the Spirit (John 3:3), and grow into the image of Jesus Christ (Ephesians 4:15). These things don't arise from our natural humanity or come about by self-effort; they are all of God, all of His grace.

It's true that we are made in the image of God, thus we have intelligence, personality, and will inherent within us. But the ability to save ourselves by "toiling" always escapes us. Like the lilies, if we are to grow beautiful in God's sight, it must be His work alone.

Father, *You are at work conforming me to the beautiful likeness of Your Son, Jesus. Day by day, let me rely upon Your grace, being confident of this very thing, that He who has begun a good work in me will complete it until the day of Jesus Christ. In His name, amen.*

**SEARCH THE WORD**

*The most beautiful flower will fade away; God's beauty in us lasts forever.*

Scripture: Luke 12:27, 28

Song: *"How Beautiful"*

*From this meditation today, I will pray . . .*

Adoration ______________________

______________________

______________________

Confession ______________________

______________________

______________________

Thanksgiving ______________________

______________________

______________________

Supplication ______________________

______________________

______________________

*From this meditation today, I will . . .*

Think ______________________

______________________

______________________

Say ______________________

______________________

______________________

Do ______________________

______________________

______________________

______________________

______________________

# God Gave Favor

*Seek the kingdom of God, and all these things shall be added to you* (Luke 12:31, *New King James Version*).

**Scripture: Luke 12:29-31**
**Song: *"God Is Good"***

***From this meditation today, I will pray . . .***

Adoration ______________________________

______________________________

______________________________

Confession ______________________________

______________________________

______________________________

Thanksgiving ______________________________

______________________________

______________________________

Supplication ______________________________

______________________________

______________________________

***From this meditation today, I will . . .***

Think ______________________________

______________________________

______________________________

Say ______________________________

______________________________

______________________________

Do ______________________________

______________________________

______________________________

______________________________

______________________________

There just wasn't enough time each week in my schedule to do all I wanted for God, so I decided to try to work three days as a scientist instead of five. I fasted and prayed. My wife agreed. Then doors opened, I found favor where there usually was none, and my request was approved. My pay and pension were cut accordingly.

The following year, the company I worked for announced that there would be no raises. God then extended more grace. You see, even though I was only working part time in a competitive field, I was given a promotion. It included a raise. Even better, with the promotion to a higher position I was considered *underpaid*—and was therefore exempt from the ban on raises! I received a second raise. As far as I can tell, God wonderfully made up a large part of what I gave up for Him. And I was able to keep blessing others in His name.

During those days, I learned a lot about seeking God's kingdom and His will for my life. As the writer of Hebrews wrote, "He is a rewarder of those who diligently seek Him" (11:6).

O, Wondrous God, *thank You for blessing Your servant. You have given me great joy in serving You. Help me remember Your goodness as I reach out to others in Your name. Through Christ, I pray. Amen.*

**SPOTLIGHT**
***Next Week's Lesson***

Make God number one, and you'll never come out second best.

# God Said a Thousand

*Do not be afraid, little flock, for your Father has been pleased to give you the kingdom* (Luke 12:32).

Not long after I truly trusted my life to Jesus, a visiting missions organizer came to our church. He began speaking in general about missions and then, surprisingly, talked at great length about the needs in one of the former states of the Soviet Union. Two members of the church volunteered to go and preach the gospel there. The only thing that remained was the money to send them. God impressed on my heart to give a thousand dollars towards the trip.

Never had I conceived of giving such a large amount to anything! I was reluctant to tell my dear wife. On the way home, though, I tentatively suggested we give substantially to the trip—"maybe several hundred dollars."

Oh, how foolish I was! My wife replied, "I felt God would have us give a thousand dollars."

I learned a lesson, and I'm still learning. We shouldn't be afraid of giving what God asks for, or of talking about it with our spouses. After all, God has already given us the kingdom.

Heavenly Father, *how great is Your wisdom and how generous You are toward me. I know I am not very wise about using the resources You have provided, but I pray that in the days ahead You will lead me to treasure Your kingdom deeply and give more generously. In Jesus' name, amen.*

**SEARCH THE WORD**

*It is never foolish to be generous toward God.*

Scripture: Luke 12:32-34

**Song:** *"He's Got the Whole World in His Hands"*

*From this meditation today, I will pray . . .*

Adoration ______________________

______________________

______________________

Confession ______________________

______________________

______________________

Thanksgiving ______________________

______________________

______________________

Supplication ______________________

______________________

______________________

*From this meditation today, I will . . .*

Think ______________________

______________________

______________________

Say ______________________

______________________

______________________

Do ______________________

______________________

______________________

______________________

______________________

# Which Airline?

*Do not put your trust in princes, in mortal men, who cannot save. When their spirit departs, they return to the ground; on that very day their plans come to nothing* (Psalm 146:3, 4).

Scripture: Psalm 146:1-7

Song: *"People Get Ready"*

***From this meditation today, I will pray . . .***

Adoration ____________________________

____________________________________

____________________________________

Confession ___________________________

____________________________________

____________________________________

Thanksgiving _________________________

____________________________________

____________________________________

Supplication _________________________

____________________________________

____________________________________

***From this meditation today, I will . . .***

Think _______________________________

____________________________________

____________________________________

Say _________________________________

____________________________________

____________________________________

Do __________________________________

____________________________________

____________________________________

____________________________________

____________________________________

At the airport, Billy was surprised to have a choice of airlines. The first airline had a sleek plane, offered champagne, hundreds of movies, and good-looking attendants. Royalty, too, was traveling on the flight.

The other airline offered just basic amenities with a smile. They did say the owner and maker of the plane would be with them. And Billy noted their guarantee to get him to his destination safely and on time. Surely, Billy thought, the other plane would do the same. "Hurry up. This is the fun flight," said the man at the fancy airline. Billy quickly got on board.

The rich food left him sick. The movies became annoying. His seat was unreasonably small. Then Billy felt strange. They were losing altitude. He saw the pilot shoot past as his parachute opened. His heart sank. In the distance he saw the other plane. Everyone was smiling. A confident man sat in their midst.

Yes, a fictional scenario. But I am glad my destination is eternal and wonderful. Jacob's God, the God of truth, is also my God. May each person choose wisely his path!

Heavenly Father, *today, let my focus be on You and not the things and troubles of this world. I pray this prayer in Jesus' name. Amen.*

**SPOTLIGHT**

***Next Week's Lesson***

No "perks" the world offers can compare to the rewards of serving Jesus.

# Family Faith

*We will not hide them from their children;*
*we will tell the next generation the praiseworthy deeds of the Lord*
(Psalm 78:4).

I knew that my mother's family had been Christians for several generations. When I began to explore the history of her family, though, I discovered the true extent.

In 1662, John Argor, one of my mother's ancestors and a Cambridge educated vicar, refused to sign the Uniformity Act. The Act required all ministers to approve the Book of Common Prayer and to acknowledge the unlawfulness of taking up arms against the king.

Argor lost his pulpit, and friends asked him how he thought he would provide for his large family. To this he answered, "God is my housekeeper, and I believe He will provide for us."

Mom never told me this story, but she lived a faithful life herself. When she developed cancer, her life and writings were an inspiration to many. After her death, one of her articles was published. She wrote that she thanked God for allowing her to have cancer because of the lessons she had learned from the experience.

Father, *thank You for our children and grandchildren. Help us to share Jesus and our faith stories with the next generation. In Jesus' name, amen.*

**SEARCH THE WORD**

*Pass the torch of God's truth to the next generation.*

Scripture: Psalm 78:1-4
Song: *"God of Our Fathers"*

***From this meditation today, I will pray . . .***

Adoration ______________________________

______________________________

______________________________

Confession ______________________________

______________________________

______________________________

Thanksgiving ______________________________

______________________________

______________________________

Supplication ______________________________

______________________________

______________________________

***From this meditation today, I will . . .***

Think ______________________________

______________________________

______________________________

Say ______________________________

______________________________

______________________________

Do ______________________________

______________________________

______________________________

January 28–31. ***Rosalie Yoakam*** *is a freelance writer and a columnist for the* Dayton Daily News. *She and her husband, Bill, live in Springboro, Ohio.*

January 29

# On a Quest

*He said to them, "Take nothing for your journey, neither a staff, nor a bag, nor bread, nor money; and do not even have two tunics apiece"* (Luke 9:3, *New American Standard Bible*).

Scripture: Luke 9:1-10

Song: *"Leaving All to Follow Jesus"*

***From this meditation today, I will pray . . .***

Adoration ____________________

Confession ____________________

Thanksgiving ____________________

Supplication ____________________

***From this meditation today, I will . . .***

Think ____________________

Say ____________________

Do ____________________

My husband, Bill, was nearing graduation from college. I was the current breadwinner, teaching elementary school. As I came in from school, Bill met me. "We're going to Findlay," he said. "They just posted a job opening for assistant city engineer."

We jumped into our old car and drove the 50 miles. Two blocks from the city engineer's office our car stalled and refused to restart. A mechanic from a nearby garage jump-started the engine, but it cost $5, all the money we had between us.

The vehicle quit again. A kind stranger pushed our disabled auto for several blocks, and then into a service station. The verdict was a bad fuel pump.

We walked five blocks to the local minister's house. His wife fed us, and then they took us back to the station, where they paid for the repairs (money we repaid later).

Bill left a note on the closed engineer's office door. But a few weeks later Bill was appointed Assistant City Engineer of Findlay, Ohio.

Dear Father in Heaven, *thank You for providing what I need as I journey through life intent upon bringing glory to Your name. In the name of the Father, the Son, and the Holy Spirit, amen.*

**SPOTLIGHT**

***Next Week's Lesson***

Even a little with God is always enough.

# Postal Moment

*Go your ways; behold, I send you out as lambs in the midst of wolves* (Luke 10:3, *New American Standard Bible*).

I was going postal. An acquaintance had hired me to teach workshops for her company. My job was to instruct attendees on how to obtain a high score on the postal exam. I had no experience with such tests, but had been trained . . . over the phone.

Preparing for the first class, because I felt insecure, I typed out everything I was to say. Before the first session, I placed the notes on the podium and went to the hallway to greet the participants.

As I collected money from the students, a competitor slipped into the classroom, stole my notes, and left. When I discovered the loss, I was terrified. However, in spite of my panic, I managed to teach the first class successfully. In fact, my presentation from memory was perhaps more effective than a rote reading from notes. It was a learning experience for me as well as the students.

I learned Jesus not only sends His little lambs among wolves. He protects them while they are there.

Dear Father, *thank You for protecting me as I go about my days. I am sometimes tempted to think that parts of my life are too small for Your attention. But remind me that You are with me in the midst of every moment. Help me to rest in Your unchanging care this day and every day. In the name of Your precious Son, my Savior, I pray. Amen.*

**SEARCH THE WORD**

*Lambs vs. Wolves is no contest when the Good Shepherd is the referee.*

Scripture: Luke 10:1-3

Song: *"Anywhere with Jesus"*

***From this meditation today, I will pray . . .***

Adoration __________

Confession __________

Thanksgiving __________

Supplication __________

***From this meditation today, I will . . .***

Think __________

Say __________

Do __________

# Peace for Troubled Households

*Whatever house you enter, first say, "Peace be to this house"* (Luke 10:5, *New American Standard Bible*).

Scripture: Luke 10:4-7
Song: *"Peace, Perfect Peace"*

***From this meditation today, I will pray . . .***

Adoration ______________________________

Confession ______________________________

Thanksgiving ______________________________

Supplication ______________________________

***From this meditation today, I will . . .***

Think ______________________________

Say ______________________________

Do ______________________________

Westin, one of my first graders, was the picture of health, stocky, with dark eyes and hair. But at the beginning of the school year his mother recounted his history. Westin had developed leukemia at age three. He must go to a clinic for periodic tests.

Tearfully, she reported at midyear: the leukemia had returned. Westin would undergo chemotherapy and be unable to attend school.

In order to continue his educational progress, I agreed to tutor the boy in his home. Once a week, after teaching a full day, I went to Westin's small white house. Before exiting the car each week, I prayed for his strength and peace.

His treatment was lengthy, lasting well into his second year. His second-grade teacher took over the tutoring until he was able to rejoin his class.

Ten years later, both teachers were invited to an anniversary party to rejoice over Westin's prolonged remission from disease. We were thrilled to celebrate with the joyful family. And I was reminded: Christian service, with compassion, brings peace to troubled households.

Dear Father, *I pray for the peace of my friends and neighbors. May I serve them with Your compassion. In Jesus' name. Amen.*

**SPOTLIGHT**
***Next Week's Lesson***

Pronounce "peace" to all you meet.

February

# RESPONDING TO GOD'S CALL

*O my people, hear my teaching . . . tell the next generation the praiseworthy deeds of the* LORD.
—Psalm 78:1a, 4b

*Photo © Jupiterimages*

# Welcome Food

*Whatever city you enter,*
*and they receive you, eat what is set before you*
(Luke 10:8, *New American Standard Bible*).

Scripture: Luke 10:8-12

Song: *"Break Thou the Bread of Life"*

***From this meditation today, I will pray . . .***

Adoration ____________________

____________________

____________________

Confession ____________________

____________________

____________________

Thanksgiving ____________________

____________________

____________________

Supplication ____________________

____________________

____________________

***From this meditation today, I will . . .***

Think ____________________

____________________

____________________

Say ____________________

____________________

____________________

Do ____________________

____________________

____________________

February 1–3. ***Rosalie Yoakam*** *is a freelance writer and a columnist for the* Dayton Daily News. *She and her husband, Bill, live in Springboro, Ohio.*

In Rostov, Russia, we met a woman who said she knew it was possible to live on just bread and salt. She had done so for a period of time during WW II. The same woman thanked my husband and me for the care packages she had received from America following the war. She credited the food contained in those packages for her survival.

Have you noticed how sharing a meal produces an atmosphere where intimate fellowship can develop? Our conversation took place in 1992 in the elderly woman's house, one of the few buildings in her neighborhood to endure the battle that once raged in her city. As we sat at her dining room table, her story was interpreted by her daughter, Lydia, an English teacher.

The events the Russian lady recalled had taken place many years before, but she had lacked the opportunity to show her gratitude. She now eagerly served a meal to the first Americans she had met since that time.

The borscht soup was delicious. And how our gracious host smiled when my husband asked for seconds!

Father, *thank You for blessing me with memories of hospitality, times when I have shared food, and Your love, with others. In Jesus' name. Amen.*

**SPOTLIGHT**

***Next Week's Lesson***

Barriers between people are broken down when food is shared.

# The Heavenly Register

*Do not rejoice in this, that the spirits are subject to you, but rejoice that your names are recorded in heaven* (Luke 10:20, *New American Standard Bible*).

My college diploma sits proudly on the shelf above my computer. It is precious to me because it took me 25 years to earn it. After high school, I completed two years of college and then dropped out of the academic scene. I married, had three daughters, and thought I would never be able to finish my education.

The Lord had other plans. When a Christian school was established in our congregation, the director asked whether I could renew my teaching license. I contacted a local college and found it was possible. Wilmington College accepted my previous credits and worked out a plan for the completion of my course of study.

Today, my name is listed as a recipient of the Bachelor of Arts degree. What a great day of celebration when I graduated! My dream had finally come true.

We will all "graduate" from this earth some day, entering an existence beyond the grave. If we're recorded on the heavenly register, what a far greater event than any other commencement day!

Dear Father, *thank You for loving me, forgiving me, and enrolling me for a heavenly eternity in fellowship with You. I am so grateful to be Your child. In the name of Jesus, Lord and Savior of all, I pray. Amen.*

**SEARCH THE WORD**

*What joy! What honor! Our names are written in Heaven.*

Scripture: Luke 10:17-20

Song: *"When the Roll Is Called Up Yonder"*

*From this meditation today, I will pray . . .*

Adoration ______________________________

______________________________

______________________________

Confession ______________________________

______________________________

______________________________

Thanksgiving ______________________________

______________________________

______________________________

Supplication ______________________________

______________________________

______________________________

*From this meditation today, I will . . .*

Think ______________________________

______________________________

______________________________

Say ______________________________

______________________________

______________________________

Do ______________________________

______________________________

______________________________

______________________________

______________________________

# Awesome Deeds

*Come and see the works of God,*
*Who is awesome in His deeds toward the sons of men*
(Psalm 66:5, *New American Standard Bible*).

Scripture: Psalm 66:5-12
Song: *"In the Hour of Trial"*

***From this meditation today, I will pray . . .***

Adoration ________________________________________

________________________________________

________________________________________

Confession ________________________________________

________________________________________

________________________________________

Thanksgiving ________________________________________

________________________________________

________________________________________

Supplication ________________________________________

________________________________________

________________________________________

***From this meditation today, I will . . .***

Think ________________________________________

________________________________________

________________________________________

Say ________________________________________

________________________________________

________________________________________

Do ________________________________________

________________________________________

________________________________________

________________________________________

________________________________________

Charity Lynch was a Quaker woman who moved with her husband and children to Ohio from South Carolina in the early 1800s. They settled in the town of Waynesville and were very happy there—until tragedy struck in 1813. Their newborn son died. The husband's death soon followed. Then Charity herself fell ill and was not expected to live. The Lynchs' seven surviving children were distributed to six different homes in four towns.

When Charity was told that her children were gone, she could only accept it as a temporary arrangement. She was determined to get them back. Slowly her health returned, and she was able to write about how she dealt with this time of intense tribulation:

"At that time I often retired to my room, shut the door, took my Bible, walked my room, and read some consoling promise of the gospel. I often was able to rejoice in the midst of grief, those days when I lived only for my dear children. For them my daily prayer was offered up to the throne of grace."

She eventually regained all her children.

*Thank You, Father, for Your awesome love and care. In the midst of the most difficult times, keep me close! In Jesus' name I pray. Amen.*

**SPOTLIGHT**
***Next Week's Lesson***

One of God's best blessings is the hope He offers lost sinners.

# The Night Meditation

*On my bed I remember you;*
*I think of you through the watches of the night*
(Psalm 63:6).

Unlike my seatmate who was asleep before the plane left the runway, I couldn't get comfortable. Whenever I closed my eyes, all I could think about was the reason I was making this trip.

The night before, I'd been surrounded by friends traveling behind a horse-drawn sleigh, listening to the sleigh bells and the sounds of horses' hoofs as they crunched through the crusty snow. Now, one night later, my thoughts were troubled as I took the overnight flight to be with my daughter who was facing a lengthy surgical procedure to eradicate cancer. Alone, with no one to talk with, I felt tears threatening to spill down my cheeks. But in the silence I also recalled a hymn I'd learned as a child, "Anywhere with Jesus I can safely go."

Whether we're facing illness, difficult times, or searing loneliness, we are invited to meditate on God's love. In the long night hours He reaches through the darkness to remind us we are never alone.

O God, *thank You for reminding me that I am never alone in this life. Help me to recollect Your abiding presence regularly, especially in the times when I'm most tempted to worry. Thank You, in Jesus' name. Amen.*

**SEARCH THE WORD**

*"Your love is better than life"* (Psalm 63:3).

Scripture: Psalm 63:1-6
Song: *"The Morning Light Is Breaking"*

**From this meditation today, I will pray . . .**

Adoration ______________________________

______________________________

______________________________

Confession ______________________________

______________________________

______________________________

Thanksgiving ______________________________

______________________________

______________________________

Supplication ______________________________

______________________________

______________________________

***From this meditation today, I will . . .***

Think ______________________________

______________________________

______________________________

Say ______________________________

______________________________

______________________________

Do ______________________________

______________________________

______________________________

February 4–10. ***Elaine Ingalls Hogg,*** *of New Brunswick, Canada is a speaker and author, having written two books and several hundred devotionals and articles.*

February 5

# He Went First

*This is he that was spoken of by the prophet Isaiah, saying, The voice of one crying in the wilderness, Prepare ye the way of the Lord, make his paths straight* (Matthew 3:3, *King James Version*).

Scripture: Matthew 3:1-6
Song: *"Prepare the Way, O Zion!"*

*From this meditation today, I will pray . . .*

Adoration ______________________________

______________________________

______________________________

Confession ______________________________

______________________________

______________________________

Thanksgiving ______________________________

______________________________

______________________________

Supplication ______________________________

______________________________

______________________________

*From this meditation today, I will . . .*

Think ______________________________

______________________________

______________________________

Say ______________________________

______________________________

______________________________

Do ______________________________

______________________________

______________________________

______________________________

______________________________

"I'm scared."

I can't remember exactly how old I was when I first uttered those words, but I do remember the circumstances with certainty. I wanted to go with my dad, but the tide was out, and his boat looked so low in the water. And I'd never climbed down a ladder before.

"I'll go first," Dad said. "I'll guide where to put your feet. All you have to do is take one step at a time and hang on." So Dad stood on the ladder, and I backed onto the first rung. Now, instead of seeing the distance to the bobbing boat below, all I saw was my father's arms around me, surrounding me, protecting me from falling, directing my footsteps onto each successive rung.

As John prepared the way for Jesus, so Jesus has gone ahead of us to prepare the way to Heaven. Why look into the distance to see all the obstacles on our journey? Instead, we can visualize His protecting arms around us and hear His gentle voice directing our way. "I'll go first," He says. And He did—at the cross.

Lord, *thank You for sending Jesus ahead of me to the grave, eternally defeating death for all who follow Him. Praise to You, in His name! Amen.*

**SPOTLIGHT**
***Next Week's Lesson***

I'll follow wherever He leads me.

# Bringing Good News

*After John was put in prison,*
*Jesus went into Galilee, proclaiming the good news of God*
(Mark 1:14).

Shortly after my daughter finished her treatments for cancer, she ran a marathon. The act of simply completing the run symbolized a great personal victory.

Historians tell us the first marathon run took place in 490 BC, when a soldier named Pheidippides ran with news from a battlefield on the plain of Marathon to the city of Athens. After a three-hour run of more than 25 miles, Pheidippides died of exhaustion—but not before he delivered this momentous message to his country's citizens: "Nike! (We conquer!)"

Pheidippides was so excited about the Greeks' victory over the Persians that he gave everything he had to tell others the good news. We too have news to share: "Jesus Christ brings victory!"

Christ died on the cross and rose again, defeating Satan and conquering death. As Christians, we have been given good news—no, better than good news. We've been given the best news of all time. Jesus Christ has paid the penalty for our sin. When we tell others of this marvelous victory, should we give less than our all?

Dear God, *impress upon me the magnitude of the news Your Son, Jesus, brought to our world. Help me to give my all so that others will know of this great victory. In the precious name of Jesus, I pray. Amen.*

**SEARCH THE WORD**

*We have the kind of good news we should be bursting to tell.*

Scripture: Mark 1:14, 15
Song: *"Victory in Jesus"*

***From this meditation today, I will pray . . .***

Adoration ____________________

Confession ____________________

Thanksgiving ____________________

Supplication ____________________

***From this meditation today, I will . . .***

Think ____________________

Say ____________________

Do ____________________

# Staying in Tune?

*I tell you, no! But unless you repent, you too will all perish* (Luke 13:5).

Scripture: Luke 13:1-5

Song: *"Repent, the Kingdom Draweth Nigh"*

***From this meditation today, I will pray . . .***

Adoration ______________________

Confession ______________________

Thanksgiving ______________________

Supplication ______________________

***From this meditation today, I will . . .***

Think ______________________

Say ______________________

Do ______________________

When I was taking piano lessons, my teacher always tried to make the instruction more appealing by telling me facts about the composers I was studying. One day we were working through a piece by Handel, and she told me of a time when Handel became impatient with one of the singers in his choir. Apparently, the chorister continued to sing his own unusual interpretations instead of following the maestro's instructions. Handel supposedly took the offending member by the legs and hung him by the heels out of a third-story window! Finally, the chorister repented and agreed to sing in the maestro's way.

Unlike Handel, God doesn't take us by the heels and hold us upside down until we agree to follow Him. Nonetheless, if we are to find peace and harmony in our lives, we will surely be led to times of repentance. This means not only saying we are sorry and asking God to forgive us for our sin. It also calls for making a 180-degree turn away from sin. Thereafter, we will intend to walk in a different direction, relying on the Spirit to keep us steady, strong, and in tune with the Maestro of our days.

Dear God, *as I look back through the days of my life, I can see where I have been guilty of rebelling against Your will and Your ways. I'm sorry. From now on, I want to do things Your way. Through Christ, amen.*

**SPOTLIGHT**

***Next Week's Lesson***

When we see a sign that says "Stop! Wrong Way!" we'd better turn around.

# One More Chance!

*"Sir," the man replied, "leave it alone for one more year, and I'll dig around it and fertilize it. If it bears fruit next year, fine! If not, then cut it down"* (Luke 13:8, 9).

There's nothing like watching a living thing grow, even as the cold blasts of winter close in all around us. A few years ago I bought an amaryllis bulb to plant. According to the instructions, I needed to give the bulb a good soaking and then water it only once a week until a green shoot would appear.

All through the month of February I watered and watched. "This thing is never going to grow!" I exclaimed after watering it for the fourth week in a row and finding no sign of life. "I should throw it out."

In the end I decided to water and fertilize it one more time, thus giving it a last chance to show some sign of life. Although slow starting, with the right amount of moisture and fertilizer, the plant grew and produced a beautiful flower.

When we allow the master to care for us in all His loving ways, we can grow and bring forth fruit. He doesn't give up on us. He patiently lets us make our mistakes or just lie dormant until we've had enough of our lonely living apart from Him. Then, watch us grow!

God, *bring forth the kind of fruits in me that demonstrate my roots go deep in Your love. Be the master gardener of my life, in Christ's name. Amen.*

**SEARCH THE WORD**

*What a bountiful harvest of fruit we'll produce if God is our gardener!*

Scripture: Luke 13:6-9

Song: *"The Water of Life"*

*From this meditation today, I will pray . . .*

Adoration ______________________________

______________________________

______________________________

Confession ______________________________

______________________________

______________________________

Thanksgiving ______________________________

______________________________

______________________________

Supplication ______________________________

______________________________

______________________________

*From this meditation today, I will . . .*

Think ______________________________

______________________________

______________________________

Say ______________________________

______________________________

______________________________

Do ______________________________

______________________________

______________________________

______________________________

______________________________

# Turn from Danger

*I preached that they should repent and turn to God and prove their repentance by their deeds* (Acts 26:20).

Scripture; Acts 26:19-23

**Song:** *"Repent! 'Tis the Voice of Jesus"*

***From this meditation today, I will pray . . .***

Adoration ______________________________

______________________________

______________________________

Confession ______________________________

______________________________

______________________________

Thanksgiving ______________________________

______________________________

______________________________

Supplication ______________________________

______________________________

______________________________

***From this meditation today, I will . . .***

Think ______________________________

______________________________

______________________________

Say ______________________________

______________________________

______________________________

Do ______________________________

______________________________

______________________________

______________________________

______________________________

Nineteen-year-old Jeff was part of a work team that went out from our church to help the victims of Hurricane Katrina in 2005. Upon his return, he told of his experiences.

Fighting back tears, he said, "When I met Don in a church parking lot, he was volunteering to help the flood victims. Although a young man like me, he'd already served jail time and had lost touch with his family.

"During the hurricane he'd found shelter in one of the few churches not already flooded. In the early morning hours, staring at the cross at the front of the church, he repented of his sins and turned to God. So complete was the change in his life that he called his family, asking for their forgiveness and reconciliation. Now, instead of being guarded in a prison cell, he was acting as a security guard at the distribution center."

Don's deeds—helping others, being trustworthy—proved his true repentance. Thankfully, God saves us while we are still *un*worthy. But He doesn't leave us in our sad state. He invites us into a brand new lifestyle.

Dear God, *I know others see You through how I conduct my life. Help me to proclaim Your matchless mercy by my life of gratefulness and good works. Through Christ my Savior, I pray. Amen.*

**SPOTLIGHT**

***Next Week's Lesson***

Repentance plugs us in to Jesus' transforming power.

# Can't Earn Heaven

*For the* Lord *watches over the way of the righteous, but the way of the wicked will perish* (Psalm 1:6).

The peace of a beautiful summer afternoon was shattered by the unmistakable sound of a man's voice crying out, *"Help!"* Someone was in danger. My heart raced as I ran to dial 9-1-1. "There's a man in the lake," I said. "He's calling for help."

"Can you tell me where you live?" the voice on the other end of the line asked. Struggling to stay calm so I could give clear directions, I said, "West Bay. Please hurry!" I went on to explain, "When you get to Cleveland there's a fork in the road. Be sure to take the road on the right because the sign marked West Bay Road doesn't actually lead to West Bay." I explained further . . .

If the emergency crew had gone the wrong way, someone could have perished. Today's psalm speaks of the moral decisions we need to make during our lifetimes. Ultimately, they are matters of life and death. Should we choose the path of our own righteousness, we will fall short of eternal life. If we choose God alone as our righteousness, we will enjoy wonderful fellowship with His Son in this life—and enjoy Heaven with Him thereafter. What a loving and gracious Lord is ours!

Dear God, *help me to listen closely to Your instructions that I might stay on the path of righteousness this day. Through my Lord Jesus Christ. Amen.*

**SEARCH THE WORD**

*A fruitful tree or chaff blowing in the wind?— it's our choice.*

Scripture: Psalm 1

**Song: *"Each Step I Take"***

***From this meditation today, I will pray . . .***

Adoration ______________________________

______________________________

______________________________

Confession ______________________________

______________________________

______________________________

Thanksgiving ______________________________

______________________________

______________________________

Supplication ______________________________

______________________________

______________________________

***From this meditation today, I will . . .***

Think ______________________________

______________________________

______________________________

Say ______________________________

______________________________

______________________________

Do ______________________________

______________________________

______________________________

______________________________

______________________________

February 11

# Egg on My Face

*He guides the humble in what is right and teaches them his way* (Psalm 25:9).

Scripture: Psalm 25:1-10
Song: *"More Like the Master"*

***From this meditation today, I will pray . . .***

Adoration ________________________

Confession ________________________

Thanksgiving ________________________

Supplication ________________________

***From this meditation today, I will . . .***

Think ________________________

Say ________________________

Do ________________________

February 11–17. ***Susan J. Reinhardt*** *is an office manager and writer who enjoys antiquing. She and her husband live in Souderton, Pennsylvania.*

I was wrestling with a computer problem, but the computer was winning. "Let me show you how this works," said my husband, who seemed to be getting a little frustrated with me. He made a number of suggestions, some of which I'd already tried without success; others, I just didn't think would work. In desperation, though, I finally swallowed my pride and listened carefully to his instructions.

Click. Click. Click. Problem solved.

This is known as "egg on my face time."

I'm sure God must shake His head when we insist on doing things our own way. We think we know the best way to handle a situation, but He can see the whole picture from beginning to end. After making a mess of things, we end up crying out for Him to rescue us. He graciously steps in, guiding us and teaching us His ways when we're finally ready to accept His direction.

Our pride can be the biggest barrier to our relationship with the Lord. It takes a humble attitude to receive truth.

Father, *thank You for Your patience when I'm in an I-can-do-it-myself mode. You whisper to my heart through Your Word until I get the message. Praise to You, in the name of Jesus! Amen.*

**SPOTLIGHT**
***Next Week's Lesson***

It's hard to hear God when pride makes us plug up our ears.

# Watching for a Mistake

*One Sabbath, when Jesus went to eat in the house of a prominent Pharisee, he was being carefully watched* (Luke 14:1).

In sixth grade, one of my classmates, Judy, was a top-notch student. I wanted to be the best, but the result was always the same: Judy came out number one, while I was the runner-up. The green-eyed monster of jealousy grabbed my heart. I avoided her like the plague.

Did I seize the opportunity to be challenged, learn from her successes, and develop a friendship with her? No. I became upset with her and swirled down into self-pity.

The Pharisees had Jesus right there with them, eating a meal with Him. He spoke to them, encouraging them to look at life through the lens of God's love and concern for a sick man. Yet they allowed pride, jealousy, and a know-it-all attitude to rob them of blessing. Instead of seeing what they could learn, they secretly watched to find some fault or weakness.

It takes a humble heart to rejoice with others. On the other hand, the Germans have a word, *schadenfreude,* meaning to "rejoice in the misfortunes of others." We have that option too. But why not choose to learn from others' mistakes—and celebrate with them in their successes?

Lord, *may I recognize You as the source of my strength and ability. Therefore, let me be thankful for the successes in my own life and in the lives of others. All the glory goes to You alone. In Jesus' name, amen.*

**SEARCH THE WORD**

*Delighting in another's misfortune may lead to our own.*

Scripture: Luke 14:1-6

Song: *"Jesus Is Passing This Way"*

***From this meditation today, I will pray . . .***

Adoration ______________________

______________________

______________________

Confession ______________________

______________________

______________________

Thanksgiving ______________________

______________________

______________________

Supplication ______________________

______________________

______________________

***From this meditation today, I will . . .***

Think ______________________

______________________

______________________

Say ______________________

______________________

______________________

Do ______________________

______________________

______________________

______________________

______________________

# SPS!

*When someone invites you to a wedding feast, do not take the place of honor, for a person more distinguished than you may have been invited* (Luke 14:8).

Scripture: Luke 14:7-9

**Song:** *"I Need Thee Every Hour"*

***From this meditation today, I will pray . . .***

Adoration ____________________

Confession ____________________

Thanksgiving ____________________

Supplication ____________________

***From this meditation today, I will . . .***

Think ____________________

Say ____________________

Do ____________________

When I was growing up, Mom tried to instill certain strong values in me. For example, she wouldn't allow bragging. Whenever I showed any signs of self-aggrandizement, she would comment, "SPS," which stood for "self-praise stinks." While she was lavish with her praise of my accomplishments and abilities, she didn't hesitate to correct me if I was becoming obnoxious.

Jesus' words usually fly in the face of human wisdom. We're told it's a dog-eat-dog world, so we have to compete aggressively and push ourselves into the limelight. But Jesus spoke of handling the everyday experiences of life with humility and grace. He told people not to grab the best seats for themselves but to take a lower place. He pointed out how embarrassing it would be if someone told them to give up their hard-won place of privilege for an even more favored guest.

Giving ourselves honor leaves us unfulfilled—and constantly vulnerable to being "taken down a peg." How much sweeter our reward when it comes by pure grace!

Father, *when I'm tempted to grab position or honor, help me to remember that self-praise ends in meager satisfaction. Let me find my joy in honoring You with a servant heart. In the precious name of Jesus I pray. Amen.*

**SPOTLIGHT**

***Next Week's Lesson***

Jockeying for position will bring us last place in life's race.

# Parade for . . . Whom?

*Everyone who exalts himself will be humbled, and he who humbles himself will be exalted*
(Luke 14:11).

In the book of Esther, Haman enjoyed great power in the king's court. Instead of being thankful, though, he longed for honor and praise. Therefore, when godly Mordecai refused to "bow and scrape" before him, Haman raged.

One day, Mordecai discovered a plot against the king, notified the authorities, and thereby saved the king's life. Mordecai didn't demand any recognition; he just went about his business. Later, however, when the king came across the account of Mordecai's good deed, he was disturbed to find this courageous whistle-blower hadn't been properly rewarded.

The king called Haman and asked him what he would do for a great man. Haman assumed the king was talking about him and suggested the equivalent of our ticker-tape parade. You can imagine Haman's shock and humiliation when the king commanded him to do all these things for Mordecai!

Someone once said, "The way up is down." If you try to set up your own ticker-tape parade, you'll likely find you've prepared it for someone else.

Father, *thank You for Your many blessings. Help me to remember that true promotion and favor come only from You. In Jesus' name, amen.*

**SEARCH THE WORD**

*"Pride goes before destruction, and a haughty spirit before a fall"*
(Proverbs 16:18).

Scripture: Luke 14:10, 11

Song: *"Have Thy Way, Lord"*

*From this meditation today, I will pray . . .*

Adoration ______________________________

______________________________

______________________________

Confession ______________________________

______________________________

______________________________

Thanksgiving ______________________________

______________________________

______________________________

Supplication ______________________________

______________________________

______________________________

*From this meditation today, I will . . .*

Think ______________________________

______________________________

______________________________

Say ______________________________

______________________________

______________________________

Do ______________________________

______________________________

______________________________

______________________________

______________________________

# No Strings Attached

*When you give a banquet, invite the poor, the crippled, the lame, the blind, and you will be blessed. Although they cannot repay you, you will be repaid at the resurrection of the righteous*
(Luke 14:13, 14).

Scripture: Luke 14:12-14
**Song:** *"Jesus Is All the World to Me"*

A mom smiles as a server puts a scoop of mashed potatoes on her child's plate. An elderly man happily chats with people at his table, glad for the company. A woman in a wheelchair is thankful she can get out of the house.

The server's back aches from hours of preparation. Her family has sacrificed their own traditions to be here. None of these people will ever invite her for dinner at their homes. Yet, her heart overflows with joy as their faces radiate hope for the future.

Jesus told His hosts not to invite their friends, relatives, or rich neighbors in hopes that they'd reciprocate in turn. Instead, He instructed them to extend hospitality to those who had no way of repaying. Such hosts would be blessed and honored by God on the day when He puts all things right.

Giving "with no strings attached" can produce great joy in our hearts. Whatever it costs us in time, money, and effort to serve the poor is far outweighed by the delight it brings to God's heart.

Heavenly Father, *give me a heart filled with compassion and love for those who can't repay the kindness You call me to share. In Jesus' name, amen.*

*From this meditation today, I will pray . . .*

Adoration ______________________________

______________________________

______________________________

Confession ______________________________

______________________________

______________________________

Thanksgiving ______________________________

______________________________

______________________________

Supplication ______________________________

______________________________

______________________________

*From this meditation today, I will . . .*

Think ______________________________

______________________________

______________________________

Say ______________________________

______________________________

______________________________

Do ______________________________

______________________________

______________________________

______________________________

______________________________

**SPOTLIGHT**
***Next Week's Lesson***

Give without expecting to get.

# Credit Where It's Due

*Whereof I was made a minister, according to the gift of the grace of God given unto me by the effectual working of his power. Unto me, who am less than the least of all saints, is this grace given, that I should preach among the Gentiles the unsearchable riches of Christ* (Ephesians 3:7, 8, *King James Version*).

As a world-renowned preacher stepped up to the pulpit, the crowd gave him its full attention, waiting for profound words of wisdom. Yet he spoke with great simplicity and humility. Afterwards, a reporter said to him, "Dr. Smith, you have a seminary degree and several doctorates. You've traveled the world and met many great leaders. How does it feel to be so honored?"

The preacher smiled and said, "I'm nothing special. Jesus Christ is the source of my abilities."

This man, like Paul, refused to rely on his heritage or academic background for his effectiveness in ministry. He stressed God's grace in his life, recognizing the ministry as a gifting from God. He was more interested in presenting the gospel than building his reputation.

We can be thankful for men and women like this, who serve the church with pure hearts. They simply give credit where all the credit is due.

Father, *when I'm tempted to bask in applause, remind me that it's You who have extended blessing. Keep working through me, in Jesus' name. Amen.*

**SEARCH THE WORD**

*Deflect personal praise back to the one who empowers you.*

Scripture: Ephesians 3:1-10

Song: *"Cleanse Me"*

*From this meditation today, I will pray . . .*

Adoration ______________________

______________________

______________________

Confession ______________________

______________________

______________________

Thanksgiving ______________________

______________________

______________________

Supplication ______________________

______________________

______________________

*From this meditation today, I will . . .*

Think ______________________

______________________

______________________

Say ______________________

______________________

______________________

Do ______________________

______________________

______________________

______________________

______________________

# Key Element of Change

*All of you, clothe yourselves with humility toward one another, because, "God opposes the proud but gives grace to the humble"* (1 Peter 5:5).

Scripture: 1 Peter 5:1-5
Song: *"I Surrender All"*

***From this meditation today, I will pray . . .***

Adoration ______________________________

______________________________

______________________________

Confession ______________________________

______________________________

______________________________

Thanksgiving ______________________________

______________________________

______________________________

Supplication ______________________________

______________________________

______________________________

***From this meditation today, I will . . .***

Think ______________________________

______________________________

______________________________

Say ______________________________

______________________________

______________________________

Do ______________________________

______________________________

______________________________

______________________________

______________________________

Her dad had abandoned Liza and her mom before her birth. Further complicating matters, her mom's family rejected them as well. As an adult, Liza was drawn to a lifestyle of partying and drinking. Several failed marriages and ill health left her a broken, addicted, suicidal woman.

But Liza's story has a happy ending. She discovered a church that embraced her with loving hearts. They told her about Jesus and how she could have a fresh start in Him. She gratefully entered the waters of baptism.

Of course, there were many things Liza didn't yet understand in the Word, but she humbly listened, thoughtfully considered, and then tried to practice what she learned. She even began reaching out to others and sharing what Jesus had done for her. Gradually, the sad, devastated woman was transformed by the power of Christ.

The key element in this change was her willingness to receive God's Word along with the counsel of mature believers. Liza's openness and humility helped her find the path of life.

Father, *please keep my heart soft and pliable. When things aren't going well, help me listen to the godly counsel of others. In Jesus' name, amen.*

**SPOTLIGHT**
***Next Week's Lesson***

Only lives humbly seeking God's help can truly be transformed.

# True Relationship with God

*You have looked into my heart, Lord, and you know all about me* (Psalm 139:1, *Contemporary English Version*).

Children believe that their parents have the uncanny ability to love them and to know every move they make. For instance, Melissa believes, "My parents have eyes in the backs of their heads." Jeff thinks, "No matter what I do, my mom can always tell when I'm lying." And Abbey says, "Mom and Dad love me, no matter what."

The psalmist expressed some of the same thoughts about his relationship with God. David knew he served an all-seeing, all-knowing, and loving God. He believed that his relationship with God was real because God knew his unspoken thoughts, understood his anger, his anxiety, even his depression.

To have a deepening relationship with God, we must believe that He understands us and His love for us is unconditional. A child put it this way, "When you pray, you get a happy feeling inside—like God just walked into your heart and is warming himself at a cozy fire."

Lord, *You know all about me, yet You invite me to come before You, freely revealing the contents of my heart. What a privilege it is to build my life around You, the one who loves me unconditionally. I thank You in the name of Jesus, my Savior and Lord. Amen.*

**SEARCH THE WORD**

*God can see right through us and still enjoys the show.*

Scripture: Psalm 139:1-6

**Song:** *"God Made Me for Himself"*

***From this meditation today, I will pray . . .***

Adoration __________

Confession __________

Thanksgiving __________

Supplication __________

***From this meditation today, I will . . .***

Think __________

Say __________

Do __________

February 18–24. ***Wesley Sharpe*** *is a retired school psychologist who writes on educational and parenting topics. He lives in Fort Bragg, California.*

# Test of a Disciple

*You cannot be my disciple, unless you love me more than you love your father and mother, your wife and children, and your brothers and sisters. You cannot come with me unless you love me more than you love your own life* (Luke 14:26, *Contemporary English Version*).

Scripture: Luke 14:25-27

Song: *"Jesus Loves Me"*

***From this meditation today, I will pray . . .***

Adoration ______________________________

______________________________

______________________________

Confession ______________________________

______________________________

______________________________

Thanksgiving ______________________________

______________________________

______________________________

Supplication ______________________________

______________________________

______________________________

***From this meditation today, I will . . .***

Think ______________________________

______________________________

______________________________

Say ______________________________

______________________________

______________________________

Do ______________________________

______________________________

______________________________

______________________________

______________________________

To love Jesus more than life must have seemed unreasonably harsh to many hearers who thought they were Jesus' disciples. And it is not easy for us to hear either. Dr. Phil McGraw, author of *Family First: Your Step-by-Step Plan for Creating a Phenomenal Family,* said, "I love my family more than anything in this world, and I want us all to be safe, healthy, happy, and prosperous in everything we do, both within our family and as we go out into the world."

It is only natural that most of us want to be good parents, and we love those closest to our hearts. Jesus knew that to ask His disciples to put their love for Him above even their closest human relationships meant they were willing to give up everything to serve Him.

Only God can claim this kind of love. Yet, thankfully, when we give Him our all, He gives us every good thing in return: "No mind has conceived what God has prepared for those who love him" (1 Corinthians 2:9).

Gracious God, *I want to build my life around You, to love You more than life itself. Thanks for Your Spirit to help me grow. In Christ's name, amen.*

**SPOTLIGHT**

***Next Week's Lesson***

Teach my heart
to love You more.

# What Is a Disciple?

*So then, you cannot be my disciple unless you give away everything you own*
(Luke 14:33, *Contemporary English Version*).

Shireen, an Iranian teenager, often listened to the Persian language broadcasts of the Radio Voice of Christ. She wrote the following letter to the station, telling of her wish to follow Jesus:

"One night I saw in a dream that Jesus was telling me, 'My child, I accept you.' I shared these dreams with one of my teachers and one of my friends. They told me if I believed in Jesus I would become an infidel. But when I realized the truth, deep in my heart, I became glad and believed."

She ended her letter with several questions and a request for a Bible and other Christian literature. "Am I a complete Christian now?" She asked. "Is it really true that I am an infidel? And when should I talk to my parents about this?"

Shireen willingly gave up everything to follow Jesus. There must be other stories like hers, because in the past 40 years the Iranian Christian Church has grown from about 5,000 to over 200,000 believers. Her commitment is the kind that Jesus asks from all His followers.

Father, *more than anything, I want to be Jesus' disciple. I know that He is always with me, asking me for room in my heart. In His name, amen.*

**SEARCH THE WORD**

*Can we sing "I Surrender All" and really mean it?*

Scripture: Luke 14:28-33

Song: *"Here I Am, Lord"*

***From this meditation today, I will pray . . .***

Adoration ______________________

______________________

______________________

Confession ______________________

______________________

______________________

Thanksgiving ______________________

______________________

______________________

Supplication ______________________

______________________

______________________

***From this meditation today, I will . . .***

Think ______________________

______________________

______________________

Say ______________________

______________________

______________________

Do ______________________

______________________

______________________

______________________

______________________

# Too Much Money

*You still lack one thing. Sell everything you have and give to the poor, and you will have treasure in heaven. Then come, follow me* (Luke 18:22).

Scripture: Luke 18:18-25

Song: *"Leaving It All with Jesus"*

*From this meditation today, I will pray . . .*

Adoration ______________________________

______________________________

______________________________

Confession ______________________________

______________________________

______________________________

Thanksgiving ______________________________

______________________________

______________________________

Supplication ______________________________

______________________________

______________________________

*From this meditation today, I will . . .*

Think ______________________________

______________________________

______________________________

Say ______________________________

______________________________

______________________________

Do ______________________________

______________________________

______________________________

______________________________

______________________________

Marzi Muhammadi, an Afghan doctor, hoped to be elected to the parliament in that country's first free election in 30 years. She was battling for a seat from her province, and to finance her campaign she sold everything she owned except her wedding ring. Yet she lost the election. Still, she willingly gave up everything for her goal.

Marzi's commitment was the kind of response Jesus had hoped for from the man in today's Scripture. But he believed his life was blameless because he followed God's Old Testament law.

Jesus knew that the true test of discipleship for this man would be to give away everything he owned and then follow Him. It was a test of character that the rich man failed. He couldn't bring himself to follow Jesus from place to place or give up his wealth to help others.

Jesus continues to say, "Follow me." If we accept His love and follow His example, we are His disciples. But we will not be perfect in our attempts. Only step by step, relying wholly on His grace, do we stay close to Him.

Lord, *I hand over the control of my life to You, and I will follow Your Spirit's leading the best I can. Thank You for the free gift of salvation that made this journey with You possible. In Jesus' name, amen.*

**SPOTLIGHT**

***Next Week's Lesson***

You can't take it with you, so why not have Jesus send it on ahead?

# High Cost of Believing

*Peter said, "Remember, we left everything to be your followers!"* (Luke 18:28, *Contemporary English Version*).

Christians in Vietnam know what it means to give up everything for their faith. Often local authorities try to persuade believers to give up their belief in Jesus. Their tactics include refusing to give monthly support money to poor Christian families. Thus some Christians give in to the pressure and abandon their beliefs; others stand firm.

Peter and the other disciples watched as Jesus spoke to the rich man. The man seemed to have his heart set on the promise of eternal life, but he wasn't willing to make the sacrifice Jesus required of His followers. Disappointed, he walked away.

Later, Peter reminded Jesus that he and the other fishermen had left their homes and families to be with Him. Peter must have realized that what they had given up for Christ would, in a sense, be repaid with eternal life.

To stay or walk away from Jesus is still the choice we face. Each of us must decide whether the benefits of committing our lives to God are worth the hardships we may have to endure. Thankfully, we need never go it alone. We have the fellowship of other believers to encourage us—along with God's own Spirit within us.

Dear God, *I come to You in obedience to Your Word, trusting in Your gracious promise to be present with me always. In Christ's name, amen.*

**SEARCH THE WORD**

*Jesus left Heaven's glories for us. What have we left for Him?*

Scripture: Luke 18:28-30

**Song:** *"Leave It There"*

*From this meditation today, I will pray . . .*

Adoration ______________________

Confession ______________________

Thanksgiving ______________________

Supplication ______________________

*From this meditation today, I will . . .*

Think ______________________

Say ______________________

Do ______________________

February 23

# A Better Way to Fish

*The men pulled their boats up on the shore. Then they left everything and went with Jesus* (Luke 5:11, *Contemporary English Version*).

Scripture: Luke 5:1-11

Song: *"Follow Me, the Master Said"*

*From this meditation today, I will pray . . .*

Adoration ______________________

______________________

______________________

Confession ______________________

______________________

______________________

Thanksgiving ______________________

______________________

______________________

Supplication ______________________

______________________

______________________

*From this meditation today, I will . . .*

Think ______________________

______________________

______________________

Say ______________________

______________________

______________________

Do ______________________

______________________

______________________

______________________

______________________

What a difference between the response of the three fishermen who had been washing their nets, and the rich man who asked Jesus the way to eternal life! While the rich man apparently couldn't imagine giving away his wealth, Peter, James, and John didn't hesitate. They left their boats, their nets, and all their other equipment by the lake to follow Jesus.

Can you imagine the disciples saying, "Wait a minute, Jesus! After we sell our fish for a good price, *then* we'll come with You." No, the men had listened to Jesus' teaching, they had witnessed a miracle, and Jesus promised they would do much more than catch fish in the days ahead. They were convinced that Jesus was God's messenger, and they were willing to drop everything to follow Him.

When Jesus turns to us and says "Come with me," there's no room for a wishy-washy response. He seeks a yes or no. And once we say "Yes!" He gives us everything we need to live a life that brings glory to His kingdom.

O God, *how I long to be counted among those faithful to Your Son in this life! Keep me close through study of the Word, prayer, and fellowship with my brothers and sisters in the church. Thank You, in Jesus' name. Amen.*

**SPOTLIGHT**

***Next Week's Lesson***

With enthusiasm the fishermen left all behind for the chance to be Jesus' disciples.

# Results of Obedience

*The Lord said to Ananias, "Go! I have chosen him to tell foreigners, kings, and the people of Israel about me"* (Acts 9:15, *Contemporary English Version*).

While traveling in the Middle East, we decided to take a side trip to Damascus, Syria, probably the oldest continually occupied city in the world. We found the ruins of the ancient Roman city, and after shopping in a crowded bazaar, we walked the bustling Straight Street mentioned in Acts 9:11. Later, we walked down a stairway to an ancient Roman road and entered a small underground chapel. Tradition says we were standing in the home of Ananias.

We don't know much about Ananias or how he became a Christian. But we do know that he swallowed his fear and immediately obeyed God. He left his home and found Saul. As a result of his obedience Saul of Tarsus became Paul the apostle, and the Christian faith spread throughout the Roman world.

Isn't that how God usually works? It may not be clear to us why He wants us to do something. Nevertheless, our task is to trust Him and to do what He has called us to do. He alone is responsible for the results.

**Precious Father,** *forgive me when I ignore You and go my own way. Give me the wisdom to recognize Your will and to do it with a joyful heart. Help me to trust You completely, each step of the way. In Jesus' name, amen.*

**SEARCH THE WORD**

*Being a disciple may mean receiving dangerous assignments. Lord, give us courage to obey.*

**Scripture: Acts 9:1-6, 11-16**

**Song: *"Trusting Jesus"***

***From this meditation today, I will pray . . .***

Adoration ______________________

Confession ______________________

Thanksgiving ______________________

Supplication ______________________

***From this meditation today, I will . . .***

Think ______________________

Say ______________________

Do ______________________

February 25

# This Is Shouting News!

*Let everything that has breath praise the LORD. Praise the LORD* (Psalm 150:6).

Scripture: Psalm 150

Song: *"Praise the Name of Jesus"*

***From this meditation today, I will pray . . .***

Adoration ______________________________

______________________________

______________________________

Confession ______________________________

______________________________

______________________________

Thanksgiving ______________________________

______________________________

______________________________

Supplication ______________________________

______________________________

______________________________

***From this meditation today, I will . . .***

Think ______________________________

______________________________

______________________________

Say ______________________________

______________________________

______________________________

Do ______________________________

______________________________

______________________________

February 25–29. ***Phillip H. Barnhart*** *has written 14 books and contributed articles to dozens of publications. Retired, he lives with his wife, Sharron, in Florida.*

The book of Psalms comes to us in five sections, each division concluding on a note of praise. In fact, this final psalm not only punctuates the fifth section with praise, but also the entire collection of 150 psalms. Yes, the last psalm has the last word, the word of praise. Yet there is one requirement: We have to be breathing. And if we are breathing, we ought to be praising.

This is very practical. If we get up in the morning, read the newspaper, and can't find our name in the obituary column, we ought to start the day on a crescendo of praise! The book of Psalms begins by inviting us to the law as a way of life and ends by inviting us to praise as the use of our very breath.

Have you considered that there is no better use of your breath than to articulate praises to the God of your blessings? In other words, the many ways God blesses us each day is "shouting news"!

Dear God, *I raise my praise for the many and varied ways You bring good things to my life, each and every day. You are gracious and generous, and I am grateful. I praise You now and always; as long as I have breath, I will praise You. In the name of Jesus I pray. Amen.*

**SPOTLIGHT**

***Next Week's Lesson***

Singing, shouting, speaking, whispering—let's use our life's breath to praise Him!

# First, Get Ready

*Then David said, "No one may carry the ark of God but the Levites, for the* Lord *has chosen them to carry the ark of God and to minister before Him forever* (1 Chronicles 15:2, *New King James Version*).

A minister was having difficulty preparing a particular sermon. Finally, he gave up. "Maybe the Holy Spirit will give me something to say," he said to himself. Standing before the congregation on Sunday morning, God did indeed tell him what to say: "Tell the people you are unprepared."

The first time David tried to move the ark to Jerusalem, he made a mess of things. *That will not happen this time,* David vows to himself and promises the people. Every possible preparation will be made, every detail attended to. David will go by the book this time.

Whatever we do for God warrants good preparation. It shouldn't be left to chance or planned haphazardly. After all, God deserves our best. We should do our homework thoroughly, thread our needles carefully, put the stones precisely in place. When we serve God, we are on a high level and in a large place; there, what we do calls for the best we have and the most we are. And before everything else, getting ready is the key to serving God.

Lord, *I want to prepare for what You call me to do. Help me ready my mind and my heart through the gifts You give me. In Jesus' name, amen.*

**SEARCH THE WORD**

*We'll never fly high in God's kingdom by just "winging it."*

Scripture: 1 Chronicles 15:1-3, 11-15

Song: *"Prepare the Way, O Zion!"*

***From this meditation today, I will pray . . .***

Adoration ______________________________

______________________________

______________________________

Confession ______________________________

______________________________

______________________________

Thanksgiving ______________________________

______________________________

______________________________

Supplication ______________________________

______________________________

______________________________

***From this meditation today, I will . . .***

Think ______________________________

______________________________

______________________________

Say ______________________________

______________________________

______________________________

Do ______________________________

______________________________

______________________________

______________________________

______________________________

February 27

# A Hallelujah Heart

*David told the leaders of the Levites to appoint their brothers as singers to sing joyful songs, accompanied by musical instruments: lyres, harps and cymbals* (1 Chronicles 15:16).

Scripture: 1 Chronicles 15:16-24
Song: *"The Hallelujah Side"*

***From this meditation today, I will pray . . .***

Adoration ______________________________

______________________________

______________________________

Confession ______________________________

______________________________

______________________________

Thanksgiving ______________________________

______________________________

______________________________

Supplication ______________________________

______________________________

______________________________

***From this meditation today, I will . . .***

Think ______________________________

______________________________

______________________________

Say ______________________________

______________________________

______________________________

Do ______________________________

______________________________

______________________________

______________________________

______________________________

David's preparation for getting the ark to Jerusalem included a context for joyful praise. The ark, representing God's covenant with His people, would be lifted to highest glory with shouts of victory and songs of adoration. In each soul would be an amen attitude; in each person gathered, a hallelujah heart.

This dimension of uninhibited joy comes through in the 3-year-old who went to church for the first time. After she and her parents had taken their seats, the lights in the sanctuary were dimmed, and the choir came down the center aisle carrying lighted candles. All was quiet until the 3-year-old started singing in a loud voice, "Happy birthday to you. Happy birthday to you!" Her joy wouldn't stay inside. What was in her heart flowed out everywhere.

Someone asked Joseph Haydn, the composer, why his music was so cheerful. He replied, "I cannot make it otherwise. When I think upon God, my heart is so full of joy, the notes dance and leap from my pen!"

Dear Heavenly Father, *there's a joy deep in my heart about who You are to me. May I put it on my face in smiles and laughter. May I put in on my lips in tributes and praises. All praise to You, in Christ's name. Amen.*

**SPOTLIGHT**
***Next Week's Lesson***

David went all out
in his celebration of praise.

# God Strengthens Us

***God gave the Levites the strength they needed to carry the chest, and so they sacrificed seven bulls and seven rams***
**(1 Chronicles 15:26, *Contemporary English Version*).**

A helpful admonition made its way some time ago into books, onto posters, and taped to refrigerator doors. It spoke of God's help in our lives, promising strength and courage: "There is nothing you and God cannot accomplish together today." It's true, isn't it, that such a combination always makes a majority?

David's first attempt to get the ark to Jerusalem failed. The second one did not. The people prepared, and help came from God. It was God who gave them strength to carry the ark to Jerusalem and get it there safely. It was God who guided each step and empowered every move.

When we look at a mountain we need to climb and fear we can't get to the top, God promises to be with us all the way. When we see a road we need to walk, one that stretches long before us and we wonder if we will ever get to its end, God promises to guide our steps and guard our feet. When we put our hands to a formidable and difficult task, we know we are not alone.

Dear God, *thank You for being with me in all things and in all places. As I begin each undertaking, I feel Your hand on mine. I am invited by Your presence, I am encouraged by Your promise, I am strengthened by Your power. In the precious name of Jesus I pray. Amen.*

**SEARCH THE WORD**

*God empowers us to do the tasks He entrusts to us.*

Scripture: 1 Chronicles 15:25-29

Song: *"O God, Our Help in Ages Past"*

***From this meditation today, I will pray . . .***

Adoration ______________________________

______________________________

______________________________

Confession ______________________________

______________________________

______________________________

Thanksgiving ______________________________

______________________________

______________________________

Supplication ______________________________

______________________________

______________________________

***From this meditation today, I will . . .***

Think ______________________________

______________________________

______________________________

Say ______________________________

______________________________

______________________________

Do ______________________________

______________________________

______________________________

______________________________

______________________________

# Blessings All Around

*When David had finished offering the burnt offering and peace offerings, he blessed the people in the name of the LORD* (1 Chronicles 16:2, *New American Standard Bible*).

*Scripture*: 1 Chronicles 16:1-6
Song: *"There Shall Be Showers of Blessing"*

***From this meditation today, I will pray . . .***

Adoration ______________________________

______________________________

______________________________

Confession ______________________________

______________________________

______________________________

Thanksgiving ______________________________

______________________________

______________________________

Supplication ______________________________

______________________________

______________________________

***From this meditation today, I will . . .***

Think ______________________________

______________________________

______________________________

Say ______________________________

______________________________

______________________________

Do ______________________________

______________________________

______________________________

______________________________

______________________________

The day the ark arrived in Jerusalem was a great day in the life of God's people. On that day past failure was forgotten and present accomplishment celebrated. All the preparation had paid off, the objective had been reached. What a day of great blessing!

A man attended a Bible study where the teacher talked of the land promised to Abraham. Thinking about that, the man said, "I already live in the promised land." He didn't have to go anywhere to claim God's promises or gain God's favor. In his daily life he already inhabited the perfect place to enjoy God's goodness. For him, there were blessings all around.

Later on in the Bible study, the discussion focused on the stress people experience these days. This same man commented, "I'm too blessed to be stressed." In a similar vein, an old Russian proverb says, "All days are beautiful . . . when you can wake up." God gives us life, and life gives us so much, if we'll only see it.

**Dear Lord,** *how extravagant You are in Your blessings! With You, the calf is always the fatted calf, the robe the best robe, the pearl a gem of great price. Your peace, too, exceeds my understanding. Every blessing You give me, I give You back in praise. In Jesus' name I pray. Amen.*

**SPOTLIGHT**
***Next Week's Lesson***

If we worship as David did, it will be skillful, heartfelt, and loud.

# March

# SIGNS OF GOD'S COVENANT

*Let everything that has breath*
*praise the* LORD.
—Psalm 150:6

*Photo © Jupiterimage*

# Credit Is Due

*The* Lord *is great and greatly to be praised; He is also to be feared above all gods* (1 Chronicles 16:25, *New King James Version*).

Scripture: 1 Chronicles 16:7-36
Song: *"Fresh as the Morning"*

*From this meditation today, I will pray . . .*

Adoration ______________________

______________________

______________________

Confession ______________________

______________________

______________________

Thanksgiving ______________________

______________________

______________________

Supplication ______________________

______________________

______________________

*From this meditation today, I will . . .*

Think ______________________

______________________

______________________

Say ______________________

______________________

______________________

Do ______________________

______________________

______________________

March 1-2. ***Phillip H. Barnhart*** *has written 14 books and contributed articles to dozens of publications. Retired, he lives with his wife, Sharron, in Florida.*

With the ark safely in Jerusalem, David weaves a song of praise from three previously penned psalms. He leaves no doubt as to where credit is due. If anyone points a finger of acclaim at him, he deflects it and points straight up to the God of all blessings. He will make everyone aware of source and resource. All will know that God has been on the move on behalf of His people.

If we think, we will thank. Here's what I mean: When we consider how good God is to us, we will surely let Him know how we feel about that. We will use at least some of the 86,400 seconds of each day to say, "Thank You." In fact, I believe we will use more and more of them until we are using all of them (in Heaven). In happy moments, we can praise God. In difficult moments, we can seek God. In every moment, we can thank God. For us, giving God credit is the constant characteristic of our lives.

Father, *whatever foundation I stand upon, I know You have put it there. Every road I take You have laid down. All the things I count my own find their origin in Your goodness. Everything I know, everything I have, began in the heart of Your love for me. Thank You, in Jesus' name. Amen.*

**SPOTLIGHT**
***Next Week's Lesson***

How can a person who sincerely meditates on God's love refrain from His praise?

# A Forever Love

*David also appointed Heman, Jeduthun, and the others chosen by name to give thanks to the* LORD, *for "his faithful love endures forever"* (1 Chronicles 16:41, *New Living Translation*).

Some 60 years ago, well-known theologian Karl Barth was lecturing at a seminary when a student asked him to sum up his theology in just a few words. The lecturer stepped from behind the podium and began singing, "Jesus loves me, this I know . . ." In a similar vein, Holocaust survivor Corrie ten Boom inspired her hearers when she said, "No problem is too big for God's power; no person is too small for God's love."

We love to hear of God's love. After the ark had been successfully delivered to Jerusalem, David made organizational arrangements to insure God's faithful love would be broadcast to the people. He told his staff to draw a circle of God's love so large around the people they could not step outside of it.

Many centuries after David, the great preacher Dwight L. Moody understood the importance of people knowing God's love. He proclaimed: "If we could only make people really believe that God loves them, what a rush we would see for the kingdom of God."

Father, *thank You for loving me, no matter what. Thank You for loving me in all circumstances and in every context. Thank You for loving me, even when I don't love You back. In the name of Your Son, Jesus. Amen.*

**SEARCH THE WORD**

*We can convert the most troubled souls if we can convince them of the depth of God's love.*

Scripture: 1 Chronicles 16:37-43

**Song:** *"When Love Is Found"*

*From this meditation today, I will pray . . .*

Adoration ______________________________

______________________________

______________________________

Confession ______________________________

______________________________

______________________________

Thanksgiving ______________________________

______________________________

______________________________

Supplication ______________________________

______________________________

______________________________

*From this meditation today, I will . . .*

Think ______________________________

______________________________

______________________________

Say ______________________________

______________________________

______________________________

Do ______________________________

______________________________

______________________________

______________________________

______________________________

March 3

# Does God Have You?

*He also chose David His servant, and took him from the sheepfolds* (Psalm 78:70, *New American Standard Bible*).

Scripture: Psalm 78:67-72

Song: *"A Sovereign Protector I Have"*

***From this meditation today, I will pray . . .***

Adoration ______________________________

______________________________

______________________________

Confession ______________________________

______________________________

______________________________

Thanksgiving ______________________________

______________________________

______________________________

Supplication ______________________________

______________________________

______________________________

***From this meditation today, I will . . .***

Think ______________________________

______________________________

______________________________

Say ______________________________

______________________________

______________________________

Do ______________________________

______________________________

______________________________

March 3–9. ***Pam Sneddon*** *and her husband live in Santa Barbara, California, and worship at Montecito Covenant Church.*

Kristen, my daughter-in-law, had been telling bedtime stories to her two children. She was using some of the passages from her Bible study group and read the segment where Ahimelech gives fugitive David a sword. At the word *sword*, Kristen's 2-year-old son, Harry, popped straight up in bed and exclaimed, "I know, the big guy! The big guy had the sword!"

"Do you mean David?" Kristen asked. "No, no," said Harry, spreading his arms as wide as he could, "the big, huge guy had the sword. Go-li-ath." Harry sounded out the syllables carefully, "Go-li-ath had the sword. David, David was the little guy—but he had God!"

Harry, of course, was remembering a previous bedtime story about David and Goliath. As Harry had learned, more important than human strength or size was the extent of one's trust in God. Yes, David had God; or rather, God had David. When God has us, He will take us even through the challenges that are obviously too big for us.

Dear Lord, *help me live with a constant sense of Your sovereignty. How thankful I am—how awed I am—that You chose me and took me from my self-centered life into the service of Your kingdom. In Jesus' name, amen.*

**SPOTLIGHT**

***Next Week's Lesson***

Perhaps David was a "man after God's heart" because he had learned how to listen.

# Pancake Offerings

*Go and tell David my servant, "Thus says the* Lord,
*'You shall not build a house for Me to dwell in'"*
(1 Chronicles 17:4, *New American Standard Bible*).

One Saturday morning as I drove up the road leading to our house, I recognized two bikes lying in the driveway of a new neighbor I hadn't yet met. I stopped just in time to see my 11-year-old twins emerging from the neighbor's house, carrying cans of soda. I asked what they were doing, and Russell answered, "Well, you always told us to welcome new neighbors, so we made something for them."

"What did you make?" I asked.

"Pancakes!"

"And how did you get pancakes here on your bikes?"

"Easy," answered Andrew, demonstrating. "We put them in our pockets!" I tried to picture the new neighbor's reaction to these unwanted gifts, but it must have been gracious, since the twins ended up with sodas.

Sometimes, in my zeal to "do something" for God, I am like my twins. I offer Him my crumpled pancakes, which He hasn't asked for, when He has so much more to give me. If I were a bit more like David, I might check in with God to see if my plans are in line with His plans.

Great Giver, *I'm not only blessed beyond imagination but given the power to accomplish what You've planned for me to do. Through Christ, amen.*

**SEARCH THE WORD**

*Only God can balance what is in our hearts with that which is for the greater good.*

Scripture: 1 Chronicles 17:1-6
Song: *"Holiness Unto the Lord"*

*From this meditation today, I will pray . . .*

Adoration ______________________

______________________

______________________

Confession ______________________

______________________

______________________

Thanksgiving ______________________

______________________

______________________

Supplication ______________________

______________________

______________________

*From this meditation today, I will . . .*

Think ______________________

______________________

______________________

Say ______________________

______________________

______________________

Do ______________________

______________________

______________________

______________________

______________________

# House Plans

*I tell you that the* LORD *will build a house for you*
(1 Chronicles 17:10, *New American Standard Bible*).

Scripture: 1 Chronicles 17:7-10
Song: *"Stepping in the Light"*

***From this meditation today, I will pray . . .***

Adoration ______________________________

______________________________

______________________________

Confession ______________________________

______________________________

______________________________

Thanksgiving ______________________________

______________________________

______________________________

Supplication ______________________________

______________________________

______________________________

***From this meditation today, I will . . .***

Think ______________________________

______________________________

______________________________

Say ______________________________

______________________________

______________________________

Do ______________________________

______________________________

______________________________

______________________________

______________________________

For years, my mother designed plans for the perfect house while our family of six lived in a tiny, two-bedroom apartment. However, what my parents were finally able to afford radically differed from her dream-house plans. We moved into a rambling, 60-year-old Victorian in disrepair, its paint long faded, covered with vines.

How that house shaped our family for years to come! We learned to adapt to strange creakings, faulty electricity, no central heating, and temperamental plumbing. But our big old house also allowed us to spread out, to develop in ways we would never have experienced in the tidy, modern home my mom had envisioned. In fact, it gave us more than a place to live; it gave us a place to *grow.*

David's vision differed from God's. The king envisioned cedar and stone, but God planned another kind of house, one that would stretch all the way to Christ. Often, we, like David, focus so intently on our own designs that we can hardly imagine God's bigger master plan. Yet He faithfully leads us into His better ways, step by step.

Lord of my life, *I am so glad that You are the Master Architect of my future! Let me be like David, quick to change my focus when my plans fall short of Your inestimable glory. In the name of the Father, the Son, and the Holy Spirit, I pray. Amen.*

**SPOTLIGHT**
***Next Week's Lesson***

When life's circumstance is the bitterest is when God's grace tastes the sweetest.

# Imperishable Inheritance

*I will set up one of your descendants after you, who shall be of your sons. . . . He shall build for Me a house, and I will establish his throne forever* (1 Chronicles 17:11, 12, *New American Standard Bible*).

My brother farms some of the same land that our great-grandfather worked in the 19th century. In fact, not long ago, my mother and brother received a plaque for having a family farm that has been operating continuously for a hundred years. A plaque is a small hint of past generations' efforts behind their plows, of men and women working hard under a baking sun. It recalls countless freezing mornings, devastating droughts, and the occasional fearsome tornadoes. The plaque proclaims appreciation for our inheritance, not so much of land, but of our ancestors' hope, strength, and persistence.

As God had promised, David's son Solomon did sit on Israel's throne. But God's promise meant much more. It pointed forward to the birth of Jesus—in His humanity, a descendent of David—whose kingdom is eternal. What a heritage we have in Christ! And our inheritance, as it says in 1 Peter 1:4 *(NASB)* can never disappear or be corrupted in any way. It "will not fade away," but is "reserved in heaven" for us.

Lord, *I am so grateful that through Jesus I have a part in Your promises and that my inheritance in Christ is imperishable. In His name I pray. Amen.*

**SEARCH THE WORD**

*There is no distance that is beyond God's reach.*

Scripture: 1 Chronicles 17:11-15
Song: *"O Come, O Come, Emmanuel"*

*From this meditation today, I will pray . . .*

Adoration ____________________

Confession ____________________

Thanksgiving ____________________

Supplication ____________________

*From this meditation today, I will . . .*

Think ____________________

Say ____________________

Do ____________________

# Not Too Far for God

*David the king went in and sat before the* Lord *and said, "Who am I, O* Lord *God, and what is my house that Thou hast brought me thus far?"* (1 Chronicles 17:16, *New American Standard Bible*).

Scripture: 1 Chronicles 17:16-19
Song: *"Amazing Grace"*

***From this meditation today, I will pray . . .***

Adoration ____________________

Confession ____________________

Thanksgiving ____________________

Supplication ____________________

***From this meditation today, I will . . .***

Think ____________________

Say ____________________

Do ____________________

Most who sing the well-loved hymn *Amazing Grace* probably don't know it was based on 1 Chronicles 17:16 and 17. Nor are many who sing it aware that the author, John Newton, was for many years a slave-ship captain. After his conversion and baptism, though, Newton left the sea, joined the crusade against slavery, and later, in 1764, became an ordained Anglican minister.

Yet, Newton never forgot his sordid past. According to one account, he once exclaimed during a sermon: "My memory is nearly gone, but I remember two things: 'That I am a great sinner, and that Christ is a great Savior!'" Likewise, David, king of all Israel, sat before the Lord in awe at what God had done in his life.

We come from very different experiences, but we too can sit before God. In fact, He calls us constantly to be still and simply acknowledge His lordship in our lives. In our stillness, recalling His greatness, we will be constantly amazed at the grace that has brought us so far into sweet fellowship with Him.

Father, *Your grace is truly amazing. You forgave me by Your Son's blood, releasing me to serve You in joy. Praise You, in Christ's name! Amen.*

**SPOTLIGHT**
***Next Week's Lesson***

God's lifeboat never leaks; when He says He will save, He will!

# Awesome and Waiting

*O* LORD, *there is none like Thee, neither is there any God besides Thee* (1 Chronicles 17:20, *New American Standard Bible*).

Annie, rebelling against her family's faith, defiantly maintained that God couldn't possibly care about her—and she didn't believe in Him anyway. In her junior year of college, Annie became pregnant. Following friends' advice, she went to an abortion clinic. However, while she was waiting, Annie asked herself, "If I don't believe in God, then why does this seem so wrong? . . . God, if you are there, help me!"

Annie later said, "It was as if God were waiting for one small sign of seeking from me, because immediately I heard a voice full of love saying, 'Now I can help you.'"

Annie quickly left the clinic. Even though it was difficult, she parented her little girl, finished college on time, and eventually met a wonderful man who loved God—and cared lovingly for Annie and her daughter.

If you are in a difficult place these days, if you have felt that God just doesn't care about you, know that He is waiting for you. Even one little sign of an open heart is enough for Him. Truly there is no God like the Lord. His love waits to enter with healing and peace, no matter how desperate the situation.

Awesome Lord, *I love You because You first loved me. I am so grateful that You provided a way to come to You through Jesus. In His name, amen.*

**SEARCH THE WORD**

*Here's a three-word sentence you will never hear God say: "I will try."*

Scripture: 1 Chronicles 17:20-22

**Song:** *"Glory to God on High"*

*From this meditation today, I will pray . . .*

Adoration ____________________

____________________

____________________

Confession ____________________

____________________

____________________

Thanksgiving ____________________

____________________

____________________

Supplication ____________________

____________________

____________________

*From this meditation today, I will . . .*

Think ____________________

____________________

____________________

Say ____________________

____________________

____________________

Do ____________________

____________________

____________________

____________________

____________________

March 9

# He Hears

*Thou, O my God, hast revealed to Thy servant that Thou wilt build for him a house; therefore Thy servant hath found courage to pray before Thee* (1 Chronicles 17:25, *New American Standard Bible*).

Scripture: 1 Chronicles 17:23-27
Song: *"Rescue the Perishing"*

***From this meditation today, I will pray . . .***

Adoration ______________________________

Confession ______________________________

Thanksgiving ______________________________

Supplication ______________________________

***From this meditation today, I will . . .***

Think ______________________________

Say ______________________________

Do ______________________________

Craig, a new Christian, was knocked from his boat into the waters off the southern California coast. He struggled for five hours to reach a buoy in the 58-degree water, praying and reciting the 23rd Psalm as he swam. Each time he was about to give up, something floated close enough for him to grab—first a blue balloon, and then a piece of driftwood. Craig finally reached the buoy, only to be repulsed by aggressive sea lions.

As he began to sink, he heard a boat engine and was soon rescued—by his brother. Unknown to Craig, his unmanned boat had covered the 25 miles to Catalina Island, crashing on the rocky shore. There a friend recognized it and called Craig's brother, who started a search.

King David's reliance on God's faithfulness gave him courage to come to God, trusting that God would hear his prayer. God extends the same faithfulness to each person who calls upon Him, whether great king or new Christian. He hears and responds with the gift of eternal life.

*Thank You,* Lord, *for not only revealing Your faithfulness in small ways, but for rescuing me by sending Jesus to pull me out of sin's deep waters. In Him, I have the courage to come before You. And in Him I pray. Amen.*

**SPOTLIGHT**
***Next Week's Lesson***

The Bible is full of God's promises to help in times of trouble. Keep reading!

# Keeping Promises

*The* LORD *swore an oath to David, a sure oath that he will not revoke: "One of your own descendants I will place on your throne"* (Psalm 132:11).

Tears shimmered in Janet's eyes as she fled her father's side. Both hands loaded with clothes, Ben watched her leave, sadness causing his mouth to droop. He then turned from his daughter to his wife. "Martha, you know I wouldn't go if the boss hadn't insisted. I'll try to get back in time for Janet's recital Friday night, but I don't know if I'll be able to get away in time."

As the evening's event approached, Janet alternated between anxiety and anticipation. She had worked so hard for this; it was important for her father to be there. Finally, Mom insisted they had to leave without him.

Ben slid into the saved seat beside his wife, just as Janet's group stepped before the lights. He saw his child's beaming smile as she found both parents' faces in the audience. As the music began and the group of girls stepped across the stage, Ben exchanged looks with his wife, leaned closer to her ear, and whispered, "After all, a promise is a promise."

Father, *as You always keep Your promises, help me to keep the promises I make to others. In the precious name of Jesus I pray. Amen.*

**SEARCH THE WORD**
*If earthly fathers want to give us their best, we can be sure our heavenly Father will do even more.*

Scripture: Psalm 132:1-12
**Song:** *"Standing on the Promises"*

***From this meditation today, I will pray . . .***

Adoration ______________________________

______________________________

______________________________

Confession ______________________________

______________________________

______________________________

Thanksgiving ______________________________

______________________________

______________________________

Supplication ______________________________

______________________________

______________________________

***From this meditation today, I will . . .***

Think ______________________________

______________________________

______________________________

Say ______________________________

______________________________

______________________________

Do ______________________________

______________________________

______________________________

March 10–16. ***Gay Ingram*** *enjoys writing from her home in East Texas. She has published two novels and a book on the history of her hometown, Big Sandy.*

# Plans Gone Amiss

*I had it in my heart to build a house as a place of rest for the ark of the covenant of the* Lord, *for the footstool of our God, and I made plans to build it* (1 Chronicles 28:2).

Scripture: 1 Chronicles 28:1-5
Song: *"Lamp of Our Feet"*

Morgana's son, Terry, stomped past her into the hall. "Since you won't let me go to the mall, now I'll have to call Jim and beg off." Just a minor inconvenience for Terry, right? But what if it were something more important, like a move to another city or the purchase of a new car? How often do we make plans, set things in motion, and then run into a brick wall?

"But I prayed about it," we say. Yes, but did we wait to listen for God's guidance, or did we just go ahead, working out the details, committing ourselves to something before really sensing a clear "Go" from above?

When the ark of the covenant arrived back in Jerusalem, King David was so happy he danced with joy before it. He surely spent lots of time planning the temple, collecting materials, designing a resting place for this ark, one worthy of the Lord's presence. Yet, though Scripture doesn't tell us, I suspect David didn't wait to hear all that God had to say about the building—and the builder—of His temple.

Heavenly Father, *teach me to seek Your wisdom in everything I undertake. Give me patience to wait for a clear word from You. In the name of Your Son, my Savior, I pray. Amen.*

***From this meditation today, I will pray . . .***

Adoration ____________________

Confession ____________________

Thanksgiving ____________________

Supplication ____________________

***From this meditation today, I will . . .***

Think ____________________

Say ____________________

Do ____________________

**SPOTLIGHT**
***Next Week's Lesson***

Learning how to read God's master blueprint helps us build a more perfect temple to His glory.

# Learning a Hard Lesson

*I will establish his kingdom forever if he is unswerving in carrying out my commands and laws, as is being done at this time (1 Chronicles 28:7).*

"You're grounded!" said Don, shaking the traffic ticket in his son's face. "There'll be no driving privileges for two weeks, Son." The young man, Joshua, struggled to keep tears of disappointment in check.

Fighting to control his angry response, the father took a deep breath and reached to place an arm around his son's shoulders. "Josh, you know the rules. With privileges come responsibilities. What if someone had been crossing the street when you ran that red light? It could have been much worse."

"I didn't mean to do it, Dad. We were late for the show, and the streets were empty; not another car was around. I didn't see the police car until he came up behind me, lights flashing."

"Getting caught isn't the problem, Son. Learning to obey the laws of the land is important. And learning to do that can help us learn to obey God too." Don Morgan tightened his grip. "After all, any authority on earth can only operate with His permission. That's something to honor, right?"

Lord, *thank You for giving us civil authorities under Your authority. Please keep our leaders attuned to their responsibilities too! In Jesus' name, amen.*

**SEARCH THE WORD**
*The more we study God's "handbook," the better we understand His desire to protect us.*

Scripture: 1 Chronicles 28:6-8

**Song:** *"Blest Is He Who Loves God's Precepts"*

*From this meditation today, I will pray . . .*

Adoration ______________________________

______________________________

______________________________

Confession ______________________________

______________________________

______________________________

Thanksgiving ______________________________

______________________________

______________________________

Supplication ______________________________

______________________________

______________________________

*From this meditation today, I will . . .*

Think ______________________________

______________________________

______________________________

Say ______________________________

______________________________

______________________________

Do ______________________________

______________________________

______________________________

______________________________

______________________________

March 13

# The Same Hand Provides

*Consider now, for the* Lord *has chosen you to build a temple as a sanctuary. Be strong and do the work* (1 Chronicles 28:10).

Scripture: 1 Chronicles 28:9, 10
Song: *"Jesus, My All in All"*

***From this meditation today, I will pray . . .***

Adoration ______________________________

Confession ______________________________

Thanksgiving ______________________________

Supplication ______________________________

***From this meditation today, I will . . .***

Think ______________________________

Say ______________________________

Do ______________________________

"But I don't feel qualified to chair the Vacation Bible School program. Find someone who's had experience."

"Mrs. Johnson, as your minister, I've been praying about this for some time, and God keeps bringing your name to mind. I recall you volunteered at the library last summer and helped with their Summer Reading Program. Could this be so much different? And you're good with kids; they really like you. I've noticed how they swarm around you during fellowship time. Just say you'll look over the materials—and get back with me in a couple days—OK?"

Open catalogs and manuals spread around her, Amy felt as if she were drowning. Close to tears, she laid her head down softly. Resting her chin on folded hands, she began to pray, "God, this is such a big job . . ."

Then a familiar Bible verse came to mind: "I can do everything through him who gives me strength"(Philippians 4:13). Maybe, she thought, it wasn't such an impossible task after all.

Father God, *I know You empower those whom You call for Your purposes. Help me to remember to look to You for strength and wisdom when I feel overwhelmed. For I know Your hand that points the way is the same hand that provides the way. In Christ's holy name I pray. Amen.*

**SPOTLIGHT**
***Next Week's Lesson***

God doesn't expect us to "do it all," but He does want us to listen for His direction.

# Help When You Need It

*"All this," David said, "I have in writing from the hand of the* Lord *upon me, and he gave me understanding in all the details of the plan"* (1 Chronicles 28:19).

Darrell stepped back and glared at his old tractor. *Why wouldn't that crazy thing run*? He'd tinkered with every part he could get his hands on. And still, the tired engine would just crank over, give a few gasps, and die.

Disgusted with his failed efforts, Darrell packed up his tools and walked away. Later that day, his friend Sam stopped by. Darrell told him about his tractor trials. So they walked, coffee cups in hand, toward the stubborn machine. "I just don't know what else to do. And I sure don't know where I'll find the money for a new tractor."

Sam nodded his head, deep in thought. "Did you set the spark plugs to spec?" Darrell replied in the affirmative. "You know, these old engines get worn after a while," Sam said. "How about adjusting to allow for some wear?" Darrell stopped in his tracks. "You know, Sam, that just might do the trick. I think God brought you over today just to give me that information."

Holy Spirit, *You are the promise of God to be teacher of all things. Even before I attempt my own efforts, help me to remember to turn first to You. Teach me to seek Your wisdom whenever I have a problem, for the work of the kingdom is Yours—and best done in Your way! In the name of God the Father, Son, and Holy Spirit, amen.*

**SEARCH THE WORD**

*Some of God's most complex plans come with very simple and direct instructions.*

Scripture: 1 Chronicles 28:11-19

**Song:** *"Did You Think to Pray?"*

*From this meditation today, I will pray . . .*

Adoration ______________________

______________________

______________________

Confession ______________________

______________________

______________________

Thanksgiving ______________________

______________________

______________________

Supplication ______________________

______________________

______________________

*From this meditation today, I will . . .*

Think ______________________

______________________

______________________

Say ______________________

______________________

______________________

Do ______________________

______________________

______________________

______________________

______________________

# He Provides the Help

*The divisions of the priests and Levites are ready for all the work on the temple of God, and every willing man skilled in any craft will help you in all the work* (1 Chronicles 28:21).

Scripture: 1 Chronicles 28:20, 21
**Song:** *"Help Somebody Today"*

***From this meditation today, I will pray . . .***

Adoration ______________________________

Confession ______________________________

Thanksgiving ______________________________

Supplication ______________________________

***From this meditation today, I will . . .***

Think ______________________________

Say ______________________________

Do ______________________________

"If I could just figure out how to finish off those wings." Gloria reached for another cookie and sipped her hot chocolate. This week's Bible study had produced a lively discussion, and the ladies continued their conversation in the kitchen. "What seems to be your problem?" asked Jane as she settled into the chair beside Gloria.

"Well, I'm working on Margaret's angel costume for the Christmas pageant, but I can't come up with some decent wings."

"I know who can help you," Sally said across the table. "Go to Walden's and talk to the lady in fabrics. She's a whiz. There isn't anything she can't do."

"That's true," said Jane. "She figured out how to attach a veil to my daughter's bridal headpiece last summer. I don't know how many times I've asked for her help. The whole wedding came together like a dream." Gloria smiled her thanks to her friends, as she reached for another cookie. And she silently gave thanks to the Lord for meeting her need.

Father, *in ancient days King David told his son how You would meet his every need in carrying out Your will. Thank You for this same concern for each need in my own life. How awesome You are! Through Christ, amen.*

**SPOTLIGHT**
***Next Week's Lesson***

God's church is like an altar; each stone provides part of the structure that brings praise to Him.

# Preparing Our Dwelling Place

*The* LORD *has chosen Zion, he has desired it for his dwelling* (Psalm 132:13).

Our lease would expire soon, and we had to find a new place that suited our plans. For months we'd searched for property to buy, consulting realtors, scanning ads, and chasing down leads. All to no avail. We were running out of time. Then while waiting on a dryer load, I scanned the laundromat's bulletin board. A handwritten note caught my attention . . . And the first time I stepped onto that piece of land, I knew I was home.

We were blessed in being able to choose our place of retirement. This will be our dwelling place for the rest of our lives, God willing.

God has a dwelling place too! First Corinthians 3:16 tells us that we are God's temple, that His Spirit dwells in us. God chose us and called us to be the embodied evidence of His reality in the world. Therefore, each day as I look about this beautiful place God prepared for us, I ask His help in keeping His own dwelling place worthy of His abiding presence.

Father, *I thank You for sending the Holy Spirit to indwell me, to be my comforter and guide. Remind me, too, that I am Your representative in my world, Your ambassador among my neighbors. Help me show forth Your love in all I do and say. I pray this prayer in the name of Jesus, my merciful Savior and Lord. Amen.*

**SEARCH THE WORD**

*We will find peace when we allow God to place us where He wants us to be.*

Scripture: Psalm 132:13-18

Song: *"Zion, Founded on the Mountains"*

*From this meditation today, I will pray . . .*

Adoration ______________________________

______________________________

______________________________

Confession ______________________________

______________________________

______________________________

Thanksgiving ______________________________

______________________________

______________________________

Supplication ______________________________

______________________________

______________________________

*From this meditation today, I will . . .*

Think ______________________________

______________________________

______________________________

Say ______________________________

______________________________

______________________________

Do ______________________________

______________________________

______________________________

______________________________

______________________________

March 17

# God's Name

*I know that the* LORD *is great, that our* Lord *is greater than all gods. The* LORD *does whatever pleases him, in the heavens and on the earth, in the seas and all their depths* (Psalm 135:5, 6).

Scripture: Psalm 135:1-5

Song: *"Jesus, Name Above All Names"*

***From this meditation today, I will pray . . .***

Adoration ______________________________

______________________________

______________________________

Confession ______________________________

______________________________

______________________________

Thanksgiving ______________________________

______________________________

______________________________

Supplication ______________________________

______________________________

______________________________

***From this meditation today, I will . . .***

Think ______________________________

______________________________

______________________________

Say ______________________________

______________________________

______________________________

Do ______________________________

______________________________

______________________________

March 17–23. ***Sally Jadlow*** *writes poetry and short stories, serves in Kansas City as a chaplain to corporations, and teaches creative writing at a Christian school.*

A lady in our study group asked, "Why not call Jesus by the name of Allah or Buddha? They're just other names for God, right?"

"If I called my husband another name," came my reply, "would he be upset?"

"Of course. You're his wife. You should know his name," she said. I nodded. "God has told us His names in the Bible. He never identified himself as Allah or Buddha. Why should we call Him something He has not called himself?"

From the very beginning, Christianity has had to challenge what is known as "syncretism"—the belief that somehow all claims to truth have equal value and must be equally accepted. Yet the Scriptures tell us that one God is greater than all other gods. And we know who this one is: the God and Father of our Lord Jesus Christ.

Almighty God, *may I honor You and Your name with heartfelt adoration, realizing You are the God above all gods, the only one worthy of my praise. In the name of Your Son, my Savior, I pray. Amen.*

**SPOTLIGHT**

***Next Week's Lesson***

Study the names of God and you will discover why He alone can meet your every need.

# What's in Your Heart?

*My father David had it in his heart to build a temple for the Name of the* LORD, *the God of Israel* (2 Chronicles 6:7).

Long ago I asked the Lord to help me make a list of the qualities He wanted for my four children's future spouses. Periodically I prayed this list back to God—reminding Him, in a sense, of the list He gave me. Eighteen years separate the first from the last child. As the children grew up, they found the persons described on the list. Today, three are married with children; one to go.

The list didn't call for good looks or big bank accounts, but for good helpmates. It asked for the establishment of godly homes where children are loved and nurtured. It sought a home environment where every family member would hear and heed God's voice.

I truly believe the Lord put these thoughts into my heart, just as He put it into David's heart to build a beautiful temple for Him. I may not live to see that last child marry, but I know I can trust God to work in his life. David didn't live to see the finished temple, but he fervently aspired to lay the groundwork for what was to come. And that attitude was critical. As mystic James Allen said: "You will become as small as your controlling desire, as great as your dominant aspiration."

Father God, *may I listen for Your direction as I pray, go with Your flow, and make Your heart glad in all my ways. In Jesus' name, amen.*

**SEARCH THE WORD**

*We are not expected to bring all God's plans to completion, only to be part of His process.*

Scripture: 2 Chronicles 6:1-11

Song: *"Sweet Will of God"*

***From this meditation today, I will pray . . .***

Adoration ______________________

______________________

______________________

Confession ______________________

______________________

______________________

Thanksgiving ______________________

______________________

______________________

Supplication ______________________

______________________

______________________

***From this meditation today, I will . . .***

Think ______________________

______________________

______________________

Say ______________________

______________________

______________________

Do ______________________

______________________

______________________

______________________

______________________

# I Promise

*O* Lord, *the God of Israel, there is no god like Thee in heaven or on earth, keeping covenant and showing lovingkindness to Thy servants who walk before Thee with all their heart*
(2 Chronicles 6:14, *New American Standard Bible*).

Scripture: 2 Chronicles 6:12-17
**Song:** *"O Jesus, I Have Promised"*

***From this meditation today, I will pray . . .***

Adoration ______________________

Confession ______________________

Thanksgiving ______________________

Supplication ______________________

***From this meditation today, I will . . .***

Think ______________________

Say ______________________

Do ______________________

"I'm really in a pinch. I promise I'll pay you back on payday," my coworker says. Payday comes. I receive excuses . . . but no repayment.

"Mom, please let me have a puppy. I promise I'll take care of it." But once the puppy grows up, I become its constant caretaker.

"If you'll take the chairmanship, I promise I'll be there to back you up, one hundred percent." The support dwindles to nearly zero by the end of my term of office.

I am guilty of the same kinds of promise-breaking, though. No matter how sincere I may be when I proclaim a promise, I sometimes lose heart before I can fulfill my best intentions.

God is different. He is absolutely, eternally trustworthy. Yet when He promises, He sometimes attaches a condition. And that's where the problem comes in. I'm fickle. I don't have the power to complete my part unless I rely on Him for the strength of heart to carry on to the end. You see, what God *calls* me to, He gives me the *strength* to do.

Faithful One, *help me to follow through on what I have promised as I reach out and receive Your strength to finish well. In Jesus' name, amen.*

**SPOTLIGHT**
***Next Week's Lesson***

We are judged not by how many promises we make, but by how many we keep.

# Hearing, Heart to Heart

*Hear Thou from heaven Thy dwelling place, and forgive, and render to each according to all his ways, whose heart Thou knowest for Thou alone dost know the hearts of the sons of men, that they may fear Thee, to walk in Thy ways as long as they live in the land which Thou hast given to our fathers* (2 Chronicles 6:30, 31, *New American Standard Bible*).

I watch a robin hop over the spring grass in my backyard. He pauses, cocks his head, and listens. With a quick peck, he leans back and pulls a worm out of the ground.

I can't imagine having ears so sharp they can hear a worm crawling underground! God's ears are even better than that, though. He can hear my prayers all the way from earth to Heaven, even if those prayers are unspoken (for He knows my heart, and prayer is more about my open, longing heart than about the words I compose).

God wants to hear from me, heart to heart. Therefore, today I will make time to quiet my heart before Him that He may say:

*"My child, come and enter in,*
*unburden your soul of cares and sin.*
*I long to hear from you today.*
*Ask me; I'll find a way."*

Lord, *forgive me when I cling to my problems, assuming You're uninterested. Reconnect me today to Your constant presence. Through Christ, amen.*

**SEARCH THE WORD**

*Since God keeps all of His promises, we can have confidence in everything else He tells us.*

Scripture: 2 Chronicles 6:18-31

**Song:** *"Sweet Hour of Prayer"*

***From this meditation today, I will pray . . .***

Adoration ______________________________

______________________________

______________________________

Confession ______________________________

______________________________

______________________________

Thanksgiving ______________________________

______________________________

______________________________

Supplication ______________________________

______________________________

______________________________

***From this meditation today, I will . . .***

Think ______________________________

______________________________

______________________________

Say ______________________________

______________________________

______________________________

Do ______________________________

______________________________

______________________________

______________________________

______________________________

March 21

# Homecoming

*He got up and came to his father. But while he was still a long way off, his father saw him, and felt compassion for him, and ran and embraced him, and kissed him. And the son said to him, "Father, I have sinned against heaven and in your sight; I am no longer worthy to be called your son"* (Luke 15:20, 21, *New American Standard Bible*).

Scripture: 2 Chronicles 6:36-39
Song: *"Nearer, My God, to Thee"*

***From this meditation today, I will pray . . .***

Adoration ______________________________

Confession ______________________________

Thanksgiving ______________________________

Supplication ______________________________

***From this meditation today, I will . . .***

Think ______________________________

Say ______________________________

Do ______________________________

At times I have gone into the far land of unforgiveness, greed, or anger. The only solution: name the land, ask God for forgiveness, and come home. Then my prayers sound like this . . .

"Father, You see me from afar. You run toward me, throw Your arms around me, and call for celebration. My heart rejoices in Your strong embrace. You declare I am no longer a slave, but a reinstated child.

"Your mercy flows like honey; Your smile, like sunshine. You wipe away my tears and dress me in fine linen, slipping the ring of rulership on my finger.

"Who am I that You should do this for me? Surely, Your mercy extends to even my generation. I bow before You, who stays closer than a brother, and then I look into Your eyes. My inmost being melts in gratitude before You, my Savior, my Lord, my God.

"And I hear You say, 'Welcome home, child.'"

Father, *thank You for Your constant vigilance for my return—and for giving Your Son to provide a way home for me. In His name I pray. Amen.*

**SPOTLIGHT**
***Next Week's Lesson***

A beautiful home is constructed with more than fine materials; it is framed with the mercy of Jesus.

# His Resting Place

*Arise, O* LORD *God, to Thy resting place*
(2 Chronicles 6:41, *New American Standard Bible*).

Imagine being an Israelite surrounded by all the lavish architectural workmanship on the day when Solomon dedicated the temple. Over here, intricately worked solid brass pillars more than 40' high. There, a beautifully fashioned gold overlay box with angels adorning the top. On the far wall, two golden lamp stands created by the finest craftsmen.

On that day, Solomon invited the Lord to come dwell in the Holy of Holies, the divine "resting place." And God graciously answered Solomon's prayer; He filled the temple with His presence in the form of a glory cloud.

In contrast, when Jesus came to earth in a body, He didn't live in a gilded temple. He had no place to lay His head in the very world He'd created. Even after death, He lay in a borrowed tomb.

Now the Lord has risen from the dead—and is still looking for a place to reside. Today Jesus asks, "May I come make my home inside your heart? May I settle in and abide there?"

Dear heavenly Father, *make my heart Your resting place. May Your roots sink down deep into me. Let nothing tear me away from You, and help me avoid any distraction that arranges my priorities apart from the kingdom work You've given me. In the name of Jesus, amen.*

**SEARCH THE WORD**

*The adage says, "Home is where the heart is." That's all the more reason for Jesus to live there.*

Scripture: 2 Chronicles 6:40-42

Song: *"You Are Awesome in This Place"*

***From this meditation today, I will pray . . .***

Adoration ____________________

____________________

____________________

Confession ____________________

____________________

____________________

Thanksgiving ____________________

____________________

____________________

Supplication ____________________

____________________

____________________

***From this meditation today, I will . . .***

Think ____________________

____________________

____________________

Say ____________________

____________________

____________________

Do ____________________

____________________

____________________

____________________

____________________

March 23

# His Power

*I am sending forth the promise of My Father upon you; but you are to stay in the city until you are clothed with power from on high* (Luke 24:49, *New American Standard Bible*).

Scripture: Luke 24:44-49

Song: *"Come, Holy Spirit"*

*From this meditation today, I will pray . . .*

Adoration ____________________

____________________

____________________

Confession ____________________

____________________

____________________

Thanksgiving ____________________

____________________

____________________

Supplication ____________________

____________________

____________________

*From this meditation today, I will . . .*

Think ____________________

____________________

____________________

Say ____________________

____________________

____________________

Do ____________________

____________________

____________________

____________________

____________________

In 1955, I read in *Life* magazine about the five missionaries martyred while they ministered to the Waodani Indians in Ecuador's eastern rainforest. I was a young Christian, and I wondered how people could have the faith to go into such a hostile place, spurning the threat of death, to preach the gospel.

Years later, I understood: They didn't rely on their own strength. They had the power of the Holy Spirit, just as the first disciples did. After Jesus walked on this earth with His followers for three years, He told them they'd receive the promised Holy Spirit to guide them after His resurrection and ascension to Heaven. Obedient, they waited until the Day of Pentecost for the Holy Spirit to come into them in fullness. Then they were ready to be Jesus' witnesses, even to death.

You and I need the Holy Spirit operating in our lives today, just as the first disciples did. Thankfully, once we are baptized, the Spirit comes to dwell within us, empowering us to serve in the deepest jungles—or in our neighbor's living room.

Father, *thanks for sending Your Holy Spirit that I may be an effective witness in any circumstance You may bring my way. In Jesus' name, amen.*

**SPOTLIGHT**

***Next Week's Lesson***

Peace is more than a state of mind. It is the assurance that Jesus is leading us.

# Freedom Through Obedience

*I run in the path of your commands, for you have set my heart free* (Psalm 119:32).

My kids, probably like yours, always wanted to do things their way. I remember watching my 2-year-old son as he brushed his teeth one day. This was back in the days when I'd need to help him, so our routine was that he would start the process and I would finish it, or vice versa. On this particular day, I said "How about if I start, and you finish?" He carefully thought about it and then replied firmly, "No, *you* start and I'll finish!"

As children, we think we know it all. However, if you're like me, as a "maturing" adult, I have become painfully aware of how limited my knowledge is. I've also experienced how wonderfully God directs our paths and learned that there is no need to run from Him. In fact, these days, instead of running from His leading, I yearn for it; I seek it.

It's in that safe place that I find the most perfect peace and joy. Strangely, obedience sets my heart free; liberty flows amidst a yielding to His commands.

Lord, *thank You for Your patience with me as I struggle to find my way in this world. And thank You for embracing me when I do eventually come running into Your wide-open arms. I pray in Jesus' holy name. Amen.*

**SEARCH THE WORD**

*Daily I must commit myself to sing, "Where He leads me, I will follow."*

Scripture: Psalm 119:25-32

Song: *"Free from the Law"*

*From this meditation today, I will pray . . .*

Adoration ______________________________

______________________________

______________________________

Confession ______________________________

______________________________

______________________________

Thanksgiving ______________________________

______________________________

______________________________

Supplication ______________________________

______________________________

______________________________

*From this meditation today, I will . . .*

Think ______________________________

______________________________

______________________________

Say ______________________________

______________________________

______________________________

Do ______________________________

______________________________

______________________________

March 24–30. ***Maralee Parker*** *markets adult degree programs at a Christian college in addition to helping plan worship services at her church.*

March 25

# So Subtle!

*In his twelfth year he began to purge Judah and Jerusalem of high places, Asherah poles, carved idols and cast images* (2 Chronicles 34:3).

Scripture: 2 Chronicles 34:1-7

Song: *"I Would Be True"*

***From this meditation today, I will pray . . .***

Adoration ______________________________

______________________________

______________________________

Confession ______________________________

______________________________

______________________________

Thanksgiving ______________________________

______________________________

______________________________

Supplication ______________________________

______________________________

______________________________

***From this meditation today, I will . . .***

Think ______________________________

______________________________

______________________________

Say ______________________________

______________________________

______________________________

Do ______________________________

______________________________

______________________________

______________________________

______________________________

Ever played the dictionary game? It's a competition in which participants create fake definitions for a word and then read them aloud—including the correct one. They then compete to determine which definition is true amid the false. To score points and win, a good player will create a unique and convincing, close-to-true definition to distract the other players from what is genuinely correct.

King Josiah didn't play the dictionary game, of course, but he was responsible for proclaiming what was true among many false distractions. Twelve years into his rule, he saw his people worshiping powerless idols. His response? He destroyed the idols, eliminating the distractions, and turned the people's eyes to the one true God.

In our day, idolatry is ever so subtle and subversive. Most of us won't turn from the Lord completely; we'll steer clear of the obvious falsities around us. But we may well be distracted by a few choice half-truths—just enough to live a thoroughly lukewarm Christian life. Perhaps that is enough to make the god of this world quite happy.

Lord, *I live in a world filled with distractions and subtle heresies. Give me a discerning heart, filled with Your wisdom! In Jesus' name, amen.*

**SPOTLIGHT**

***Next Week's Lesson***

One who truly cares will remove all of life's distractions and debris to expose the truth.

# Mom Too

*The men did the work faithfully*
(2 Chronicles 34:12).

I remember it well. The special Bible had a beautiful rendition of Jesus with children on its cover, as well as many colorful pictures inside. A small gold cross hung from the zipper that enclosed it.

Using her meager factory wages, our Primary Department Sunday school teacher had sacrificially purchased five of these Bibles to present to her students. This woman dedicated herself to telling kids of God's love for them. Not only did she faithfully take her own children to church regularly, she determined to help others learn of Him.

She faithfully served in our little country church in whatever way she could. Even with her limited 8th-grade education, she could still invite children to Sunday school. She could still drive them to church. She could still buy a few Bibles with a picture of Jesus-and-the-children on the cover. She could still serve God.

Just like the men in today's Scripture reading, this humble woman quietly and faithfully served God in any way she could. She also built a solid legacy in the process, as that faithful woman was my mother.

Father, *how thankful I am for the long train of dedicated men and women who have served you faithfully from the very beginnings of the church! May I someday be added to that marvelous list. Through Christ, amen.*

**SEARCH THE WORD**

*A sincere Christian servant sees sacrifice as a secure investment in eternity.*

Scripture: 2 Chronicles 34:8-18
Song: *"Find Us Faithful"*

***From this meditation today, I will pray . . .***

Adoration ______________________

______________________

______________________

Confession ______________________

______________________

______________________

Thanksgiving ______________________

______________________

______________________

Supplication ______________________

______________________

______________________

***From this meditation today, I will . . .***

Think ______________________

______________________

______________________

Say ______________________

______________________

______________________

Do ______________________

______________________

______________________

______________________

______________________

March 27

# Personal Faith

*Great is the* Lord*'s anger that is poured out on us because our fathers have not kept the word of the* Lord (2 Chronicles 34:21).

Scripture: 2 Chronicles 34:19-21

Song: *"Gracious God, My Heart Renew"*

Severe hearing loss is hereditary on my father's side of the family. He had 12 siblings, and many of them shared this "family curse."

My brother also inherited it. He was sent to a school for the deaf as a 6-year-old, where he learned how to read lips.

I have cousins whose children inherited this disability, and I also have second cousins whose children have inherited it. My son hasn't had children yet, but I do worry about them.

Thus far, deafness has missed me personally, and I am thankful for that. But of greater concern to me than my physical heredity is my spiritual heritage. Unlike Josiah, I've truly benefited from my family's good spiritual influence over the years. But unless I personally accept Jesus' sacrificial death on the cross and receive His forgiveness and salvation, I will miss out on that blessing altogether. Whether or not I benefit from my spiritual heritage depends upon my personal choice.

God, *thank You for providing eternal life through Jesus. I am grateful for the opportunity to accept Him as my Savior. I rejoice in knowing that Christ has paid the full penalty for my sins. In His precious name, amen.*

*From this meditation today, I will pray . . .*

Adoration ______________________

Confession ______________________

Thanksgiving ______________________

Supplication ______________________

*From this meditation today, I will . . .*

Think ______________________

Say ______________________

Do ______________________

**SPOTLIGHT**

***Next Week's Lesson***

Eternal life comes not from what we inherit or achieve, but from the one in whom we believe.

# Jesus, PhD?

*Because your heart was responsive and you humbled yourself before God . . . I have heard you, declares the* LORD (2 Chronicles 34:27).

At work this week, I overheard some coworkers energetically discussing a problem in the hall outside of my office. One person said, "Your opinion doesn't count until you have a doctorate after your name." I couldn't believe what I was hearing! What an arrogant comment (coming from someone with a doctorate, actually).

Not a great way to win friends and influence people. But worse, it's an ineffective way to represent Jesus, isn't it? I think of how our Savior interacted so intimately with the lowliest of people in His day: the woman at the well; the woman who poured expensive perfume on His feet; Zacchaeus, the tax collector, with whom no one else would associate.

In further humble service, Christ washed His own disciples' feet, instead of the other way around. Time after time, Jesus lived out a perfect example of how to humble ourselves before God—with no PhD required.

Almighty and everlasting God, *may my heart be humble, realizing that everything I have is from You. Every breath I breathe is because of You. Every day I live is because You've willed it to be so. I praise You and humbly thank You for Your love for me, in spite of my undeserving ways. In the holy name of Jesus, my Lord and Savior, I pray. Amen.*

**SEARCH THE WORD**

*Eyes of faith see eternity, "I's" of arrogance see no farther than themselves.*

Scripture: 2 Chronicles 34:22-28

Song: *"Blest Are the Humble Souls That See"*

***From this meditation today, I will pray . . .***

Adoration ______________________________

Confession ______________________________

Thanksgiving ______________________________

Supplication ______________________________

***From this meditation today, I will . . .***

Think ______________________________

Say ______________________________

Do ______________________________

March 29

# Heart and Soul

*The king stood by his pillar and renewed the covenant in the presence of the* LORD*—to follow the* LORD *and keep his commands, regulations and decrees with all his heart* (2 Chronicles 34:31).

Scripture: 2 Chronicles 34:29-33

Song: *"I Surrender All"*

***From this meditation today, I will pray . . .***

Adoration ______________________________

______________________________

______________________________

Confession ______________________________

______________________________

______________________________

Thanksgiving ______________________________

______________________________

______________________________

Supplication ______________________________

______________________________

______________________________

***From this meditation today, I will . . .***

Think ______________________________

______________________________

______________________________

Say ______________________________

______________________________

______________________________

Do ______________________________

______________________________

______________________________

______________________________

______________________________

I was 15 years old, attending a Christian summer camp for the very first time. Coming from a small rural church with few teens, I thought I'd entered Heaven—along with 150 other young people.

I had such great fun that week! I sang, I swam, I ate, I made lifelong friends. More importantly, I was challenged to deepen my faith in the most practical ways. The special speaker for the week asked, "Whose side will you choose to be on? Will it be God's side, or . . . the other side? You can't walk the fence. You must choose."

That was exactly what I had been doing—walking the fence. I was the perfect Christian young lady on Sundays when I attended church, and the typical self-centered teenager when in school. Not surprisingly, few of my schoolmates knew I was a Christian.

In our Scripture reading today, King Josiah renewed His commitment to follow the Lord with all of his heart and soul. That week at camp, I did the same. And I haven't looked back since.

Lord, *keep before me this day the precious decrees of Your goodness and love that come to me in the Scriptures. Thank You, in Jesus' name. Amen.*

**SPOTLIGHT**

***Next Week's Lesson***

Others can't see Jesus in us until we put Him front and center in our lives.

# Safe and Sound

*Turn my eyes away from worthless things*
(Psalm 119:37).

Most autistic people have a hard time looking into another person's eyes. They find it quite difficult and threatening. My daughter has Asperger's syndrome, a high functioning form of autism. She keeps her gaze down when she's with others, rarely looking someone in the eye. That usually only happens when she starts feeling emotionally "safe" with someone.

Today's Scripture reading reminds us to turn our eyes to God's Word for our guidance in daily life. There God reveals what is right and wrong, and what will bring us genuine joy. Turning our eyes from the temporary thrills of this world to the eternal purposes of God is a sure way to stay spiritually "safe," as it will keep our priorities in good order.

It's comforting to know that we can "gaze" into God's heart, isn't it? We do it through prayer, through studying His Word, through listening to that still, small voice as the Holy Spirit guides us through each day. We can feel safe, too, in His returning gaze, knowing that He is completely trustworthy.

My loving heavenly Father, *I lift my eyes up to the hills. Where does my help come from? It comes from You, the creator of Heaven and earth. Please remind me that I am safe, forever, in Your care. I pray this prayer in the name of Jesus, my merciful Savior and Lord. Amen.*

**SEARCH THE WORD**

*Focus your eyes on Jesus and keep all else in your peripheral vision.*

Scripture: Psalm 119:33-40
Song: *"Look to the Lamb of God"*

***From this meditation today, I will pray . . .***

Adoration ______________________________

______________________________

______________________________

Confession ______________________________

______________________________

______________________________

Thanksgiving ______________________________

______________________________

______________________________

Supplication ______________________________

______________________________

______________________________

***From this meditation today, I will . . .***

Think ______________________________

______________________________

______________________________

Say ______________________________

______________________________

______________________________

Do ______________________________

______________________________

______________________________

______________________________

______________________________

March 31

# Waiting to Hear from Us

*O* LORD, *I call to you; come quickly to me.*
*Hear my voice when I call to you*
(Psalm 141:1).

Scripture: Psalm 141:1-4

Song: *"I Will Call Upon the Lord"*

***From this meditation today, I will pray . . .***

Adoration ______________________________

______________________________

______________________________

Confession ______________________________

______________________________

______________________________

Thanksgiving ______________________________

______________________________

______________________________

Supplication ______________________________

______________________________

______________________________

***From this meditation today, I will . . .***

Think ______________________________

______________________________

______________________________

Say ______________________________

______________________________

______________________________

Do ______________________________

______________________________

______________________________

March 31. ***Dan Nicksich*** *serves as senior minister of First Christian Church, Somerset, Pennsylvania. He and wife Donna have two sons, Andrew and Derek.*

A.W. Tozer once suggested that the Christian is a rather odd person: "He feels supreme love for One whom he has never seen; talks familiarly every day to Someone he cannot see; expects to go to Heaven on the virtue of Another; empties himself in order to be full; admits he is wrong so he can be declared right; goes down in order to get up; is strongest when he is weakest; richest when he is poorest and happiest when he feels the worst."

We understand David's prayer in similar, paradoxical fashion. We ask the One who is already here to "come" to us. We ask the One who never slumbers, the One who already knows our every need, to "hear" us as we call to Him. Yet David understands that *God wants to hear from us.* He delights in our expressions of dependence upon Him.

The power is in the appeal. God wants to hear from you, is patiently *waiting* to hear from you. He delights in those who take the time to seek His favor, who call upon Him, knowing He hears and answers.

O Lord, *I thank You for your comforting presence and that I can turn to You whenever I need. Keep me attentive to Your gentle responses as You guide me each step along Your paths of peace. In Jesus' name, amen.*

**SPOTLIGHT**

***Next Week's Lesson***

The greatest gains in life's journeys come when we lose ourselves and allow God to give the directions.

# April

# THE COVENANT IN EXILE

*O Lord, hear my voice. Let your ears be attentive to my cry for mercy.*
—Psalm 130:2

*Photo © Jupiterimage*

April 1

# Evil Empire

*The* LORD *delivered Jehoiakim king of Judah into his hand, along with some of the articles from the temple of God* (Daniel 1:2).

Scripture: Daniel 1:1, 2
Song: *"We Will Glorify"*

***From this meditation today, I will pray . . .***

Adoration ______________________________

Confession ______________________________

Thanksgiving ______________________________

Supplication ______________________________

***From this meditation today, I will . . .***

Think ______________________________

Say ______________________________

Do ______________________________

April 1–6. ***Dan Nicksich*** *serves as senior minister of First Christian Church, Somerset, Pennsylvania. He and his wife Donna have two sons, Andrew and Derek.*

The New York Yankees are one of the most successful sports franchises ever. That means sports fans either love 'em or hate 'em. Detractors have dubbed them "The Evil Empire"; nothing good ever comes from the Yankees.

Amazingly, we sometimes see God using evil empires for His good purposes. For instance, a stubborn, pagan Pharaoh arose to his position so that God could demonstrate His power. In another case, the prophet Habakkuk discovered that vicious Babylonians would actually be God's instrument to deal with evil in the land of Israel. In the Gospels, Jesus told Pilate that his power to pronounce a death sentence could only come from above.

So we shouldn't be surprised that, in Daniel's day, God used Nebuchadnezzar to discipline his wayward people. To the human eye, Israel fell to a greater kingdom. But Scripture affirms that the Lord himself remained in control. This account gives us a wonderful personal application: Never be quick to assume that evil is winning the day.

Father, *I marvel at how You use the unwilling, the uncaring, even the ones adamantly opposed to You. What a sovereign God! Through Christ, amen.*

**SPOTLIGHT**
***Next Week's Lesson***
God uses both sinners and saints for His purposes.

# Worthy by His Grace

*Bring . . . young men without any physical defect, handsome, showing aptitude for every kind of learning, well informed, quick to understand, and qualified to serve in the king's palace* (Daniel 1:3, 4).

Mighty Moses thought he couldn't speak in public. The great King David's brothers once ridiculed him as a child and tried to send him home. And valiant warrior Gideon initially saw himself as the weakest of all the Israelites.

In our Scripture passage today, Daniel, Hananiah, Mishael, and Azariah were selected for training in order to enter the Babylonian king's service. Only those who met the highest physical and intellectual standards were chosen. So imagine the boost to one's self-esteem should he "get the call."

We often doubt ourselves, our abilities, or our worthiness to serve God. Yet God sees all that is hidden from our view. He looks past outward appearances and into our hearts. Even so, He does not save us based on our potential or any human quality within us. He calls us by pure grace and prepares us for His service through the working of His Spirit within us. Bottom line: We are "worthy" only as He makes us so.

Lord, *You have selected and gifted each of us for Your service. No ability, no talent, no matter how meager it may seem, is insignificant. Help me to use all that You have given me for Your glory alone. In Jesus' name, amen.*

**SEARCH THE WORD**

*Success is determined by how you partner with God in His service.*

Scripture: Daniel 1:3-7

Song: *"In the Service of the King"*

*From this meditation today, I will pray . . .*

Adoration ____________________

____________________

____________________

Confession ____________________

____________________

____________________

Thanksgiving ____________________

____________________

____________________

Supplication ____________________

____________________

____________________

*From this meditation today, I will . . .*

Think ____________________

____________________

____________________

Say ____________________

____________________

____________________

Do ____________________

____________________

____________________

____________________

____________________

April 3

# Resolved!

*Daniel resolved not to defile himself with the royal food and wine, and he asked the chief official for permission not to defile himself this way* (Daniel 1:8).

Scripture: Daniel 1:8-10

Song: *"Dare to Be a Daniel"*

*From this meditation today, I will pray . . .*

Adoration ______________________________

______________________________

______________________________

Confession ______________________________

______________________________

______________________________

Thanksgiving ______________________________

______________________________

______________________________

Supplication ______________________________

______________________________

______________________________

*From this meditation today, I will . . .*

Think ______________________________

______________________________

______________________________

Say ______________________________

______________________________

______________________________

Do ______________________________

______________________________

______________________________

______________________________

______________________________

It has been estimated that most New Year's resolutions are broken within a few short days. Some apparently don't even last the night! But not so with Daniel. He resolved not to defile himself with any food God had declared unclean, and he stuck to it. For him, even the demands of a king took second place to the laws of God.

God's people have always realized that sin defiles them in the sight of God and weakens their fellowship with Him. There really are no justifications that might excuse us from obedience to our loving Lord. And that is good—for our own good—because of sin's destructive power.

In the book of Genesis, Joseph faced temptation, day after day, from Potiphar's wife. But he resolved not to sin against God.

Let us consider today: What special circumstances tend to make it difficult for us to obey God? Do certain acquaintances bring temptations with them? Do certain environments put us at risk? May we rightly proceed with caution amidst circumstances that will try our souls. Thus may our resolve never be defiled.

Lord, *I can be weak, easily tempted, so quick to make poor choices. May the resolve of Daniel inspire me to stand firm this day. In Jesus' name, amen.*

**SPOTLIGHT**

***Next Week's Lesson***

It's better not to make a promise than to break a promise.

# Daniel: A +

*Please test your servants for ten days:*
*Give us nothing but vegetables to eat and water to drink*
(Daniel 1:12).

While some may enjoy watching a film like *Arachnophobia,* one friend of mine can't even stand to watch the previews. For someone who actually suffers from that particular phobia, there's no entertainment value in watching marauding spiders intent on inflicting mayhem. But the people I feel for most are those stricken with testophobia. Nothing fancy in this word; it's exactly what it sounds like—a fear of taking tests.

Though he didn't face a classroom setting, Daniel welcomed his special test, a test of faith in God. What an opportunity to demonstrate the superiority of God's wisdom in all things—even nutrition! So Daniel proposed a 10-day test between those eating the rich, royal foods and the four young Hebrew men (Daniel included) who would eat only what God had declared appropriate.

Daniel understood that God's laws aren't meant to restrict us, but to enhance us. Royal food would defile; God's way would bless. In other words, pass the test of obedience . . . and reap your blessing!

Dear Lord, *when the way seems cloudy, when it seems another way holds greater promise, remind me of the wisdom of Your ways, of the blessings inherent in Your plans for me. For this day, keep me walking in obedience as You assure me of Your constant presence. In Jesus' name, Amen.*

**SEARCH THE WORD**

*Commit yourself to truth, and you will find yourself at war with those who commit to no truth.*

Scripture: Daniel 1:11-14
Song: *"Wonderful Words of Life"*

*From this meditation today, I will pray . . .*

Adoration ______________________________

______________________________

______________________________

Confession ______________________________

______________________________

______________________________

Thanksgiving ______________________________

______________________________

______________________________

Supplication ______________________________

______________________________

______________________________

*From this meditation today, I will . . .*

Think ______________________________

______________________________

______________________________

Say ______________________________

______________________________

______________________________

Do ______________________________

______________________________

______________________________

______________________________

______________________________

# It Is Enough

*To these four young men God gave knowledge and understanding of all kinds of literature and learning. And Daniel could understand visions and dreams of all kinds* (Daniel 1:17).

Scripture: Daniel 1:15-17
Song: *"The Bible Stands"*

***From this meditation today, I will pray . . .***

Adoration ______________________________

______________________________

______________________________

Confession ______________________________

______________________________

______________________________

Thanksgiving ______________________________

______________________________

______________________________

Supplication ______________________________

______________________________

______________________________

***From this meditation today, I will . . .***

Think ______________________________

______________________________

______________________________

Say ______________________________

______________________________

______________________________

Do ______________________________

______________________________

______________________________

______________________________

______________________________

John Murray lay in bed ill, and his son was reading the Bible to him. Upon hearing the words of Psalm 8:8, "All that swim the paths of the seas," Murray asked the boy to repeat the phrase. Hearing it the second time, Murray said, "It is enough if the Word of God says there are paths in the sea; they must be there, and I am going to find them." Within a few years he had discovered and was charting ocean currents. This 19th-century Canadian is now considered the father of modern oceanography.

Notice Murray's faith: If the Word of God says it is so . . . It was enough, too, for our four young men, that God said it was so. Daniel and his friends trusted the wisdom of God's dietary laws and were blessed accordingly.

To those with faith, God's Word is more than a guide for getting to Heaven. It is also the wisdom of God for successful living in this present world. And, most wonderfully, such wisdom remains readily available, as the apostle James tells us: "If any of you lacks wisdom, he should ask God, who gives generously to all" (James 1:5).

*Help me,* Father, *to stand upon Your Word as firmly as those who have preceded me in the faith with such laudable lives. In Christ's name, amen.*

**SPOTLIGHT**
***Next Week's Lesson***

If we read God's Word discerningly, we will discover His wisdom!

# None Equal

*The king talked with them, and he found none equal to Daniel, Hananiah, Mishael and Azariah; so they entered the king's service* (Daniel 1:19).

We measure intelligence with a test that gives us a numeric rating we call our "intelligence quotient," or IQ. Marilyn vos Savant achieved the highest IQ ever recorded, 228. I enjoy reading her newspaper column, in which she answers various questions posed by readers. I've yet to see her struggling to answer, and I marvel at her wit and wisdom.

In this way, I can relate to an ancient king who enjoyed talking with four young Hebrew men. To this mighty ruler, the young men surpassed all the other supposed wise men of his kingdom. The king's discerning investigation was the only "IQ test" that mattered, and his word was this: there were none wiser than these four youths.

Few of us can say there are "none equal" to us in any particular field. And, of course, we may never stand before a king. But God's wisdom, encased within His Word, will bring His blessing to those who live accordingly. Build your house on the solid foundation of His Word, and others may well marvel at the depth of your wisdom and understanding.

Lord, *guide me in Your wisdom lest I go astray. As I heed Your indwelling Spirit, may Your glory be my only claim to fame. Through Christ, amen.*

**SEARCH THE WORD**

*With the wisdom from above, we can fill in the gaps of our understanding.*

Scripture: Daniel 1:18-21

Song: *"Standing on the Promises"*

*From this meditation today, I will pray . . .*

Adoration __________

Confession __________

Thanksgiving __________

Supplication __________

*From this meditation today, I will . . .*

Think __________

Say __________

Do __________

April 7

# The Lord Our Helper

*My help comes from the* Lord,
*who made the heavens and the earth!*
(Psalm 121:2, *New Living Translation*).

Scripture: Psalm 121:1-4
Song: *"I Will Call Upon the Lord"*

***From this meditation today, I will pray . . .***

Adoration ______

Confession ______

Thanksgiving ______

Supplication ______

***From this meditation today, I will . . .***

Think ______

Say ______

Do ______

April 7–13. ***Marty Prudhomme,*** *of Mandeville, Louisiana, is a Bible teacher, singer, and speaker who leads an evangelistic ministry called "Adopt-a-Block."*

As Hurricane Katrina blew across Louisiana, Annie's husband, Mack, was airlifted to safety from his room in a New Orleans hospital. Not knowing where Mack had been taken, Annie was forced to live for weeks by herself in the downtown convention center. After the waters receded, Annie searched for two weeks and finally found Mack in a Lafayette hospital, 160 miles west of New Orleans. Annie lost her home, all that she owned, and almost lost her husband.

Lafayette overflowed with evacuees, as shelters and churches housed thousands. Many took strangers into their homes, including my niece, Pixan. She met Annie at an ice cream parlor near the hospital and could almost hear God whisper, "She's the one I want you to help." Pixan prayed with Annie, brought her home, and cared for her needs. After Mack's release from the hospital, God miraculously led them to the last available rental house in Lafayette. When you are lost, hurting, or alone, God knows right where you are. He'll send help.

Lord, *when I despair of finding any help amidst my daily difficulties, refocus my vision on Your infinite power and love! Through Christ, amen.*

**SPOTLIGHT**
***Next Week's Lesson***

When the storm clouds are the darkest, God's light is still there waiting to break through.

# Sudden Trouble

*As soon as they heard the sound of the horn, flute, zither, lyre, harp and all kinds of music, all the peoples, nations and men of every language fell down and worshiped the image of gold that King Nebuchadnezzar had set up (Daniel 3:7).*

A great raging wall of water crashed into the Gulf Coast with a fury unknown in U.S. history, destroying everything in its path. Living in Louisiana, I watched with horror as our stunned government officials bowed in fear before the devastation of Hurricane Katrina. While many shuddered at the magnitude of the damage, God was raising up a mighty force, the church, to respond with compassion and practical help. Thus, in a sense, God was the "first responder."

God shows His love and care amidst the worst catastrophes. Surely God's people felt it a sudden, tragic turn of events when King Nebuchadnezzar set up his golden image for idolatrous worship. In horror they heard the sound of the horns and knew that death could be imminent. Yet God used King Nebuchadnezzar's fearsome decrees as part of His plan to bless Daniel and the captive nation. Whether nature harasses us—or even our own secular leaders—we can remain confident amidst every raging wind: God's will prevails.

Lord, *instead of bowing down under the weight of my problems, let me rise up, strong and courageous, in Your strength. In Jesus' name, amen.*

**SEARCH THE WORD**

*For those enveloped in darkness, the smallest light brings hope.*

Scripture: Daniel 3:1-7

Song: *"Peace When Trouble Blows"*

*From this meditation today, I will pray . . .*

Adoration ______________________________

______________________________

______________________________

Confession ______________________________

______________________________

______________________________

Thanksgiving ______________________________

______________________________

______________________________

Supplication ______________________________

______________________________

______________________________

*From this meditation today, I will . . .*

Think ______________________________

______________________________

______________________________

Say ______________________________

______________________________

______________________________

Do ______________________________

______________________________

______________________________

______________________________

______________________________

# In Flood or Fire

*If you do not worship [the idol], you will be thrown immediately into a blazing furnace. Then what god will be able to rescue you from my hand?* (Daniel 3:15).

Scripture: Daniel 3:8-15

Song: *"We Have an Anchor"*

*From this meditation today, I will pray . . .*

Adoration ______________________________

______________________________

______________________________

Confession ______________________________

______________________________

______________________________

Thanksgiving ______________________________

______________________________

______________________________

Supplication ______________________________

______________________________

______________________________

*From this meditation today, I will . . .*

Think ______________________________

______________________________

______________________________

Say ______________________________

______________________________

______________________________

Do ______________________________

______________________________

______________________________

______________________________

______________________________

My brother, Billy, and sister-in-law, Delores, are from St. Bernard Parish, Louisiana. For them, Katrina's floods came even more unexpectedly than for others. You see, they thought they were safe living in an area that *never* floods. But their front door burst open one morning, and within two minutes they stood waist deep in water.

They broke down the back door and climbed up the outside garage stairs onto the roof, barely making it out before the entire house flooded. A neighbor with a boat rescued them and brought them to a local community center, where they stayed for three days without food or water. All the while, the family was praying for them, not knowing where they were or if they were even alive. (Billy has diabetes and could have been in really big trouble.)

Six days later we found them all in Baton Rouge. They were extremely dirty and starving, but "OK." Billy had no medication for the entire time. He could have died in a diabetic coma, but our God was able to deliver him. What a miracle! No matter what troubles you—freezing flood waters or a blazing furnace—God can rescue you.

God, *I won't be forced to worship an idol today, but I am often tempted by lesser gods. Help me cling to You a bit tighter! Through Christ, amen.*

**SPOTLIGHT**

***Next Week's Lesson***

When our ship seems out of our control, God takes over the helm.

# Best Defense: None

*If we are thrown into the blazing furnace, the God we serve is able to save us from it, and he will rescue us from your hand, O king* (Daniel 3:17).

Marty works for a large corporation where he manages dozens of salesmen. He is honest, hardworking, and well-regarded by his superiors. But two years ago, his work situation changed drastically. Marty's new supervisor was "offended" by his Christianity and did everything she could to make him look incompetent, even embarrassing him publicly at a large manager's meeting.

Marty's response? He prayed for her, determining to trust in God's favor. By the end of the year, he was worn out, but at the last sales manager's meeting, the CEO announced Marty's group as the top sales group in the entire company. They honored him with a large bonus and a nice vacation. And . . . the CEO transferred Ben's supervisor to another area of the company—she has not been heard of since.

Notice in our Scripture today that the three Hebrew men didn't defend themselves. They allowed God to do the talking for them. It seems that when we stand up for God, even in total silence, He will fight for us.

Almighty Lord, *You see my trials and You are fully able to defend me when I cannot defend myself. Thank You, my rock, my shield, my strength, and my redeemer. In Christ's holy name I pray. Amen.*

**SEARCH THE WORD**

*Rescue will come in God's good timing.*

Scripture: Daniel 3:16-23

Song: *"He Is My Defense"*

***From this meditation today, I will pray . . .***

Adoration ______________________________

______________________________

______________________________

Confession ______________________________

______________________________

______________________________

Thanksgiving ______________________________

______________________________

______________________________

Supplication ______________________________

______________________________

______________________________

***From this meditation today, I will . . .***

Think ______________________________

______________________________

______________________________

Say ______________________________

______________________________

______________________________

Do ______________________________

______________________________

______________________________

______________________________

______________________________

# He's There!

*He said, "Look! I see four men walking around in the fire, unbound and unharmed, and the fourth looks like a son of the gods"* (Daniel 3:25).

Scripture: Daniel 3:24-27

**Song:** *"'Tis So Sweet to Trust in Jesus"*

***From this meditation today, I will pray . . .***

Adoration ______________________________

Confession ______________________________

Thanksgiving ______________________________

Supplication ______________________________

***From this meditation today, I will . . .***

Think ______________________________

Say ______________________________

Do ______________________________

I hope you aren't tired of hearing about Hurricane Katrina. For those of us who lived in Louisiana during those howling winds, fearsome memories still linger. At the moment, I'm thinking of the six pine trees that smashed through Ron and Caron's roof. Every room in the house was ruined as trees and water burst through.

The couple went into shock, totally overwhelmed, but God held them in His hands. Ron and Caron moved in with a family friend and, one by one, work crews from churches around the country began to show up for them. People they didn't know cut trees, cleared the yard, and removed the damaged sections of the house. Months later, after many tears and many prayers, the house stands rebuilt.

The trials have been great, the stress difficult, but God walked with them in the midst of their "fiery furnace." They are coming up out of the fire without even the smell of smoke on their clothes. What was impossible for human strength, God accomplished with divine power. In fact, He was right there with them the whole time.

God, *You've promised to walk with me through flood or fire. Even if I perish, I'm determined to walk with You through it all. In Jesus' name, amen.*

**SPOTLIGHT**

***Next Week's Lesson***

Why are we surprised when God comes through? He's been delivering His followers for thousands of years.

# Amazing Reversals

*I decree that the people of any nation or language who say anything against the God of Shadrach, Meshach and Abednego be cut into pieces and their houses be turned into piles of rubble, for no other god can save in this way* (Daniel 3:29).

Decades ago, Sara received a letter warning, "Do not return to East Germany, or you will be arrested. And don't smuggle any more Bibles into this country." She prayerfully obeyed God, however, and on her next trip she entered another communist country, Poland. I went with her—on my first mission trip.

Sara knew God was able to deliver her from her enemies. Once, while crossing into Germany (before the wall came down) an SS officer interrogated her. As he drew back his fist to strike her, she prayed for God's protection. The officer's arm froze in midair, and Sara shared the gospel with him. The upshot was that Sara soon had a friend to protect her whenever she came through his checkpoint at the border.

God Almighty has been working such amazing reversals among His people for centuries. A blaspheming king becomes a defender of Israel's God; a Gestapo torturer turns into a compassionate helper. Who but the Lord could save the day in this way?

Lord, *keep me trusting You, even in dangerous situations. Help me recall the miraculous ways You deliver Your children. In Christ's name, amen.*

**SEARCH THE WORD**

*The world can't understand why Christians believe; we can't understand why the world ignores the evidence.*

Scripture: Daniel 3:28-30

Song: *"Almighty Father, Lord Most High"*

*From this meditation today, I will pray . . .*

Adoration ______________________

______________________

______________________

Confession ______________________

______________________

______________________

Thanksgiving ______________________

______________________

______________________

Supplication ______________________

______________________

______________________

*From this meditation today, I will . . .*

Think ______________________

______________________

______________________

Say ______________________

______________________

______________________

Do ______________________

______________________

______________________

______________________

______________________

April 13

# Storm Protection

*The* LORD *will keep you from all harm—he will watch over your life* (Psalm 121:7).

Scripture: Psalm 121:5-8
**Song: *"Trusting Jesus"***

***From this meditation today, I will pray . . .***

Adoration ______________________________

Confession ______________________________

Thanksgiving ______________________________

Supplication ______________________________

***From this meditation today, I will . . .***

Think ______________________________

Say ______________________________

Do ______________________________

The house moaned—I could see the walls moving in and out with the force of Katrina. The winds screamed as they passed between the houses. Three mighty oak trees groaned an unearthly cry as they were torn from their roots, falling on the left side of the house. They toppled over, one after another, like heavy giants, shaking the world with their impact.

Next the winds whipped around the house, and a tree came crashing down in the backyard. But instead of falling in the same direction as the others, it had fallen at a 90-degree angle across the back. An eternity seemed to pass while the terror went on and on. Then several large branches tore off the trees in the front yard, falling in front of the door.

When the winds finally ended, my house stood safe amidst a mass of uprooted and broken trees. I don't know why some suffer such tragedy and others are untouched, but I know God is faithful to all who call on Him. He watches over their lives, preserving them here in the reality we know on earth—or taking them to be with Him in the ultimate reality that awaits all who love Him.

God, *You deliver from trials, not by always changing the circumstances but in transforming my heart. Thanks for Your peace! Through Christ, amen.*

**SPOTLIGHT**
***Next Week's Lesson***

Christians are not promised a world without pressure, but we are promised a deliverer.

# No Excuse, Please!

*Though the wicked bind me with ropes, I will not forget your law* (Psalm 119:61).

"He hit me first!" offers 8-year-old Steven, who had just been fighting with his brother. Typical childhood explanation for less than exemplary behavior, right?

But don't we adults often apply this "because he did a bad thing to me" logic to justify our sins? We may well feel justified in forgetting what's truly right when someone seriously wrongs us. We drop a tidbit of juicy gossip about her, we make it hard for him, we overestimate the damages, or we exaggerate (or under report) on our tax forms. Yet, two wrongs do not make a right.

The psalmist understood this. Daniel understood it too: Obedience to God offers no loopholes or compromises. Hard times, insults, injuries—none justify evil on our part. If, like the psalmist, we promise to obey God, seek God with all our hearts, consider all our ways, and are quick to obey God's commands, then—if we have integrity—we will not forget God's law, even though the wicked bind us with ropes.

Father, *You know my desire to love and obey You—and my tendency to forget Your law, especially when others have hurt me. Help me to respond as Your Son always did, in obedience and love. Through Him, amen.*

**SEARCH THE WORD**

*When we are tempted to lash out, we must remember the grace we were given.*

Scripture: Psalm 119:57-64

Song: *"In Christ Alone"*

*From this meditation today, I will pray . . .*

Adoration ______________________________

______________________________

______________________________

Confession ______________________________

______________________________

______________________________

Thanksgiving ______________________________

______________________________

______________________________

Supplication ______________________________

______________________________

______________________________

*From this meditation today, I will . . .*

Think ______________________________

______________________________

______________________________

Say ______________________________

______________________________

______________________________

Do ______________________________

______________________________

______________________________

April 14–20. ***Andrew Parris*** *lives with his wonderful wife, Regula, and delightful son, Michael, in Colorado. As an engineer, he works on the Atlas rocket program.*

April 15

# Character, or Just Position?

*Daniel so distinguished himself among the administrators and the satraps by his exceptional qualities that the king planned to set him over the whole kingdom* (Daniel 6:3).

Scripture: Daniel 6:1-4

Song: *"Make Me a Captive, Lord"*

*From this meditation today, I will pray . . .*

Adoration ______________________________

______________________________

______________________________

Confession ______________________________

______________________________

______________________________

Thanksgiving ______________________________

______________________________

______________________________

Supplication ______________________________

______________________________

______________________________

*From this meditation today, I will . . .*

Think ______________________________

______________________________

______________________________

Say ______________________________

______________________________

______________________________

Do ______________________________

______________________________

______________________________

______________________________

______________________________

Most of us know the story of Daniel in the lions' den, which unfolds here in chapter 6. We know of Daniel and his obedience, and we recall how God rescued him from hungry lions' jaws.

We may be less familiar with King Darius, who plays a key role in this story. In these next few days, let us consider and contrast Daniel and King Darius. I believe we'll gain some insights into the differences between the kingdom of God and human kingdoms, between a man who knows, loves, and obeys God, and a man who knows power, loves himself, and obeys his own desires.

Today's passage reveals a difference in the origins of their power. Darius had power because of his position, because he ruled the kingdom and could direct the affairs of his subjects as he pleased. He assumed he was accountable only to himself. Daniel, on the other hand, had power because of his exceptional qualities, because he was trustworthy, incorruptible, conscientious, and skillful. Kingdom people are known not so much by their *position,* but by their *character.*

Lord, *develop in me the qualities shining so brightly in Daniel's life. May I too come to be known as a person of character. In the name of Jesus, amen.*

**SPOTLIGHT**

***Next Week's Lesson***

Live your life to get what you "deserve," and you will live far below what God has intended for you.

# Really Number One?

*Anyone who prays to any god or man during the next thirty days, except to you, O king, shall be thrown into the lions' den* (Daniel 6:7).

O King / Queen ________________ *(fill in your own name)*, live forever! The world has agreed that you deserve the best and most luxurious house, car, vacations, toys, tools, games, and pleasure. You deserve to be adored and admired by everyone for your accomplishments, your good looks, your good deeds, your power, and your possessions. You are, in effect, King Darius.

This vain monarch found it perfectly natural that everyone should bow to him, and so he happily wrote a decree that he alone must be worshiped for a solid 30 days (for starters). In contrast, Daniel humbly worshiped God alone, coming before Him with praises and petitions.

Hundreds of advertisements each day—and many well-intentioned people—try to convince me that I deserve the best, that I should live luxuriously, and that, really, the world ought to worship me. It makes me wonder: How tempted am I to secretly agree, like King Darius, that I'm Number One in the universe?

O God, *help me to center my life around You, for You alone are worthy of devotion and praise. Help me to resist the world's temptations to vanity and pride. I come humbly to You daily to seek Your presence, Your will, Your power, Your grace, and Your mercy. In Christ's name, amen.*

**SEARCH THE WORD**

*If you are the center of your world, you are missing a universe you would enjoy.*

Scripture: Daniel 6:5-9

**Song:** *"Humble Thyself in the Sight of the Lord"*

***From this meditation today, I will pray . . .***

Adoration ______________________

______________________

______________________

Confession ______________________

______________________

______________________

Thanksgiving ______________________

______________________

______________________

Supplication ______________________

______________________

______________________

***From this meditation today, I will . . .***

Think ______________________

______________________

______________________

Say ______________________

______________________

______________________

Do ______________________

______________________

______________________

______________________

______________________

# Impractical Behavior

*[Daniel] went home to his upstairs room where the windows opened toward Jerusalem . . . [and] got down on his knees and prayed . . . just as he had done before* (Daniel 6:10).

Scripture: Daniel 6:10-14

Song: *"This Little Light of Mine"*

***From this meditation today, I will pray . . .***

Adoration ______________________________

______________________________

______________________________

Confession ______________________________

______________________________

______________________________

Thanksgiving ______________________________

______________________________

______________________________

Supplication ______________________________

______________________________

______________________________

***From this meditation today, I will . . .***

Think ______________________________

______________________________

______________________________

Say ______________________________

______________________________

______________________________

Do ______________________________

______________________________

______________________________

______________________________

______________________________

While clearly an excellent administrator, Daniel isn't primarily a "practical" man. He does not compromise his walk with God or his testimony in order to be politically correct or to protect his personal interests. He does not selfishly conceal his relationship with God for 30 days until the decree expires.

There was nothing magical about praying with open windows towards Jerusalem three times a day. Yet, to hide his prayers in this circumstance would be to give in to his enemies' attack on his integrity as servant of the living God.

The world says, "Be practical. Compromise your walk with God in order to get along and fit in. Talk about sports, the weather, politics, and even sex, but don't talk about Jesus, sin, or salvation. Gossip about people's outrageous lifestyles, but don't pass moral judgment on them. Worship the world's idols, but not the Lord God."

It won't be easy, but I hope today to follow Daniel's impractical example. Will you join me?

Living God, *I want to grow in my walk with You, and I want my life to testify to Your glory and goodness. May the manner of my life today humbly testify to the world that You are Lord of All. In Jesus' name, amen.*

**SPOTLIGHT**

***Next Week's Lesson***

The outcome of unrighteous compromise is predictable: it stresses the soul.

# It's Too Late

*The king returned to his palace and spent the night without eating and without any entertainment being brought to him. And he could not sleep* (Daniel 6:18).

You slam on the brakes, but you know it's too late. In a few seconds you'll hit the car in front of you, and you can do nothing to prevent it. Or you speak angry words that you immediately regret. Those words hurt the one you love, but you can't take them back.

There comes a time when we can't undo what we've done—and when we can't *stop* doing what we've always been doing. That's when we may realize our helplessness and cry out to God for help, as did King Darius. Probably only sickness, wars, or rumors of wars ever prevented the king from enjoying his nightly sensual indulgences. But this night was different. The king, who seemed accustomed to sending people to the lions' den, suffered helplessly in a trap he himself had been caught in.

If we must be caught, let it be like Daniel, entwined in righteousness, wrapped up in obedience to God—not like the king, who languished in the jaws of foolish vanity.

Lord God of Heaven and earth, *You know my weaknesses and vanities and, Lord, You know my desire to serve You in righteousness and obedience. Purify my heart. Help me to walk with You along the pathways of life, free from the chains of my sins. I pray this prayer in the name of Jesus, my merciful Savior and Lord. Amen.*

**SEARCH THE WORD**

*While the righteous rest, the unrighteous wrestle with justifications.*

Scripture: Daniel 6:15-18

Song: *"Purify My Heart"*

*From this meditation today, I will pray . . .*

Adoration ____________________

Confession ____________________

Thanksgiving ____________________

Supplication ____________________

*From this meditation today, I will . . .*

Think ____________________

Say ____________________

Do ____________________

# Winning a Heart

*The king was overjoyed and gave orders to lift Daniel out of the den* (Daniel 6:23).

Scripture: Daniel 6:19-23

Song: *"All for Jesus"*

***From this meditation today, I will pray . . .***

Adoration ________________________

Confession ________________________

Thanksgiving ________________________

Supplication ________________________

***From this meditation today, I will . . .***

Think ________________________

Say ________________________

Do ________________________

Eager children run into the living room on Christmas morning to see what presents await them. Distraught women went early on the third day to the tomb where Jesus was laid. And the anguished King Darius got up at the first light of dawn, hurrying to see whether Daniel was still alive.

Clearly, the king cared deeply for Daniel, not merely as a valued administrator, but apparently as a close friend. Daniel and the king obviously had very different religious beliefs and value systems. Yet Daniel's excellence, loyalty to the king, and consistent service to God bridged the gap between them. He so touched the king's heart that Darius was thrilled to find Daniel alive.

The king observed genuine faith in action. Even in this most trying situation, Daniel treated King Darius not with coldness, bitterness, or disdain, but with warmth, grace, and respect. What an example for us today! A godly life benefits not only believers but also our relationships with, and testimony among, those with seeking hearts.

Dear God, *help me to love the world as You love it. Help me to be its salt and light for Your glory. And thank You for the example of Daniel's life, of a believer who won the heart of a king through excellence, loyal friendship, and continual service to You. I pray in Jesus' name. Amen.*

**SPOTLIGHT**

***Next Week's Lesson***

It's impossible to appraise the true value of a faithful friend.

# God Is More Than We Know

*I issue a decree that in every part of my kingdom people must fear and reverence the God of Daniel. For . . . his kingdom will not be destroyed, his dominion will never end* (Daniel 6:26).

Have you ever been introduced with words that seemed to leave out a lot of information? Maybe you were introduced as a gifted musician or a smart student, yet you wanted to say: "But I'm *more* than that!"

We generally first grasp new ideas by relating them to familiar concepts, although these limited concepts do not enable us to fully comprehend the new ideas. Here's what I mean: Daniel knew God deeply from a lifetime of walking with Him. In contrast, it appears that powerful King Darius was just beginning to know God, and in his proclamation he began with what he readily grasped: God's *power.* Yet, while God is powerful, He is also much more.

As Daniel knew, God is also faithful, righteous, compassionate, forgiving, just, gracious . . . the list could go on forever. For God will always be greater than our limited understanding of Him.

Let us walk constantly with Him, then, as Daniel did, so our lives and testimonies will grow fuller as we come to know God more deeply. That adventure has no end.

Almighty God, *You are great and awesome, infinitely beyond my understanding. Nevertheless, I love and worship all that You have revealed of Yourself. Thank You for showing me Your goodness this day. In Jesus' name, amen.*

**SEARCH THE WORD**

*It will take us eternity to discover the depth of our friendship with God.*

Scripture: Daniel 6:24-28

Song: *"Crown Him with Many Crowns"*

*From this meditation today, I will pray . . .*

Adoration ______________________________

______________________________

______________________________

Confession ______________________________

______________________________

______________________________

Thanksgiving ______________________________

______________________________

______________________________

Supplication ______________________________

______________________________

______________________________

*From this meditation today, I will . . .*

Think ______________________________

______________________________

______________________________

Say ______________________________

______________________________

______________________________

Do ______________________________

______________________________

______________________________

______________________________

______________________________

# Wait in the Cherry Tree

*I wait for the* LORD, *my soul waits, and in his word I put my hope* (Psalm 130:5).

Scripture: Psalm 130

**Song:** *"Surely the Presence of the Lord"*

*From this meditation today, I will pray . . .*

Adoration ______________________________

______________________________

______________________________

Confession ______________________________

______________________________

______________________________

Thanksgiving ______________________________

______________________________

______________________________

Supplication ______________________________

______________________________

______________________________

*From this meditation today, I will . . .*

Think ______________________________

______________________________

______________________________

Say ______________________________

______________________________

______________________________

Do ______________________________

______________________________

______________________________

April 21–27. ***Rhonda Brunea*** *is a single mother of four. She loves to read and also to collect amusing and pretty much useless pets, like sheep.*

In the beloved literary classic *Anne of Green Gables,* we meet the charming waif, Anne, as she waits alone at a train station. Another child might have been frightened, but not Anne. When Matthew finally arrives, she cheerily informs him that she didn't mind his tardiness a bit. She had made up her mind to climb into a wild cherry tree and spend the night entranced by moonlight and white blossoms, confident that someone would come for her in the morning.

The life of faith often feels like a long wait at a train station. We think God must have forgotten us, and we begin to fret. We wonder why He's late. But God is never late; He holds the master schedule, and He knows exactly when to move. Meanwhile, we wait, and if there is nothing else to be done about it, we may as well wait with all our might, like Anne. Confidence in the one for whom we wait gives us the freedom to wait with joy. Thus we clamber into the boughs of a wild cherry tree and perch there, deeply content among fragrant, moonlit blossoms.

Lord, *today give me the patient attitude of trust. So much of what I'll experience today depends on what I choose to experience. In Christ, amen.*

**SPOTLIGHT**

***Next Week's Lesson***

Waiting on God should lead us to the expectation that He has greater opportunities in store.

# Look at Me!

*I turned to the* Lord *God and pleaded with him in prayer and petition, in fasting, and in sackcloth and ashes* (Daniel 9:3).

"Mommy!" A small boy has been trying unsuccessfully for several minutes to get his mother's attention. Finally, he drags a chair next to her and climbs up on it, raising him to his mother's eye level. Placing both hands flat against her cheeks, he pulls her face in his direction and demands, "*Look* at me!"

God isn't hard of hearing, nor does He become distracted, as an earthly parent might. However, the principle of persistent prayer abounds in Scripture. God strengthens our faith by making us flex our prayer muscles.

Seemingly unanswered prayer can make believers feel like that small boy. But when the answer seems overly long in coming, it's time to dig in with all the determination of the undaunted child. To fast, mourn, and pray as Daniel did is like dragging a very big chair next to our Father. Then, with the daring of a child who knows that he's loved, we place our hands on His strong face and demand, "Look at me!" Well pleased at such trusting audacity, a smiling Father-God turns to regard His child.

Father, *I know You always hear me. You are El Roi, the God Who Sees Me. You love me with an indestructible love, and no one can snatch me from Your hand. Knowing this truth, let me be determined in petition and sacrificial in intercession for others. In the precious name of Jesus I pray. Amen.*

**SEARCH THE WORD**

*The bolder our address to God, the more prepared we must be to receive His answer.*

Scripture: Daniel 9:1-3

Song: *"His Eye Is on the Sparrow"*

*From this meditation today, I will pray . . .*

Adoration __________

Confession __________

Thanksgiving __________

Supplication __________

*From this meditation today, I will . . .*

Think __________

Say __________

Do __________

# Reinvent Yourself?

*We have sinned and done wrong. We have been wicked and have rebelled; we have turned away from your commands and laws* (Daniel 9:5).

Scripture: Daniel 9:4-10

Song: *"Create in Me a Clean Heart"*

"It's never too late to reinvent yourself," the speaker assured his audience. A weary and disillusioned young woman straightened in her chair. Something about the phrase "reinvent yourself" snagged her imagination. Could she really make herself into someone new?

No, not from the inside out. Our inability to do so stands at the heart of our need for God's amazing grace. Through our baptism and by the power of the indwelling Holy Spirit, though, we can indeed enjoy soul-deep reinvention. But to benefit from God's beautiful offer of a fresh start, we must first be willing to look frankly into our lives and see the truth: "I have sinned."

Daniel admitted that painful truth on behalf of an entire people, and it was the first step to a brand new day for them. For God reveals our faults not to punish, but to correct that which keeps us from experiencing all the fullness of His good plans for us. Alone, we are helpless to reinvent ourselves. In Christ, we are new creations.

My God, *I thank You for loving me too much to settle for mediocrity. Help me to abandon my life into Your strong and creative hands. Mold it like soft clay in the hands of the master craftsman. Wonderful Lord, reinvent my life; make me more like You. In the name of Jesus I pray. Amen.*

***From this meditation today, I will pray . . .***

Adoration ______

Confession ______

Thanksgiving ______

Supplication ______

***From this meditation today, I will . . .***

Think ______

Say ______

Do ______

**SPOTLIGHT**

***Next Week's Lesson***

If we want God to truly fill us, we have to be willing to empty ourselves first.

# Training His Child

*The* Lord *did not hesitate to bring the disaster upon us, for the* Lord *our God is righteous in everything he does; yet we have not obeyed him* (Daniel 9:14).

Children dread this statement: "This is going to hurt me more than it hurts you!" They doubt the claim, but a good parent knows that discipline supplies healthy boundaries—and sometimes painful corrections. Without limits, a child will stay self-centered and remain incapable of growth.

God is the ultimate good parent, isn't He? He wants the very best for His children and won't hesitate to apply whatever encouragement is required to reap the essential changes. Some of His children are particularly obstinate and require firmer training. But the wise realize the futility of refusing their Father's correction, for it would go against their own best interests.

God's training program is a permanent facet of life. For He longs to give His children good things, as they learn to follow their own deepest longing to its ultimate Source. And consider this: Providing our adoption into His family (via the cross) really did hurt God more than it hurt us. Would such a loving Father then leave us to raise ourselves?

My loving Father, *I trust You to know what is necessary for my training. Help me bend to Your loving discipline. In Jesus' name, amen.*

**SEARCH THE WORD**

*The more mature we become, the more we appreciate God's parenting skills.*

Scripture: Daniel 9:11-14

Song: *"Have Thine Own Way, Lord"*

*From this meditation today, I will pray . . .*

Adoration ______________________

Confession ______________________

Thanksgiving ______________________

Supplication ______________________

*From this meditation today, I will . . .*

Think ______________________

Say ______________________

Do ______________________

# We Have Heard

*Give ear, O God, and hear; open your eyes and see the desolation of the city that bears your Name. We do not make requests of you because we are righteous, but because of your great mercy* (Daniel 9:18).

Scripture: Daniel 9:15-19
Song: *"Jesus Died for You"*

***From this meditation today, I will pray . . .***

Adoration ______________________________

______________________________

______________________________

Confession ______________________________

______________________________

______________________________

Thanksgiving ______________________________

______________________________

______________________________

Supplication ______________________________

______________________________

______________________________

***From this meditation today, I will . . .***

Think ______________________________

______________________________

______________________________

Say ______________________________

______________________________

______________________________

Do ______________________________

______________________________

______________________________

______________________________

______________________________

The dusty traveler stands before the imposing doors of a great man's house. "I beg an audience with your master," he tells the servant who answers his knock. "Who are you to beg favors of my lord?" the servant asks. "Why should my master see you?"

"It's true," the traveler says. "I'm not an important man. But I am a man in great distress, and I believe your master may help me, if only he will hear me. I have heard of his reputation. They say he is merciful as well as wise."

"Why should he hear you? What have you to give him?"

The traveler bows his head, clutching his hat in his hands. "Truly, sir, I have nothing to offer except . . ."

"Except?"

"Except my gratitude and eternal devotion."

The servant smiles. He pulls the great doors open and stands aside to admit the dusty traveler.

"That is the price of admission, good sir. What you have heard is true; enter, and ask what you will."

Great and merciful God, *I come before You with nothing to offer but gratitude and love. I ask for Your favor not because I deserve it but because of who You are, my powerful and gracious Savior. Through Christ, amen.*

**SPOTLIGHT**
***Next Week's Lesson***

It is a gentle, sincere plea that catches the attention of God.

# What a Confidence Builder!

*As soon as you began to pray, an answer was given* (Daniel 9:23).

Matt's heart pounded so hard he thought it would burst out of his chest. There she was—the girl he loved—sitting alone at a library table. He had to ask her to the youth-group party before somebody else did. *Just do it!* he coached himself. The worst she can say is, "Why would I want to be seen with a guy like you?"

Matt swallowed hard and strolled over, trying to look casual and confident. "Hey, Tina. So, uh . . . how's it going?" *I can't think of anything to say! Why is she just sitting there? I think I'm going to be sick.* "So . . . got a date for the party yet?"

"Nope. You?"

"Nope." Now, now! *Ask!*

Most of us can recall similar adolescent scenes of reticence to step forward, fearing to ask, avoiding assertion. And in almost every area of life, as grown-ups, we've learned to move forward, confidently, with any legitimate request. But can we do so in approaching our God?

Angel Gabriel told Daniel that, even as his lips began to ask, the answer was already given. When it comes to prayer, what better confidence-builder can we have than that?

Lord, *I believe You are waiting with answers even before I ask. Help me trust Your love enough to ask boldly for every need. In Jesus' name, amen.*

**SEARCH THE WORD**

*Our relationship with the Father is strengthened when we learn to trust Him enough to ask for His help.*

Scripture: Daniel 9:20-23

*Song: "Seek Ye First"*

***From this meditation today, I will pray . . .***

Adoration ______________________

______________________

______________________

Confession ______________________

______________________

______________________

Thanksgiving ______________________

______________________

______________________

Supplication ______________________

______________________

______________________

***From this meditation today, I will . . .***

Think ______________________

______________________

______________________

Say ______________________

______________________

______________________

Do ______________________

______________________

______________________

______________________

______________________

April 27

# Moment by Moment

***Seventy "sevens" are decreed . . . to finish transgression, to put an end to sin, to atone for wickedness, to bring in everlasting righteousness, to seal up vision and prophecy and to anoint the most holy* (Daniel 9:24).**

Scripture: Daniel 9:24-27

**Song:** *"One More Day's Work for Jesus"*

***From this meditation today, I will pray . . .***

Adoration ______________________________

______________________________

______________________________

Confession ______________________________

______________________________

______________________________

Thanksgiving ______________________________

______________________________

______________________________

Supplication ______________________________

______________________________

______________________________

***From this meditation today, I will . . .***

Think ______________________________

______________________________

______________________________

Say ______________________________

______________________________

______________________________

Do ______________________________

______________________________

______________________________

______________________________

______________________________

Why does human nature so predictably resist a deadline? Students wait until the last minute to write their term papers, often pulling an "all-nighter." Taxpayers send in their returns at midnight on the final day—or file for an extension. We keep saying to ourselves, "There's still a little more time . . ."

The phrase "seventy 'sevens' are decreed" suggests there is only so much time, and then the time runs out. A sense of urgency pervades this passage. "Time is limited," it shouts. "Act now!" God does have a timetable, and He's not inclined to accommodate stragglers.

Each of us has a limited span of time to use while we're visiting planet Earth. We may spend it as we please, but when it's gone, it's gone. The end of our opportunity to serve in God's great rescue effort will arrive, and none of us knows when. We are wise, then, to ponder carefully the best use of our precious time. Not just for the week ahead, but for the next few moments let us make the most of the time we have.

Sovereign Lord, *how comforting to know that Your plans for the universe cannot be thwarted. You have determined times and seasons for all things, and You've given me a part to play. Thank You, in Jesus' name. Amen.*

**SPOTLIGHT**

***Next Week's Lesson***

It's hard to imagine any better time than now to accept God's unconditional love.

# Accept This Blessing

*Blessed are those who dwell in your house; they are ever praising you* (Psalms 84:4).

I can't remember ever being hugged by my father. He was an unhappy man, quick to anger, slow to praise. It's no surprise, then, that I grew up believing I had to earn my heavenly Father's love and affection. I just couldn't wrap my mind around the idea of unconditional love.

One weekend, when my husband and kids were out of town, I called an older couple in the church to see if I could spend the night at their house. What they did for me that weekend changed my life forever. From serving my favorite food to moving the recliner so I could sit in front of the fireplace, Vic and Carol treated me like their favorite child.

I'd never been so "loved on" in all my life. I went home and cried like a baby, finally realizing that God loves me that much, and so much more. Since then, I've grown in God's love—so blessed to be one of His favored kids. The same love and favor of God is there for all of us who call upon Him. We need not earn it, but only accept it.

Father, *help me grasp how wide and long and high and deep Your love is for me. Reveal Your love that goes beyond knowledge—that I might be utterly filled with Your sweet presence. In Christ's name, amen.*

**SEARCH THE WORD**

*Any love we experience here is but a sample of what God has in store for us for eternity.*

Scripture: Psalms 84:1-4

Song: *"How Great Is Your Love"*

*From this meditation today, I will pray . . .*

Adoration ______________________

______________________

______________________

Confession ______________________

______________________

______________________

Thanksgiving ______________________

______________________

______________________

Supplication ______________________

______________________

______________________

*From this meditation today, I will . . .*

Think ______________________

______________________

______________________

Say ______________________

______________________

______________________

Do ______________________

______________________

______________________

April 28–30. ***Barb Haley****, of San Antonio, is a widely published author and has worked as a school teacher, Bible quiz coach, and private piano instructor.*

April 29

# Choose Your Thoughts

*This is what the* Lord *Almighty says:*
*"Give careful thought to your ways"* (Haggai 1:7).

Scripture: Haggai 1:1-11

Song: *"The Thought of God"*

*From this meditation today, I will pray . . .*

Adoration ______________________________

______________________________

______________________________

Confession ______________________________

______________________________

______________________________

Thanksgiving ______________________________

______________________________

______________________________

Supplication ______________________________

______________________________

______________________________

*From this meditation today, I will . . .*

Think ______________________________

______________________________

______________________________

Say ______________________________

______________________________

______________________________

Do ______________________________

______________________________

______________________________

______________________________

______________________________

"You are what you think." True statement? A Christian counselor once explained to me that thoughts heavily influence feelings and actions. When I think on happy things, I am likely to become happier. When I replay painful events in my mind, I struggle with grief, anger, and even bitterness. These feelings then help determine how I behave.

There's a story about Ronald Reagan, as a kid, going into town with his aunt to order a new pair of shoes. But Reagan couldn't decide whether he wanted round or square toes. To his surprise, when he returned to the store a few days later, the shoemaker handed him one shoe with a square toe and the other with a round toe. "This will teach you not to let people make your decisions for you," the shoemaker cautioned. Reagan said that he learned right then that "if you don't make your own decisions, someone else will." Rather than sitting passively by, take charge of your life by choosing your thoughts carefully. Every action needs a thought to get it started.

Father Almighty, *as I realize the power of my thoughts, I pray You would reveal any false beliefs that might negatively affect my actions. Teach me to line up my thoughts with Your Word, that I might walk in the freedom of Truth. In the name of Your Son, my Savior, I pray. Amen.*

**SPOTLIGHT**

***Next Week's Lesson***

God can only lead us in the right direction once we make the choice to follow.

# God Never Lets Go

*Haggai, the* LORD'S *messenger, gave this message of the* LORD *to the people: "I am with you," declares the* LORD (Haggai 1:13).

Have you ever taught a child how to ride a bicycle? Most likely, you ran alongside, holding the bike upright as the child learned to balance, pedal, and steer. Eventually, you slipped behind the bike where the child could no longer see you. "I'm still here," you promised, as the child repeatedly turned to check. Finally, when the child acquired enough confidence and skill, you let go of the bike to show the child that he could, indeed, keep going on his own, even far out of your sight.

Not so with our heavenly Father! He will never let go. Deuteronomy 31:8 promises that "the Lord himself goes before you and will be with you; He will never leave you nor forsake you."

Why wouldn't God want us to be able to keep going on our own? Because He desires to achieve His will and purpose in our lives by working through us. As He holds us with His righteous right hand, His Spirit more fully influences our lives, enabling us to continue with confidence and skill while relying on His power.

Dear Father, *thank You for Your promise to stay by my side—to love, guide, and support me. I give myself to the leading of Your Holy Spirit that I might accomplish all that You have planned for my life. Teach me to listen to Your voice and trust Your direction. Through Christ I pray. Amen.*

**SEARCH THE WORD**

*If God created the way to Heaven, why wouldn't He want to help us along the path?*

Scripture: Haggai 1:12-15

**Song:** *"Forever Grateful"*

***From this meditation today, I will pray . . .***

Adoration ______________________________

______________________________

______________________________

Confession ______________________________

______________________________

______________________________

Thanksgiving ______________________________

______________________________

______________________________

Supplication ______________________________

______________________________

______________________________

***From this meditation today, I will . . .***

Think ______________________________

______________________________

______________________________

Say ______________________________

______________________________

______________________________

Do ______________________________

______________________________

______________________________

______________________________

______________________________

*I will listen to what*
*God the* Lord *will say;*
*he promises peace to*
*his people, his saints*
*—but let them not*
*return to folly.*
—Psalm 85:8

# May

# RESTORATION AND COVENANT RENEWAL

*I will praise you, O LORD, with all my heart . . .*
*and will praise your name for your love and your faithfulness.*
—Psalm 138:1, 2

May 1

# God Glasses

*Many . . . who had seen the former temple, wept aloud when they saw the foundation of this temple being laid, while many others shouted for joy* (Ezra 3:12).

**Scripture: Ezra 3:8-13**

**Song:** *"Give Thanks to God, for He Is Good"*

***From this meditation today, I will pray . . .***

Adoration ______________________________

______________________________

______________________________

Confession ______________________________

______________________________

______________________________

Thanksgiving ______________________________

______________________________

______________________________

Supplication ______________________________

______________________________

______________________________

***From this meditation today, I will . . .***

Think ______________________________

______________________________

______________________________

Say ______________________________

______________________________

______________________________

Do ______________________________

______________________________

______________________________

May 1–4. ***Barb Haley,*** *of San Antonio, is a widely published author and has worked as a school teacher, Bible quiz coach, and private piano instructor.*

A remnant of Jewish people had returned to Jerusalem to rebuild the destroyed temple. With the foundation laid, the people stopped to give praise to the Lord. Some shouted for joy; some wept.

What made the difference in the people's reactions? I believe it had something to do with their perspectives. No doubt some looked back to what once was and mourned the loss, while others looked forward to what was to be and rejoiced with excitement. What they already held in their hearts determined what they saw.

Too often, we judge solely by what we see on the surface. Thankfully, our heavenly Father looks much deeper. We may see failure, while God appreciates effort and improvement. We might see hopelessness while God sees the first small steps toward a bright future. It's been said that we only see what we are *prepared* to see. We would all do well, then, to reflect often on the character of God. As we do, we will learn to see all things through His eyes.

Father, *search my heart and examine my thoughts. Remind me to focus on others' hearts more than outward appearances. Through Christ, amen.*

**SPOTLIGHT**

***Next Week's Lesson***

Vision can never be caught by gazing backwards.

# Faith—My Working Energy

*Then the peoples around them set out to discourage the people of Judah and make them afraid to go on building* (Ezra 4:4).

If anyone ever owned the right to be discouraged, it had to be Helen Keller. In her book *Let Us Have Faith,* Helen said, "I know that faith made my life possible and that of many others like me. . . . Reason hardly warranted Anne Sullivan's attempt to transform a little half-human, half-animal, deaf-blind child into a complete human being. Neither science nor philosophy had set such a goal, but faith, the eye of love did. . . . In my doubly shadowed world, faith gives me a reason for trying to draw harmony out of a marred instrument. Faith is not a cushion for me to fall back upon; it is my working energy."

Anne Sullivan stepped into Helen's life and cared enough to stay and make a difference. No doubt Anne, herself, suffered great discouragement in the process. But she didn't give up.

In your life these days, who needs a friend to step in and make a difference? Might you be just that person? Refuse to give up as you allow your faith in God to become your working energy.

Dear Father in Heaven, *may I keep on doing Your will, even in the midst of discouraging circumstances. Help me remember that my strength comes from You as I strive to make a difference in someone's life today. In the name of the Father, the Son, and the Holy Spirit, I pray. Amen.*

**SEARCH THE WORD**

*What a privilege it is to change a life by being a friend.*

Scripture: Ezra 4:1-4

Song: *"God Will Make a Way"*

*From this meditation today, I will pray . . .*

Adoration ______________________________

______________________________

______________________________

Confession ______________________________

______________________________

______________________________

Thanksgiving ______________________________

______________________________

______________________________

Supplication ______________________________

______________________________

______________________________

*From this meditation today, I will . . .*

Think ______________________________

______________________________

______________________________

Say ______________________________

______________________________

______________________________

Do ______________________________

______________________________

______________________________

______________________________

______________________________

# All in a Day's Work

*Then Zerubbabel son of Shealtiel and Jeshua son of Jozadak set to work to rebuild the house of God in Jerusalem. And the prophets of God were with them, helping them*
(Ezra 5:2).

Scripture: Ezra 5:1-5

Song: *"Building Day by Day"*

***From this meditation today, I will pray . . .***

Adoration ____________________

______________________________

______________________________

Confession ____________________

______________________________

______________________________

Thanksgiving ____________________

______________________________

______________________________

Supplication ____________________

______________________________

______________________________

***From this meditation today, I will . . .***

Think ____________________

______________________________

______________________________

Say ____________________

______________________________

______________________________

Do ____________________

______________________________

______________________________

______________________________

______________________________

Having explained the meaning of *humility* to my fourth-grade class, I asked whether the students knew anyone who was humble. When one child named her pastor, another raised his hand and blurted, *"My* pastor humiliates himself every Sunday!" Out of the mouths of babes . . .

In our Scripture passage for today, God had spoken to the Jewish people, instructing them to rebuild the temple. The people immediately went to work, including the prophets of God.

What a great example of humility in leadership! Colossians 3:23, 24 says, "Whatever you do, work at it with all your heart, as working for the Lord, not for men, since you know that you will receive an inheritance from the Lord as a reward. It is the Lord Christ you are serving." Whether spreading peanut butter on bread for the kids, cleaning restrooms for a booming corporation, or speaking at an international religious conference, we can serve Jesus, if that is our goal.

Dear Father, *once again, I surrender my life to You. Take my hands, my mouth, and my feet. Use my whole being to accomplish Your purposes in my world today. In the name of Jesus, my Savior, I pray. Amen.*

**SPOTLIGHT**

***Next Week's Lesson***

When doing God's will is at the heart of our efforts, He will support our cause.

# Mission Impossible?

*If it pleases the king, let a search be made in the royal archives of Babylon to see if King Cyrus did in fact issue a decree to rebuild this house of God in Jerusalem. Then let the king send us his decision in this matter* (Ezra 5:17).

Enemies of God's people, determined to stop the rebuilding of the temple, wrote a letter to the king, asking him to confirm that the work was authorized. Unable to deter the work with their own lies and threats, these enemies attempted to stir up strife at the very highest level. But their efforts backfired when King Cyrus supported the work and further authorized that all expenses be paid from the royal treasury.

I recall praying about a situation that seemed incredibly hopeless. "I don't even know what to ask for," I told the Lord. And immediately these words of Scripture came to mind: "[He] is able to do immeasurably more than all we ask or imagine, according to his power that is at work within us" (Ephesians 3:20).

When we know we are doing God's will, we know we have His power within us. We may not know exactly what to ask, but we can certainly imagine the Lord having the power and the plan to set everything right, in spite of any determined opposition. Isn't that enough?

Dear Father, *I am sure to face opposition today in a society bent on leaving all moral absolutes behind. Work through me, in Christ's name. Amen.*

**SEARCH THE WORD**

*Nothing is more important than having God's blessing and authorization.*

Scripture: Ezra 5:6-17

**Song:** *"Our God Is an Awesome God"*

*From this meditation today, I will pray . . .*

Adoration ______________________________

______________________________

______________________________

Confession ______________________________

______________________________

______________________________

Thanksgiving ______________________________

______________________________

______________________________

Supplication ______________________________

______________________________

______________________________

*From this meditation today, I will . . .*

Think ______________________________

______________________________

______________________________

Say ______________________________

______________________________

______________________________

Do ______________________________

______________________________

______________________________

______________________________

______________________________

# Homesick

*By the rivers of Babylon we sat and wept when we remembered Zion* (Psalm 137:1).

Scripture: Psalm 137:1-7

Song: *"I'll Fly Away"*

***From this meditation today, I will pray . . .***

Adoration ______________________________

______________________________

______________________________

Confession ______________________________

______________________________

______________________________

Thanksgiving ______________________________

______________________________

______________________________

Supplication ______________________________

______________________________

______________________________

***From this meditation today, I will . . .***

Think ______________________________

______________________________

______________________________

Say ______________________________

______________________________

______________________________

Do ______________________________

______________________________

______________________________

May 5–11. ***Patty Duncan*** *loves kids and children's books. She enjoys working with both in her fifth-grade classroom at Eugene (Oregon) Christian School.*

I suffered my first bout of homesickness at the age of 5. During a visit, my aunt and uncle persuaded my parents to send me with them to play with my favorite cousin for a few days. My relatives lived in another town, and it was my first extended time away from Mom and Dad. During the day I was fine, happily playing with dolls and coloring books. At night, however, my spirits sagged.

Things were different here! My aunt sewed button eyes on my teddy bear, even though I liked him just as he was. When bedtime came, we said our prayers, and Aunt Fran tucked us in. Then my thoughts again turned toward Mom and Dad. What were they doing right now? Did they miss me?

In the darkness, I buried my head in the pillow and quietly cried. My wise aunt and uncle recognized the symptoms, and the next day my parents picked me up. Homesickness can debilitate, but it displays the strength of ties to home and family. Surely the Israelites had every reason to weep in their foreign land of captivity.

Father, *thank You that someday I'll change addresses, and all the comfort of this house will pale compared to living in Your presence. In Christ, amen.*

**SPOTLIGHT**

***Next Week's Lesson***

When we know Heaven is our home, all other residences become temporary lodgings.

# Good Grief

*"The wall of Jerusalem is broken down, and its gates have been burned with fire." When I heard these things, I sat down and wept* (Nehemiah 1:3, 4).

"Dad's gone." I heard my sister-in-law's voice over the phone, but struggled to accept her words. "Oh no," I responded, disbelieving.

For months we'd expected this news. Doctors said the congestive heart failure was terminal. A counselor helped Daddy plan his funeral and set his finances in order. He was almost 93 years old, after all, but it still seemed too soon to lose him. And my brother and I worried about our mother. Dad had always been the strong one, and she went along with his decisions. How would she manage?

In the grief that followed, Mom struggled with loneliness, often feeling hopeless. The protective "walls" of her marriage were gone, and the "gates" of decision-making provided by her husband were destroyed. She felt deeply sad and helpless. Attending a class for widows comforted her, however, and helped her learn how to survive the hard work of grieving. To our surprise, she regained her gentle cheerfulness and even began to make her own choices. A few years later she moved into a retirement center . . . and thrived.

**Father,** *Your Son was "a man of sorrows and acquainted with grief." Thanks for staying close when we lose our loved ones. In Him, amen.*

**SEARCH THE WORD**

*Those who hope in the Lord have help in this life.*

Scripture: Nehemiah 1:1-4

Song: *"He Giveth His Beloved Sleep"*

***From this meditation today, I will pray . . .***

Adoration ____________________

____________________

____________________

Confession ____________________

____________________

____________________

Thanksgiving ____________________

____________________

____________________

Supplication ____________________

____________________

____________________

***From this meditation today, I will . . .***

Think ____________________

____________________

____________________

Say ____________________

____________________

____________________

Do ____________________

____________________

____________________

____________________

____________________

# Pray the Scriptures

*Remember, I pray, the word that You commanded Your servant Moses* (Nehemiah 1:8, *New King James Version*).

Scripture: Nehemiah 1:5-11

Song: *"Prayer Is the Key"*

***From this meditation today, I will pray . . .***

Adoration ______________________________

Confession ______________________________

Thanksgiving ______________________________

Supplication ______________________________

***From this meditation today, I will . . .***

Think ______________________________

Say ______________________________

Do ______________________________

Wednesday night prayer meetings were anything but boring at San Jose Christian College, when I attended in the late 1960s. Woodrow Phillips, our beloved president, brought the sessions to life. Woody, as we knew him, always opened a chapter of the Bible, read a section, and explained it. Then he'd apply it to our lives and invite us to "pray it" with him.

The way he linked the Bible to dating, studying for finals, and curfews made it uniquely personal for us. He'd alternate reading, then praying through the Word, for the entire meeting, drawing from his deep well of relationship with God. He encouraged us to bring God's Word before Him in prayer, just as Nehemiah did, "reminding" the Lord of what He'd already said about our concerns.

God certainly doesn't need reminders! But we do, especially when a situation looks bleak from all outward appearances. "Lord, You said . . ." is a great way to build our faith when we pray, helping us embrace His will in His presence.

Wonderful Counselor, *Powerful Healer, Loving Father, remember now Your promises to me and to others who need Your touch. Though You really need no reminder, please remind me of Your close presence throughout this day. In Your Holy name I pray. Amen.*

**SPOTLIGHT**

***Next Week's Lesson***

Why should we be amazed when God cares for us as He promised?

# Amazed, Astonished, Astounded

*The king said to me, "What do you request?"*
(Nehemiah 2:4, *New King James Version*).

I really needed a job. Even though I stayed busy with substitute teaching, I needed the stability of full-time work. Besides, I wanted my own classroom, my own kids to nurture. Then one afternoon the phone rang, and the principal of the Christian school my now-grown kids had attended invited me to interview for a position.

Invited . . . *me!* I was amazed. After the interview, I talked to a teacher on the hiring committee, seeking feedback on how I'd come across. She said mine was the strongest interview she'd seen.

Recalling my nervousness, I was astonished. When I got the job and went for the initial meeting with the principal, she confided that she'd been wanting to hire me for three years, ever since I'd earned my degree in education. She'd known me as a parent at the school and believed I'd make a fine teacher.

I was astounded. And Nehemiah must have felt the same way when he allowed the king to see his sorrow after concealing it for four months. How could he have known the king would extend such wonderful favor?

**Jehovah-jireh,** *You truly are the one who provides in overwhelming ways. I thank You so much for the wonderful way You brought me to my school. I don't deserve Your favor—but thank You for it anyway! In Christ, amen.*

**SEARCH THE WORD**

*When God answers prayer in amazing ways, we just want to sing His praise.*

Scripture: Nehemiah 2:1-10
Song: *"Your Love Is Reaching Me"*

***From this meditation today, I will pray . . .***

Adoration ____________________

Confession ____________________

Thanksgiving ____________________

Supplication ____________________

***From this meditation today, I will . . .***

Think ____________________

Say ____________________

Do ____________________

May 9

# First Step, Diagnosis

*And I went out by night . . . and viewed the walls of Jerusalem which were broken down and its gates which were burned with fire* (Nehemiah 2:13, *New King James Version*).

Scripture: Nehemiah 2:11-16

Song: *"My Soul Follows Hard After Thee"*

***From this meditation today, I will pray . . .***

Adoration ______________________________

______________________________

______________________________

Confession ______________________________

______________________________

______________________________

Thanksgiving ______________________________

______________________________

______________________________

Supplication ______________________________

______________________________

______________________________

***From this meditation today, I will . . .***

Think ______________________________

______________________________

______________________________

Say ______________________________

______________________________

______________________________

Do ______________________________

______________________________

______________________________

______________________________

______________________________

My youngest son has an impressive orthopedic history. Before he reached high school, he broke bones in a foot, a thigh, an arm (a couple of times) and his other elbow—twice. In all those trips to the emergency room and follow-up visits to the Orthopedic and Facture Clinic, I learned the importance of X-rays.

Always the first step in treating my son involved taking an X-ray. Then the doctor would slide the large film into the clips and turn on the light box behind it. "Here is the fracture," he'd say, pointing with a pen to the jagged edges of some misshapen bone. It wasn't difficult to accept his diagnosis, seeing it pictured in stark black and white, and I had no trouble agreeing to the treatment plan.

Nehemiah recognized the importance of diagnosis as a first step and took a donkey ride by moonlight to survey the damage to Jerusalem's wall. It's a good strategy for tackling any problem. Take time to gain a good understanding of what's amiss before proceeding to fix it.

Lord, *help me pause when troubles surface. Help me move into quietness that I might ask Your expert advice—and then spend plenty of time listening for Your still, small voice of guidance. May I always trust Your plan for overcoming any obstacles in my journey with You. In Jesus' name, amen.*

**SPOTLIGHT**

***Next Week's Lesson***

Time spent analyzing a problem is never wasted.

# Recruit a Team

*I said to them . . . "Come and let us build the wall of Jerusalem" . . . So they said, "Let us rise up and build"*
(Nehemiah 2:17, 18, *New King James Version*).

As a new teacher, I'm learning all the time. This year I took an idea from a magazine and created a long list of jobs for my fifth-grade students. They eagerly volunteered to clean the white board, lead the pledges, and hand out papers. I was a little surprised at their willingness to help, but recognized a good thing when I saw it.

When their parents came for Back to School open-house night, the trend continued as moms and dads volunteered to drive on field trips, make copies, and grade papers. So many signed up that I had to create a calendar scheduling them for alternating weeks!

Needless to say, it's been a wonderful year. I bring less work home and leave school earlier. Chatting with moms when they come in has built strong relationships, and the classroom runs smoothly because all the students share the workload.

Nehemiah's dynamic leadership followed the same principle: recruiting an army of volunteers for the task at hand. Rarely can we do it all alone.

Lord, *thank You for calling Your people to work together in the kingdom. We'd miss so much if we tried to manage everything without help. May we always work hand-in-hand for Your glory. Through Christ, amen.*

**SEARCH THE WORD**

*God knows that His people are stronger when they serve together.*

Scripture: Nehemiah 2:17-20
Song: *"In the Family of God"*

***From this meditation today, I will pray . . .***

Adoration ____________________

Confession ____________________

Thanksgiving ____________________

Supplication ____________________

***From this meditation today, I will . . .***

Think ____________________

Say ____________________

Do ____________________

May 11

# A Crying Prayer

*In the day when I cried out, You answered me, and made me bold with strength in my soul* (Psalm 138:3, *New King James Version*).

Scripture: Psalm 138:1-5
Song: *"As the Deer"*

*From this meditation today, I will pray . . .*

Adoration ____________________

Confession ____________________

Thanksgiving ____________________

Supplication ____________________

*From this meditation today, I will . . .*

Think ____________________

Say ____________________

Do ____________________

During a short-term missions trip to Brazil, I spent three weeks living in the home of a family who welcomed us with overwhelming graciousness. Our hostess, Nair, eagerly helped me learn a little Portuguese and taught me how to cook the savory black-bean mixture she served over rice.

My most memorable lesson, however, occurred not in the kitchen but in a garage. She took me to a prayer meeting of women from the church, held in the white stucco carport of one of the church women. As usual, with ladies everywhere, the gathering began with enthusiastic chatter. Then they started to pray.

Although I understood only a few words of the language, there was no mistaking the fervor of their intercessions. Nair squinted her eyes shut and cried out in a loud voice, tears streaming down her face. I watched in wonder. It wasn't the volume of her voice, nor the lowliness of the setting, but the intensity of her spirit that ignited mine. My hostess cried out to God, just as the psalmist did.

O God, *when Your Son prayed in the garden, He prayed so intently that drops of blood fell from His brow. Make me bold, Lord, and give me courage to open my heart in all sincerity to Your love. In Christ I pray. Amen.*

**SPOTLIGHT**
***Next Week's Lesson***

We should keep the lines of communication open to God so we know His voice in our time of need.

# Trust This Rock

*I call as my heart grows faint; lead me to the rock that is higher than I* (Psalm 61:2).

The children squeal with delight as I push the merry-go-round. "Faster—*faster!*" they cry, hanging on with all their might. Their innocent trust is so precious.

As for me, sometimes I feel life is a merry-go-round that goes too fast. Problems come one upon another, and my heart grows faint. I can't see the next step, and my soul cries, "Stop the world; I want to get off!"

Then I can drag my feet in a desperate attempt to control my own destiny. I can announce to Heaven that my problems are too big for God, that I must handle them myself. Or I can abandon myself to God, trusting that He will never fail or forsake me.

Yes, I can hold tightly to Him, my strong tower, my refuge, my rock. I can rest under the shelter of His wings and cry with Job, "Though He slay me, yet will I trust Him" (13:15, *NKJV*).

God is in control, either way. But when I choose trust, I end up having more peace, more hope, more joy—and I soon learn again just how much I'm loved.

Lord of my life, *today I want You to have control of my every word and deed. And keep reminding me that You are capable of handling each problem that comes my way. In the name of Jesus, my Lord and Savior, amen.*

**SEARCH THE WORD**

*God and I together accomplish much more than I ever do alone.*

Scripture: Psalm 61:1-5

Song: *"Strengthen for Service, Lord"*

*From this meditation today, I will pray . . .*

Adoration ______________________________

______________________________

______________________________

Confession ______________________________

______________________________

______________________________

Thanksgiving ______________________________

______________________________

______________________________

Supplication ______________________________

______________________________

______________________________

*From this meditation today, I will . . .*

Think ______________________________

______________________________

______________________________

Say ______________________________

______________________________

______________________________

Do ______________________________

______________________________

______________________________

May 12–19. ***Nancy Hagerman*** *lives in Colorado with her husband, Steve, director of Turkish World Outreach. She loves reading to her grandchildren.*

May 13

# It's the Little Things

*What they are building—if even a fox climbed up on it, he would break down their wall of stones!* (Nehemiah 4:3).

Scripture: Nehemiah 4:1-6

Song: *"Eternal God, Whose Power Upholds"*

***From this meditation today, I will pray . . .***

Adoration ______________________________

______________________________

______________________________

Confession ______________________________

______________________________

______________________________

Thanksgiving ______________________________

______________________________

______________________________

Supplication ______________________________

______________________________

______________________________

***From this meditation today, I will . . .***

Think ______________________________

______________________________

______________________________

Say ______________________________

______________________________

______________________________

Do ______________________________

______________________________

______________________________

______________________________

______________________________

If I were a senior devil instructing less-experienced imps as in C. S. Lewis's *Screwtape Letters,* I know just what I'd say. "Remember, the little foxes spoil the whole vineyard! Don't attack your assigned believer with major catastrophes; he will just run to our Enemy. Send in the little foxes, the everyday irritations. Bring misunderstandings into his relationships, get him into debt, fill his life with a thousand minor distractions. Those are the things he'll consider too small to bring to You Know Who.

"And keep him busy, busy, busy! Don't allow him any time for fellowship, prayer, or reading that horrible black book. He'll soon become tired, confused, and begin to believe the Enemy doesn't care for them. In next to no time . . . he'll be yours."

My point: Don't assume that anything in your life is beneath God's attention. It's the little discouragements that do so much damage, if we let them. That is how Sanballat and his friends hoped to wear down the builders of Jerusalem's walls. But Nehemiah and his people refused to give in. We, likewise, can stand firm in God.

Father, *help me never forget how much I matter to You. Today I commit my life into Your hands, even amidst naysayers and discouragers. Thank You for Your loving care in all situations. In Jesus' name, amen.*

**SPOTLIGHT**

***Next Week's Lesson***

**If we allow God to deal with the daily distractions, we will defeat the devil.**

# Not So Formidable

*When Sanballat, Tobiah, the Arabs, the Ammonites and the men of Ashdod heard that the repairs to Jerusalem's walls had gone ahead . . . they were very angry* (Nehemiah 4:7).

Sanballat, Tobiah, the Arabs, the Ammonites, and the men of Ashdod—formidable enemies against a handful of God's elect. Yet God's people have often faced insurmountable odds. David stood before nine-foot-tall Goliath with five stones and a sling. Moses stood against Pharaoh with only a wooden staff. Elijah confronted a wicked queen and 450 prophets of Baal with a simple stone altar and a stack of wet wood. And Jehoshaphat defeated the armies of Ammon and Moab simply by standing still and waiting on God.

Our Lord's victories do not depend on our strength, but they do make use of our faith. Even today, He can still walk through fire with us, shut the mouths of lions, and knock down walls—or build them up again. Our Lord can divide the Red Sea as easily today as He did so many years ago. He is the same yesterday, today, and forever. Remembering this truth makes it easier to calm my spirit, to allow His perfect love to cast out my fears as I face my own daily giants.

Precious Lord, *I thank You that victory in Jesus does not depend on my strength but on Yours. Guide my thoughts and actions today. Help me remember to wait on You, for You are my strength. In Jesus' name, amen.*

**SEARCH THE WORD**

*When we turn our enemies over to God, they don't stand a chance!*

Scripture: Nehemiah 4:7-11

Song: *"Faith Is the Victory"*

*From this meditation today, I will pray . . .*

Adoration ______________________________

______________________________

______________________________

Confession ______________________________

______________________________

______________________________

Thanksgiving ______________________________

______________________________

______________________________

Supplication ______________________________

______________________________

______________________________

*From this meditation today, I will . . .*

Think ______________________________

______________________________

______________________________

Say ______________________________

______________________________

______________________________

Do ______________________________

______________________________

______________________________

______________________________

______________________________

# Do Something!

*Don't be afraid of them. Remember the* LORD*, who is great and awesome, and fight for your brothers, your sons and your daughters, your wives and your homes* (Nehemiah 4:14).

**Scripture: Nehemiah 4:12-15**
**Song: *"Onward, Christian Soldiers"***

***From this meditation today, I will pray . . .***

Adoration ________________________________

________________________________

________________________________

Confession ________________________________

________________________________

________________________________

Thanksgiving ________________________________

________________________________

________________________________

Supplication ________________________________

________________________________

________________________________

***From this meditation today, I will . . .***

Think ________________________________

________________________________

________________________________

Say ________________________________

________________________________

________________________________

Do ________________________________

________________________________

________________________________

________________________________

________________________________

Some time ago a teacher in Colorado was fired for keeping a Bible on his desk. It was not a teaching aid. He simply kept it there to read while he ate his lunch.

And in a case that was later overturned, the Ninth Circuit Court of Appeals ruled the Pledge of Allegiance unconstitutional because of the words, "under God." Hearing of the case, Jay Leno quipped, "With hurricanes, flooding, fires, earthquakes tearing up the world from one end to the other, are we sure this is a good time to take God out of the pledge of allegiance?"

British orator Edmund Burke said, "All that's necessary for the triumph of evil is that good men do nothing." Nehemiah must have known that doing nothing in the face of his enemies would lead to their assured triumph. Instead, he called the people to bring swords, spears, and bows to the wall. They'd need to form a strong defense.

Even today, Christians under attack will often have to rouse themselves. Doing nothing as a once great culture crumbles will bring no honor to themselves or to the God who ultimately governs all peoples.

Lord, *help me to be Your hands, Your voice, Your heart within a struggling society that's dying to find Your salvation. In Jesus' name I pray. Amen.*

**SPOTLIGHT**
***Next Week's Lesson***

To vanquish evil we need powerful weapons: God's Word and prayer.

# How Are You Today?

*From that day on, half of my men did the work, while the other half were equipped with spears, shields, bows and armor* (Nehemiah 4:16).

"How are you?" my friend asked politely as I entered the church building. Smiling, I gave the standard reply, "Fine!" Actually, I was screaming inside. I'd just moved, boxes filled the house, and my daughter was seriously ill. I felt overwhelmed and hopeless, on the verge of despair. Had I been honest with my friend, she stood ready to offer prayer, compassion, and practical help. But I allowed pride to keep me from the warm support of Christian fellowship.

No doubt here's where we can learn from Nehemiah, who designated half of his people for support while the others worked. Yet we can't support one another if we don't know what's needed—and what help is available.

One day a small child was trying to lift a heavy stone as his father watched. The rock wouldn't budge, and the boy began to weep. "Are you using all your strength?" his father asked.

"Yes, I am!" the frustrated boy cried.

"No, you're not," the father said evenly. "You haven't asked me to help you."

Lord, *deliver me from any pride that keeps me from the support I need from my Christian brothers and sisters. Thank You, in Jesus' name. Amen.*

**SEARCH THE WORD**

*Stretch your prayer life before you strain yourself!*

Scripture: Nehemiah 4:16-23

Song: *"Brothers, Joining Hand to Hand"*

***From this meditation today, I will pray . . .***

Adoration ______________________

______________________

______________________

Confession ______________________

______________________

______________________

Thanksgiving ______________________

______________________

______________________

Supplication ______________________

______________________

______________________

***From this meditation today, I will . . .***

Think ______________________

______________________

______________________

Say ______________________

______________________

______________________

Do ______________________

______________________

______________________

______________________

______________________

# Grapes and Diamonds

*I prayed, "Now strengthen my hands"*
(Nehemiah 6:9).

Scripture: Nehemiah 6:1-14
Song: *"I Need Thee Every Hour"*

***From this meditation today, I will pray . . .***

Adoration ______________________________

Confession ______________________________

Thanksgiving ______________________________

Supplication ______________________________

***From this meditation today, I will . . .***

Think ______________________________

Say ______________________________

Do ______________________________

A grape must be crushed before it can be made into wine. Silver must withstand the hottest part of the fire to become pure. Diamonds form only through prolonged exposure to high pressure and temperature. And believers grow spiritually mature and complete through trials and testing.

Men and women of God aren't formed overnight. Joseph suffered in Pharaoh's dungeon. David faced Goliath and even death at the hand of his king. Daniel was taken captive and carried hundreds of miles from home before he became counsel to a pagan king. Even Jesus learned obedience from the things He suffered (see Hebrews 5:8). Every trial brings a choice. We can shake our fist at God and ask, "Why me?" Or we can humbly pray, "Now, strengthen my hands."

Lilias Trotter writes in her *Parables of the Cross:* "Take the hardest thing in your life—the place of difficulty, outward or inward—and expect God to triumph gloriously in that very spot. Just there He can bring your soul into blossom."

Heavenly Father, *I trustingly place myself in Your hands. Help me wait patiently for the unfolding of Your purposes in my life. I present my body a living sacrifice that You might make it holy and acceptable. In the name of Your Son, my Savior, I pray. Amen.*

**SPOTLIGHT**
***Next Week's Lesson***

God can use our struggles to strengthen us and astound the unbeliever.

# Impossible? His Specialty

*When all our enemies heard about this . . . [they] were afraid and lost their self-confidence, because they realized that this work had been done with the help of our God* (Nehemiah 6:16).

The orphans had dinner and were tucked into bed. They had no idea the orphanage had no money or food for breakfast the next day. But God had called George Mueller to care for these children. Though he did not know how, he was confident the Lord would provide.

Committing the care of the orphans to God, Mr. Mueller went to bed. The next morning he went for a walk, praying for God to supply the needs. During his walk he met a friend who asked him to accept some money for the orphanage. Mr. Mueller thanked his friend, but didn't tell him about the pressing need. Instead, he praised God for the answer to prayer and went back to the orphanage for breakfast.

God finishes what He starts. He can tear down walls and build them up again. He opens doors no one can shut and closes doors that can't be opened. As Nehemiah's enemies learned, no one can change God's plans or force His hand. God specializes in the impossible.

Dear heavenly Father, *thank You for Your faithfulness. My heart trusts in You, and You have never failed me—nor will You. Please help me to walk by faith in joyful anticipation of the blessings that await me. In my precious Savior's name I pray. Amen.*

**SEARCH THE WORD**

*When you don't know the next step, you can trust your Tour Guide on life's most extreme adventure.*

Scripture: Nehemiah 6:15-19

**Song:** *"He Is Able to Deliver Thee"*

*From this meditation today, I will pray . . .*

Adoration ______________________________

______________________________

______________________________

Confession ______________________________

______________________________

______________________________

Thanksgiving ______________________________

______________________________

______________________________

Supplication ______________________________

______________________________

______________________________

*From this meditation today, I will . . .*

Think ______________________________

______________________________

______________________________

Say ______________________________

______________________________

______________________________

Do ______________________________

______________________________

______________________________

______________________________

______________________________

# Is a Quick Fix Worth It?

*Wait for the* LORD; *be strong,*
*and let your heart take courage; yes, wait for the* LORD
(Psalm 27:14, *New American Standard Bible*).

Scripture: Psalm 27:11-14
Song: *"Wait, O My Soul, Thy Maker's Will"*

*From this meditation today, I will pray . . .*

Adoration ________________________________

________________________________

________________________________

Confession ________________________________

________________________________

________________________________

Thanksgiving ________________________________

________________________________

________________________________

Supplication ________________________________

________________________________

________________________________

*From this meditation today, I will . . .*

Think ________________________________

________________________________

________________________________

Say ________________________________

________________________________

________________________________

Do ________________________________

________________________________

________________________________

May 19-25. ***Judith Ward,*** *a retired Head Start teacher, lives in Kentucky, where she enjoys writing children's stories and playing with her grandchildren.*

While visiting my niece, I was accused of "trying to control everything." I accepted the fact that what I had done upset my niece. But I could not accept her characterization of the motive. I felt the motive was love.

I was hurt and went to my room to read my Bible and pray. Soon it became clear to me that I must not defend myself but wait upon God to heal this breech.

Nevertheless, I still tried to fix the problem! And you can imagine what happened; the hurtful words we said to each other caused even more pain on both sides.

Eventually, we "agreed to disagree" and parted with hugs. God in His own time healed both of our hearts, but my attempt at a quick fix had contributed little. I learned much, though: Waiting on God isn't always easy, but the benefits far outweigh the consequences of impatient and misguided controlling behaviors.

Lord, *let me realize the fulfillment of Your promise—that if I wait on You, my heart can take courage and I can have strength to obey You. Thank You for showing me mercy and forgiveness when I rush ahead of Your will. In Christ's precious name I pray. Amen.*

**SPOTLIGHT**
***Next Week's Lesson***

It is helpful to remember that in God's time all issues will be seen as they really are.

# It Didn't Happen

*All native-born Israelites are to live in booths so your descendants will know that I had the Israelites live in booths when I brought them out of Egypt. I am the* LORD *your God* (Leviticus 23:42, 43).

One day while I was walking my 5-year-old grandson, Kevin, home from the park, I noticed a big dog watching us from across the street. Knowing Kevin's fear of dogs, I immediately shielded him from seeing the dog. Kevin joyfully went on his merry way, unaware of the potential danger.

I wonder how many times God has sheltered me that way. When I pray in thankfulness to Him, I'm reminded these days to include gratitude, not only for the blessings I've received, but for the unknown tragedies from which God has surely shielded me.

God's people in the days of Moses enjoyed the great blessing of God's direct protection, as He even instructed them in building their shelters. This reminds me of the Scripture in Psalm 61:3, where David says to God, "You have been my refuge, a strong tower against the foe." It also helps me form a picture of Jesus, who shelters us from every form of spiritual opposition.

Dear God, *help me to remember that You have provided shelter for me, just as You sheltered the Israelites in the wilderness. Teach me a daily, heartfelt gratitude for Your loving care. Through Jesus Christ my Lord, amen.*

**SEARCH THE WORD**
*When we need an attitude adjustment, we should consider how things might have been without God.*

Scripture: Leviticus 23:33-43
Song: *"The Sheltering Rock"*

*From this meditation today, I will pray . . .*

Adoration ______________________

______________________

______________________

Confession ______________________

______________________

______________________

Thanksgiving ______________________

______________________

______________________

Supplication ______________________

______________________

______________________

*From this meditation today, I will . . .*

Think ______________________

______________________

______________________

Say ______________________

______________________

______________________

Do ______________________

______________________

______________________

______________________

______________________

# Frazzled or Joyful?

*The* Lord *your God will bless you in all your harvest and in all the work of your hands, and your joy will be complete* (Deuteronomy 16:15).

Scripture: Deuteronomy 16:13-17
Song: *"He Keeps Me Singing"*

***From this meditation today, I will pray . . .***

Adoration ______________________________

______________________________

______________________________

Confession ______________________________

______________________________

______________________________

Thanksgiving ______________________________

______________________________

______________________________

Supplication ______________________________

______________________________

______________________________

***From this meditation today, I will . . .***

Think ______________________________

______________________________

______________________________

Say ______________________________

______________________________

______________________________

Do ______________________________

______________________________

______________________________

______________________________

______________________________

While attending a writer's conference, I ran into a friend I hadn't seen in years. As we were eating lunch, I noticed how nervous and exhausted she appeared. She shared with me that she wished she could be more joyful about serving God . . . but she was simply worn out.

I sensed that she'd overextended herself in church activities. "When do you have time to write?" I asked.

"That is exactly my problem," she said. "I really thought God wanted to use my writing to encourage others, but I can't find time to do it! I feel I am disobeying God."

A few months later I ran into her again. This time, she shared that she'd read Eugenia Price's book, *A Woman's Choice,* and it had spoken deeply to her heart. She even quoted these lines: "Millions of women are simply expecting too much of themselves. God does not expect us to be superwomen. He only expects us to be His women and to take the daily provision He yearns to give us."

I couldn't have said it better!

Heavenly Father, *just as You helped my friend, let me stay tuned to the Holy Spirit's leading so I too can have my joy complete in You. I pray the work of my hands today will glorify You. In Jesus' name, amen.*

**SPOTLIGHT**
***Next Week's Lesson***

Lifted spirits come after the heart is bowed down before God.

# Bow to Him

*Ezra blessed the* Lord, *the great God. And all the people answered, Amen, Amen, with lifting up their hands: and they bowed their heads, and worshipped the* Lord *with their faces to the ground*
(Nehemiah 8:6, *King James Version*).

They worshiped with their faces to the ground? What do you make of that?

Meditating on what genuine renewal means, my thoughts drifted back to my treasured Sunday school teacher in Deland, Florida, years ago. Her every word and action demonstrated a heart consumed with Jesus. With humble countenance and demeanor, she ministered His love to everyone. Mrs. Thompson had true humility because she sat at the feet of Jesus daily.

Andrew Murray in his book *Humility* says, "We may find that we have been delighting in beautiful thoughts and feelings, in solemn acts of consecration and faith, while the only sure mark of the presence of God—the disappearance of self—was all the time wanting. Come and let us flee to Jesus, and hide ourselves in Him." Perhaps this principle might motivate a people to worship with faces—or knees—pressed to the ground. But when did you last bow, literally, to God at a worship service?

Lord, *often I think more highly of myself than I should. Help me pray today in a posture that shows my willingness to hear Your voice and submit to Your will. In Christ's name I pray. Amen.*

**SEARCH THE WORD**

*Downcast eyes and a humble heart help us see Jesus.*

Scripture: Nehemiah 8:1-6

**Song: *"Before the Lord We Bow"***

***From this meditation today, I will pray . . .***

Adoration ______________________________

______________________________

______________________________

Confession ______________________________

______________________________

______________________________

Thanksgiving ______________________________

______________________________

______________________________

Supplication ______________________________

______________________________

______________________________

***From this meditation today, I will . . .***

Think ______________________________

______________________________

______________________________

Say ______________________________

______________________________

______________________________

Do ______________________________

______________________________

______________________________

______________________________

______________________________

May 23

# Still Hearing the Word?

*They read from the Book of the Law of God, making it clear and giving the meaning so that the people could understand what was being read* (Nehemiah 8:8).

Scripture: Nehemiah 8:7-12

Song: *"We Have a Sure Prophetic Word"*

***From this meditation today, I will pray . . .***

Adoration ______________________________

________________________________________

________________________________________

Confession ______________________________

________________________________________

________________________________________

Thanksgiving ______________________________

________________________________________

________________________________________

Supplication ______________________________

________________________________________

________________________________________

***From this meditation today, I will . . .***

Think ______________________________

________________________________________

________________________________________

Say ______________________________

________________________________________

________________________________________

Do ______________________________

________________________________________

________________________________________

________________________________________

________________________________________

My husband and I had moved to a new city and were searching for a church home. We didn't realize that we hadn't been "fed" very well from the Bible—until we heard clear and powerful proclamation from the Book, just as in Nehemiah's day. We were like sponges; we couldn't get enough of the Scripture in this new church.

Is it harder to find such good preaching today? I've certainly noticed many preachers embellish the Word by decorating it with their own favorite spin.

Ezra and Nehemiah awakened a hunger in the people to know more about God—directly from the Word of God. And, thankfully, the Word that so powerfully convicted the people of Nehemiah's day is the same Scripture that convicts and blesses us today; plus, we have the New Testament too. What a shame it would be to ignore this treasure or listen to explanations of it that fall short of its glorious message: the word of sin and repentance, of forgiveness and eternal salvation.

I praise You, *God the Father, God the Son, and God the Holy Spirit, for the many preachers who continue faithfully to feed their flocks with the precious Word that leads us to Christ our Lord. Help me to faithfully lift up our pastors and teachers in prayer. In Christ's name, amen.*

**SPOTLIGHT**

***Next Week's Lesson***

How can God's Word be a lamp to our feet if we never light its flame?

# Let Us Keep the Feast

*[Ezra] read from the book of the law of God daily, from the first day to the last day. And they celebrated the feast seven days, and on the eighth day there was a solemn assembly according to the ordinance* (Nehemiah 8:18, *New American Standard Bible*).

One of my favorite authors is the 19th-century preacher Charles Spurgeon. He has such a way of giving us word pictures to help us understand Scripture. In one of his books, *Twelve Sermons on Holiness,* he enlightens us regarding the word *feast:* "Let us keep the feast, nourishing souls with Christ's sacrifice, making our hearts glad by reflecting upon the blessing which this has brought us. It should always be feast time with God's servants. Let's feast by feeding upon Christ; he was slain to be fed upon. Only Jesus is the true feast. Our keeping of the feast is not a matter for times and seasons, for festivals and holidays, it is always our position, our daily lifelong fellowship with Jesus."

As we see Ezra and the people feasting for seven days on the law of God, and as we see how Spurgeon offers such a beautiful view of what holy feasting is, we can learn also to feast on God's Word daily.

My awesome Father, *thank You for Jesus the Lamb who was sacrificed for my sins. And thank You for speaking to me through the Bible, which I treasure so highly. As I feast on the written Word and the living Word, grow me into the kingdom servant You call me to be. Through Christ, amen.*

**SEARCH THE WORD**

*The Christian's life can be feast or famine—it depends on how much we eat of His bread!*

Scripture: Nehemiah 8:13-18

**Song:** *"Feasting with My Lord"*

*From this meditation today, I will pray . . .*

Adoration ______________________________

______________________________

______________________________

Confession ______________________________

______________________________

______________________________

Thanksgiving ______________________________

______________________________

______________________________

Supplication ______________________________

______________________________

______________________________

*From this meditation today, I will . . .*

Think ______________________________

______________________________

______________________________

Say ______________________________

______________________________

______________________________

Do ______________________________

______________________________

______________________________

______________________________

______________________________

# Help or Harm?

*Keep back thy servant also from presumptuous sins; let them not have dominion over me: then shall I be upright, and I shall be innocent from the great transgression* (Psalm 19:13, *King James Version*).

Scripture: Psalm 19:7-14

Song: *"What A Friend We Have in Jesus"*

*From this meditation today, I will pray . . .*

Adoration ______________________________

Confession ______________________________

Thanksgiving ______________________________

Supplication ______________________________

*From this meditation today, I will . . .*

Think ______________________________

Say ______________________________

Do ______________________________

Most mothers like to think they have "the gift of helps" in relation to their children. We love to help our children—but do we love it too much? Once our married children leave the nest, they may see our helping gift in a whole new light.

One holiday while visiting our daughter, I started to do what I always do: match my grandson's socks. Since our daughter has a large family, I always thought that doing something practical like that was quite helpful. But this time, as I picked up a sock to take upstairs, my daughter said, "Don't do that."

I was shocked. It came out that I was offending her by getting into the children's dresser drawers.

A presumptuous sin? I began to see it that way. Yes, after much embarrassment and agonizing, I finally saw it from my daughter's viewpoint—and apologized. Of course, I hope I'll keep back from presumption with God too. That may be harder to see, harder to define. I'll ask Him to help me here!

Lord, *let me not offend You or others with my words and actions. Thank You for being my friend always, even when I goof! Through Christ, amen.*

**SPOTLIGHT**

***Next Week's Lesson***

We presume far too much if we think we are as wise as God.

# Needing Wisdom Today?

*The child grew and became strong;*
*he was filled with wisdom, and the grace of God was upon him*
(Luke 2:40).

Our small group members began sharing their prayer requests. One by one, they made their needs known.

"Our daughter's new neighbors are spreading lies about her. She needs wisdom regarding how to deal with the situation."

"We found drugs in our son's room. Pray that we'll know how to talk to him about it."

"Our daughter-in-law was taken to the hospital after a drug overdose. Pray for wisdom for our son."

All these friends had knowledge of God and His promises. They knew the Scriptures. But now they needed more; they needed to know how to *apply* the Word to the situations they faced.

We all need such wisdom. Solomon asked the Lord for it, believing it was more important to him than vast riches. And even Jesus, in His human nature, grew in wisdom.

What crisis are you experiencing today? It may be a family illness, a broken relationship, a spiritual dryness. Ask the Lord for wisdom, and He will give it to you.

Dear Lord, *I am so thankful for Your promise to guide me into Your wise ways. Keep my heart attentive to Your leading. In Jesus' name, amen.*

**SEARCH THE WORD**

*God is wise enough to remedy any of our shortcomings.*

Scripture: Proverbs 8:22-31

Song: *"I Want to Be Like Jesus"*

*From this meditation today, I will pray . . .*

Adoration ______________________________

______________________________

______________________________

Confession ______________________________

______________________________

______________________________

Thanksgiving ______________________________

______________________________

______________________________

Supplication ______________________________

______________________________

______________________________

*From this meditation today, I will . . .*

Think ______________________________

______________________________

______________________________

Say ______________________________

______________________________

______________________________

Do ______________________________

______________________________

______________________________

May 26–31. ***Donna Goodrich,*** *of Mesa, Arizona, is a freelance writer, editor, and conference leader. She and her husband, Gary, have three children.*

May 27

# God Speaks, Even to Me

*In the past God spoke to our forefathers through the prophets at many times and in various ways* (Hebrews 1:1).

Scripture: Hebrews 1:1-5
Song: *"Speak to My Soul"*

*From this meditation today, I will pray . . .*

Adoration ______

Confession ______

Thanksgiving ______

Supplication ______

*From this meditation today, I will . . .*

Think ______

Say ______

Do ______

I caught my breath as I drove through the beautiful northern Michigan hills, passing lush pine trees on both sides. I could almost hear God's whisper, "I created this beauty for you."

Years earlier, tears had come to my eyes as our son-in-law held up our first grandchild. I'd thought back to our daughter's illness during the first three years of her life, and I could almost hear God whisper, "I healed Janet so she could be the mother of this precious baby."

And in 1984, doubts filled my heart as I stood by the side of my comatose mother. "Why, Lord?" I implored. "She's such a good woman." And I could almost hear God's whisper, "She's been faithful to me all these years. It's time for her to come home."

God speaks to us in many ways: in the beauty of nature, in the wonder of childbirth, even in the valley of death. Thankfully, no matter the trial we face, we can always take a moment to listen for His voice. For God has been speaking to His beloved human beings down through the centuries, calling them to himself. He is just that good, just that personal, and just that interested in you and me.

Lord, *as the psalmist says, let me be still today and know that You are God. I pray to listen more closely, through Christ, my Savior. Amen.*

**SPOTLIGHT**
***Next Week's Lesson***

It's amazing!
Although we are one of billions,
God knows our every need.

# Just Add Light

*The light shines in the darkness,*
*but the darkness has not understood it* (John 1:5).

What a dark time in the life of my friend Charles! First, his mother died. Shortly afterwards, he lost his younger sister to pneumonia. Then one day he came home to find his grandmother lifeless on the kitchen floor. Adding to his problems was an inability to keep a job because of his addiction to alcohol.

But then Charles met the Lord. "When my grandma died," he told me, "I knew that if I didn't change the way I was heading, I would very quickly be next."

The months following his baptism weren't easy for Charles, but he determined to leave his old ways behind. When I saw him a year later, he was sober, neatly dressed, and fully employed.

When the darkness of our tough times seems to overwhelm us, we can remember that Christ came not only to give *life*, but to give *light*. After all, He is the light of the world (see John 8:12). And the best way to fight any darkness is simply to add more light.

Dear Father, *I am so thankful that You have brought the light of Christ into my life. And I am thankful, too, that no matter how hard the prince of darkness tries, he can never gain a complete victory. Through Christ and His cross, the war against sin and death has been won. I give all glory to You, in the name of the Father, and the Son, and the Holy Spirit. Amen.*

**SEARCH THE WORD**

*When God comes near,*
*the shadows flee.*

Scripture: John 1:1-5

Song: *"The Light of the World Is Jesus"*

***From this meditation today, I will pray . . .***

Adoration ______________________________

______________________________

______________________________

Confession ______________________________

______________________________

______________________________

Thanksgiving ______________________________

______________________________

______________________________

Supplication ______________________________

______________________________

______________________________

***From this meditation today, I will . . .***

Think ______________________________

______________________________

______________________________

Say ______________________________

______________________________

______________________________

Do ______________________________

______________________________

______________________________

______________________________

______________________________

# He Reigns!

*About the Son he says, "Your throne, O God, will last for ever and ever, and righteousness will be the scepter of your kingdom"* (Hebrews 1:8).

Scripture: Hebrews 1:6-9
Song: *"God Is Still on the Throne"*

***From this meditation today, I will pray . . .***

Adoration ______________________________

______________________________

______________________________

Confession ______________________________

______________________________

______________________________

Thanksgiving ______________________________

______________________________

______________________________

Supplication ______________________________

______________________________

______________________________

***From this meditation today, I will . . .***

Think ______________________________

______________________________

______________________________

Say ______________________________

______________________________

______________________________

Do ______________________________

______________________________

______________________________

______________________________

______________________________

I once read a story in a Sunday school paper that ended with these words: "She prayed, and everything turned out all right." While I definitely know that prayer changes things, I'm more inclined to go along with the saying that "prayer changes people, and people change things."

More powerful than both these statements, however, is the promise in God's Word that no matter how rough the situation we're going through, His Son is still on the throne, and His rule makes everything right.

His rule took Joseph out of prison and made him prime minister of Egypt.

His rule delivered Daniel from the lions' den.

His rule brought three Hebrew men out of a fiery furnace, without even a trace of smoke remaining on them.

His rule brought down the walls of Jericho after the Israelites had marched around the city seven times.

Are you in a prison today of illness or depression? walking through the fire? facing a wall? God is still on the throne. In due time, He will make everything right.

Father, *thank You that every situation may be redeemed for Your glory—even if only as a way of purifying me through fiery trials. Keep me strong and faithful, then, amidst all circumstances! In Your Son's name, amen.*

**SPOTLIGHT**
***Next Week's Lesson***

In an ever-changing world, God's care is constant.

# Some Things Never Change

*You remain the same, and your years will never end*
(Hebrews 1:12).

I walked into the empty chapel on the campgrounds. Things didn't look the same as they did when I was a teen and my family spent 10 days there every summer. Gleaming restrooms replaced the wooden structures across the road. A beautiful nursery made it convenient for mothers to enjoy the services. No more ceiling fans; air conditioners had taken their place. "Everything's different," I thought wistfully.

No, not everything. For across the front of the chapel stretched the grey stone altar rail, stained with the tears of many seekers over the years. I thought of all the prayers offered at that altar: for salvation, for renewal, for guidance in ministry and mission. There were so many prayers of intercession for loved ones or prayers for strength and encouragement. And one more thing hadn't changed: The God I met summer after summer at those camp meeting services is the same God I serve today.

Perhaps things have radically changed in your life. You've lost a family member; you've had to make a move; your children are gone. Take heart. God is still there for you, and He never changes.

Father, *the older I get, the harder it is to accept changes in my world. Yet how reassuring is Your unchanging faithfulness! In Jesus' name, amen.*

**SEARCH THE WORD**

*If the distance between you and God has lengthened, be assured God hasn't moved.*

Scripture: Hebrews 1:10-12
**Song: *"Yesterday, Today, Forever"***

***From this meditation today, I will pray . . .***

Adoration ______________________

______________________

______________________

Confession ______________________

______________________

______________________

Thanksgiving ______________________

______________________

______________________

Supplication ______________________

______________________

______________________

***From this meditation today, I will . . .***

Think ______________________

______________________

______________________

Say ______________________

______________________

______________________

Do ______________________

______________________

______________________

______________________

______________________

# Jesus Is Here with Us

*The Word became flesh and made his dwelling among us. We have seen his glory* (John 1:14).

Scripture: John 1:14-18

**Song:** *"Thou Didst Leave Thy Throne"*

*From this meditation today, I will pray . . .*

Adoration ______________________________

______________________________

______________________________

Confession ______________________________

______________________________

______________________________

Thanksgiving ______________________________

______________________________

______________________________

Supplication ______________________________

______________________________

______________________________

*From this meditation today, I will . . .*

Think ______________________________

______________________________

______________________________

Say ______________________________

______________________________

______________________________

Do ______________________________

______________________________

______________________________

______________________________

______________________________

The baby girl wasn't expected to live through the night. But when a friend walked into the hospital room the next morning, the infant was cooing and smiling. The friend looked at the exhausted, but thankful, parents and said, "Jesus must have been here."

A young woman who had suffered from depression for 18 months awoke one morning and told her husband, "I'm going to make it." Joy filled the room. Jesus must have been there.

A teenage girl arose from prayer and shared with those gathered around her, "The aching loneliness I had inside is gone." Jesus must have been there.

It's true that none of us has seen the face of God, nor His Son, in the flesh. But who can deny that we have seen His glory over and over again—in His touch on our bodies, our minds, and our hearts? How God must love us—to become one of us and to let us see like that!

I am going to look around me today and make a note of all the places where I might see glimpses of His glory. I know it will encourage and strengthen my heart.

Dear Father, *thank You for loving me so deeply. Thank You for sending Your Son to live on this earth that He might understand all the things I'm going through. I love You, in Jesus' name. Amen.*

**SPOTLIGHT**

***Next Week's Lesson***

In order to find Jesus, start the search in your heart.

# June

# IMAGES OF CHRIST IN HEBREWS

*He is the image of the invisible God,*
*the firstborn over all creation.*
—Colossians 1:15

Photo © iStock

# Angelic Encouragement

*Are not all angels ministering spirits sent to serve those who will inherit salvation?*
(Hebrews 1:14).

Scripture: Hebrews 1:13, 14
Song: *"God Will Take Care of You"*

*From this meditation today, I will pray . . .*

Adoration ______________________

______________________

______________________

Confession ______________________

______________________

______________________

Thanksgiving ______________________

______________________

______________________

Supplication ______________________

______________________

______________________

*From this meditation today, I will . . .*

Think ______________________

______________________

______________________

Say ______________________

______________________

______________________

Do ______________________

______________________

______________________

June 1. ***Donna Goodrich,*** *of Mesa, Arizona, is a freelance writer, editor, and conference leader. She and her husband, Gary, have three children.*

I sat in Detroit Metro airport, exhausted. Shortly after my mother's death, my elderly stepfather had come to spend five months with us, and I had just taken him home. On the plane I was seated next to a gentlemen who turned out to be a Christian singer. I shared with him my reason for the trip, and he promised to pray for me.

When I changed planes in Chicago, my new seatmate was reading a book written by an inspirational author I knew. We, too, had an uplifting conversation. Then, as I embarked on the third leg of my flight—from St. Louis to Phoenix—my new seatmate and I discovered we had a mutual friend in the church she attended.

Back home, my husband greeted me and said, "You must be tired."

"No," I replied. "God sent three 'angels' to minister to me. I feel renewed!" And I wondered: Who might need my own angelic encouragements in the week ahead?

Dear Father, *sometimes I get so caught up in my own problems, I fail to look for those who may need my help. Lead me to someone today who needs encouragement, just as You have ministered to me. I pray this prayer in the name of Jesus, my merciful Savior and Lord. Amen.*

**SPOTLIGHT**
***Next Week's Lesson***

Unlike men, God has perfect knowledge of when and how we need His intervention.

# Something God Forgets

*I will forgive their iniquity, and their sin I will remember no more* (Jeremiah 31:34, *New King James Version*).

How is your memory? Ever forget anything? I have forgotten so many things that . . . I could never remember them all! At least I've never forgotten my wife's birthday or our anniversary.

However, I did forget her name once. Yes, shortly after our wedding, I was leading worship and wanted to say something about my new wife. Since I was nervous anyway, my mind seemed to go blank at just the wrong moment. How did I recover? I spoke of "my beautiful bride" (avoiding saying her name at all). She thought I was being romantic; I didn't tell her otherwise!

Has it occurred to you that nothing "occurs" to God? God knows everything, yet our passage says that He chooses not to remember our sin. Unlike us, God can choose what to remember and what to forget. And when God forgets, it really is gone, forgotten right out of existence.

Dear Father, *how thankful I am that You have chosen to deal with my sin problem through Your own personal sacrifice in Jesus, Your Son. I lift my heart in praise for the saving work He did for me at Calvary. Thanks to You for loving sinners and forgetting their sins. In my Savior's name, amen.*

**SEARCH THE WORD**

*God can help us in our darkest hour and still forget what brought us to that point.*

Scripture: Jeremiah 31:31-34

**Song:** *"Jesus Loves Even Me"*

*From this meditation today, I will pray . . .*

Adoration ________________________________

________________________________

________________________________

Confession ________________________________

________________________________

________________________________

Thanksgiving ________________________________

________________________________

________________________________

Supplication ________________________________

________________________________

________________________________

*From this meditation today, I will . . .*

Think ________________________________

________________________________

________________________________

Say ________________________________

________________________________

________________________________

Do ________________________________

________________________________

________________________________

June 2–8. ***Peter Anderson*** *is a school teacher, who lives in Ocala, Florida, along with his wife and younger son. His hobbies include taking mission trips.*

# God Is So Generous!

*Abraham took a tenth of all he had captured in battle and gave it to Melchizedek* (Hebrews 7:2, *New Living Translation*).

Scripture: Hebrews 7:1-3
Song: *"Something for Thee"*

*From this meditation today, I will pray . . .*

Adoration ______________________________

Confession ______________________________

Thanksgiving ______________________________

Supplication ______________________________

*From this meditation today, I will . . .*

Think ______________________________

Say ______________________________

Do ______________________________

I've heard it said that if you want to clear a church building, just announce you'll be taking up an offering. And, apparently, there is no subject worse than tithing in certain churches. But I hope I haven't lost you, faithful reader, because of this topic. Like it or not, our Scripture discusses giving a tenth.

Our passage today has Abraham giving a tenth of all he had gained to Melchizedek. And just who is Melchizedek? Just the priest who is "like the Son of God" (see verse 3). Abraham knew it was God who provided the victories and spoils in all his battles. So as an act of worship, Abraham gave back a tenth of all he had graciously been given. Similarly, it is God who has blessed us with everything we have, even the air we breathe.

I know it can be difficult to follow and trust God completely. But we can begin by returning at least some portion of that with which He has blessed us. That portion will no doubt grow much larger over the years. For God is faithful, always overwhelming His children with a generosity that goes far beyond what they expect.

Dear Father, *help me to view everything in my life as on loan from Your gracious hand. As I lift up a thankful heart for all Your goodness, help me, as well, to give back with genuine gratitude. In Jesus' name, amen.*

**SPOTLIGHT**
***Next Week's Lesson***

Whether it is money or time, God expects us to be responsible for handling what He has loaned us.

# Conquering Who?

*Blessed be God Most High, who has defeated your enemies for you* (Genesis 14:20, *New Living Translation*).

"Don't count your years. Make your years count." That's what my refrigerator magnet says. An older couple (older than we are) had left us that magnet as a gift when we bought their house. My wife and I noticed it there on the frig almost immediately. And I've taken the advice to heart, trying to make my years count rather than counting the years as they seem to fly by, ever faster and faster.

It helps to learn to slow down each day, to pay attention—not just to the days but to moments within those days. Thus God calls to us in the Psalms: "Be still, and know that I am God" (Psalm 46:10).

It is this God who helps us through every day, every moment, every situation. He never fails us in our times of need.

But what particular "enemy" will you face today? Will it be a genuine thwarter of God's will or just an unnecessary obstacle of our own making? I like to remember the pithy words of writer Elbert Hubbard along these lines: "An enemy is anyone who tells the truth about you." In such a case, may God help us to conquer ourselves.

Heavenly Father, *help me to remember that all of my resources are sacred gifts, as they come from Your hand. Use me to make a difference today, by the power of Your indwelling Spirit. Through Christ, I pray. Amen.*

**SEARCH THE WORD**

*God stations himself beside us daily. Shouldn't that motivate us to use our time very wisely?*

Scripture: Genesis 14:17-20

Song: *"Holy Ground"*

***From this meditation today, I will pray . . .***

Adoration ______________________________

______________________________

______________________________

Confession ______________________________

______________________________

______________________________

Thanksgiving ______________________________

______________________________

______________________________

Supplication ______________________________

______________________________

______________________________

***From this meditation today, I will . . .***

Think ______________________________

______________________________

______________________________

Say ______________________________

______________________________

______________________________

Do ______________________________

______________________________

______________________________

______________________________

______________________________

# Who Is Really Blessed?

*Without question, the person who has the power to give a blessing is greater than the one who is blessed* (Hebrews 7:7, *New Living Translation*).

Scripture: Hebrews 7:4-17

Song: *"Hail, Thou Source of Every Blessing"*

***From this meditation today, I will pray . . .***

Adoration ______________________

______________________

______________________

Confession ______________________

______________________

______________________

Thanksgiving ______________________

______________________

______________________

Supplication ______________________

______________________

______________________

***From this meditation today, I will . . .***

Think ______________________

______________________

______________________

Say ______________________

______________________

______________________

Do ______________________

______________________

______________________

______________________

______________________

On my mission trips to Romania, I always took tissues, shampoo, soap, pain relievers, and an assortment of common things we easily find at our local discount stores in America. These items were to be delivered to the "gypsies" (the Roma) of Romania.

Upon entering the homes of many of the Roma, I was humbled to recall how richly blessed I have been over the years, beyond measure, from God's hand. While I was a blessing to them, they ended up being such a blessing to me.

What an awesome challenge—to *bless* someone else! When we have the resources to bless others, we should do so. I opened my heart to the Roma of Romania, and they opened their homes to me. I gave them supplies, but they gave me friendship. Really, who received the greater blessing? As Victor Hugo once said: "As the purse is emptied, the heart is filled."

Almighty and gracious God, *You have blessed me beyond all measure. Now help me to be a blessing to someone today. May I open my eyes to the needs around me—and also open my heart and billfold to the people You bring across my path. In the name of the Father, the Son, and the Holy Spirit, I pray. Amen.*

**SPOTLIGHT**

***Next Week's Lesson***

Only when I empty myself of worldly possessions can I hope to find room for His wealth.

# Satisfaction Guaranteed

*(For the law made nothing perfect),*
*and a better hope is introduced, by which we draw near to God*
(Hebrews 7:19).

The song says it best: "My hope is built on nothing less than Jesus' blood and righteousness." Quick question: Which would you prefer? The law or the grace of Jesus? We are made perfect through Christ Jesus, while the law can only show us our shortcomings. (I prefer the grace of Jesus.)

Christ Jesus is our better hope. When He comes into our lives, He gives us purpose. Through the work of the Holy Spirit, we draw near to God. When we accept Christ's sacrificial death on the cross for the remission of our sin, we gain that better hope for all eternity. Entering the waters of baptism in His name, we will be with Jesus forever.

Not only do we gain eternity, we gain Jesus as our "priest." He is our intercessor before God the Father, ever guaranteeing that our covenant with God stays in place. I like that word: *guarantee*. I can build my hope of eternity on Him, satisfaction guaranteed.

O great merciful Father, *thank You for Jesus, my Savior. He is indeed my hope and my guarantee of eternity. I praise His name. Help others to see Jesus living in me so that You will be glorified in my life—and become the hope in others' lives. I pray this prayer in the name of Jesus, my Savior and Lord. Amen.*

**SEARCH THE WORD**

*While other hope may be based on chance, hope in Christ comes with a guarantee.*

Scripture: Hebrews 7:18-24
**Song:** *"The Solid Rock"*

*From this meditation today, I will pray . . .*

Adoration ______________________

______________________

______________________

Confession ______________________

______________________

______________________

Thanksgiving ______________________

______________________

______________________

Supplication ______________________

______________________

______________________

*From this meditation today, I will . . .*

Think ______________________

______________________

______________________

Say ______________________

______________________

______________________

Do ______________________

______________________

______________________

______________________

______________________

June 7

# Save to the Uttermost

*Therefore He is also able to save to the uttermost those who come to God through Him, since He always lives to make intercession for them* (Hebrews 7:25, *New King James Version*).

Scripture: Hebrews 7:25, 26
Song: *"Jesus Saves!"*

***From this meditation today, I will pray . . .***

Adoration ______________________________

______________________________

______________________________

Confession ______________________________

______________________________

______________________________

Thanksgiving ______________________________

______________________________

______________________________

Supplication ______________________________

______________________________

______________________________

***From this meditation today, I will . . .***

Think ______________________________

______________________________

______________________________

Say ______________________________

______________________________

______________________________

Do ______________________________

______________________________

______________________________

______________________________

______________________________

Of all household duties, doing the laundry is arguably one of the least favorite chores. First you sort the dirty clothes, then place them in the washing machine. Following the wash, you throw the clothes in the dryer (unless you hang them out to dry). Finally, you must fold them or hang them up in their proper places. And this chore never seems to end.

But what would you do if that shirt you placed in the washing machine came out still dirty? You would probably wash it again, since you want your shirts completely clean, not just partially clean.

Now, I don't want to equate laundry with our souls, because the analogy will soon break down. But when Jesus comes into our hearts, He does cleanse us completely. That is what it means "to save to the uttermost" in our passage today. *Completely* saved, not just partially. This is no halfway job, since He washes away our sin. And who could imagine the Lord of All doing a less than perfect work for us?

Merciful Lord, *thank You for saving my soul and cleansing me from sin. Help me to live the Christian life so that others can see You, the living Christ, living in me. In Your name, I pray. Amen.*

**SPOTLIGHT**
***Next Week's Lesson***

God can't and won't do anything less than perfect.

# Just Once

*Unlike the other high priests, he does not need to offer sacrifices day after day, first for his own sins, and then for the sins of the people. He sacrificed for their sins once for all when he offered himself* (Hebrews 7:27).

April 15 comes just once a year. We all know the date as "Tax Day" in the United States, the deadline for paying our income taxes (unless we file for an extension). Either I pay my taxes by that deadline, or I must pay "late penalties" for missing the date. I'm just glad this day comes around only once a year.

While I still pay my taxes every year, Jesus paid my "sin debt" once and for all when He died on a Roman cross. He doesn't have to die "all over again" every time I sin; that debt is paid in full. And while Jesus intercedes on my behalf with His precious blood, He doesn't have to sacrifice Himself anymore.

That truth, "He sacrificed for their [my] sins once for all when he offered himself," leads me to praise God on this Lord's Day. As we worship today, we can offer thanks to a loving God who would sacrifice himself on our behalf. We deserve death; He gives us life. Once and for all!

Dear heavenly Father, *thank You so much for loving me and saving my soul. Thank You for Jesus! Help me to radiate Christ in my life today, that others may come to know Him. In the name of the Father, the Son, and the Holy Spirit, I pray. Amen.*

**SEARCH THE WORD**

*There will be no credit cards in Heaven; Christ has paid off all debts for its inhabitants.*

Scripture: Hebrews 7:27, 28

Song: *"At the Cross"*

*From this meditation today, I will pray . . .*

Adoration ______________________________

______________________________

______________________________

Confession ______________________________

______________________________

______________________________

Thanksgiving ______________________________

______________________________

______________________________

Supplication ______________________________

______________________________

______________________________

*From this meditation today, I will . . .*

Think ______________________________

______________________________

______________________________

Say ______________________________

______________________________

______________________________

Do ______________________________

______________________________

______________________________

______________________________

______________________________

June 9

# Lost in the Crowd

*God is spirit,*
*and his worshipers must worship in spirit and in truth*
(John 4:24).

**Scripture: John 4:21-26**
**Song: *"Sweet, Sweet Spirit"***

***From this meditation today, I will pray . . .***

Adoration ______________________________

______________________________

______________________________

Confession ______________________________

______________________________

______________________________

Thanksgiving ______________________________

______________________________

______________________________

Supplication ______________________________

______________________________

______________________________

***From this meditation today, I will . . .***

Think ______________________________

______________________________

______________________________

Say ______________________________

______________________________

______________________________

Do ______________________________

______________________________

______________________________

June 9–15. ***Jimmie Oliver Fleming*** *is writing a book titled* Clinging to God's Word. *She also teaches a children's Sunday school class at her church*

"There was a much better spirit in our old church," the man complained. "Now I just feel like a number."

"Yeah, I know what you mean," the other man agreed. "The number zero."

What had happened? These two church members apparently felt they had gotten lost in the crowd. While they supported the construction of their new church building, they weren't enjoying the change.

Jesus explained to the Samaritan woman that the *place* of worship was not as important as the *spirit* of worship: "A time is coming when you will worship the Father neither on this mountain nor in Jerusalem" (John 4:21).

Our two modern-day worshipers were facing the question that lay heavy on the Samaritan woman's heart. *Where is the best place to go for closeness to God?* Thankfully, God has chosen to dwell in us; He goes with us to our various places of worship. If only we will keep our spirits open to Him there!

*Thank You,* Lord, *for Your love and Your Spirit of truth. Help me learn to look within before I look out into the crowd and feel lost. In Jesus' precious name, amen.*

**SPOTLIGHT**
***Next Week's Lesson***

The most beautiful cathedral is no match for a heart filled with the presence of God.

# Truly Everlasting

*When Christ came as high priest of the good things that are already here, he went through the greater and more perfect tabernacle that is not man-made* (Hebrews 9:11).

The batteries I'd placed in my portable radio lasted so long that I wondered whether the brand name could be taken literally. But the batteries couldn't really last forever; they were merely man-made. (Besides, so often, just when I needed them most—zap, they'd go dead.)

All man-made products will eventually stop working, even when they're "built to last." (Actually, I sometimes wonder what, exactly, that claim can mean. Is the product built to last for . . . a week? a month? a year? or indefinitely? The phrase simply hangs in the air, uncommitted to any specific length of time.)

What a contrast with Christ, our high priest! With His precious blood as an offering for our sins, He entered a tabernacle that was not man-made: Heaven itself. Now He sits at the right hand of the Father, evermore making intercession for us. Thus He is our advocate, always available to plead our case before the throne. No man-made tabernacle and no more man-made sacrifices. Only the everlasting accomplishment of Jesus will do for our salvation.

**Heavenly Father,** *thank You for sending Your Son, Jesus, to offer an eternal sacrifice for the sins of the world. In His name I pray. Amen.*

**SEARCH THE WORD**

*We must be eternally grateful for a defense attorney with pure motives and control over our destinies.*

Scripture: Hebrews 9:11-15

Song: *"Nothing but the Blood"*

*From this meditation today, I will pray . . .*

Adoration ______________________________

______________________________

______________________________

Confession ______________________________

______________________________

______________________________

Thanksgiving ______________________________

______________________________

______________________________

Supplication ______________________________

______________________________

______________________________

*From this meditation today, I will . . .*

Think ______________________________

______________________________

______________________________

Say ______________________________

______________________________

______________________________

Do ______________________________

______________________________

______________________________

______________________________

______________________________

# Why Blood?

*He said, "This is the blood of the covenant, which God has commanded you to keep." In the same way, he sprinkled with the blood both the tabernacle and everything used in its ceremonies* (Hebrews 9:20, 21).

Scripture: Hebrews 9:16-24
Song: *"There Is Power in the Blood"*

Moses told the people in his day about the covenant that God expected them to keep with Him. Then the covenant was "ratified," so to speak, by blood. Why? The answer comes by analogy. Think of a will. It can only go into effect once someone has actually died. Similarly, God's promises of our inheritance can only go into effect if the perfect sacrifice for sin has been accomplished for us.

Before the coming of Christ, in Moses' day, the law required that everything be cleansed with the blood of animals. Today, we look back to the blood of Jesus, the perfect Lamb of God, for the cleansing of salvation. As the Scripture reminds us, without the shedding of blood there is no forgiveness (see Hebrews 9:22).

Sadly, many people today consider it crude or unenlightened to speak of Christ's mission in the world being a sacrificial offering. They prefer to consider Jesus a great teacher, a moral influence, or simply a good man. But in light of the clear teachings of Scripture, we do not have that option, do we?

O God, *I seek Your cleansing and forgiveness, and I lift up a thankful heart that Jesus has shed His blood for just this longing. In His name, amen.*

***From this meditation today, I will pray . . .***

Adoration ______________________________

______________________________

______________________________

Confession ______________________________

______________________________

______________________________

Thanksgiving ______________________________

______________________________

______________________________

Supplication ______________________________

______________________________

______________________________

***From this meditation today, I will . . .***

Think ______________________________

______________________________

______________________________

Say ______________________________

______________________________

______________________________

Do ______________________________

______________________________

______________________________

______________________________

______________________________

**SPOTLIGHT**
***Next Week's Lesson***

The life of Christ gave us a perfect example; His death was a perfect sacrifice.

# Cant' Earn This!

*Just as man is destined to die once, and after that to face judgment, so Christ was sacrificed once to take away the sins of many people* (Hebrews 9:27, 28).

In ancient Israel, the high priest entered the Most Holy Place every year with blood that was not his own. Although the sacrifices came only once a year, they still had to be offered over and over again. They were temporary "coverings" for the sins of the nation.

In contrast, Christ died *once* to take away the sins of the world. Furthermore, He rose from the dead and will appear a second time. His mission will be different at that time, but it will still be the result of the one sacrifice, eternally offered before the Father.

What great salvation Christ has accomplished for us! And the most wonderful thing of all is that we do not need to try to earn it. Instead, let us be so grateful for this gift to us that we serve our Lord with joyful and thankful hearts. This is always the motive for our good works—not that we could become worthy of Christ's sacrifice, but that we might proclaim it's surpassing goodness by our own manner of life. And even this we can only do by His spirit working within us.

Heavenly Father, *I know that I can pray no prayer more fitting than to simply thank You for Your Son, Jesus, whom You sent into this world as the ultimate sacrifice for sin. In His name I pray. Amen.*

**SEARCH THE WORD**

*No insurance policy on earth has comprehensive coverage like the "Heaven covenant" offered by Jesus Christ.*

Scripture: Hebrews 9:25-28

Song: *"Behold the Glories of the Lamb"*

*From this meditation today, I will pray . . .*

Adoration ____________________

Confession ____________________

Thanksgiving ____________________

Supplication ____________________

*From this meditation today, I will . . .*

Think ____________________

Say ____________________

Do ____________________

# Pointing to the Ultimate

*The law is only a shadow of the good things that are coming—not the realities themselves* (Hebrews 10:1).

Scripture: Hebrews 10:1-10

**Song:** *"Jesus, Priceless Treasure"*

*From this meditation today, I will pray . . .*

Adoration ______________________________

______________________________

______________________________

Confession ______________________________

______________________________

______________________________

Thanksgiving ______________________________

______________________________

______________________________

Supplication ______________________________

______________________________

______________________________

*From this meditation today, I will . . .*

Think ______________________________

______________________________

______________________________

Say ______________________________

______________________________

______________________________

Do ______________________________

______________________________

______________________________

______________________________

______________________________

When I first saw the old man's cluttered little office, I thought the plaque hanging above his desk referred to his profession. Actually, no one seemed to know the old man's line of work. He'd just always been there in the neighborhood to lend a listening ear and to occasionally give advice. "*Good* advice," everyone agreed.

Everyone also agreed it was a "good thing" the old man had remained in the neighborhood all those years. In explaining the plaque above his desk, he said, "I just saw it one day, and I liked it." What did the plaque say? I moved closer to read the small print: "Good things come in small packages."

True! And it's also true that sometimes good things are foreshadowed before they actually appear in reality. That's the idea in our Scripture today. The Old Testament sacrificial system served the good purpose of pointing to Christ. It could never match the greatness of the perfect, eternal sacrifice of the cross. However, it could hint.

Sometimes when I leave the office of that kind old man I lift up a prayer to my heavenly Father. The man seems to point me there . . .

Lord God in Heaven, *may I use every opportunity to point to my Savior in all I do or say this day. Thank You, in Jesus' name. Amen.*

**SPOTLIGHT**

***Next Week's Lesson***

Consider the small things you do for others. They may be what leads them to Jesus.

# An Exciting Drama

*Day after day every priest stands and performs his religious duties; again and again he offers the same sacrifices, which can never take away sins* (Hebrews 10:11).

Did the priest mentioned in our Scripture ever get bored with his everyday duties? If so, we can no doubt identify with seemingly never-ending duties, especially the ones we have to do day after day. However, it's been said that doing the hard part first will make our work seem easier.

Jesus, the perfect priest, came to do what everyday duties couldn't accomplish: take away our sins. And He certainly did the hard part first—He went to the cross, giving up all His heavenly privileges, to die like a common criminal. Then came the resurrection, the ascension, and His eternal reign in glory. Thankfully, He then sent His Spirit to dwell in our hearts until His coming again.

Nothing boring here! That's because this is the greatest drama ever enacted in the history of the universe. The key for you and me is to ask ourselves daily: Am I a vital part of this drama? Does my own life show that all Christ did for me makes a practical difference?

Lord, *thank You for forgiving my sins. May I now serve You with a joyful and thankful heart, realizing it's a privilege rather than a duty. And when I become bored with my daily routines, give me a fresh awareness of Your indwelling presence. In Jesus' name, amen.*

**SEARCH THE WORD**

*Life's drama (Act One) has to be played out properly so Heaven (Act Two) is understood and appreciated.*

Scripture: Hebrews 10:11-14

**Song: *"Jesus, Help Me"***

*From this meditation today, I will pray . . .*

Adoration ______________________________

______________________________

______________________________

Confession ______________________________

______________________________

______________________________

Thanksgiving ______________________________

______________________________

______________________________

Supplication ______________________________

______________________________

______________________________

*From this meditation today, I will . . .*

Think ______________________________

______________________________

______________________________

Say ______________________________

______________________________

______________________________

Do ______________________________

______________________________

______________________________

______________________________

______________________________

June 15

# Once and for All?

*Their sins and lawless acts I will remember no more*
(Hebrews 10:17).

Scripture: Hebrews 10:15-18
Song: *"Great Is Thy Faithfulness"*

***From this meditation today, I will pray . . .***

Adoration ______________________________

________________________________________

________________________________________

Confession ______________________________

________________________________________

________________________________________

Thanksgiving ____________________________

________________________________________

________________________________________

Supplication ____________________________

________________________________________

________________________________________

***From this meditation today, I will . . .***

Think __________________________________

________________________________________

________________________________________

Say ____________________________________

________________________________________

________________________________________

Do _____________________________________

________________________________________

________________________________________

________________________________________

________________________________________

The young mother had spoken stern words. "Now, you listen to me, Tyler. I'm telling you once and for all—behave yourself. Stop bothering your sister!"

While dining at a local restaurant, I overheard such words from a mother to her son at least 10 different times. The "once and for all rule" just hadn't held up—no matter how many times it was proclaimed. (I could identify with her. I've used this same rule with my own sons on occasion—with similar result.)

According to the author of Hebrews, in God's unfolding plan of salvation, no sacrifice of animals could *once and for all* remove human sin. Only Christ, the perfect sacrifice, could do that. Being fully human, He could atone for humans. And being fully God, He could atone with eternal result. So you see, He removed the need for animal sacrifices once and for all.

When we're forgiven, our wrongdoings are remembered no more. As someone has said, "God buries our sins in the deepest sea, and puts up a sign: No Fishing!"

Dear Father, *when I'm tempted to resurrect all my old failings and sins, draw me nearer to the cross of Your precious Son. There my sins were nailed with Him. There all of Your love and acceptance come to me forever. Thank You, in the name of my Savior, Jesus Christ. Amen.*

**SPOTLIGHT**
***Next Week's Lesson***

How often does God have to remind us that He has the final say before we believe Him?

# Barn Choir

*He will fill your barns with grain,*
*and your vats will overflow with good wine*
(Proverbs 3:10, *New Living Translation*).

During a severe winter cold-snap, I was in the milking parlor at 2:00 AM preparing to milk 250 cows lounging in the attached barn. I was frustrated, struggling against the cold weather. But in my heart raged an even bigger wrestling match—with God. I resented my financial pressures. Despite all I was doing, it seemed as if God just wasn't providing enough. "Where is Your provision when I need it?" I questioned. "What more can I do? " I railed.

As the hours passed, the parlor slowly warmed with the heat given off by the cattle. Then I noticed a new sound. I turned to see first one, then several, and eventually dozens of sparrows descending from the barn's rafters to eat grain that had spilled on the parlor floor. Not seeming to notice the cold, dark night, they began to sing.

Songs of thanksgiving? Songs of praise? A sparrow choir had arrived to thank God for His provision. My heart soared.

Dear Father, *thank You for every simple reminder of Your care for me and for every one of Your creatures. And please melt the coldness and hardness in my heart that grips me when I forget You are the only sustenance I need. Through Christ my Savior, I pray. Amen.*

**SEARCH THE WORD**

*Our possessions and worries about them often stand as a wall between us and simple faith.*

Scripture: Proverbs 3:5-12

Song: *"His Eye Is on the Sparrow"*

***From this meditation today, I will pray . . .***

Adoration ______________________

______________________

______________________

Confession ______________________

______________________

______________________

Thanksgiving ______________________

______________________

______________________

Supplication ______________________

______________________

______________________

***From this meditation today, I will . . .***

Think ______________________

______________________

______________________

Say ______________________

______________________

______________________

Do ______________________

______________________

______________________

June 16–22. ***Ron Silflow*** and his wife, ***Laura***, *reside in Bozeman, Montana, where they enjoy friends, conversation, coffee, books, campfires, and mountains.*

# For Now, the Author Allows

*Let us fix our eyes on Jesus, the author and perfecter of our faith, who for the joy set before Him, endured the cross, scorning its shame, and sat down at the right hand of the throne of God* (Hebrews 12:2).

Scripture: Hebrews 12:1-3

Song: *"I Love to Tell the Story"*

What kind of author writes stories that include personal tragedy, sickness, accidents, and even death? Apparently, the same storyteller who authors my life story. So, I ask myself whether that is really very good news.

Often, I pray about how I'd like the next sentences and paragraphs of my story to read. My prayers never include confusion or darkness, pain or disappointment. But Jesus, the author of my faith, allows these elements into my earthly days and invites me to follow Him right through to the same joy that He entered. Yes, His story included injustice. Yes, His story included sorrow, pain, and death. But His story didn't end there. Death led to a life at home alongside His Father.

Can you and I accept this kind of story teller as the author of our lives? He called His story good. Can you and I call our stories good? We can, if we see that this is not yet the best of all possible worlds for us. We are not yet home.

Lord, *I know that in Your wisdom You are allowing the forces of evil to have some sway here on earth. Remind me that sin's power is temporary and that nothing enters my life without Your approval. In Jesus' name, amen.*

***From this meditation today, I will pray . . .***

Adoration ______________________________

______________________________

______________________________

Confession ______________________________

______________________________

______________________________

Thanksgiving ______________________________

______________________________

______________________________

Supplication ______________________________

______________________________

______________________________

***From this meditation today, I will . . .***

Think ______________________________

______________________________

______________________________

Say ______________________________

______________________________

______________________________

Do ______________________________

______________________________

______________________________

______________________________

______________________________

**SPOTLIGHT**

***Next Week's Lesson***

Suffering is part of the human experience; it is also part of the growing experience.

# Downward Mobility

*God is educating you; that's why you must never drop out. He's treating you as dear children. The trouble you're in isn't punishment; it's training* (Hebrews 12:7, *The Message*).

To be pursued by someone who loves me is a great experience. It makes me feel important. Yet it surprises me, because sometimes I don't feel I'm *worth* pursuing. So when I read a story about Jesus loving me so much that He took the hard downward path of humility, suffering, and punishment to the death, my heart perks up.

Because He took the descending path, I am made clean and acceptable. I don't have to prove that I am worthy of love; I am now God's adopted son. Writer Henri Nouwen speaks of it this way: "My whole life I have been surrounded by well-meaning encouragement to go 'higher up—you can do so much good there, for so many people.' But these voices calling me to upward mobility are completely absent from the gospel." As I take time to reflect on various circumstances in my life that are difficult to understand, I may need to view them differently. Was that recent loss of my job, for instance, really a *punishment*? Or was it *training*—and an opportunity to grow in faith? In other words, isn't downward mobility a good thing?

My Pursuing Father, *thank You for the intensity of Your desires toward me. I rest in Your presence with me on paths that I don't understand right now—paths of learning and training. Sustain me, through Christ. Amen.*

**SEARCH THE WORD**

*Self-made men are often proud and inflexible. The humble, however, are putty in God's hands.*

Scripture: Hebrews 12:4-7

**Song: *"Blessed Are the Sons of God"***

***From this meditation today, I will pray . . .***

Adoration ______________________

______________________

______________________

Confession ______________________

______________________

______________________

Thanksgiving ______________________

______________________

______________________

Supplication ______________________

______________________

______________________

***From this meditation today, I will . . .***

Think ______________________

______________________

______________________

Say ______________________

______________________

______________________

Do ______________________

______________________

______________________

______________________

______________________

# Untamed God

*No discipline seems pleasant at the time, but painful. Later on, however, it produces a harvest of righteousness and peace for those who have been trained by it* (Hebrews 12:11).

Scripture: Hebrews 12:8-11

Song: *"Stand Up and Bless the Lord"*

***From this meditation today, I will pray . . .***

Adoration ______________________________

______________________________

______________________________

Confession ______________________________

______________________________

______________________________

Thanksgiving ______________________________

______________________________

______________________________

Supplication ______________________________

______________________________

______________________________

***From this meditation today, I will . . .***

Think ______________________________

______________________________

______________________________

Say ______________________________

______________________________

______________________________

Do ______________________________

______________________________

______________________________

______________________________

______________________________

I love the story of the interaction between God and Job in the Old Testament. Job was being severely tested, and I see myself in him as he tries to get God to recognize his righteousness and end his sufferings. Finally, God responds to Job's complaint and begins a beautiful history lesson for him (and me): "Where were you when I laid the earth's foundation? Tell me, if you understand" (Job 38:4). At the other end of this history lesson, Job discovers that the two things he's been trying to produce on his own—peace and righteousness—can only come from God.

I don't think God is angry with me when I complain and try to convince Him to change my circumstances. But He isn't a tame God. In a very real sense, He is wild and uncontrollable and . . . good.

Like Job, when you and I come to the end of our futile attempts to manage and manipulate God, can we find what we've always longed for? His peace? His righteousness? If so, it will be because we have received these blessings as gifts from His generous heart.

Father, *help me see that the discipline You bring into my life has a good purpose. You wish to produce a harvest of peace and righteousness in me. So help me give up my efforts at total control. In Jesus' name, amen.*

**SPOTLIGHT**

***Next Week's Lesson***

God knows the "big picture" so much better than we do. We must wait as He reveals it to us.

# My Weakness, His Strength

*Wherefore lift up the hands which hang down, and the feeble knees*
(Hebrews 12:12, *King James Version*).

The river was flowing swiftly as I let it carry me toward the safety of a small island. "I'll be OK," I thought—until I discovered the current had carried me downstream past the lower end of the island. At that point, the strength of the current doubled. I was in trouble. I turned to swim back to shore, but when I saw the distance, I panicked.

My energy was sapped, and now, filled with fear, I felt helpless. My friends and family, watching my flailing efforts, were concerned, but unaware of how weak and vulnerable I felt.

Eventually, I made it far enough out of the strong current to be able to stand, shakily, in knee-deep water. Bent over, my hands on my knees, I gasped for the oxygen I craved.

What swift current of circumstances in your life makes you feel threatened, out of control, vulnerable, foolish, or ashamed at the moment? Join me in lifting a weary, discouraged, struggling heart to God. He's a Lord who loves to come through for us. How has He met with you in your weakness?

God of my salvation, *I come before You acknowledging my inadequacies, my sins, my failures. In this place of neediness, I lift up my hands that hang down, and on feeble knees I look to You. Through Christ, amen.*

**SEARCH THE WORD**

*To panic is human;*
*to persevere takes faith.*

Scripture: Hebrews 12:12, 13

**Song:** *"From Out the Depths I Cry, O Lord"*

***From this meditation today, I will pray . . .***

Adoration ______________________

______________________

______________________

Confession ______________________

______________________

______________________

Thanksgiving ______________________

______________________

______________________

Supplication ______________________

______________________

______________________

***From this meditation today, I will . . .***

Think ______________________

______________________

______________________

Say ______________________

______________________

______________________

Do ______________________

______________________

______________________

______________________

______________________

June 21

# Make Beautiful Harmony

*Fulfil ye my joy, that ye be likeminded, having the same love, being of one accord, of one mind* (Philippians 2:2, *King James Version*).

Scripture: Philippians 2:1-4

Song: *"O Thou That Hear'st When Sinners Cry"*

***From this meditation today, I will pray . . .***

Adoration ______________________________

______________________________

______________________________

Confession ______________________________

______________________________

______________________________

Thanksgiving ______________________________

______________________________

______________________________

Supplication ______________________________

______________________________

______________________________

***From this meditation today, I will . . .***

Think ______________________________

______________________________

______________________________

Say ______________________________

______________________________

______________________________

Do ______________________________

______________________________

______________________________

______________________________

______________________________

I love it when my son, Zach, returns from guitar lessons. He shares with me things he's learned—like how to listen to the *texture* of music; how to enjoy the way different instruments blend with each other to make a sound bigger and more beautiful than they can produce individually.

In a similar vein, my friend Tim loves to talk about musical harmony. Then he makes his point, explaining how relationships between people include differences in personalities, differences in opinion, differences in perspective. Yet these differences can work in harmony too.

I admit that being "likeminded" with people is hard for me. I often feel threatened by others' viewpoints as I argue for my own. My feelings can get hurt, and many times I've lashed out at those who disagree with me.

Yet have you noticed that the people we most often disagree with are those closest to us? usually family or friends? Join me in asking God for help to move towards these folks with humility and love rather than withdrawing into relational disharmony.

God, *Your love for me penetrates my heart and helps me see how I can harmonize with others whom You also dearly love. Through Christ, amen.*

**SPOTLIGHT**

***Next Week's Lesson***

How boring life would be if color had no hues, music had no overtones, and people had no distinctives!

# Never Alone

*Surely I am with you always, to the very end of the age*
(Matthew 28:20).

Close friends invited my wife and me to join them in their anniversary celebration. Their relationship has been filled with serious challenges. But instead of evaluating whether their marriage had gotten better, they chose to speak about how they enjoyed being together, even through the most difficult times.

I have heard many say that our attitudes spring from our choices. I agree, but honestly, I really struggle with making consistently right choices. And there is something deeper that my heart longs for than just "getting it right."

As I look at the closeness Jesus enjoyed with the Father, even as He moved into suffering, I realize that's the deep thing my heart longs for. Closeness with God.

What are the biggest challenges in your life these days? Are you worn out trying to make life better, easier, more comfortable? Join me in thanking Jesus, not only for His incarnation, but for His promise of continued closeness. Let Him come alongside you.

Dear God, *I don't want to face today's struggles alone. Please forgive me for attitudes that come across as a demand for You to make my life better. I do thank You for pursuing me and walking alongside me, for my heart can only truly rest in Your presence. I pray in Jesus' holy name. Amen.*

**SEARCH THE WORD**

*Lasting relationships with Jesus and others are focused more on friendship than on mere familiarity.*

Scripture: Philippians 2:5-11

Song: *"I Want Jesus to Walk with Me"*

*From this meditation today, I will pray . . .*

Adoration ______________________

______________________

______________________

Confession ______________________

______________________

______________________

Thanksgiving ______________________

______________________

______________________

Supplication ______________________

______________________

______________________

*From this meditation today, I will . . .*

Think ______________________

______________________

______________________

Say ______________________

______________________

______________________

Do ______________________

______________________

______________________

______________________

______________________

June 23

# Can God Provide?

*It is better to trust in the* LORD *than to put confidence in man*
(Psalm 118:8, *New King James Version*).

Scripture: Psalm 118:5-9
Song: *"Trust and Obey"*

***From this meditation today, I will pray . . .***

Adoration ______________________________

Confession ______________________________

Thanksgiving ______________________________

Supplication ______________________________

***From this meditation today, I will . . .***

Think ______________________________

Say ______________________________

Do ______________________________

My husband and I responded to the call of God to serve Him in overseas missions. There was no salary, though, and my husband suggested we sell our house to finance the first trip.

*Sell the house?* I rebelled. We had worked hard on that house, and it was our security. I fought with God and was miserable. Then I thought: If I were killed on the road tomorrow, the burden of the house would be lifted. So . . . why not let it go today?

We never regretted our decision. When our own money ran out, there was always just enough for us—and for others with very great needs. Fifteen years later we retired to a home of our own—all we need and more—absolutely amazed at the way God provides for all things.

Now we live on a pension from my husband's former job in the British Health Service, but our faith clings ultimately to God. A pension merely relies on the stability of the stock market. God is much more reliable than that!

*Thank You, Father, for the ability to earn my own living. But my trust goes far beyond my own skills. It is You I can trust to provide for my family and myself, even when all else fails. Through Christ my Lord, amen.*

**SPOTLIGHT**
***Next Week's Lesson***
**Investing ourselves in Heaven's security ultimately means divesting ourselves of trust in earthly holdings.**

June 23–29. ***Marion Turnbull,*** *of Middlesbrough, England, has worked with her husband in overseas missions. Now retired, they enjoy their 13 grandchildren.*

# Jesus, Supreme

*He is the head of the body, the church;*
*he is the beginning and the firstborn from among the dead,*
*so that in everything he might have the supremacy* (Colossians 1:18).

When the queen of England decides to visit a city, great preparations ensue, and no expense is spared to make her visit a happy one. Parks and gardens are trimmed to perfection, roads and buildings repaired. The red carpet of welcome comes out, the mayor waits, and we welcome the queen in our best new clothes.

The city is at her disposal as we honor her. City leaders stop looking important and bow down. The security men get headaches when she goes walking around among her people, but she decides, and they follow. Nobody argues with, or walks ahead of, the queen.

But kings, queens, and presidents live under the authority of our Lord Jesus, whether they acknowledge the fact or not. He is supremely in control, and nothing escapes His notice. Ironically, men and nations struggle for power—which has already been given to Him!

Today's reading delights my heart. How good to know that ultimate control rests in Christ's capable hands. Let us never be ashamed to acknowledge Him and give Him all the honor He is due.

Father, *I am so glad that Your Son reigns supreme over all. In this quiet moment, I joyfully bow before Him, and in His holy name I pray. Amen.*

**SEARCH THE WORD**

*Man's power and prestige are fleeting; God's preeminence, however, lasts forever.*

Scripture: Colossians 1:15-20
Song: *"Jesus! the Name High over All"*

*From this meditation today, I will pray . . .*

Adoration ______________________

______________________

______________________

Confession ______________________

______________________

______________________

Thanksgiving ______________________

______________________

______________________

Supplication ______________________

______________________

______________________

*From this meditation today, I will . . .*

Think ______________________

______________________

______________________

Say ______________________

______________________

______________________

Do ______________________

______________________

______________________

______________________

______________________

June 25

# Opening Our Homes

*Do not forget to entertain strangers*
(Hebrews 13:2).

Scripture: Hebrews 13:1-6
**Song:** *"He Walked Where I Walk"*

Manchester, my city in England, is full of political asylum seekers, foreign students, and people of various nationalities and cultures. In theory, this should enrich and challenge us, but we do tend to withdraw into our own cultural groups, because we feel more comfortable there. Nothing wrong with that, I suppose. But if we never open up our hearts and homes to strangers, we miss something important and blessed.

Overseas students like to visit a home in the country, but if Christians don't invite them, those students may lose an opportunity for hearing the gospel. And so many of these folks are delightful people!

Perhaps we are wary of inviting desperate asylum seekers who may take advantage of us. But I read in the Bible that God actually *favors* the poor and defenseless. And I have no doubt that extending simple human kindness and hospitality is a great way to show our faith in action. Even if I have only one small room, I can offer that to Jesus—and to the stranger He loves.

Father, *I would exercise my faith in these things too. Yet I need Your wisdom and protection for my family members, as they are willing to participate. Continue to guide and encourage me as I remember that whatever I offer to You, You will pour back into my life with even greater blessings. I pray this prayer in the name of Jesus, my merciful Savior and Lord. Amen.*

*From this meditation today, I will pray . . .*

Adoration ______________________________

______________________________

______________________________

Confession ______________________________

______________________________

______________________________

Thanksgiving ______________________________

______________________________

______________________________

Supplication ______________________________

______________________________

______________________________

*From this meditation today, I will . . .*

Think ______________________________

______________________________

______________________________

Say ______________________________

______________________________

______________________________

Do ______________________________

______________________________

______________________________

______________________________

______________________________

**SPOTLIGHT**
***Next Week's Lesson***

Discovering God's blessings is like a treasure hunt through the lives of people and information around you.

# Be Yourself in Him

*Remember your leaders who spoke the word of God to you. Consider the outcome of their way of life and imitate their faith* (Hebrews 13:7).

I'm thinking of a man who once brought the Word of God to our church in a powerful way. He was much loved and revered, and he certainly lived the life that he preached. In fact, some young men revered him so much that when they preached, they copied our friend's mannerisms, even his tone of voice. Someone said, "They're just his clones!"

Time, however, showed that they were not clones, because they had their own deep faith in God. Eventually their own personalities came through in their living and preaching. The same message, the same God, was proclaimed. But each could be himself in Him.

It is the *faith* of the leader we are encouraged to follow, as we see that faith lived out. We need not imitate the man or woman, but follow their faith in the one who never changes. My faith, like the leader's faith, must rest solely in Jesus.

Dear heavenly Father, *I thank You for all the men and women who have helped me grow in my Christian life. I pray for my present church leaders and Sunday school teachers—and for all of us—that we may be good examples to those who follow You. In the name of the Father, the Son, and the Holy Spirit, I pray. Amen.*

**SEARCH THE WORD**

*We are certain to be blessed if we get to know Jesus by imitating those who are closest to Him.*

Scripture: Hebrews 13:7-9

Song: *"For All the Saints"*

*From this meditation today, I will pray . . .*

Adoration ______________________________

Confession ______________________________

Thanksgiving ______________________________

Supplication ______________________________

*From this meditation today, I will . . .*

Think ______________________________

Say ______________________________

Do ______________________________

# Outside the Camp

*Let us, then, go to him outside the camp, bearing the disgrace he bore. For here we do not have an enduring city, but we are looking for the city that is to come* (Hebrews 13:13, 14).

Scripture: Hebrews 13:10-16

Song: *"My Song Is Love Unknown"*

*From this meditation today, I will pray . . .*

Adoration ______________________________

______________________________

______________________________

Confession ______________________________

______________________________

______________________________

Thanksgiving ______________________________

______________________________

______________________________

Supplication ______________________________

______________________________

______________________________

*From this meditation today, I will . . .*

Think ______________________________

______________________________

______________________________

Say ______________________________

______________________________

______________________________

Do ______________________________

______________________________

______________________________

______________________________

______________________________

I recall the story of a mother who watched her soldier son marching in a parade. She observed to her friend, "Why is everybody out of step but my Jamie?"

As Christians in this world, I suppose we have all experienced times when we feel "out of step" with everyone else. Our interests, values, and perspectives often don't mesh with the "man on the street," do they?

One of my young friends was expected to attend an office party. As a Christian, she felt totally out of place among all the drunken revelry and soon ordered a taxi home. "Now some of my colleagues avoid me, and I feel like such an outsider," she complained. But she was in good company. Jesus was also rejected, just for being true to himself. And He calls us to follow Him and live with Him "outside the camp."

Of course, my friend still loved her colleagues and prayed for them. But she finally had to admit that she was not one of them. She belonged with Jesus.

Dear God, *You have won my heart. This world has its attractions and delights, but You are better to me than all of them. Your Son was despised and rejected by this world, and I will follow Him, even if I am the only one. In the holy name of Jesus, my Lord and Savior, I pray. Amen.*

**SPOTLIGHT**

***Next Week's Lesson***

Our witness is effective only when it is distinctive and demonstrated.

# Taking Possession

*I press on to take hold of that for which Christ Jesus took hold of me* (Philippians 3:12).

On his daughter's 21st birthday, a very rich man gave her a present. It was an envelope containing the deed to a house. She flung her arms around his neck and thanked him, then put the deed in a drawer and just left it there. Her father was very disappointed, because he intended the house to be lived in.

A house is for possession. God, at great cost, gave me the "deed" of my salvation. I didn't have to earn it, but I do have to take hold of it and live in it.

The apostle Paul was obviously enjoying the salvation God had given to him. But he knew there was more, and he intended to take hold of everything God had meant for him.

I know there is more for me to take hold of in my life: more doors and windows to open up, more rooms to be filled with God's presence, more of my garden to clear so that good works may flower and blossom. It's easy to let gifts lie in a drawer; possession takes some effort.

*Thank You,* Father, *for all the blessings of the past. But I want to take hold of everything You have given me in Christ Jesus. I open up all the doors and windows of my heart and life to You and ask You to come and fill this house. May Your love in me flow out to all I meet this day. In the name of Jesus, Lord and Savior of all, I pray. Amen.*

**SEARCH THE WORD**

*To be at home with God can begin whenever we seek to be fully in His presence.*

Scripture: Philippians 3:12-16

**Song: *"O Breath of Life"***

*From this meditation today, I will pray . . .*

Adoration ______________________

______________________

______________________

Confession ______________________

______________________

______________________

Thanksgiving ______________________

______________________

______________________

Supplication ______________________

______________________

______________________

*From this meditation today, I will . . .*

Think ______________________

______________________

______________________

Say ______________________

______________________

______________________

Do ______________________

______________________

______________________

______________________

______________________

# Avoiding the Shame

*As I have often told you before and now say again even with tears, many live as enemies of the cross of Christ* (Philippians 3:18).

Scripture: Philippians 3:17-21
Song: *"Here Is Love, Vast as the Ocean"*

*From this meditation today, I will pray . . .*

Adoration ______

Confession ______

Thanksgiving ______

Supplication ______

*From this meditation today, I will . . .*

Think ______

Say ______

Do ______

The Scottish Covenanters, severely persecuted for their faith, sang hymns in the carts that carried them to the gallows. They sang farewell to earthly sun and moon; they sang of the doors of Heaven opening before them and of seeing Christ in all His glory.

Many in our present day face death for their faith in Christ, and all Christians experience some kind of rejection in this world. As Jesus said, we must take up our cross and follow Him.

When someone carried a cross in those ancient days, everyone knew he was on his way to crucifixion. We, too, will often face the choice of suffering rejection or evading the shame of the cross. Sadly, at those times, we may opt for living comfortably with the world.

It's sobering to realize that the "enemies of the cross of Christ" were believers—but with their minds set on earthly things. So it's no wonder Paul wept. Nevertheless, by grace, I want to be like our Lord, who scorned not the cross but the shame of avoiding it.

Dear God, *keep me from professing Your name while still living as though the cross never existed. Let the cross of Your Son mean everything to me! If I am privileged to suffer for You, let me even rejoice. In Jesus' name, amen.*

**SPOTLIGHT**
***Next Week's Lesson***
The best way to overcome our darkest hours is to imagine the delights the Lord has prepared for us!

# Delighting in the Lord

*He will delight in the fear of the Lord. He will not judge by what he sees with his eyes, or decide by what he hears with his ears* (Isaiah 11:3).

Best-selling author Stephen King once spoke of a story concept that occurred to him: "I was too overawed with delight to do more than think about it for days." I understand his emotion. As a fiction writer, I recently had an inspiration for an intriguing novel. Excitement grew as I discussed possible plot points and characters with fellow writers. I enjoyed thinking about it and writing down ideas as they surfaced.

I may never achieve novel-writing success, but I can dream of making this book a reality. Perhaps someday I'll hold the complete manuscript in my hands, and then I'll probably do a "Snoopy Dance" over the achievement—even though the book may never make it to the bookstores.

As I've grown in my Christian faith and become more familiar with my Savior, I've learned to rest in Him and His wisdom. As I bask in His love this day, I realize that Jesus is truly worthy of my delight.

God, *I delight in Your love and mercy. Help me to keep You foremost in my mind, even in the midst of ordinary tasks. In Jesus' name, amen.*

**SEARCH THE WORD**

*Spend time imagining the glories of Heaven; then rest assured knowing they are a hundred times better.*

Scripture: Isaiah 11:1-3

Song: *"Joyful, Joyful, We Adore Thee"*

***From this meditation today, I will pray . . .***

Adoration ______________________

Confession ______________________

Thanksgiving ______________________

Supplication ______________________

***From this meditation today, I will . . .***

Think ______________________

Say ______________________

Do ______________________

June 30. ***Bonnie Doran*** *is a part-time bookkeeper for her church. She enjoys writing, reading, and cooking.*

*His love
endures forever.*
—Psalm 118:1b

Photo © dreamstime

# July

# IMAGES OF CHRIST IN THE GOSPELS

*God is one and there*
*is no other but him. . . . love him.*
—Mark 12:32, 33

Photo © iStock

July 1

# Need Recharging Today?

*Jesus returned to Galilee in the power of the Spirit, and news about him spread through the whole countryside* (Luke 4:14).

**Scripture: Luke 4:14, 15**

**Song:** *"Just a Closer Walk with Thee"*

***From this meditation today, I will pray . . .***

Adoration ______________________________

______________________________

______________________________

Confession ______________________________

______________________________

______________________________

Thanksgiving ______________________________

______________________________

______________________________

Supplication ______________________________

______________________________

______________________________

***From this meditation today, I will . . .***

Think ______________________________

______________________________

______________________________

Say ______________________________

______________________________

______________________________

Do ______________________________

______________________________

______________________________

July 1–6. ***Bonnie Doran*** *is a part-time bookkeeper for her church. She enjoys writing, reading, and cooking*

Apparently, Jesus relied on the power of the Spirit to energize Him for His mission on earth. I would love to take up that habit! In fact, I sometimes wish I came with an alarm that would beep when I get spiritually, emotionally, or physically drained. I do need constant re-energizing.

God created us with amazing stamina, but we're not little pink bunnies that can bang a drum forever. We need to check our energy levels daily. Have we spent time with the power source of the universe to recharge our spiritual batteries? Do we power up emotionally by taking time to examine a rose or admire a sunset? Or are we hunched over a steering wheel in a never-ending traffic circle of errands?

My prayer is that I'll learn to rely on the recharger of my life, rather than depending on the all-too-weak batteries of my own strength.

Father, *thank You for Jesus' example of relying on Your power rather than His human strength. In His divine nature, He was all-powerful, but in His human nature, He showed the way for every human: to depend on heavenly help in all endeavors. In His precious name I pray. Amen.*

**SPOTLIGHT**

***Next Week's Lesson***

The Holy Spirit provides our second wind as we boldly run the racetrack of life.

# Power or Timidity?

*All the people were amazed and said to each other, "What is this teaching? With authority and power he gives orders to evil spirits and they come out!"* (Luke 4:36).

The people of Palestine had never heard such a speaker. Here was an uneducated carpenter from the wrong side of the tracks, and he was a better orator than their usual synagogue teacher. And something else made them scratch their heads. His message had authority, backed by powerful action.

I'm usually a timid witness when someone asks me about the hope within me. I don't want to offend. I don't want a potential friend to turn her back on me. And I certainly don't welcome ridicule—or being labeled as a religious fanatic. So I whisper that I'm a Christian and often act as if I'm ashamed.

Yet the same Lord who ordered demonic forces to flee now lives within me, ready to calm my anxiety and enable me to speak boldly for Him. Through His Holy Spirit, I can stand strong against real or imagined opposition.

We serve an awesome God. He has the authority to act in our lives and has the power to motivate us to action too. That's a message worth shouting from the rooftops.

Lord, *help me throw off the shackles of my timidity and serve as a courageous witness for You. Yet may my words always be seasoned with gentleness and my actions wrapped in love. Through Christ, I pray. Amen.*

**SEARCH THE WORD**

*Failing to share the gospel of Christ with a friend now could mean missing a friend in Heaven.*

Scripture: Luke 4:31-37

Song: *"Awesome God"*

***From this meditation today, I will pray . . .***

Adoration ____________________

Confession ____________________

Thanksgiving ____________________

Supplication ____________________

***From this meditation today, I will . . .***

Think ____________________

Say ____________________

Do ____________________

July 3

# In His Grip

*The people all tried to touch him, because power was coming from him and healing them all* (Luke 6:19).

Scripture: Luke 6:17-23

Song: *"He Touched Me"*

*From this meditation today, I will pray . . .*

Adoration ______________________________

______________________________

______________________________

Confession ______________________________

______________________________

______________________________

Thanksgiving ______________________________

______________________________

______________________________

Supplication ______________________________

______________________________

______________________________

*From this meditation today, I will . . .*

Think ______________________________

______________________________

______________________________

Say ______________________________

______________________________

______________________________

Do ______________________________

______________________________

______________________________

______________________________

______________________________

Dr. Fritz Talbot of the Children's Clinic in Düsseldorf, fought against infant mortality in the 1940s. When a child was hopelessly wasting away, the physician would scrawl a prescription on the chart: Old Anna.

Anna was a grandmotherly woman on the ward, often seated in a large rocker with a baby on her lap. She held and stroked the failing patients. In most cases, those children began to thrive. In fact, she had more success with her "rocking chair therapy" than any of the doctors in the clinic.

Jesus knew the power of touch. He could heal with a word, and sometimes did. More often, though, He accompanied his healing with touch.

I used to view God working only through intermediaries—His encouragement through the written Word, His "hug" from a friend, His challenge from a sermon. Now I experience Him as personally reaching into my life. My prayers aren't directed merely to a so-called higher power in the clouds, but to the Lord who stays ever so close. He touches me on the shoulder, reaches out to grasp my hand, and holds me steady in His grip.

Jesus, *thank You that You love me personally and up close. Help me to sense Your presence and rely on Your grip. Through Christ, amen.*

**SPOTLIGHT**

***Next Week's Lesson***

Reaching out to touch the distressed and the different might result in a hug from God.

# The Measure of Success

*Woe to you when all men speak well of you, for that is how their fathers treated the false prophets* (Luke 6:26).

I like approval. I love to receive compliments about my clothes, appreciation for my writings, and gratitude for my delicious dinners. However, I know that I need to seek approval from the right people. For example, some less-than-sincere folks may speak kindly of my "fashion sense" when they really mean that I tend to hide my excess pounds pretty well.

True friends won't steer me wrong. A comment about my weight stings, but a friend will encourage me when I finally pass up the French silk pie.

One youth worker described to me a tough-looking teen: he was wearing black clothes and chains, had tattoos, and sported a Mohawk gelled into six-inch spikes. As the worker talked with him, he discovered a sensitive and deeply spiritual young man. After a while, the worker asked him why he dressed as he did. "So I know who my friends are," he responded.

Ouch. Do I wear my designer blouses to get the approval of people who aren't real friends? Or am I willing to act contrary to custom in order to win approval from God, the one who really counts?

Lord, *too often I've craved the spotlight of others rather than a "well done" from You. Help me to put You first! In Jesus' name, amen.*

**SEARCH THE WORD**

*Remind us often, Lord, that You look past our appearances and into our hearts.*

Scripture: Luke 6:24-26

Song: *"You Are My All in All"*

*From this meditation today, I will pray . . .*

Adoration ____________________

____________________

____________________

Confession ____________________

____________________

____________________

Thanksgiving ____________________

____________________

____________________

Supplication ____________________

____________________

____________________

*From this meditation today, I will . . .*

Think ____________________

____________________

____________________

Say ____________________

____________________

____________________

Do ____________________

____________________

____________________

____________________

____________________

July 5

# Holocaust Forgiveness

*Love your enemies and pray for those who persecute you* (Matthew 5:44).

Scripture: Matthew 5:38-45

**Song:** *"Hiding in Thee"*

***From this meditation today, I will pray . . .***

Adoration ________________________

Confession ________________________

Thanksgiving ________________________

Supplication ________________________

***From this meditation today, I will . . .***

Think ________________________

Say ________________________

Do ________________________

On February 28, 1944, the Nazis arrested the ten Boom family. Their crime: hiding Jewish refugees and helping them escape German-occupied Holland. Corrie ten Boom and her sister, Betsie, were sent to the Ravensbrück concentration camp in Germany. Betsie died; Corrie was released in December 1944, weak and emaciated.

When she recovered, Corrie began speaking on the theme of forgiveness throughout Europe. After one meeting in Germany in 1947, a man approached her—one of her cruelest Ravensbrück guards. Could Corrie now practice what she preached?

She prayed for the ability to forgive this man, then reached out to clasp his hand. In her book, *Tramp for the Lord,* she wrote, "For a long moment we grasped each other's hands, the former guard and the former prisoner. I had never known God's love so intensely as I did then."

Although our natural inclination is to seek revenge, Jesus commanded us to love our enemies. How radical! It's only possible through the love God supplies to us.

Lord God, *I am helpless in the face of hatred. Yet through Your Son, You forgave the sins of the world, though You had no part in them. Please work Your forgiving ways into my own soul, day by day. Thank You, in the holy name of Jesus, my Lord and Savior. Amen.*

**SPOTLIGHT**

***Next Week's Lesson***

True forgiveness has been the prescription that has healed many broken hearts.

# More Surgery!

*"Tell us by what authority you are doing these things," they said. "Who gave you this authority?"* (Luke 20:2).

Recently a doctor told me I needed surgery, a second operation in 10 months. Although the news distressed me, I was glad the surgeon who performed the first operation was the one who called. I trusted her, and I preferred her scalpel to anyone else's.

I now have three small incisions from the laparoscopic procedure, in addition to my hip-to-hip scar from hernia repair. My surgeon jokingly offered a "buy-one-get-one-free" deal on any future operations, but I declined. (Hey, I'm running out of parts.)

If a truck driver had told me I needed surgery, he would have been correct, but a truck driver has no training in making accurate diagnoses; he has no authority in that area. And though it's true that a self-proclaimed expert could tell us all kinds of things about our health, I want to know that the person has genuine credentials to back up his claims.

Jesus is no pretender with a mail-order diploma. He's the authority on spiritual life and death. Although I might cringe at the thought of "spiritual surgery," I know and trust the Great Physician to work wonders on my soul.

God, *I acknowledge Your sovereignty in this world and in my own life. I yield myself to You as the ultimate authority. Through Christ, amen.*

**SEARCH THE WORD**

*We might diagnose our problems, but no one cures like Jesus!*

Scripture: Luke 20:1-8

Song: *"All Hail the Power of Jesus' Name"*

***From this meditation today, I will pray . . .***

Adoration ____________________

Confession ____________________

Thanksgiving ____________________

Supplication ____________________

***From this meditation today, I will . . .***

Think ____________________

Say ____________________

Do ____________________

# Living in His Favor

*The time of the* L*ORD's favor has come*
(Isaiah 61:2, *New Living Translation*).

Scripture: Isaiah 61:1-4
Song: *"Set My Spirit Free"*

*From this meditation today, I will pray . . .*

Adoration ________________________________

________________________________

________________________________

Confession ________________________________

________________________________

________________________________

Thanksgiving ________________________________

________________________________

________________________________

Supplication ________________________________

________________________________

________________________________

*From this meditation today, I will . . .*

Think ________________________________

________________________________

________________________________

Say ________________________________

________________________________

________________________________

Do ________________________________

________________________________

________________________________

July 7–13. ***Paula Moldenhauer*** *is passionate about her relationship with Jesus. She writes from her home in Colorado, where she home-schools her four children.*

As a young wife I sat in my bedroom reading Romans 8:1, which says there's no condemnation for those who belong to Christ Jesus. I remember a strange feeling, as if the Spirit wanted to communicate something I didn't quite grasp. Frustrated, I set my Bible aside. Later, God revealed to me what I hadn't understood in 20 years as Christian: God completely accepts me. He doesn't look at me with condemning eyes, but with eyes of favor.

Somehow, I'd gotten the wrong message. I believed Jesus forgave sins and gave me an eternal inheritance, but that my job was to "live up" to that gift. Perfection eluded me, though, and I wrapped myself in a cloak of self-loathing. I just couldn't be "good enough."

What a joyous day when I finally realized that Jesus came not only to give me Heaven in the future, but also His peace in the present. When He stood in the synagogue and read the prophecy of Isaiah, Jesus proclaimed His mission to my approval-hungry heart.

Dear Lord, *help me more fully grasp Your favor and live as one unconditionally loved. Thank You for setting my heart free and turning the ashes of my life into something beautiful for Your glory. In Jesus' name, amen.*

**SPOTLIGHT**
***Next Week's Lesson***

Feelings can be deceptive and destructive. Be sure to test them with the Scriptures.

# No Longer a Victim

*He cast out many demons*
(Mark 1:34, *New Living Translation*).

I don't know whether I believe that demons can live in a Christian—all the theology of the spirit world is bigger than I can grasp at the moment. But I do know that for many years I was in bondage to what I can only describe as demonic lies. Were they indeed lies of the devil? In any case, it seemed I was being "told" that I was unworthy to serve Jesus—that I was a failure. I thought God must grow so tired of my constant mistakes.

I also kept recalling past hurts, so that, too often, my thoughts swirled with anger and fear. I felt my heart was in prison.

One day some caring people spent several hours praying with me. They encouraged me to confess my sins of pride, unforgiveness, and perfectionism. As we shared together, they explained some of the misconceptions I'd held about God and myself. Then they showed me the truth: the chains I'd been living in were shattered at the cross. They had no power over me. I no longer needed to be victim to the demons who'd chased me.

Heavenly Father, *thank You for setting me free from perfectionism and pride. Keep me close to You throughout this day. And make me ever more wise to the ways of the enemy, so that my thoughts reflect only the truths of Your eternal Word. I pray through my deliverer, Jesus. Amen.*

**SEARCH THE WORD**

*The cross of Jesus marks the dividing line between man's solo journey and his walk with a friend.*

Scripture: Mark 1:29-34

**Song: *"Master, the Tempest Is Raging"***

***From this meditation today, I will pray . . .***

Adoration ______________________________

______________________________

______________________________

Confession ______________________________

______________________________

______________________________

Thanksgiving ______________________________

______________________________

______________________________

Supplication ______________________________

______________________________

______________________________

***From this meditation today, I will . . .***

Think ______________________________

______________________________

______________________________

Say ______________________________

______________________________

______________________________

Do ______________________________

______________________________

______________________________

______________________________

______________________________

# Time for a Time-out?

*Everyone is looking for you*
(Mark 1:37, *New Living Translation*).

Scripture: Mark 1:35-39
Song: *"In the Garden"*

*From this meditation today, I will pray . . .*

Adoration ______________________________

Confession ______________________________

Thanksgiving ______________________________

Supplication ______________________________

*From this meditation today, I will . . .*

Think ______________________________

Say ______________________________

Do ______________________________

My friend was on the phone, crying, while my teenage son kept giving me "the look"—the one that says, "Get off the phone; I need you, Mom."

Then my daughter poked her head in and whispered, "I really need to talk to you." The doorbell rang as I heard a thud downstairs, followed by a wail, and the shriek of my younger children calling for me. I wanted to scream.

Either I'm a very important person . . . or my life is totally out of control. It feels like the latter.

I once read that John Wesley's mother would throw her apron over her head when she couldn't take it anymore (she gave birth to 19 children in all). That was the signal to her brood that Mom needed to pray and not be interrupted.

Jesus, too, spent His days being pulled in a million directions. But it didn't seem to ruffle Him as it does me. He always seemed to know which cries to answer immediately, and which ones could wait. And I notice that when people pulled at Him, He often slipped away by himself and prayed. Did He understand the great value of a time-out?

Father, *help me to recognize the signal when I need a time-out from the demands of my world. Instead of blowing my cool, help me to choose time alone with You. Thank You, in Jesus' name. Amen.*

**SPOTLIGHT**
***Next Week's Lesson***

Reaching to God through prayer can bring perspective to the pandemonium of life.

# Touched

*Moved with compassion, Jesus reached out and touched him*
(Mark 1:41, *New Living Translation*).

The doctor raised an eyebrow as I cuddled my fevered child. "It's very contagious," he said. But I couldn't help it. My little one needed the comfort of his mother's arms.

I washed my hands, took lots of showers, and changed my clothes often, but I refused to ignore the longing in Sam's eyes. He was hurting. I couldn't make the virus go away, but I could hold him.

When I hurt, I long for the touch of Jesus. Unlike me, Jesus has the power to make all the pain go away, but sometimes He doesn't do that. In those times it can be hard to trust Him.

I've been known to whine, complain, and even throw little fits about the hard stuff in my life. But as I've grown in my relationship with Jesus, I've come to understand that even when He doesn't take away the difficult circumstances, my pain always moves Him. He doesn't stand aloof, afraid of the germs in my life. He gets right down there in the middle of my messes and holds me. For that I am eternally thankful.

Lord God in Heaven, *thank You for caring about every single thing I go through. Your touch is what I need, so please help me to slow down long enough to experience it. In the name of the Father, the Son, and the Holy Spirit, I pray. Amen.*

**SEARCH THE WORD**

*If Jesus would touch a leper, He will not hesitate to hold us during our hardships.*

Scripture: Mark 1:40-45

Song: *"The Touch of His Hand on Mine"*

***From this meditation today, I will pray . . .***

Adoration ______________________________

______________________________

______________________________

Confession ______________________________

______________________________

______________________________

Thanksgiving ______________________________

______________________________

______________________________

Supplication ______________________________

______________________________

______________________________

***From this meditation today, I will . . .***

Think ______________________________

______________________________

______________________________

Say ______________________________

______________________________

______________________________

Do ______________________________

______________________________

______________________________

______________________________

______________________________

# With Us

*Soon the house where he was staying was so packed with visitors that there was no more room, even outside the door* (Mark 2:2, *New Living Translation*).

Scripture: Mark 2:1, 2

Song: *"Heaven Came Down"*

***From this meditation today, I will pray . . .***

Adoration ______________________

______________________

______________________

Confession ______________________

______________________

______________________

Thanksgiving ______________________

______________________

______________________

Supplication ______________________

______________________

______________________

***From this meditation today, I will . . .***

Think ______________________

______________________

______________________

Say ______________________

______________________

______________________

Do ______________________

______________________

______________________

______________________

______________________

When the president visited our town, we got tickets to the rally held in an amphitheater nestled in the Red Rocks outside of Denver. As the day grew closer, our anticipation mounted. We arrived early. Standing in line for an hour didn't faze us; we waited patiently for the security check.

The afternoon progressed as the excitement heightened. Secret Service men positioned themselves all around the stage, hiding in the rocks above us, their weaponry both menacing and comforting. Then a low buzz started at the front of the crowd and moved our way. He was coming! The crowd went wild, and we cheered with the best of them, our children's eager faces alight with the thrill.

People flocked to Jesus too. Only He didn't hire Secret Service men with swords or make those who came to see him stand in a security line. He let them crowd around Him. He ate with them, laughed with them, healed their diseases, cast out their demons, and blessed them. He modeled the heart of our Father who wants always to be near to us.

O God, *I'm amazed that You don't hold yourself aloof or lock yourself away behind celestial guards. You long to be with me—so much that You choose to dwell in my heart. Thank You, in Jesus' name. Amen.*

**SPOTLIGHT**

***Next Week's Lesson***

The difference between whether Jesus feels near or far may depend on where we are choosing to stand.

# Crowded Out

*They couldn't bring him to Jesus because of the crowd* (Mark 2:4, *New Living Translation*).

Last summer I went through a crazy, busy season. Company, Cub Scout camp, conferences, and family demands kept me rushing around at full speed. I didn't get much time alone with the Lord, and guilty feelings descended upon me.

Jesus seemed to be standing on the other side of the crowd of my life. I couldn't push through to Him. Finally, I asked Him whether He was displeased. He showed me that loving my husband, my company, and my children was a way of being with Him at this time. Jesus wasn't far away; He was with me in every moment of those days.

I'm awed by the story of Brother Lawrence, who said he felt as close to God when he washed the dishes in a busy kitchen as when he prayed in solitude. I'm not there, though. My time alone with God feels so much sweeter than any other time. But I'm learning that Jesus is always with me, and I shouldn't evaluate our relationship by missed quiet times. He's there whether I'm curled up in my recliner reading my Bible or rushing around loving His people. Nothing can crowd out the presence of the one who lives within me.

Dear Lord, *thank You that You are always with me. Help me to focus on Your presence in both solitude and service. In Christ's name, amen.*

**SEARCH THE WORD**

*We should stop long enough to evaluate if the events in our busy lives will have eternal consequences.*

Scripture: Mark 2:3-5

**Song:** *"Every Day with Jesus"*

*From this meditation today, I will pray . . .*

Adoration ______________________________

______________________________

______________________________

Confession ______________________________

______________________________

______________________________

Thanksgiving ______________________________

______________________________

______________________________

Supplication ______________________________

______________________________

______________________________

*From this meditation today, I will . . .*

Think ______________________________

______________________________

______________________________

Say ______________________________

______________________________

______________________________

Do ______________________________

______________________________

______________________________

______________________________

______________________________

July 13

# Wonderful Acts of Jesus

*Everything he does is wonderful*
(Mark 7:37, *New Living Translation*).

Scripture: Mark 7:31-37
**Song:** *"His Name Is Wonderful"*

***From this meditation today, I will pray . . .***

Adoration ______________________________

______________________________

______________________________

Confession ______________________________

______________________________

______________________________

Thanksgiving ______________________________

______________________________

______________________________

Supplication ______________________________

______________________________

______________________________

***From this meditation today, I will . . .***

Think ______________________________

______________________________

______________________________

Say ______________________________

______________________________

______________________________

Do ______________________________

______________________________

______________________________

______________________________

______________________________

Though a young woman, Kim used to walk with a cane. She had a perpetual stomachache, dizziness, and frequent memory loss. She was also consumed with the shame of enduring 13 years of sexual abuse, which began when Kim was 3 years old. When she asked for prayer, Kim always appeared wounded and frightened.

A friend prayed for Kim, identifying both her emotional scars and physical disabilities, and God answered. The first thing Kim noticed was that her stomach didn't hurt anymore. Within a few days the dizziness was gone. Kim put her cane on the shelf and never again picked it up.

Before God healed her, Kim's lips were sealed. She didn't tell anyone of the abuse, and speaking in front of people petrified her. Her ears were closed to hearing God's whispers of affirmation. Now, though, she's open to God's loving words and tells people across the country how He set her free, not only from serious medical conditions, but also from the shame that haunted her for so many years. When I think of Kim, I can see that, indeed, God does everything well.

*Thank You,* God, *for Your wonderful acts of love. You heal broken hearts and bodies, opening souls to the wonder of yourself. I pray in the name of Jesus, the great physician. Amen.*

**SPOTLIGHT**
***Next Week's Lesson***

We should determine that we will not hold on to our sin and shame longer than God does.

# Love Hurts

*The punishment that brought us peace was upon him*
(Isaiah 53:5).

When I was young, my parents frequently disciplined me for doing wrong. I often deserved reprimand, and my parents did so out of love, patiently teaching me right from wrong.

They always said that punishing me hurt *them*. And I remember thinking, "Sure it does!" Now that I am a parent, I understand what they meant. I cannot express the deep love I have for my child; I want him to be happy, never to feel pain or sadness, and always to know my love. When my child has done wrong, we punish him from our deep desire that he live life on the right pathways—for his own good. But, yes, it does hurt us to punish him.

When we sin, it surely grieves God's heart. After all, sin is the ultimate form of self-destructive behavior, and no parent enjoys watching his child hurt himself. It must be horrible for God to see it happening all the time. Thus He actively did what was necessary to heal our self destructiveness: He took our sin and its punishment upon himself. What a great God is ours!

Father, *thank You for Jesus. I can't imagine the pain it caused You to send Your Son to the cross. Have mercy on me, in Christ's name. Amen.*

**SEARCH THE WORD**

*To receive God's discipline for a season is better than rejecting it and losing eternity.*

Scripture: Isaiah 53:4-6

Song: *"Why Do I Sing About Jesus?"*

*From this meditation today, I will pray . . .*

Adoration ______________________

______________________

______________________

Confession ______________________

______________________

______________________

Thanksgiving ______________________

______________________

______________________

Supplication ______________________

______________________

______________________

*From this meditation today, I will . . .*

Think ______________________

______________________

______________________

Say ______________________

______________________

______________________

Do ______________________

______________________

______________________

July 14–20. ***Amy Neighbors*** *is a stay-at-home mom of two preschoolers. She enjoys reading and writing devotions from her home in middle Georgia.*

July 15

# Cleansed by Love

*He got up from the meal, took off his outer clothing, and wrapped a towel around his waist. After that, he poured water into a basin and began to wash his disciples' feet, drying them with the towel that was wrapped around him* (John 13:4, 5).

Scripture: John 13:1-5

Song: *"O the Deep, Deep Love of Jesus"*

***From this meditation today, I will pray . . .***

Adoration ______________________________

______________________________

______________________________

Confession ______________________________

______________________________

______________________________

Thanksgiving ______________________________

______________________________

______________________________

Supplication ______________________________

______________________________

______________________________

***From this meditation today, I will . . .***

Think ______________________________

______________________________

______________________________

Say ______________________________

______________________________

______________________________

Do ______________________________

______________________________

______________________________

______________________________

______________________________

While recovering from surgery, I required assistance for a simple bath. Thankfully, I knew three people I could ask for help with such a private task without owing anything in return—my husband, my mother, or my sister. I could have asked my brothers, too, but that just wasn't an event they'd care to share with me!

Jesus had loved His disciples as family, but the time had come for Him to return to His heavenly Father. So He reached out to the disciples in a simple but deeply personal gesture—He washed their feet. Not merely to help with their hygiene, but to demonstrate the principle of servanthood that should characterize all Kingdom leadership in the centuries that would follow. It was an act of pure love and humble service, offered with no strings attached.

God's love comes to us freely and unconditionally. No matter what we have done or where we may go, His love will be with us. In response, let us reach out to others through the power of that love. All it takes is a simple act of service done in His name.

Father, *thank You for living out Your love on earth through Your Son. Please help me to share Him with others today. In His name, amen.*

**SPOTLIGHT**

***Next Week's Lesson***

The most menial act of love can have the most profound effect.

# What Great Humility!

*"No" said Peter, "you shall never wash my feet." Jesus answered, "Unless I wash you, you have no part with me." "Then Lord" Simon Peter replied, "not just my feet but my hands and my head as well!"* (John 13:8, 9).

"What is Your direction for my life and work?" In prayer, I waited for God's guidance. Several times over the coming months, an answer presented itself, one that seemed perfect, and I eagerly jumped into what I thought was a wonderful opportunity. Yet down the road a bit, I discovered that I had jumped too quickly!

Rather than hearing or heeding a humble solution, I dove into the grander schemes. I would compare all the perks and choose the very best. In doing so, I seemed to miss God's point. How was I to grow in faith, if I never faced any daunting challenges?

Jesus had no grand plan by the world's standards. To the very end, some of His disciples failed to grasp that. The idea was to model humility in the smallest acts of service. And the sobering fact is this: If we refuse such servanthood, we refuse Christ as well.

Heavenly Father, *Your Son, Jesus, taught that Your grand plan is not of this world. Yet I so often limit my vision to the here and now, making my decisions based on personal comfort and advantage. I thank You for using my mistakes to teach me that Your plans are perfect. Draw me closer to You this day, I pray, in the name of Christ my Lord. Amen.*

**SEARCH THE WORD**

*When Jesus washed His disciples' feet, it was a powerful lesson: you sacrifice nothing when serving others!*

Scripture: John 13:6-11

**Song:** *"Savior, Teach Me Day by Day"*

*From this meditation today, I will pray . . .*

Adoration ______________________

______________________

______________________

Confession ______________________

______________________

______________________

Thanksgiving ______________________

______________________

______________________

Supplication ______________________

______________________

______________________

*From this meditation today, I will . . .*

Think ______________________

______________________

______________________

Say ______________________

______________________

______________________

Do ______________________

______________________

______________________

______________________

______________________

# It's Beautiful

*Now that I, your Lord and Teacher, have washed your feet, you also should wash one another's feet. I have set you an example that you should do as I have done for you* (John 13:14, 15).

Scripture: John 13:12-17

Song: *"God, Our Author and Creator"*

*From this meditation today, I will pray . . .*

Adoration ____________________

Confession ____________________

Thanksgiving ____________________

Supplication ____________________

*From this meditation today, I will . . .*

Think ____________________

Say ____________________

Do ____________________

I grew up in a small town where my parents owned and operated their own business, always treating their customers with care and respect. We heard the Golden Rule often: "Do unto others as you would have others do unto you." And my parents lived it. Everywhere my siblings and I went, people expected proper behavior because of our parents' example and stellar reputations. We learned not only from their words but also from their actions.

Jesus' disciples were, in a sense, a big family. Therefore, anyone observing from afar probably expected certain behavior to come from them. And Jesus knew that a key indicator of their character would be this: How they treated one another.

The same is true today for the followers of Christ. People will often "tune out" a sermon, but it is quite difficult to ignore a group of people who sacrificially serve one another with the purest of motives. In them, the surpassing beauty of Christ shines through.

Father, *Your Son left a legacy for me to live—a legacy of love for You and for others. Please help me to carry out that legacy with grace, every day of my life. In Jesus' precious name, amen.*

**SPOTLIGHT**

***Next Week's Lesson***

Our actions can preach sermons even when we aren't in the pulpit.

# Where Betrayal Can't Live

*I am not referring to all of you; I know those I have chosen. But this is to fulfill the scripture: "He who shares my bread has lifted up his heel against me"* (John 13:18).

I am blessed with many friends whom I hold close to my heart. I share just about everything with them, considering their love and support to be priceless. These precious folk know my heart—sometimes better than I know it.

Jesus' disciples were not only His friends, they were like a family. He knew them, through and through, just as He knows our own hearts. We cannot hide from Him, and this ought to make great impact on how we pray. For example, when we are tempted with selfishness or lust, we often say in our prayers, "Lord, you know I don't want to do that." But, really, wouldn't it be more honest to let the Lord know that, at some level, we really *do* want to do it?

The key is to keep our true hearts always open to Him. In closing off any part of our lives to Him, we hinder the growth of the relationship. And a deep and abiding relationship with us is exactly what the Lord seeks. In such a context, betrayal has no chance.

Heavenly Father, *when I falter in my faith, please forgive me and protect me from evil. Heal my life and my heart, and use me to show Your glory to the world. In Jesus' precious name, amen.*

**SEARCH THE WORD**

*A spiritual family can be stronger than a house full of related strangers.*

Scripture: John 13:18-20

Song: *"Amazing Grace"*

*From this meditation today, I will pray . . .*

Adoration ______________________

______________________

______________________

Confession ______________________

______________________

______________________

Thanksgiving ______________________

______________________

______________________

Supplication ______________________

______________________

______________________

*From this meditation today, I will . . .*

Think ______________________

______________________

______________________

Say ______________________

______________________

______________________

Do ______________________

______________________

______________________

______________________

______________________

# Safe and Secure

*"What is it you want?" he asked. She said, "Grant that one of these two sons of mine may sit at your right and the other at your left in your kingdom"* (Matthew 20:21).

**Scripture: Matthew 20:20-23**
**Song:** *"In Heavenly Love Abiding"*

***From this meditation today, I will pray . . .***

Adoration ______________________________

______________________________

______________________________

Confession ______________________________

______________________________

______________________________

Thanksgiving ______________________________

______________________________

______________________________

Supplication ______________________________

______________________________

______________________________

***From this meditation today, I will . . .***

Think ______________________________

______________________________

______________________________

Say ______________________________

______________________________

______________________________

Do ______________________________

______________________________

______________________________

______________________________

______________________________

As new parents, my husband and I sat down to prepare a will. We named a guardian for our son and outlined financial matters in the event something should happen to us. Our estate may not amount to much, but we wanted to provide him with as much stability as we could.

There are more important matters than earthly security for our son. By being involved in church, reading the Bible, and praying with him, we pass on the tools for living a strong Christian life. We cannot secure a place in Heaven for our son, but we can do all within our ability to show him the right path.

The mother of James and John, understandably, wanted a secure future for her sons with Jesus. The three only dimly understood the kingdom, however. It was a realm in which servanthood would be the goal, in which giving up one's earthly life would be the means to eternal life. Yes, security would follow, but only as a blessed result of pursuing the Lord's will, first and foremost.

O God, *I know that my time on this earth is limited. It is not a secure existence—and sometimes not a pretty one. Thank You for preparing a place in Heaven for me to spend eternity with You. As I grow in faith, keep my thoughts on bringing glory to You. In Jesus' precious name, amen.*

**SPOTLIGHT**
***Next Week's Lesson***

A spiritual heritage where one invests in forming eternal security bonds can never be lost in probate.

# Life Worth Living

*Whoever wants to become great among you must be your servant, and whoever wants to be first must be your slave (Matthew 20:26, 27).*

Having made many job changes, I began to pray diligently, seeking to find the "me" God intended—and the perfect vocation to go with it. Yet with each promising new move, I found little peace.

When motherhood finally became my "career," I heeded the deep desire to be at home with my child. I thought I'd finally found my life's purpose. However, the yearnings barely diminished.

Only when I stopped my human reasoning could I begin practicing what I like to call "faith reasoning." Have you tried it? The upshot was that I began helping with ministries at church and opened up my life for God's use. Much of what I do now is volunteer work, even though money is tight. But I wouldn't trade my newfound areas of service for anything. They make use of the "real me" (my spiritual gifts) as nothing ever has before.

In all my previous years of employment, I was successful with the help of my heavenly Father. But nothing ever satisfied me until I used my life in joyful, wholehearted servanthood.

Lord, *You plan blessings for me far greater than I can imagine. Help me to live my life as Your servant today and always. In Jesus' name, amen.*

**SEARCH THE WORD**

*While we are saved by grace, our search for God's presence usually begins and ends with our service to Him.*

Scripture: Matthew 20:24-28

*Song: "Jesus Is Lord of All"*

*From this meditation today, I will pray . . .*

Adoration ________________

Confession ________________

Thanksgiving ________________

Supplication ________________

*From this meditation today, I will . . .*

Think ________________

Say ________________

Do ________________

# Watch Out for Flying Plywood

*When you pass through the waters, I will be with you; and when you pass through the rivers, they will not sweep over you. When you walk through the fire, you will not be burned; the flames will not set you ablaze* (Isaiah 43:2).

Scripture: Isaiah 43:1-7

Song: *"It Is Well with My Soul"*

***From this meditation today, I will pray . . .***

Adoration ______________________

______________________

______________________

Confession ______________________

______________________

______________________

Thanksgiving ______________________

______________________

______________________

Supplication ______________________

______________________

______________________

***From this meditation today, I will . . .***

Think ______________________

______________________

______________________

Say ______________________

______________________

______________________

Do ______________________

______________________

______________________

July 21–27. ***Jeanette Gardner Littleton*** *has been a published author for close to 30 years. She lives with her husband and kids in Kansas City, Missouri.*

When I saw the plywood fly by the window, I knew it was time to stop looking for flashlight batteries and get downstairs with my husband and crying children. When the sirens stopped and we exited our home, we saw where the tornado had been. One neighbor's roof was in our front yard. On the other side of him, homes were completely demolished, with chairs, underwear, and other items draped in the trees. Amazingly, our home was fine; we just lost a couple of trees.

I thought of that tornado when I read Isaiah 43:1-7. Though these words were written to the Israelites, they also apply to us. Sometimes bad things will happen. Storms will cover us, or we'll swirl in rivers of troubles up to our neck. God never promised to keep the storms and tragedies of life out of our neighborhoods. But He does promise to be with us when they strike.

Lord, *when I see the plywood flying and feel the winds blowing in my life, help me remember that You are the Master of all literal and figurative winds. Help me trust in You. Through Christ, amen.*

**SPOTLIGHT**

***Next Week's Lesson***

**In a world filled with crises, perhaps our favorite name for Jesus should be "protector."**

# Jesus from A to Z

*"But what about you?" he asked.*
*"Who do you say I am?"*
(Matthew 16:15).

About a dozen or so teenagers gathered in the unfinished basement of one teen's home. It wasn't the best setting in the world, but the minds of the teens in the Bible club were able to go beyond the setting.

Our activity was to go from A to Z. As each letter was named, teens called out words that described Jesus to them. Sure, the kids used a lot of the expected names: Savior, Lord, Emmanuel, Holy One. But they also used words we may not think about: Rescuer, Compassionate One, Eloquent, and more. Seventeen-year-old Dennis grinned mischievously as he announced "Xtra Special" for the letter X.

It's been 20 years since I co-sponsored that Bible club. But sometimes I still see those teens' reverent faces as they thought about all Jesus meant to them. It still encourages me to line a paper with A to Z sometimes and list all the things Jesus is. In fact, that might be a good spiritual exercise for all of us today.

Dear heavenly Father, *just as Peter had the discernment to know exactly who You are in a world that was confused about You, open my eyes to the many facets of Your eternal being. And as I come to know You better, increase my ability to speak of You to others. Thank You, in the name of Jesus, Your incomparable Son. Amen.*

**SEARCH THE WORD**

*Rehearsing the ways Jesus has blessed us should reaffirm His lordship and revive our commitment.*

Scripture: Matthew 16:13-16

**Song:** *"Jesus, High in Glory"*

***From this meditation today, I will pray . . .***

Adoration ______________________

______________________

______________________

Confession ______________________

______________________

______________________

Thanksgiving ______________________

______________________

______________________

Supplication ______________________

______________________

______________________

***From this meditation today, I will . . .***

Think ______________________

______________________

______________________

Say ______________________

______________________

______________________

Do ______________________

______________________

______________________

______________________

______________________

July 23

# Blurt the Good Stuff

*Jesus replied, "Blessed are you, Simon son of Jonah, for this was not revealed to you by man, but by my Father in heaven"* (Matthew 16:17).

Scripture: Matthew 16:17-20

Song: *"May the Words of My Mouth"*

*From this meditation today, I will pray . . .*

Adoration ______________________________

______________________________

______________________________

Confession ______________________________

______________________________

______________________________

Thanksgiving ______________________________

______________________________

______________________________

Supplication ______________________________

______________________________

______________________________

*From this meditation today, I will . . .*

Think ______________________________

______________________________

______________________________

Say ______________________________

______________________________

______________________________

Do ______________________________

______________________________

______________________________

______________________________

______________________________

Peter is probably the disciple I relate to most closely. You see, I'm also likely to make mistakes, get myself into trouble, or just plain sin by thoughtlessly spouting the wrong words. Likewise, Peter seemed to put his foot in his mouth regularly. He bragged about never leaving Christ—and then abandoned Him, even lied about Him. On the mountain when Elijah and Moses talked with Christ, Peter was the one who wanted to settle down there with those legends permanently. So Jesus, once again, had to correct this impulsive disciple.

However, in our Scripture passage today, blurting out an answer was a good thing for Peter to do—in fact, Jesus told him that God was working through him at just that moment. Peter might have had some issues with his mouth, but he apparently also kept his mind contemplating Christ and pondering what God was doing. As he kept his thoughts trained on God, God revealed the most marvelous truths to him. Maybe I'd like to be more like Peter, after all.

Dear Father, *how thankful I am for Your incarnate Son! Please help me to focus on Him so that if I must blurt out things, they'll be words that reveal His wonderful qualities. In His name, I pray. Amen.*

**SPOTLIGHT**

***Next Week's Lesson***

Engaging the mind before the tongue is a decision that can improve our effectiveness as Christians.

# Who's Making the Plans?

*Jesus turned and said to Peter, "Get behind me, Satan! You are a stumbling block to me; you do not have in mind the things of God, but the things of men"* (Matthew 16:23).

In his few unkind moments in life, my husband has said that I'm bossy, that I think my way is the only way to do things. In his kinder moments, my easygoing husband sits back and lets me make the plans—knowing that otherwise nothing may ever happen in our family!

I do have administrative gifts. I'm quite analytical, and I'm pretty good at planning things, thinking through the details to figure out the best way to proceed. But I guess the downside is that I get used to being in control. Also, I'm often reluctant to think outside my own plans.

In today's Scripture, Peter didn't like what Jesus was saying about the future. Perhaps it didn't line up with his plans on how things really ought to unfold.

As I've often been reminded—and as Peter was reminded—it's OK to make our plans, or perhaps nothing will ever get done. But even as we make our plans and envision our futures, we still have to keep God in the center of the equation. That way, we'll be ready for Him to reveal more of His perfect will at any moment.

Dear God, *help me remember to make no plans without consulting You and to accept Your ways as the best ways. When I don't understand, give me Your peace that surpasses understanding. In Jesus' name, amen.*

**SEARCH THE WORD**

*Since God ultimately controls our plans, it is best to consult Him before we jump too far ahead.*

Scripture: Matthew 16:21-23

**Song: *"Turn Your Eyes Upon Jesus"***

*From this meditation today, I will pray . . .*

Adoration ____________________

Confession ____________________

Thanksgiving ____________________

Supplication ____________________

*From this meditation today, I will . . .*

Think ____________________

Say ____________________

Do ____________________

July 25

# On the Mountaintop

*Peter said to Jesus, "Lord, it is good for us to be here. If you wish, I will put up three shelters—one for you, one for Moses and one for Elijah"* (Matthew 17:4).

Scripture: Matthew 17:1-4
Song: *"Lord, Be Glorified"*

***From this meditation today, I will pray . . .***

Adoration ______________________________

Confession ______________________________

Thanksgiving ______________________________

Supplication ______________________________

***From this meditation today, I will . . .***

Think ______________________________

Say ______________________________

Do ______________________________

My 17-year-old stepdaughter spent most of her time last summer at a place called God's Mountain. She worked there for a week in the early summer helping with a kids' camp. While she worked with the children, God touched her own heart, leading her to dedicate her life to Christ.

We saw the change in her life as soon as she arrived back home. And for most of the summer, she returned often to the camp to help with the different sessions and simply to relish the atmosphere—being with people who focused on Christ. She didn't want to leave that mountain when the summer ended, because so many amazing things happened there in her spiritual growth.

We've all had our "mountaintop experiences" with the Lord, times when we've just wanted to stay in His presence forever. Like Peter, we want to pitch permanent tents and bask in the glory. But life goes on and demands that we join it. However, we can ask God to keep His glory alive in our hearts.

Heavenly Father, *help me find the "glory stops" in my days—moments when I can bask in Your presence without any other agenda. Then energize me by Your Spirit to walk into my world with the matchless message of Your goodness. In the precious name of Your Son, Jesus, I pray. Amen.*

**SPOTLIGHT**
***Next Week's Lesson***

Whether in a physical location or because of a precious memory, we benefit by discovering a place for spiritual renewal.

# He's Pleased with You

*While he was still speaking, a bright cloud enveloped them, and a voice from the cloud said, "This is my Son, whom I love; with him I am well pleased. Listen to him!"* (Matthew 17:9).

I was as pleased as could be when I saw my 8-year-old son tenderly helping his 3-year-old sister. I was so proud that he was watching out for her without being asked. I love those moments in parenting when I'm just so happy with my children that I could burst.

Apparently God the Father was pretty pleased with God the Son in the Scripture for today. Just as at Jesus' baptism, the Father's voice broke through the sky, proclaiming His pleasure with His Son. The Father didn't wait until Jesus had finished the whole task set before Him on earth. He was proud of His Son and pleased with His daily obedience and commitment.

Have you ever thought about God's pleasure with you? He doesn't wait until we're finished with our work here on earth; He's pleased with us now, as we walk in day-by-day commitment to Him. He's pleased each time we make right choices and go where He leads. And even when we fail, His love never lessens, His care is never withdrawn.

*Thank You,* Lord, *for loving me as tenderly and joyfully as a mom and dad love their kids. Help me to live in the power of this love, especially when I'm tempted to see nothing but my failures. Through Christ, amen.*

**SEARCH THE WORD**

*To know we are serving a proud Father should keep us from going down a wrong path.*

Scripture: Matthew 17:5-8

Song: *"Oh, How He Loves You and Me"*

*From this meditation today, I will pray . . .*

Adoration ______________________

______________________

______________________

Confession ______________________

______________________

______________________

Thanksgiving ______________________

______________________

______________________

Supplication ______________________

______________________

______________________

*From this meditation today, I will . . .*

Think ______________________

______________________

______________________

Say ______________________

______________________

______________________

Do ______________________

______________________

______________________

______________________

______________________

*July 27*

# Ready to Burst!

*As they were coming down the mountain, Jesus instructed them, "Don't tell anyone what you have seen, until the Son of Man has been raised from the dead"* (Matthew 17:9).

Scripture: Matthew 17:9-13

Song: *"I'm Gonna Sing"*

***From this meditation today, I will pray . . .***

Adoration ______________________________

______________________________

______________________________

Confession ______________________________

______________________________

______________________________

Thanksgiving ______________________________

______________________________

______________________________

Supplication ______________________________

______________________________

______________________________

***From this meditation today, I will . . .***

Think ______________________________

______________________________

______________________________

Say ______________________________

______________________________

______________________________

Do ______________________________

______________________________

______________________________

______________________________

______________________________

Has anything so exciting ever happened to you that you were just ready to burst with the telling? I have felt that way a few times, especially a few years ago when I learned I was pregnant with my youngest child. I couldn't wait to proclaim the news to my friends and family.

Can you imagine how excited Peter, James, and John were? They'd watched Jesus glow with an internal fire, they'd actually seen Moses and Elijah, and then they heard the literal voice of God. Wouldn't their report just blow away a small group meeting? Jesus held them back though, until finally, after the resurrection, they could spread the good news far and wide.

Poet Robert Frost once said: "Half the world is composed of people who have something to say and can't, and the other half who have nothing to say and keep on saying it." We can be different from either group; we have something eternally worth saying, and we can say it, as the Spirit gives us the will and the words.

Lord, *I thank You for revealing yourself to human beings through such creative ways. When You work in my life and I'm ready to burst, give me opportunities to tell others—Christians or not—about the marvelous things You've done. In Jesus' name, amen.*

**SPOTLIGHT**

***Next Week's Lesson***

Seeking daily reminders of His perfect love for us will keep our spirits fresh and our faith strong.

# Perfection in the Fire

*Let patience have her perfect work,*
*that ye may be perfect and entire, lacking nothing*
(James 1:4, *King James Version*).

Our minister told of being in a pottery class, fashioning a colorful bowl. A four-step process was required, in which the bowl would be glazed, then baked, and then baked a third and fourth time. Impatient to see the final product, he only put the bowl in the kiln twice, at the beginning and at the end of the process. The first time he used the bowl, it cracked, and all of his hard work went to waste.

We too are like bowls in a potter's hand, and James tells us that our trials can help mold a stronger faith in us. Our hard times can be like a fire that, though painful, works to strengthen our commitment to the Lord.

It is easy to praise the Lord when circumstances unfold to our liking, and everything happens according to our own "perfect" time schedules. But we do need to develop patience. And how shall we do that unless we face delays, even prayers that seem to go unanswered for years on end? It is when the answer seems delayed and the need dire that the fire of endurance solidifies our patience.

*Thanks,* Lord, *for Your workmanship in my life. Help me trust that these trials are strengthening me and not destroying me. In Jesus' name, amen.*

**SEARCH THE WORD**

*Knowing that God isn't done with us yet must mean that He has something really good for us in Heaven!*

Scripture: James 1:1-4
Song: *"Refiner's Fire"*

*From this meditation today, I will pray . . .*

Adoration ______________________

______________________

______________________

Confession ______________________

______________________

______________________

Thanksgiving ______________________

______________________

______________________

Supplication ______________________

______________________

______________________

*From this meditation today, I will . . .*

Think ______________________

______________________

______________________

Say ______________________

______________________

______________________

Do ______________________

______________________

______________________

July 28–31. ***Colleen Yang,*** *mother of two children, was a missionary in Japan for 10 years. She now lives in Illinois, working as a writer and illustrator.*

# Ask and Believe

*If any of you lacks wisdom, he should ask God, who gives generously to all without finding fault, and it will be given to him. But when he asks, he must believe and not doubt, because he who doubts is like a wave of the sea, blown and tossed by the wind* (James 1:5, 6).

Scripture: James 1:5-8

Song: *"My Hope Is Built"*

*From this meditation today, I will pray . . .*

Adoration ____________________

____________________

____________________

Confession ____________________

____________________

____________________

Thanksgiving ____________________

____________________

____________________

Supplication ____________________

____________________

____________________

*From this meditation today, I will . . .*

Think ____________________

____________________

____________________

Say ____________________

____________________

____________________

Do ____________________

____________________

____________________

____________________

____________________

My autistic son struggles with fear and is particularly frightened of bugs. Every day before we go out, he asks me whether the bugs are going to get him. I assure him they will not bother him, and then he runs off to play with an unburdened spirit.

One day he approached a group of little boys who had caught a grasshopper in a jar. "Is the bug going to get me?" he asked.

"Yeah, look, it's *on* you!" they teased. Horrified, my son ran to me, frantically trying to brush the imagined grasshopper off his back. It took me some time to convince him that he was out of danger.

Sometimes I'm like that with God. I come to Him, asking for wisdom and reassurance; later, I easily doubt the word I've received in the face of countless real or imagined crises. In my flurry of emotion, I somehow avoid resting in the good and loving words of my Lord.

*Thank You, Lord, for Your wisdom. Help me to remember it, though, and trust it, even when the world seems to contradict Your wise words. I pray this prayer in the name of Jesus, my Savior and Lord. Amen.*

**SPOTLIGHT**

***Next Week's Lesson***

God seems never to tire of repeating His story of love for His children.

# God Honors the Poor

*The brother in humble circumstances ought to take pride in his high position. But the one who is rich should take pride in his low position, because he will pass away like a wild flower* (James 1:9, 10).

Our society seems to associate "poor" with "shameful." It wasn't until I became a missionary, though, that I truly began to comprehend this in all its power. We were poor, rarely knowing where our next meal would come from. Yet never did the Lord fail to provide. Relying on Him like that was hardly a thing of shame! In fact, soon dependence upon Him became an exhilarating experience as we saw our needs being met, time after time.

Coming back to America, I realized that it was far too easy to take a regular paycheck for granted. So for me, our Scripture verse contains a gentle challenge: Always look at things through Heaven's eyes. Thus I can see that any level of financial well-being is a gift to be received humbly.

Are you in need at the moment? God honors you and will provide. Are you doing well? You are being humbled by God's great provision.

Dear Father in Heaven, *help me never forget to thank You for humbling me by giving me so much. Help me also to remember to thank You for needs that arise, needs that turn my heart back to dependence upon Your daily bread. In the name of Your Son, my Savior, I pray. Amen.*

**SEARCH THE WORD**

*Why are we surprised when the God who owns the universe supplies our every need?*

Scripture: James 1:9-11

**Song:** *"Give Thanks"*

*From this meditation today, I will pray . . .*

Adoration ______________________

______________________

______________________

Confession ______________________

______________________

______________________

Thanksgiving ______________________

______________________

______________________

Supplication ______________________

______________________

______________________

*From this meditation today, I will . . .*

Think ______________________

______________________

______________________

Say ______________________

______________________

______________________

Do ______________________

______________________

______________________

______________________

______________________

July 31

# Rules of Engagement

*Temptation comes from our own desires which entice us and drag us away* (James 1:14, *New Living Translation*).

Scripture: James 1:12-15

Song: *"He Will Not Let Me Fall"*

*From this meditation today, I will pray . . .*

Adoration ______________________________

______________________________

______________________________

Confession ______________________________

______________________________

______________________________

Thanksgiving ______________________________

______________________________

______________________________

Supplication ______________________________

______________________________

______________________________

*From this meditation today, I will . . .*

Think ______________________________

______________________________

______________________________

Say ______________________________

______________________________

______________________________

Do ______________________________

______________________________

______________________________

______________________________

______________________________

One of the first principles you learn in the martial arts is that you should never let the attacker set the rules of engagement. For example, one scientific study looked at women who were attacked by men. The women who shouted "No!"—and fought back—had a much greater chance of survival than those who succumbed to fear and submissively allowed the attacker to have his way.

We could view Satan as a mugger. He throws temptations in our path and convinces us that we must give in, either by bullying us with shame or seducing us with myriad "innocent" justifications. Yet we are called to fight back with an aggressive counterattack, just as Jesus countered Satan's temptations in the wilderness.

What temptation hounds you right now? Are you letting the enemy set the rules of engagement? One effective counterattack is to simply avoid the people and places that make you most vulnerable. As someone once said, it is better to shun the bait than struggle in the snare.

Lord, *give me discernment to see temptations coming well before I am thrust into the heat of battle. Help me form good habits of prayer and Bible reading, strengthening my defenses. Most of all, continue to assure me of Your constant presence and love. For it is Your power, ultimately, that wins every spiritual battle. In Jesus' name, amen.*

**SPOTLIGHT**

***Next Week's Lesson***

How boldly we defend ourselves may determine whether Satan makes his goal.

August

# IMAGES OF CHRIST IN US

*Christ is all, and is in all.*
—Colossians 3:11

Photo © iStock

# Loud Tongues, Deaf Ears

*My dear brothers, take note of this: Everyone should be quick to listen, slow to speak and slow to become angry* (James 1:19).

Scripture: James 1:16-21

Song: *"My Soul in Silence Waits for God"*

***From this meditation today, I will pray . . .***

Adoration ______________________________

______________________________

______________________________

Confession ______________________________

______________________________

______________________________

Thanksgiving ______________________________

______________________________

______________________________

Supplication ______________________________

______________________________

______________________________

***From this meditation today, I will . . .***

Think ______________________________

______________________________

______________________________

Say ______________________________

______________________________

______________________________

Do ______________________________

______________________________

______________________________

August 1–3. ***Colleen Yang,*** *mother of two children, was a missionary in Japan for 10 years. She now lives in Illinois, working as a writer and illustrator.*

A Native American saying goes like this: "Listen, or thy tongue will keep thee deaf." I have found myself struggling with this principle in raising small children, especially when shouting orders seems the best way to go. It's all too easy, when I'm feeling particularly tired, to jump to conclusions and just react without truly listening to what my children have to say. I've often had to apologize for unjust reprimands.

I have realized, too, that sometimes I really don't *want* to hear what my children have to say. Yet a little bit of eye contact and a gentle smile goes so far with them.

God has been reminding me that a listening heart is a humble heart. And the humbler I am before Him, the more I will be able to hear others before contributing my "two-cents' worth." As another saying goes (this one from Arabia): "When you have spoken a word, it reigns over you. When it is unspoken, you reign over it."

*Thank You, Father, for being quick to listen to me when I come to You in prayer. Help me develop a listening ear and a humble heart in my interactions with others, that I might witness to Your love. In Christ, amen.*

**SPOTLIGHT**

***Next Week's Lesson***

To listen and learn is better than to speak and suffer.

# Telltale Tongue

*If anyone considers himself religious and yet does not keep a tight rein on his tongue, he deceives himself and his religion is worthless* (James 1:26).

The destructive power of words was vividly demonstrated by how water crystals changed their structure—according to words spoken to them! In an article in *Christian Today,* researcher Masaru Emoto, author of *The Hidden Messages of Water,* showed that water crystals which had positive words like "love" and "thanks" spoken to them changed into the most beautiful snowflake-like shapes. On the other hand, words like "fool" or "stupid" caused the water to break down.

We know that our bodies contain a high percentage of water. Is it possible, then, that words could literally tear a person apart?

No wonder the Lord places such importance on our words, making their quality equal to the quality of our religion. Yet why is it so hard, especially within our own families, to speak consistently with kindness? I'm sobered by the enormous physical and spiritual influence my words can have on the ones I dearly love. Is it your prayer today to make that influence a positive, life-giving one?

God, *in light of their power for good or ill, let my words be ordered by You. I know I can speak with kindness, if You will help me recollect all of the good things You have spoken to me in Your Word. In Jesus' name, amen.*

**SEARCH THE WORD**

*How you choose your words may determine who will listen.*

Scripture: James 1:22-27

Song: *"They'll Know We Are Christians by Our Love"*

*From this meditation today, I will pray . . .*

Adoration ____________________

____________________

____________________

Confession ____________________

____________________

____________________

Thanksgiving ____________________

____________________

____________________

Supplication ____________________

____________________

____________________

*From this meditation today, I will . . .*

Think ____________________

____________________

____________________

Say ____________________

____________________

____________________

Do ____________________

____________________

____________________

____________________

____________________

August 3

# Blessings for the Day

*It is good to proclaim your unfailing love in the morning, your faithfulness in the evening* (Psalm 92:2, *New Living Translation*).

Scripture: Psalm 92:1-8

Song: *"Thy Faithfulness, Lord, Each Moment We Find"*

***From this meditation today, I will pray . . .***

Adoration ______________________________

Confession ______________________________

Thanksgiving ______________________________

Supplication ______________________________

***From this meditation today, I will . . .***

Think ______________________________

Say ______________________________

Do ______________________________

Mornings are hard for me because I work late into the night. So I'm often tired when morning dawns, and my quiet times then become less than inspiring. I can easily begin to feel spiritually depleted.

There is hope for me, though! In fact, the psalmist hit upon an important principle that I began trying in my own quiet times with God. I felt challenged to take a few minutes each morning to "proclaim"—or meditate upon—the divine attribute that I need most during the day: God's unfailing love. As I did this, I pictured a mighty hand holding and sustaining me through the stress of the day. Then at the end of the day before I lay down to sleep, I took a few minutes to reflect on how God had revealed His love for me during the day.

After a few days of this simple spiritual exercise, I felt better able to handle my daily stresses and strains. More importantly, I sensed a closer connection with the indwelling Lord.

We're often called to be more faithful, or to do more for God. But I believe we often just need to stop and remember how much He loves us, no matter what.

*Thank You, Father, for Your nurturing hand of love, which is my source of strength today. In the precious name of Jesus, I pray. Amen.*

**SPOTLIGHT**

***Next Week's Lesson***

If we can condition ourselves to sense God's continual presence, we can change the condition of our lives.

# When the Boss Isn't Watching

*All the nations will be gathered before him, and he will separate the people one from another as a shepherd separates the sheep from the goats* (Matthew 25:32).

What is really in our hearts shows through when we think no one is watching. At my workplace some employees get busy when the boss walks in, but they put forth less effort when he walks out of sight. Employees like that merely want to look good for the boss.

Christ calls us to go well beyond a concern for mere appearances. He wants our genuine compassion for those in need. It's really the difference between His sheep and the goats ("fake sheep"). Sheep not only have a heart for the Lord, but also for His people and His business—even when they aren't aware that He is watching.

While we are on this earth, we can be transformed from goats into sheep. And we need to let God's Spirit do that work in us, day by day. Because once we step into eternity, the matter will already be settled.

Lord God, *help me see where I have the heart of a goat and help me change fully into a sheep. And may my sheep's heart influence others so they may spend eternity in the place You prepared for people, not in the place prepared for the devil and his angels. In the name of the Father, the Son, and the Holy Spirit, I pray. Amen.*

**SEARCH THE WORD**

*A physical heart condition affects the flow of blood; our spiritual heart condition affects the flow of our service for God.*

Scripture: Matthew 25:31-46

Song: *"The Shepherd's Fold on High"*

*From this meditation today, I will pray . . .*

Adoration ______________________________

______________________________

______________________________

Confession ______________________________

______________________________

______________________________

Thanksgiving ______________________________

______________________________

______________________________

Supplication ______________________________

______________________________

______________________________

*From this meditation today, I will . . .*

Think ______________________________

______________________________

______________________________

Say ______________________________

______________________________

______________________________

Do ______________________________

______________________________

______________________________

August 4–10. ***Coloradan Dianne E. Butts*** *writes for Christian magazines and compilation books. She also enjoys riding her motorcycle with her husband, Hal.*

August 5

# No Room at the Inn

*If you show special attention to the man wearing fine clothes and say, "Here's a good seat for you," but say to the poor man, "You stand there" or "Sit on the floor by my feet," have you not discriminated among yourselves and become judges with evil thoughts?* (James 2:3, 4).

Scripture: James 2:1-4

Song: *"God in Heaven Hath a Treasure"*

***From this meditation today, I will pray . . .***

Adoration ______________________________

______________________________

______________________________

Confession ______________________________

______________________________

______________________________

Thanksgiving ______________________________

______________________________

______________________________

Supplication ______________________________

______________________________

______________________________

***From this meditation today, I will . . .***

Think ______________________________

______________________________

______________________________

Say ______________________________

______________________________

______________________________

Do ______________________________

______________________________

______________________________

______________________________

______________________________

My husband, Hal, and I parked near the motel's office after a long, hard day of riding motorcycles. I was hot and sweaty, and my helmet had matted my hair to my head. I went in to get us a room. "Sorry," the clerk said. "We're full."

We rode to the next motel. This time Hal went in and got us a room. As I waited for him to do business with the clerk, I remembered seeing only two or three cars in the parking lot of that previous motel. And the clerk said they were full! Maybe it's Hal's looks—or the way his helmet doesn't mat his short hair—but since that day Hal has gotten our rooms while I wait outside . . . and we get turned away far less often.

We would have been good customers for the first motel—honest, trustworthy, a blessing as we let the light of Christ shine through us. But we were turned away, and the motel's owners may have lost more than they know.

Lord, *help me to see the value in each person You bring across my path. And give me the wisdom to distinguish earthly treasures from eternal treasures in setting my own priorities. Through Christ I pray. Amen.*

**SPOTLIGHT**

***Next Week's Lesson***

There will be no fashion checks or cash registers at Heaven's entrance.

# Upside Down?

*Are they not the ones who are slandering the noble name of him to whom you belong?* (James 2:7).

Several years ago, author Bill Myers wrote a children's book series called Journeys to Fayrah. When the characters in the story found themselves in the land of Fayrah, everything seemed upside down. But the characters soon learned the truth: the world was right side up; *they* were upside down.

Sin can so skew our thinking that we may not know what is right. Because of sin, everything in our word can get turned inside out, down side up, upside down, wrong side out, right side in, backside front, and front side back. Whew! It's tough to tell right from wrong in such a situation. That's why we need God to guide us.

To us, things seem backwards. We think of the rich as possessing kingdoms and the poor as possessing little or nothing. Yet today's verses tell us that those who are poor "in the eyes of the world" are rich in faith and will inherit the kingdom because they sincerely love God. Those who may have riches and power—yet slander Christ's name—truly are the poorest of the poor.

Lord, *let me never be counted among the ones who are slandering Your noble name. Instead, help me to live as one who loves You with a sincere and dedicated passion. And may each person I meet today see something of Your nobility in me. In Jesus' precious name, I pray. Amen.*

**SEARCH THE WORD**

*The myth that money can buy anything ruins many rich men and causes unnecessary jealousy for the countless poor.*

Scripture: James 2:5-7

Song: *"O, Could I Speak the Matchless Worth"*

***From this meditation today, I will pray . . .***

Adoration ______________________________

______________________________

______________________________

Confession ______________________________

______________________________

______________________________

Thanksgiving ______________________________

______________________________

______________________________

Supplication ______________________________

______________________________

______________________________

***From this meditation today, I will . . .***

Think ______________________________

______________________________

______________________________

Say ______________________________

______________________________

______________________________

Do ______________________________

______________________________

______________________________

______________________________

______________________________

August 7

# Short List of Sins?

*Whoever keeps the whole law and yet stumbles at just one point is guilty of breaking all of it* (James 2:10).

Scripture: James 2:8-11

Song: *"Grace Greater Than Our Sin"*

*From this meditation today, I will pray . . .*

Adoration ________________________________

________________________________

________________________________

Confession ________________________________

________________________________

________________________________

Thanksgiving ________________________________

________________________________

________________________________

Supplication ________________________________

________________________________

________________________________

*From this meditation today, I will . . .*

Think ________________________________

________________________________

________________________________

Say ________________________________

________________________________

________________________________

Do ________________________________

________________________________

________________________________

________________________________

________________________________

A prominent attorney in a town where we once lived told my husband, "The Ten Commandments would be pretty good if it weren't for that one about adultery." Within a few years we heard of circumstances that revealed the likely reason for his point of view.

We all tend to gasp at other's sins, yet we quickly excuse our own. Christian comedian Mike Warnke once said that, after describing his former life of sin, some people would say to him, "Well, I never did anything *that* bad!"

He would reply, "Yes, and you were headed to the same hell as I was!"

We often stand amazed at spectacular testimonies and conversion stories. But Mike Warnke also pointed out that it takes little common sense for a drowning person to reach out to grab a floating branch and cling to it for salvation. But what of someone who has lived a basically clean life, someone in no obvious need to escape the deadly clutches of sin? For that person to recognize his need for a Savior . . . Well, perhaps that's the bigger miracle.

Father, *when I view my list of sins as much shorter than others', I'm in danger of minimizing the very things that sent Your Son to the cross. Help me to see all sin as devastating and destructive. And help me to love others as if their sin list is as short as I imagine mine to be. In Jesus' name, amen.*

**SPOTLIGHT**

***Next Week's Lesson***

**If every living person just sins once, Christ's abundant mercy is still needed. Consider the real depth of His love!**

# Twice Blest

***Judgment without mercy will be shown to anyone who has not been merciful. Mercy triumphs over judgment!*** **(James 2:13).**

I know of a woman who grew up in a home filled with harshness and anger. Now an adult, she still goes home and cares for her once-abusive parent. When I questioned this, she said she knew that she could hang onto the pain and return hurt for hurt. Some would think she has that right. After all, aren't parents supposed to "bless" their children, to bring good things into their lives?

"But maybe I was placed in this home so I myself could be the blessing," she said. "It's not always about what we get, but what we give."

How could she treat her parent so well after the way she was treated? "I was just as hateful toward God," she said. "But He showed me mercy in forgiving my sins. How can I refuse to show mercy in return? My Lord was so generous in mercy to me, and as a result I am a friend of God. I chose to extend mercy to my parent, and now I have gained a loving friend."

Indeed, mercy triumphs over judgment. And as Shakespeare wrote: "Mercy is twice blest: It blesseth him that gives and him that takes."

**Dear Father,** *thank You so much for the mercy You have shown me, mercy too deep for me to fathom. Give me the courage to extend mercy to others, even when I have been wrongly treated. I pray in Jesus' name. Amen.*

**SEARCH THE WORD**

*Only parents of returning prodigals can imagine how Christ will feel when His children praise Him for His mercy!*

**Scripture: James 2:12-17**

**Song:** ***"There's a Wideness in God's Mercy"***

***From this meditation today, I will pray . . .***

Adoration ______________________________

______________________________

______________________________

Confession ______________________________

______________________________

______________________________

Thanksgiving ______________________________

______________________________

______________________________

Supplication ______________________________

______________________________

______________________________

***From this meditation today, I will . . .***

Think ______________________________

______________________________

______________________________

Say ______________________________

______________________________

______________________________

Do ______________________________

______________________________

______________________________

______________________________

______________________________

August 9

# Fingerprints of Faith

*You believe that there is one God. Good!*
*Even the demons believe that—and shudder* (James 2:19).

Scripture: James 2:18-20
**Song:** *"Firmly I Believe and Truly"*

*From this meditation today, I will pray . . .*

Adoration ______________________________

______________________________

______________________________

Confession ______________________________

______________________________

______________________________

Thanksgiving ______________________________

______________________________

______________________________

Supplication ______________________________

______________________________

______________________________

*From this meditation today, I will . . .*

Think ______________________________

______________________________

______________________________

Say ______________________________

______________________________

______________________________

Do ______________________________

______________________________

______________________________

______________________________

______________________________

When a person merely says, "I believe in God," it is not enough to bring salvation. Even the demons can assent to cold, hard facts of reality—while continuing to work evil. But when we who hear the gospel respond in true faith, that faith will show through in what we do.

We can do nothing without leaving evidence behind. Even a burglar sneaking through a house leaves traces of his presense: a footprint in the carpet, a fallen hair with DNA, a fingerprint on a doorknob. Similarly, where faith exists, evidence marks it as genuine.

Satan and his demons have been in the very presence of God and of the preincarnate Christ. They know who Christ is and proved it when they screeched at Him, "What do you want with us, Jesus of Nazareth? . . . I know who you are—the Holy One of God!" (Mark 1:24). Yet what does the evidence of their actions say about them?

Good works are the evidence of a genuine faith, the evidence left behind wherever faith has gone. In other words, right action is the fingerprint of faith.

Dear Father in Heaven, *as I walk through this life, help me to live in such a way that I leave behind a trail of evidence of my faith in You. And let that evidence be sufficient so that someone might follow the trail to You. I pray in the name of Jesus, my merciful Savior and Lord. Amen.*

**SPOTLIGHT**
***Next Week's Lesson***

How we live our lives shows who is in control of our lives.

# Actions Reveal Belief

*You see that a person is justified by what he does and not by faith alone* (James 2:24).

This verse doesn't contradict the truth that salvation comes through faith alone. It simply tells us that talk is cheap. We can say anything, but what we truly believe in our hearts will seep out in our actions. When we say we are followers of Christ, we may mean our words sincerely. But those words are worthless until action backs them up. In other words, *show* me, don't just *tell* me you have faith.

And the kind of "showing" we do should benefit those around us. As J. S. Whale wrote in *Christian Doctrine:* "Faith without ethical consequences is a lie. Good works must necessarily follow faith. God does not need our sacrifices, but he has, nevertheless, appointed a representative to receive them, namely our neighbor. The neighbor always represents the invisible Christ."

We can say anything. But our actions betray what our hearts truly believe. If we speak like a saint but treat others like dirt, how could we ever be justified?

Dear heavenly Father, *keep reminding me that my actions will always speak louder than my words. In order to grow in good works, let me focus on the exemplary life of Your Son. The more I get to know Him, the clearer I see the power of good works done in the power of the Spirit. Thank You for giving yourself, through Him, to the world. In His name, amen.*

**SEARCH THE WORD**

*Our walk with Christ is exactly that—a walk, not a nap.*

Scripture: James 2:21-26

Song: *"A Charge to Keep I Have"*

***From this meditation today, I will pray . . .***

Adoration ______________________

______________________

______________________

Confession ______________________

______________________

______________________

Thanksgiving ______________________

______________________

______________________

Supplication ______________________

______________________

______________________

***From this meditation today, I will . . .***

Think ______________________

______________________

______________________

Say ______________________

______________________

______________________

Do ______________________

______________________

______________________

______________________

______________________

August 11

# Anonymous Notes

*A gentle answer turns away wrath, but a harsh word stirs up anger* (Proverbs 15:1).

Scripture: Proverbs 15:1-4
**Song:** *"The Bond of Love"*

***From this meditation today, I will pray . . .***

Adoration ______________________________

______________________________

______________________________

Confession ______________________________

______________________________

______________________________

Thanksgiving ______________________________

______________________________

______________________________

Supplication ______________________________

______________________________

______________________________

***From this meditation today, I will . . .***

Think ______________________________

______________________________

______________________________

Say ______________________________

______________________________

______________________________

Do ______________________________

______________________________

______________________________

August 11–17. ***Drexel Rankin*** *has served the Christian Church (Disciples of Christ) as an ordained minister for more than 35 years*

Someone had placed the note in the offering plate in response to an opinion I had voiced in the sermon. I hadn't considered that my view was controversial, but I had obviously touched a nerve with at least one person in the congregation.

The comment piqued my attention because I was not aware of the particular information forwarded to me in the terse note. Unfortunately, I had no method of dialoguing with the writer. The note was unsigned.

It's difficult to exchange ideas or to grow in knowledge if we cannot speak to or listen to one another directly. This applies to criticisms as well as compliments, disagreeable subjects as well as agreeable ones.

Face-to-face conversations can help to clear up misunderstandings and at least give us a chance to apply the proverb above: if we know who is angry with us, we can at least know who it is that needs a gentle answer.

Loving God, *make me aware that it is so easy to disagree with one of my brothers or sisters in Christ. Sometimes the difference is petty; sometimes I think it is immense. Help me to ponder my words before I speak (or write) so that I might always disagree in love. In Christ I pray. Amen.*

**SPOTLIGHT**
***Next Week's Lesson***
Angry words conveyed anonymously are like a Frisbee® mistakenly thrown over a cliff—uncontrollable, then useless.

# Stumbling Through Life

*We all stumble in many ways. If anyone is never at fault in what he says, he is a perfect man, able to keep his whole body in check* (James 3:2).

I wanted to do something special for the children's sermon that might surprise the kids or show them a fascinating aspect of God's world. I decided to demonstrate, through a science experiment, how acts of love can "lift up" someone's spirits. The experiment was simple—add enough salt to a bowl of water, and the salt will lift to the surface an egg that had sunk in the clear tap water.

On Saturday, I tried this experiment at home, just to be sure it would work. Twice, it went off trouble-free.

But on Sunday morning with the children gathered around me—in front of a packed room of adults—the experiment flopped. (Eventually it did work, but only after I had made a mess on my pulpit robe and spilled water across the carpet—which amused both the children and everyone else.)

Oh well. We all stumble and look foolish occasionally. Once again, I'm reminded that God alone is in control.

*I confess,* Lord, *that there are times when I mess up my life—and sometimes the lives of those around me. Help me always to be aware of Your presence and to let You take control. You, alone, have the right plan for my life if I will remain quiet and listen for Your voice. In the wonderful name of Christ I pray. Amen.*

**SEARCH THE WORD**

*It is better to stumble over our words than to use our words to cause a friend to stumble.*

Scripture: James 3:1-4

**Song: *"Search Me, O God"***

*From this meditation today, I will pray . . .*

Adoration ____________________

Confession ____________________

Thanksgiving ____________________

Supplication ____________________

*From this meditation today, I will . . .*

Think ____________________

Say ____________________

Do ____________________

August 13

# In Remembrance

*With the tongue we praise our Lord and Father, and with it we curse men, who have been made in God's likeness* (James 3:9).

Scripture: James 3:5-9

Song: *"In Remembrance"*

*From this meditation today, I will pray . . .*

Adoration ______

Confession ______

Thanksgiving ______

Supplication ______

*From this meditation today, I will . . .*

Think ______

Say ______

Do ______

We sang "In Remembrance of Me" as our communion hymn during worship. The song begins with Jesus offering the cup and bread to His disciples. He asks them to eat and drink in remembrance.

As the hymn unfolds, the vision of remembering Christ expands: "In remembrance of me, heal the sick. In remembrance of me, feed the poor. In remembrance of me, open the door, and let your brother in." [rodentregatta.com.article/4560/and-on-the-third-day]

I knew that receiving the cup and bread brought Christ's presence to me on Sunday. Now, the words suggested a special way to know Christ's presence every day: do some tangible act of love in remembrance of Him. Feed a hungry person, open a door, send a card, cry with a friend, hug a child, say a gracious word to a neighbor. But pause and do your act deliberately in Jesus' name.

This approach makes our words, too, particularly powerful. A word of kindness—spoken in remembrance of all that Christ has done for us—becomes an extension of His own heavenly love through our earthly tongue.

O God, *I know that You love all of Your creation. Today, show me some person whom I can serve as an act of remembrance of Christ. And let my words, too, convey His goodness to all who hear. In Jesus' name, amen.*

**SPOTLIGHT**

***Next Week's Lesson***

If we envision each statement we make first passing through the lips of Jesus, our words will bless many.

# What Spills Out?

*Can both fresh water and salt water flow from the same spring? My brothers, can a fig tree bear olives, or a grapevine bear figs? Neither can a salt spring produce fresh water* (James 3:11, 12).

As I drove across the speed bump, the filled-to-the-brim coffee mug that I held in my hand spilled over the side of my cup and slopped coffee on my pants. I was upset at myself for being so careless. Yet I knew that it could have been worse. I might have been drinking grape juice or a raspberry smoothie!

Also, I realized that when I am "bumped" in life, the contents of my inner being often will spill out. What I think and do when I am "bumped" shows whether or not Christ is powerfully present in my life.

So I have to ask myself: When the contents of my inner self spill out, what will others see or hear?

When someone cuts me off in traffic, how do I react? When others scuttle my schedule for the day, am I willing to alter my plans to meet their needs? When I hit the inevitable speed bumps in life, what spills out? Is my cup filled with the love and mercy of Christ?

Dear Lord in Heaven, *I know that there are times when I'll encounter difficulties along the road of life. As I meet others on my travels, give me the calmness of Your Spirit that I may bless them in the name of Jesus Christ. It is in His name that I pray. Amen.*

**SEARCH THE WORD**

*Words chosen with integrity may or may not have their intended effect, but they will not dishonor the speaker.*

Scripture: James 3:10-12

Song: *"'Mid All the Traffic of the Ways"*

*From this meditation today, I will pray . . .*

Adoration ______________________________

______________________________

______________________________

Confession ______________________________

______________________________

______________________________

Thanksgiving ______________________________

______________________________

______________________________

Supplication ______________________________

______________________________

______________________________

*From this meditation today, I will . . .*

Think ______________________________

______________________________

______________________________

Say ______________________________

______________________________

______________________________

Do ______________________________

______________________________

______________________________

______________________________

______________________________

# Whom Do You Bless?

*Who is wise and understanding among you? Let him show it by his good life, by deeds done in the humility that comes from wisdom* (James 3:13).

Scripture: James 3:13-16

**Song:** *"Make Me a Blessing"*

*From this meditation today, I will pray . . .*

Adoration ______________________

______________________

______________________

Confession ______________________

______________________

______________________

Thanksgiving ______________________

______________________

______________________

Supplication ______________________

______________________

______________________

*From this meditation today, I will . . .*

Think ______________________

______________________

______________________

Say ______________________

______________________

______________________

Do ______________________

______________________

______________________

______________________

______________________

I eagerly await December, knowing that I will watch the 1940s film *It's A Wonderful Life* at least once during the month. James Stewart portrays George Bailey, a small business owner, husband, and father, who grew up in Bedford Falls. George comes to think his life is worthless—until the angel Clarence shows him a nightmarish alternative universe. It's the picture of a Bedford Falls as if George had never lived, never touched the lives of so many people, even in the smallest ways.

As a small-town banker, George had selflessly invested in the trials and tribulations of his neighbors. Thus, when George became desperate, those same neighbors, one by one, offer him their money. As each comes forward, George utters their names in loving awe. Those people had been deeply blessed by the life of George Bailey, a life of good deeds done in humility.

Never discount the worth of your smallest deed in the name of our Lord Jesus Christ. You have no idea whom you might bless.

*Make me aware,* O Loving God, *that I have opportunities each day to bless the lives of people who cross my path. May Jesus shine out of my life as You make me a blessing to someone today. In the name of Christ, amen.*

**SPOTLIGHT**

***Next Week's Lesson***

Life's most significant statements are usually made without the herald of a trumpet blast.

# Quiet Moments

*Peacemakers who sow in peace raise a harvest of righteousness* (James 3:18).

I awoke that morning with a raw, raspy throat. I had laryngitis. Barely did an intelligible sound break forth from my mouth. My children, of course, were delighted. I was unable to bark orders at them to do this or to do that—to wear clothes to school that I deemed suitable, to move faster in order to be at school on time, to eat a solid breakfast that would nourish them. Not today. There was no voice.

It didn't take long to realize just how calmly and peacefully breakfast proceeded that morning. When someone asked something of me, I could respond only in a weak whisper. And everyone else began talking softly too! They responded to me in the same manner in which I spoke—calmly, quietly.

Right there in the midst of eating my oatmeal, I realized what was happening. The tone of my voice had influenced the mood of the whole morning.

Amazing, the lessons we learn in the quiet moments.

*From time to time,* God, *remind me that I can hear You and I can hear others so clearly when the noise and clamor of my inner life are silenced for a few moments. May Your still small voice speak to me and through me each day, as I make some space for You. In the name of the Father, the Son, and the Holy Spirit, I pray. Amen.*

**SEARCH THE WORD**

*If God can speak effectively through a still, small voice, we should try to do the same.*

Scripture: James 3:17, 18

Song: *"Come and Find the Quiet Center"*

***From this meditation today, I will pray . . .***

Adoration ______________________________

______________________________

______________________________

Confession ______________________________

______________________________

______________________________

Thanksgiving ______________________________

______________________________

______________________________

Supplication ______________________________

______________________________

______________________________

***From this meditation today, I will . . .***

Think ______________________________

______________________________

______________________________

Say ______________________________

______________________________

______________________________

Do ______________________________

______________________________

______________________________

______________________________

______________________________

August 17

# Ripples of Words

*The wise in heart are called discerning, and pleasant words promote instruction* (Proverbs 16:21).

Scripture: Proverbs 16:21-24
Song: *"Pass It On"*

***From this meditation today, I will pray . . .***

Adoration ______________________________

Confession ______________________________

Thanksgiving ______________________________

Supplication ______________________________

***From this meditation today, I will . . .***

Think ______________________________

Say ______________________________

Do ______________________________

I stand at the edge of the pond and toss a pebble into the water. Ripples spread from the center in an ever-widening circle until they move out of sight.

Recently, I received an e-mail from a minister in Pennsylvania who said he had chanced upon my e-mail address. For some time he had wanted to tell me that the mentoring I had done with him while he was a seminary student was, in large part, the reason he had remained in ministry and was content in his calling. I had been his supervisor nearly a quarter of a century ago. Today, I can't put a face with the name.

The smallest words that we speak are like a pebble dropped into water. They spread far enough away that we can no longer detect them. Yet lives are touched daily by such ripples.

Our lives can send out ripples of faith that affect countless people, known and unknown. It may seem hard to believe, but our ripples can change the face of the world in which we live.

*Help me to remember,* loving God, *that I am Your face, Your hands, and Your voice in this world where I move daily. May others see You and know of Your goodness because they see You in me. In the name of Jesus, Lord and Savior of all, I pray. Amen.*

**SPOTLIGHT**
***Next Week's Lesson***

Who knows the distance a kind, well-chosen word will travel?

# A Wise Choice

*She will guide you down delightful paths; all her ways are satisfying* (Proverbs 3:17, *New Living Translation*).

While I was in college, I thought the wisest thing I could do was pledge to a sorority and get to know all the right people (those who were popular). "Then I'll have it made," I thought.

But Janie, one of the workers for Campus Crusade for Christ, had different advice for me. "Come to our Bible study," she suggested. But what was wise advice seemed foolish to me at the time. I partied while my GPA plummeted. Yet I still was not satisfied.

One night as I stood wondering why a particular frat party didn't seem as fun as parties usually seemed, I remember thinking, "What am I doing? I could be at home studying." I was finally on the path to wisdom.

I took Janie's advice, as well, and reconnected with the source of wisdom himself. That's what the writer of Proverbs suggests. Like a parent or a wise friend, he touts the value of wisdom. What you gain by grasping her is more satisfying than anything you might seek. Have you discovered that yet?

Lord, *Your wisdom truly cried out to me and delighted to embrace me. Thank You for seeking me when I didn't seek You. Through Christ, amen.*

**SEARCH THE WORD**

*Words, like a spiritual anesthesia, may take longer to affect a person whose metabolism is slower.*

Scripture: Proverbs 3:13-18

**Song:** *"More Love, More Power"*

*From this meditation today, I will pray . . .*

Adoration ____________________

Confession ____________________

Thanksgiving ____________________

Supplication ____________________

*From this meditation today, I will . . .*

Think ____________________

Say ____________________

Do ____________________

August 18–24. ***Linda Washington,*** *a former staff editor in Christian publishing, now works as a freelance editor and writer in Carol Stream, Illinois.*

# Fruitless War

*You want something but don't get it. You kill and covet, but you cannot have what you want. You quarrel and fight. You do not have, because you do not ask God* (James 4:2).

Scripture: James 4:1-3

Song: *"I Do Not Ask, O Lord"*

***From this meditation today, I will pray . . .***

Adoration ______________________________

Confession ______________________________

Thanksgiving ______________________________

Supplication ______________________________

***From this meditation today, I will . . .***

Think ______________________________

Say ______________________________

Do ______________________________

My roommate and I were at war, because I believed my boyfriend preferred her to me. Actually, I was the one at war. Just the previous week, my boyfriend came to me with the suggestion that we take a break from our relationship. So when I returned home one night and found him in my apartment talking with my roommate, I went ballistic.

Within weeks, I moved out, full of injured pride and accusations. I was angry at them and especially at God. "You knew this would happen when I moved in with her! Why didn't you warn me?" I fired at God in prayer.

"You didn't ask," was His quiet response.

I had to admit that I hadn't asked God about my relationship or living situation—or about much of anything. I did what I wanted and suffered the consequences. Like an explorer who claims a piece of land simply because he stumbled upon it, I tried to claim what I thought was mine. How many battles I've fought over people, possessions, or places without God's guidance!

Dear God, *I'm sorry for coveting instead of asking for Your will. But I'm also grateful for Your healing touch when I hurt myself through my own mistakes. In Jesus' name I pray. Amen.*

**SPOTLIGHT**

***Next Week's Lesson***

We will never be able to see all God wants us to see if our focus is only on ourselves.

# The Pride Slide

*God opposes the proud but favors the humble*
(James 4:6, *New Living Translation*).

He leveled his finger at me as I stood ready to hand him a tract on a New Orleans street corner. After berating me for "spoiling his fun," he suddenly stopped. "For many years, I wanted God to speak to me in an audible voice," he said, with an honesty that surprised both of us, seeing as how I hadn't asked him. "But He didn't." He then chose to avoid God, because God didn't respond the way he'd hoped.

I couldn't help thinking of his response years later, when I too was angry with God over a series of financial setbacks, and I demanded that He answer my request for help and direction—*right now.* As I discussed the situation with my younger brother, he quietly said, "You need to humble yourself before God."

I didn't want to hear that. I wanted God to speak in the time and fashion I chose. But once I took my brother's advice, I could accept God's clear response.

It seems I had fallen into the trap of pride. God resisted my demands until I willingly relinquished my "rights" in favor of honoring Him.

Lord of Heaven and earth, *I'm beginning to see that I can't have my way and Yours at the same time. Help me choose to honor You, instead of grasping for my own glory. Through Christ I pray. Amen.*

**SEARCH THE WORD**
*Be sure God receives credit for the results when He allows you to be His spokesperson.*

Scripture: James 4:4-7
Song: *"Take My Life and Let It Be"*

***From this meditation today, I will pray . . .***

Adoration ______________________________

______________________________

______________________________

Confession ______________________________

______________________________

______________________________

Thanksgiving ______________________________

______________________________

______________________________

Supplication ______________________________

______________________________

______________________________

***From this meditation today, I will . . .***

Think ______________________________

______________________________

______________________________

Say ______________________________

______________________________

______________________________

Do ______________________________

______________________________

______________________________

______________________________

______________________________

August 21

# Come Close

***Come close to God, and God will come close to you. Wash your hands, you sinners; purify your hearts, for your loyalty is divided between God and the world*** **(James 4:8, *New Living Translation*).**

Scripture: James 4:8-10

**Song: *"Purify Me"***

***From this meditation today, I will pray . . .***

Adoration ______________________________

Confession ______________________________

Thanksgiving ______________________________

Supplication ______________________________

***From this meditation today, I will . . .***

Think ______________________________

Say ______________________________

Do ______________________________

Near my college dorm lived a squirrel with an odd habit of running up to people instead of shying away from human contact. I found the behavior disconcerting because of rumors that the squirrel was rabid. (Actually, the squirrel was simply used to being fed by students.)

One day as I tried to enter the dorm, the squirrel met me at the front door. The closer to him I moved, the closer to me he moved. So I backed away, immediately feeling foolish for doing so.

I have a tendency to retreat from God, as well, especially in the midst of a struggle. Sometimes the fault lies with my divided loyalties, the kind James talks about in this passage (being torn between wanting success according to the world's standard and wanting to live for God.) But sometimes I directly resist conforming my ways to God's. Yet James assures his readers that drawing close to God will result in His drawing close as well—like a magnet drawing another. And that which draws also purifies. We can't remain the same when a holy God is near.

Loving God, *I need Your Spirit to calm me enough to draw close to You. Heal my tendency to resist or run, through Christ my Lord. Amen.*

**SPOTLIGHT**

***Next Week's Lesson***

When God seems far away, we need to double check our spiritual compass.

# Quick to Criticize?

*There is only one Lawgiver and Judge, the one who is able to save and destroy. But you—who are you to judge your neighbor?* (James 4:12).

I gleefully shared with my family the story of a neighbor in my apartment building who claimed to write songs for famous musicians. "She's lost touch with reality," I proclaimed. Another family, I reported, needed therapy because of their habit of fighting in the hallway.

I soon felt guilty. Not only had I speedily passed on information about others, I had shown anything but grace to my neighbors, who were members of the family of God. I was quick to judge them for their foibles, but I couldn't as readily see my own critical spirit. Of course, judging them was far easier than praying for them—or with them—in ways that preserved their dignity.

As James taught, God is the only qualified judge. And judging others is hardly a way to promote peace and good will. Instead, it demotes and devalues. It also shows what we need most: God.

Quick to critically quip? Try being "faster on the draw" to draw nearer to God.

**Dear God,** *when I'm tempted to judge others, remind me of the ways I have failed You. Let me see the log in my own eye before pointing to the speck in another's eye. Then armed with Your forgiveness, help me to accept others as You accept them. Thank You, in Jesus' name. Amen.*

**SEARCH THE WORD**

*We are more likely to reach God by pulling others alongside rather than stepping over them.*

**Scripture: James 4:11-14**

**Song:** *"Savior, Like a Shepherd Lead Us"*

***From this meditation today, I will pray . . .***

Adoration ______________________________

______________________________

______________________________

Confession ______________________________

______________________________

______________________________

Thanksgiving ______________________________

______________________________

______________________________

Supplication ______________________________

______________________________

______________________________

***From this meditation today, I will . . .***

Think ______________________________

______________________________

______________________________

Say ______________________________

______________________________

______________________________

Do ______________________________

______________________________

______________________________

______________________________

______________________________

August 23

# Making Plans

*What you ought to say is,*
*"If the Lord wants us to, we will live and do this or that"*
(James 4:15, *New Living Translation*).

Scripture: James 4:15-17

**Song:** *"Jesus, All for Jesus"*

***From this meditation today, I will pray . . .***

Adoration ______________________________

______________________________

______________________________

Confession ______________________________

______________________________

______________________________

Thanksgiving ______________________________

______________________________

______________________________

Supplication ______________________________

______________________________

______________________________

***From this meditation today, I will . . .***

Think ______________________________

______________________________

______________________________

Say ______________________________

______________________________

______________________________

Do ______________________________

______________________________

______________________________

______________________________

______________________________

Ever been so convinced of the future that you announce it to everyone before you're truly assured of it? I was so certain that two potential writing projects were "a go" that I told everyone about them and even planned my schedule around both. I didn't have a backup plan. So when the "No" came for both projects, I reeled into a tailspin of depression.

During that bleak time, I slowly realized that when I'd prayed about both projects, I never received a clear sense of God's Yes. Instead, I followed my own plans and called them His. I felt foolish as I told the same people I'd boasted to before, "Looks like I was mistaken."

I then asked God, "Well, what can I do now?" I ended up working on two entirely different projects!

Announcing a presumed outcome is a bigger gamble than discerning tomorrow's weather. As an outcome-forecaster, I'm often quite wrong. Maybe that's why James warned so strongly against "boasting about your own plans" (see James 4:16, *NLT*).

Holy One, *forgive me for the times when I follow my own path before seeking Your direction. When I fail to discern Your guidance, I lose more than I gain. Thank You for guiding me through Your Word, through circumstances, and through the wise counsel of others. In Christ's name, amen.*

**SPOTLIGHT**

***Next Week's Lesson***

Experiencing God's will does not occur if we ask Him to close His eyes while we plan our schemes.

# Glow in the Dark

*Do not participate in the unfruitful deeds of darkness, but instead even expose them; for it is disgraceful even to speak of the things which are done by them in secret* (Ephesians 5:11, 12, *New American Standard Bible*).

When I was a kid, I loved anything that promised to glow in the dark. I was fascinated by how exposure to light caused a package or toy to take on an unearthly glow in the darkness. My brothers and I used to spend hours wiggling the items under lamps, then waving them around the darkest closet or the deepest corner of the basement.

Light can work in other ways. The light of God's truth exposes the wrongs we do. Like the time I told one of the ministers of my church how "unfair" God was for taking so long to answer my prayer for employment. He gently rebuked me for resting on my laurels (i.e., waiting on God to act instead of doing something myself). Mostly, I needed to repent of my attitude toward my circumstances.

If we are to live as people of the light, our unfruitful deeds need exposure to the cleansing light of Christ. In that way, we believers will "glow" in a dark world.

My dear heavenly Father, *sometimes I fail to reflect Your light. When I require the exposing light of Your truth, give me the humility to submit instead of balking. Then help me to let that light shine out for Your glory in all I do or say. Through Christ's name I pray. Amen.*

**SEARCH THE WORD**

*We will never experience God's radiance if our paths are not in the Sonlight.*

Scripture: Ephesians 5:8-11

Song: *"Be the Centre"*

*From this meditation today, I will pray . . .*

Adoration ______________________________

______________________________

______________________________

Confession ______________________________

______________________________

______________________________

Thanksgiving ______________________________

______________________________

______________________________

Supplication ______________________________

______________________________

______________________________

*From this meditation today, I will . . .*

Think ______________________________

______________________________

______________________________

Say ______________________________

______________________________

______________________________

Do ______________________________

______________________________

______________________________

______________________________

______________________________

# God's Will for Us

*Do not put out the Spirit's fire*
(1 Thessalonians 5:19).

## Scripture: 1 Thessalonians 5:16-22

**Song: *"I Am Resolved"***

***From this meditation today, I will pray . . .***

Adoration ______________________________

________________________________________

________________________________________

Confession ______________________________

________________________________________

________________________________________

Thanksgiving ______________________________

________________________________________

________________________________________

Supplication ______________________________

________________________________________

________________________________________

***From this meditation today, I will . . .***

Think ______________________________

________________________________________

________________________________________

Say ______________________________

________________________________________

________________________________________

Do ______________________________

________________________________________

________________________________________

August 25–31. ***Cos Barnes*** *is an experienced freelance writer, living in Virginia, whose favorite hobby is playing hand bells in her church.*

As I notice the date of this devotional, I'm reminded of my son who celebrates his birthday today. I remember my little "preemie" who is now white-haired, stands six-feet-two, and towers over his three daughters. His role now, like mine of yesteryear, is to care for his family and nurture his children in their development. The hereditary mantle has passed to him.

We know Silas and Timothy were as dear to Paul as sons, and he was preparing them for the mantle of leadership. The earliest of his epistles, Thessalonians, was written by Paul in conjunction with these two young men, his protégés. Paul encouraged sobriety of life, constant watchfulness, respect for church officials, consideration of the needy, and cultivation of spiritual gifts as duties of the Christian life.

Difficulties are natural to a new church, of course. But Paul was building his life into disciples who keep the Spirit's fire burning bright. Like Paul, we too can offer our young people practical and wise advice on maintaining what has been accomplished in our congregations.

*Thank You,* God, *for the words of Paul that spell out our duties as Christians and our responsibilities to You. Amen.*

**SPOTLIGHT**
***Next Week's Lesson***

Becoming a leader in God's kingdom is a growing process that occurs as we seek His priorities.

# Turn Loose of Things

*Your wealth has rotted, and moths have eaten your clothes. Your gold and silver are corroded. . . . You have hoarded wealth in the last days* (James 5:2, 3).

People of my vintage are getting rid of their "stuff." Material things that were so essential and loved in earlier years no longer seem so important. Many of us have had to dismantle the homes of our parents and in-laws, and we've found that some of the treasures saved through the years hold little attraction for us anymore. In fact, most of us have much more stuff than we need, our attics and basements overflowing. And many of our children don't want what we have saved. Their lifestyles, home decors, and tastes are different from ours.

Among the things that I love are my great-grandmother's bed and my grandmother's clock. But will any of my children take the time to tuck linens neatly at the footboard or wind the clock weekly? I doubt it.

Think about James, a fisherman on the Sea of Galilee, who worked in partnership with Peter and Andrew. Can you imagine him having many "things" to hoard and carry around with him?

Dear Father, *I live in such a commercial world, where the almighty dollar reigns supreme. Teach me to discern what is important and what is not. And help me convey the values of Your kingdom to my children, day by day. In the name of Your Son, my Savior, I pray. Amen.*

**SEARCH THE WORD**

*We discover how much less time and desire we have for other things when we serve the king wholeheartedly.*

Scripture: James 5:1-6

Song: *"Wonderful Grace of Jesus"*

***From this meditation today, I will pray . . .***

Adoration ______________________________

______________________________

______________________________

Confession ______________________________

______________________________

______________________________

Thanksgiving ______________________________

______________________________

______________________________

Supplication ______________________________

______________________________

______________________________

***From this meditation today, I will . . .***

Think ______________________________

______________________________

______________________________

Say ______________________________

______________________________

______________________________

Do ______________________________

______________________________

______________________________

______________________________

______________________________

August 27

# Patience Is a Virtue

*You have heard of Job's perseverance and have seen what the Lord finally brought about* (James 5:11).

Scripture: James 5:7-12

Song: *"Work, for the Night Is Coming"*

*From this meditation today, I will pray . . .*

Adoration ______________________________

______________________________

______________________________

Confession ______________________________

______________________________

______________________________

Thanksgiving ______________________________

______________________________

______________________________

Supplication ______________________________

______________________________

______________________________

*From this meditation today, I will . . .*

Think ______________________________

______________________________

______________________________

Say ______________________________

______________________________

______________________________

Do ______________________________

______________________________

______________________________

______________________________

______________________________

James exhorted the church at Thessalonica to have patience in their sufferings. He used Job as an example, a man who lost his health, his wealth, his children, and his honor among peers. He was willing to go to the ash heap, to suffer horrible sores that covered his body, to lose his standing in the community, and to separate himself from his friends—all with the result of growing from the experience. His life was transformed, his faith surely strengthened.

James's object in writing this letter to the early Christians was to confront the sins and errors they were committing, while encouraging them in all the trials they faced. He stressed the importance of patience in the Christian life.

We who live in an instant-gratification society would do well to heed James's advice. For many of us, patience seems hard to come by. Yet God is more concerned with our relationship to Him than with our accomplishments for Him. As the great medieval poet John Milton put it, having lost his sight in middle age: "They also serve who only stand and wait."

Father God, *we who want things done yesterday need to slow down and wait for Your perfect timing. Teach me patience and perseverance, and help me to accept that it will require times of waiting. In Jesus' name, amen.*

**SPOTLIGHT**

***Next Week's Lesson***

Health and hope may help you in the sprint, but patience and prayer are essentials for cross-country living.

# Pray with Me

*Is any one of you in trouble? He should pray. Is anyone happy? Let him sing songs of praise* (James 5:13).

Miss Ina was my prayer partner. I visited her regularly over the years, in her home, in the hospital, and finally in a nursing facility. "Let's pray," I would begin, and then she would chime in, her words a wonderful complement to mine. It was always a beautiful, synchronized prayer, with each of us praying for different things but communing with God in close harmony.

Miss Ina also loved flowers. One day, I told her of the garden I was growing at our church, in memory of my husband. "Go into my backyard, and dig up the hydrangea," she insisted, "and plant it in your garden." I did as she instructed me.

Years passed. Returning from a trip, I called my church to catch up on happenings.

"Miss Ina died," my minister told me.

I went later that day to water the garden. The hydrangea was a mass of blue blooms. When I saw it, I felt as if Miss Ina were still praying for me.

James told the early church that prayer was the great resource of Christians in need. Could we use it a bit more often?

Father, *I know how powerful prayer is. Help me use it often, eagerly seeking Your best for my brothers and sisters in Christ. In His name, amen.*

**SEARCH THE WORD**

*The loving Father must savor the moment each time one of His children turns to Him in prayer.*

Scripture: James 5:13-15

Song: *"Prayer Is the Soul's Sincere Desire"*

*From this meditation today, I will pray . . .*

Adoration ______

Confession ______

Thanksgiving ______

Supplication ______

*From this meditation today, I will . . .*

Think ______

Say ______

Do ______

# Power in Prayer

*The effective prayer of a righteous man can accomplish much*
(James 5:16, *New American Standard Bible*).

Scripture: James 5:16-18

Song: *"Rise, My Soul, to Watch and Pray"*

*From this meditation today, I will pray . . .*

Adoration ______________________________

______________________________

______________________________

Confession ______________________________

______________________________

______________________________

Thanksgiving ______________________________

______________________________

______________________________

Supplication ______________________________

______________________________

______________________________

*From this meditation today, I will . . .*

Think ______________________________

______________________________

______________________________

Say ______________________________

______________________________

______________________________

Do ______________________________

______________________________

______________________________

______________________________

______________________________

How can we pray effectively, as James urges? Several years ago someone sent me "The Five-Finger Prayer" in an e-mail. It can help us organize our prayers like this:

Your thumb is nearest to you, so begin by praying for those closest to you—family and friends.

Next comes the pointing finger. Pray for those who teach, instruct, and heal, including teachers, doctors and ministers. They need support and wisdom in pointing others in the right direction.

The longest finger reminds us of our leaders, those who shape our nation and guide public opinion. Pray for our president and other leaders in business and industry.

The ring finger is considered the weakest. It should remind us to pray for those who are weak, in trouble, or in pain.

The smallest of all, the little finger reminds us of how we should think of ourselves in relation to God and others. Your pinkie can remind you to pray for yourself. By the time you have prayed for the other four groups, your own needs will find their proper perspective.

O Lord, *help me shed my self-centeredness that I might sincerely and effectively bring before You the needs of others. I believe, with James, that the real power in living comes only from You. In Jesus' name, amen.*

**SPOTLIGHT**
***Next Week's Lesson***

A Christian with a fervent prayer life is magnetic, drawing others into the presence of the Lord.

# Such a Great Privilege

*Whoever turns a sinner from the error of his way will save him from death and cover over a multitude of sins* (James 5:20).

At a recent prayer meeting at my church, our minister asked people to share about how they came to Christ. One man answered that he prayed for salvation in a revival meeting when he was 13 years old. Another responded that he was baptized after a youth group meeting when he was 12 years old. Others mentioned Sunday school teachers who had been instrumental in leading them to know Christ. Some named parents and grandparents.

My minister went on to ask us whether we still feel the excitement, the emotion, the joy we felt when we first entered the waters of baptism. I remember crying all the way down the aisle on that Easter Sunday morning, at 12 years old, when I made my profession of faith.

Sometimes we become complacent about the great gift of salvation that God extends to every human being. We forget to show others our faith and use our influence to win them to Christ. Yet it is our Christian responsibility to do so. And James ends his letter by telling us what a great work it is. Can you imagine covering a multitude of sins? What a privilege!

Father, *help me frequently to recall today the hour when I first believed. And help me retain my childlike faith so that others may see Your glory through me and turn to You in faith. Through Christ I pray. Amen.*

**SEARCH THE WORD**

*Every Christian is grafted into a large family tree, rooted in and sustained by Jesus.*

Scripture: James 5:19, 20

Song: *"Brighten the Corner Where You Are"*

*From this meditation today, I will pray . . .*

Adoration ______________________________

______________________________

______________________________

Confession ______________________________

______________________________

______________________________

Thanksgiving ______________________________

______________________________

______________________________

Supplication ______________________________

______________________________

______________________________

*From this meditation today, I will . . .*

Think ______________________________

______________________________

______________________________

Say ______________________________

______________________________

______________________________

Do ______________________________

______________________________

______________________________

______________________________

______________________________

# With Paul in Ephesus

*I pray that out of his glorious riches he may strengthen you with power through his spirit in your inner being* (Ephesians 3:16).

Scripture: Ephesians 3:14-21

Song: *"I Know That My Redeemer Liveth"*

*From this meditation today, I will pray . . .*

Adoration ________________________________

________________________________

________________________________

Confession ________________________________

________________________________

________________________________

Thanksgiving ________________________________

________________________________

________________________________

Supplication ________________________________

________________________________

________________________________

*From this meditation today, I will . . .*

Think ________________________________

________________________________

________________________________

Say ________________________________

________________________________

________________________________

Do ________________________________

________________________________

________________________________

________________________________

________________________________

I think of Rembrandt's fine portrait of Paul in prison (the place from which Paul wrote his letter to the Ephesians). Light from above falls on Paul's aged face. One shoe is kicked off, perhaps to relieve a tired foot. He is deep in thought with pen in hand, contemplating what he will write next to encourage the Lord's people.

Recently it was my privilege to tour Ephesus, one of the greatest ruined cities in the western world and Turkey's architectural pride. The Grande Theatre looms in awesome splendor, built by the Romans to hold a capacity audience of 24,000. It was here that Paul preached during his stay in Ephesus between AD 53 and 55. Until a year ago it was used for music concerts, but wear and tear on the structure have made this no longer possible.

As I climbed the steps and surveyed the massive, magnificent structure, I could almost hear Paul proclaiming, "I pray that you . . . may have power, together with all the saints, to grasp how wide and long and high and deep is the love of Christ" (Ephesians 3:17, 18).

*Thank You,* God, *for Your saints who have gone before me to teach me of Your love. As You transform my heart, day by day, give me a concern for the spiritual growth of my fellow believers. In Jesus' name, amen.*

**SPOTLIGHT**

***Next Week's Lesson***

The master architect desires to construct in us an elaborate tower of strength and faith.

# STANDARD COMPANION DEVOTIONS

2007-2008

## 365 DAILY BIBLE READINGS AND MEDITATIONS TO HELP YOU . . .

- Read a Scripture passage every day
- Memorize a Scripture verse each day
- Sing a song, hymn, or spiritual song
- Meditate on an inspirational or devotional thoug
- Look ahead to the upcoming Sunday school lesso
- Journal your daily expressions of prayer

***The Companion Devotions*** supports the International Sunday School Lessons for September 2007–August 2008, such as those found in the popular *Standard Lesson Commentary*®. It is an ideal companion for your *personal* or *family time* with God. The easy-to-read format supplements the daily Scripture passages with meditations that will lead you to the Sunday school lesson each week.

***The Companion Devotions*** is an inspirational devotional that correlates with the *Standard Lesson Commentary*®. Used *daily,* it will help Sunday school *teachers and students* alike to prepare for the weekly International Sunday School Lesson.

***The Companion Devotions*** features the same daily Bible readings and meditations that are available in the curriculum quarterly editions of *Devotions* and the annual *365 Devotions,* which follows a calendar-year arrangement (January–December), and adds special space for journaling and setting goals for life change.

***The Companion Devotions***® is an ideal companion for *any* International Sunday School Lesson study.

$9.99 US / $14.99 C

CHURCH & MINISTRY / MINISTRY RESOURCES / TEACHING HELPS

ISBN 0-7847-2081-9

9 780784 720813

05008 ADUL

Standard PUBLISHING

www.standardpub.com